SHAKESPEARE SURVEY

ADVISORY BOARD

1. Shakespeare and his Stage
2. Shakespearian Production
3. The Man and the Writer
4. Interpretation
5. Textual Criticism
6. The Histories
7. Style and Language
8. The Comedies
9. *Hamlet*
10. The Roman Plays
11. The Last Plays (with an index to *Surveys* 1–10)
12. The Elizabethan Theatre
13. *King Lear*
14. Shakespeare and his Contemporaries
15. The Poems and Music
16. Shakespeare in the Modern World
17. Shakespeare in His Own Age
18. Shakespeare Then Till Now
19. *Macbeth*
20. Shakespearian and Other Tragedy
21. *Othello* (with an index to *Surveys* 11–20)
22. Aspects of Shakespearian Comedy
23. Shakespeare's Language
24. Shakespeare: Theatre Poet
25. Shakespeare's Problem Plays
26. Shakespeare's Jacobean Tragedies
27. Shakespeare's Early Tragedies
28. Shakespeare and the Ideas of his Time
29. Shakespeare's Last Plays
30. *Henry IV* to *Hamlet*
31. Shakespeare and the Classical World (with an index to *Surveys* 21–30)
32. The Middle Comedies

SHAKESPEARE SURVEY

AN ANNUAL SURVEY OF
SHAKESPEARIAN STUDY AND PRODUCTION

32

EDITED BY
KENNETH MUIR

CAMBRIDGE UNIVERSITY PRESS

CAMBRIDGE

LONDON   NEW YORK   NEW ROCHELLE

MELBOURNE   SYDNEY

Published by the Press Syndicate of the University of Cambridge
The Pitt Building, Trumpington Street, Cambridge CB2 1RP
32 East 57th Street, New York, NY 10022, USA
296 Beaconfield Parade, Middle Park, Melbourne 3206, Australia

First published 1979

Shakespeare Survey was first published in 1948. For the first eighteen
volumes it was edited by Allardyce Nicoll under the sponsorship of the
University of Birmingham, the University of Manchester, the Royal
Shakespeare Theatre and the Shakespeare Birthplace Trust

Printed in Great Britain by
Western Printing Services Ltd, Bristol

The Library of Congress originally catalogued Vol. I of this serial as follows:

Shakespeare Survey; an annual survey of Shakespearian study & production. 1 – Cambridge [Eng.] University Press, 1948 –
v. illus, facsims. 26 cm.

Editor: v. 1 –   Allardyce Nicoll.

'Issued under the sponsorship of the University of Birmingham, the
Shakespeare Memorial Theatre, the Shakespeare Birthplace Trust.'

1. Shakespeare, William – Societies, periodicals, etc. 2. Shakespeare,
William – Criticism and interpretation. 3. Shakespeare, William – Stage
history. 1. Nicoll, Allardyce, 1894 – ed.

PR2888.C3   822.33   49–1639

ISBN 0 521 22753 4

EDITOR'S NOTE

The central theme of *Shakespeare Survey 33*, as already announced, will be *King Lear*. The theme of Number 34 will be 'Characterisation in Shakespeare'. It will include some papers from the 1980 International Shakespeare Conference at Stratford-upon-Avon. Other contributions on that, or on other topics, should reach the new Editor, Dr Stanley Wells (40 Walton Crescent, Oxford OX1 2JQ) by 1 September 1980 at the latest. Contributors should leave generous margins, use double spacing, and follow the style and layout of articles in the current issue. A style-sheet is available on request. Contributions should not normally exceed 5,000 words. Books for review should be sent to the Editor at the above address, not to the publisher. The retiring Editor wishes to thank the Advisory Board for their advice and support.

K.M.

CONTRIBUTORS

HAROLD F. BROOKS, *Emeritus Professor of English, Birkbeck College, University of London*

JOHN F. COX, *Lecturer in English, Avondale College, Cooranbong, New South Wales*

STANTON B. GARNER, JR, *Princeton University*

NANCY K. HAYLES, *Assistant Professor of English, Dartmouth College*

R. F. HILL, *Senior Lecturer in English, King's College, University of London*

EDITH HOLDING, *Research Associate in English, University of Michigan*

RUSSELL JACKSON, *Fellow of the Shakespeare Institute, University of Birmingham*

JOAN LARSEN KLEIN, *Associate Professor of English, University of Illinois at Urbana*

ELLIOT KRIEGER, *Assistant Professor of English, University of Massachusetts, Boston*

JERZY LIMON, *Lecturer in English Literature, University of Poznań*

M. M. MAHOOD, *Professor of English, University of Kent*

J. M. NOSWORTHY, *formerly Rendel Professor of English, University College of Wales, Aberystwyth*

D. J. PALMER, *Professor of English, University of Manchester*

✝ E. D. PENDRY, *Lecturer in English, University of Bristol*

✝ S. J. SCHÖNFELD, *Haifa*

GUSTAV UNGERER, *Lecturer in English, University of Berne*

ROGER WARREN, *Lecturer in English, University of Leicester*

KARL P. WENTERSDORF, *Professor of English, Xavier University, Cincinnati*

GEORGE WALTON WILLIAMS, *Professor of English, Duke University*

M. R. WOODHEAD, *Lecturer in English, University College of Swansea*

CONTENTS

List of Plates   *page* viii

Shakespeare's Middle Comedies: A Generation of Criticism   *by* M. M. MAHOOD   1

'Perfect Types of Womanhood': Rosalind, Beatrice and Viola in Victorian Criticism and Performance   *by* RUSSELL JACKSON   15

The Stage Representation of the 'Kill Claudio' Sequence in *Much Ado About Nothing*   *by* J. F. COX   27

As You Like It Adapted: Charles Johnson's *Love In A Forest*   *by* EDITH HOLDING   37

Social Relations and the Social Order in *Much Ado About Nothing*   *by* ELLIOT KRIEGER   49

Sexual Disguise in *As You Like It* and *Twelfth Night*   *by* NANCY K. HAYLES   63

Twelfth Night and the Myth of Echo and Narcissus   *by* D. J. PALMER   73

'Smiling at Grief': Some Techniques of Comedy in *Twelfth Night* and *Così Fan Tutte*   *by* ROGER WARREN   79

'My Lady's a *Catayan*, we are politicians, *Maluolios* a Peg-a-ramsie' (*Twelfth Night* II, iii, 77–8)   *by* GUSTAV UNGERER   85

The Importance of Being Marcade   *by* J. M. NOSWORTHY   105

A Hebrew Source for *The Merchant of Venice*   *by* S. J. SCHÖNFELD   115

The Marriage Contracts in *Measure for Measure*: A Reconsideration   *by* KARL P. WENTERSDORF   129

Richard III: Antecedents of Clarence's Dream   *by* HAROLD F. BROOKS   145

Deep Plots and Indiscretions in 'The Murder of Gonzago'   *by* M. R. WOODHEAD   151

'What is't to leave betimes?' Proverbs and Logic in *Hamlet*   *by* JOAN LARSEN KLEIN   163

The Tempest: Language and Society   *by* STANTON B. GARNER, JR   177

Pictorial Evidence for a Possible Replica of the London Fortune Theatre in Gdansk   *by* JERZY LIMON   189

A Year of Comedies: Stratford 1978   *by* ROGER WARREN   201

The Year's Contributions to Shakespearian Study:

   1   Critical Studies   *reviewed by* R. F. HILL   211

   2   Shakespeare's Life, Times and Stage   *reviewed by* E. D. PENDRY   227

   3   Textual Studies   *reviewed by* GEORGE WALTON WILLIAMS   237

Index   249

PLATES

BETWEEN PAGES 88 AND 89

I A *Twelfth Night*, New York, 1904. Viola Allen and James Young as Viola and Sebastian
[*Reproduced by permission of the Harvard Theatre Collection*]

B *As You Like It*, Stratford-upon-Avon and New York, 1885. Mary Anderson as Rosalind
[*Reproduced by permission of the Harvard Theatre Collection*]

C *As You Like It*, produced by Oscar Asche at His Majesty's Theatre, London, 1907. Lily Brayton as Rosalind and Henry Ainley as Orlando

II A Engraving by Peter Willer showing the south-western corner of the Main City in Gdansk, with a public theatre on the right

B An enlarged detail of II A showing the Fencing School in Gdansk, i.e., the actual theatre

III *The Taming of the Shrew*, Royal Shakespeare Theatre, 1978. Directed by Michael Bogdanov, designed by Chris Dyer. The final scene, with Paola Dionisotti as Kate (standing, left) and Jonathan Pryce as Petruchio (seated, right)
[*Photo: Joe Cocks*]

IV *The Tempest*, Royal Shakespeare Theatre, 1978. Directed by Clifford Williams, designed by Ralph Koltai. Michael Hordern as Prospero, Ian Charleson as Ariel
[*Photo: Joe Cocks*]

V *The Tempest*, Royal Shakespeare Theatre, 1978. David Suchet as Caliban
[*Photo: Joe Cocks*]

VI *The Merchant of Venice*, The Other Place, Stratford, 1978. Directed by John Barton, designed by Christopher Morley. Patrick Stewart as Shylock
[*Photo: Joe Cocks*]

VII *Measure for Measure*, Royal Shakespeare Theatre, 1978. Directed by Barry Kyle, designed by Christopher Morley. Michael Pennington as the Duke and Paola Dionisotti as Isabella at the Moated Grange
[*Photo: Joe Cocks*]

VIII *Love's Labour's Lost*, Royal Shakespeare Theatre, 1978. Directed by John Barton, designed by Ralph Koltai. From left to right: Michael Pennington as Berowne, Paul Whitworth as Dumaine, Richard Griffiths as the King, Carmen du Sautoy as the Princess, Jane Lapotaire as Rosaline, Sheridan Fitzgerald as Maria, Avril Carson as Katherine
[*Photo: Joe Cocks*]

SHAKESPEARE'S MIDDLE COMEDIES:
A GENERATION OF CRITICISM

M. M. MAHOOD

On one point, and one alone, critics of the past twenty-five years can be said to have reached agreement about *Much Ado About Nothing*, *As You Like It*, and *Twelfth Night*: they belong to a group of plays which are Shakespeare's finest achievement in comedy. A generation ago such an assertion would have been open to challenge by those who had rediscovered the forgotten strengths of the last plays, but in 1961 Frank Kermode, contributing to *Early Shakespeare* (edited by J. R. Brown and B. Harris), dared to let it be known that he thought 'The Mature Comedies' better plays than the Romances, and his judgment has persisted and prevailed.

Mature is not the most fortunate name. Is the chestnut spire less mature than the fruit? 'Middle', though a drab term, has the advantage of neutrality over epithets such as happy, gay, golden, festive, joyous, all of which have proved counter-productive: A. P. Rossiter (*Angel with Horns*, 1961) reminds us of the '*Decameron*-like hardness' of *Much Ado About Nothing*, and Ralph Berry detects much aggression in the abrasive encounters of *As You Like It*, while unnumbered critics stress the underlying sadness of *Twelfth Night*. Perhaps we have become wary of adjectives suggestive of jollity and contentment because they came rather easily to all those eminent figures invited, around the quatercentennial year, to say a few words in appreciation of Shakespeare. J. Dover Wilson's *Shakespeare's Happy Comedies* (1962) is, however, far from such bumbling. Based on ideas shaped in the nineteen-twenties when the author was helping Arthur Quiller-Couch to edit the Comedies, it pays no heed to post-war critical discussion. Yet it would be an impertinence in both the Elizabethan and the modern sense to complain that the book is old-fashioned in its attribution of an independent life to dramatic characters. Over the course of half a century, the plays had indeed become 'another Nature' to Wilson, so that for him Olivia was 'real' enough to plight her troth to Sebastian 'in the very chantry that she had erected to her brother's memory'. And in such responses Wilson is always rubbing shoulders with an Elizabethan audience that he knew as well as it can be known.

'Q''s rather skimpy presentation of the Comedies was virtually the only annotated edition available to English readers in the nineteen-fifties. Although the New Arden was then under way, *As You Like It* and *Twelfth Night* did not appear until 1975 and as yet there is no *Much Ado About Nothing*. The needs of students in the greatly expanded universities of the nineteen-sixties were served at first by the Signet paperbacks and later, from 1967 and 1968, by Penguin editions of all three comedies. The want of a fully scholarly apparatus was more apparent than real, since these plays require less editorial intervention and explanation than most. Their dates, give or take a year, are agreed upon, and their texts present no massive problems. The major sources of each play, in a new translation when necessary, have been available since 1958 in the second volume of Geoffrey Bullough's *Narrative and Dramatic Sources of Shakespeare* (1957–75). This enables us to read, say, an important article such as Robert C. Melzi's 'From Lelia to Viola' (*Renaissance Drama*, 9, 1966) with some relevant texts at our elbow; moreover, both Bullough and Kenneth Muir (*Shakespeare's Sources*, 1957) provide lucid critical discussions of their own. Probably the chief usefulness of annotated editions in the period under review has lain in their introductions, and here one would wish to pick out Agnes Latham's sensible and crisply-worded introduction to the New Arden *As You Like It*.

The guidance traditionally afforded by editors has been supplemented in this period from new sources. There are for example the students' guidebooks aimed largely at readers outside the U.K. and the U.S. I shall be returning to G. K. Hunter's workmanlike *Writers and their Work* booklet (*Shakespeare: the Late Comedies*, 1962; revised 1969). Gareth Lloyd Evans, in *Shakespeare III* (1971), chances his arm more freely, as when he finds all the heroines a little sad – not all readers will share his conviction that Beatrice, after telling us she was born under a dancing star, leaves the stage in tears. The general introduction I would most readily direct the student towards is not an undergraduate guidebook but the essay 'Shakespeare's Comedies' in F. P. Wilson's posthumous *Shakespearian and Other Studies* (1969) edited by Helen Gardner. Intended for the Elizabethan Drama volume of the *Oxford History of English Literature*, it is a model of what such history should be. Wilson writes in the security of a marvellously full knowledge which enables him to present the plays with a Johnson-like independence, common sense, and gusto.

The needs of the new student public have also been met by those slim monographs which would once have been dubbed Bazaar Notes but which nowadays, in the hands of critics

such as Barbara Hardy (*Twelfth Night*, 1962), J. R. Mulryne (*Much Ado About Nothing*, 1965) and Michael Jamieson (*As You Like It*, 1965) can often breathe new vigour into elderly academic reading. Another 'aid to study' is the collection of essays; it has its dangers because it may leave the reader confident he has all the evidence in the case, and at the same time reluctant to trust his own experience of the play; but it has the compensating merit that it can bring back into circulation essays from little-known or defunct periodicals. This is especially the virtue of L. D. Lerner's *Shakespeare's Comedies* (Harmondsworth, 1967). The really enterprising undergraduate now has his own bibliographical guide in Gāmini Salgādo's chapter on these plays in *Shakespeare: Select Bibliographical Guides* (edited by Stanley Wells, Oxford, 1973).

The existence of other bibliographical guides, notably the annual bibliography in *Shakespeare Quarterly* and the annual review of criticism in *Shakespeare Survey*, makes my task rather different from that undertaken in the articles which introduced earlier volumes of the *Survey*. In the safe knowledge that all the books and articles on the middle comedies subsequent to John Russell Brown's review in *Shakespeare Survey 8* can be located through these and other reference works, I have taken the risk of being idiosyncratically selective. My plan is, first, to try to define the direction of critical principle and practice in books on Shakespearian comedy, which these plays represent at its best; then to review studies of certain features common to these three plays; and finally to review interpretations of them one by one. I am only too aware that some real gold must have slipped through my sieve, but in honesty I have to add that some of the three score and upward of articles devoted to each of these plays in the last twenty-five years are not named here because my reaction to them was: 'O what men dare do! What men **may** do!'

II

Re-reading the books and articles on Shakespeare's comedies which have been published in the last twenty-five years is like turning the leaves of the family photograph album: did we really all look like that, not so very long ago? The fashion of the fifties was for the *leitmotiv*, the theme, the governing idea. It was a healthy and necessary reaction against mere gustatory relish: Shakespeare had to be shown to have something to say in these comedies. In his presidential address to the English Association in 1958, 'The Nature of Comedy and Shakespeare', E. M. W. Tillyard claimed that 'Shakespeare tells us' this in *Much Ado About Nothing*, and 'tells us' that in *As You Like It*. In *Free Shakespeare* (1974) (the title is a slogan rather than a description), J. R. Brown gazes rather ruefully at himself when young: 'The comedies, so long enjoyed without conscious moral reflection, have been presented by scholarship as treatments of "Love's Order", "Love's Wealth", "Love's Truth", each play having its implicit judgement on human relationships.' Actually *Shakespeare and His Comedies* (1957) is far from being a dated book, thanks to Brown's insistence that the meaning of each play is not an extractable element but implicit in its whole action. Other critics, however, in their search for the pattern in the carpet – and 'pattern' was the in-word of the decade – arbitrarily picked up this or that thread, and some odd distortions resulted from the process. Critics of the fifties, murmuring 'themes, themes' with the ecstasy of Kipps contemplating 'chubes, chubes', tended to take the view of a play that a medical drawing takes of the human frame. We were often presented with a diagram of veins or muscles or bones; occasionally with a skilfully complete, transparent model of the whole body; but scarcely ever with an image of the living play.

A living play is more than actors on a stage interpreting a text: it is a communal event in time, an occasion created by actors and audience together. The recognition of this made C. L. Barber's *Shakespeare's Festive Comedy* (Princeton, N.J., 1959) a turning-point in criticism. Barber's argument moved forward from an alternative form of pattern-making, that represented by the earlier writings of Northrop Frye. 'Model' would be a better word than 'pattern' here, since Frye did not trace the designs of individual plays but rather evolved the poetics of comedy in defining a comic structure so compelling that Shakespeare, whatever his story, had to respond to its 'comic drive'. Like Frye, Barber views Shakespearian comedy as a fruit of the union between classical comedy and the 'folk' element, but for him the all-important aspect of the Saturnalian tradition is its communal character. The audience does not merely witness the archetypal progress 'through release to clarification'. Because the play's context is traditional revelry, it experiences this archetypal progress for itself.

It was some time before this awareness of the participating audience became a critical assumption. Bertrand Evans's book, *Shakespeare's Comedies* (Oxford, 1960), recognises the audience's share, in that his subject is dramatic irony, the comic exploitation of differences of awareness among characters, and between the characters and ourselves. But for him the audience's function is to judge rather than share; each play offers a hierarchy of knowingness, with ourselves as the omniscient gods and such characters as Dogberry in the lowest depths of ignorance. Even when Evans acknowledges our involvement in the great scenes of *Twelfth Night* he speaks of it as 'a sense of personal responsibility'. Surely it is not responsibility which leads people to 'jump up' in the Trinidad or Brixton Carnival.

In 1965 three works appeared which all in their different ways reflected the increasing concern with comedy as a communal experience.

3

Francis Berry, in *The Shakespeare Inset*, studied one set of dramaturgical devices by which Shakespeare manipulates our involvement. His discussion of *Twelfth Night* IV, ii is particularly sensitive. R. G. Hunter's *Shakespeare and the Comedy of Forgiveness* (Columbia) identifies a traditional role of the spectators of comedy: they are called upon to forgive the central character, however erring, in the way that they once concurred in forgiving *humanum genus* in the medieval miracle play. Most interesting of all was the third chapter of Northrop Frye's *A Natural Perspective* (New York, 1965). Here, our varying abilities to participate in comedy's ritual of identity lost and identity rediscovered in a new social order – that archetype which so much fascinated the structuralist sixties – is shown to be provided for by characters who embody the part of our mind which holds back from, or even rejects, the comic imbroglio: the fool and the *idiotes*, as they are paired in Dogberry and Don John, Touchstone and Jaques, Feste and Malvolio. Philip Edwards has spoken up well for such loners in *Shakespeare and the Confines of Art* (1968).

The multi-consciousness of the dramatist, matching the multifariousness of audience responses, has become a leading critical interest of the present decade. Two pointers to it were Norman Rabkin's *Shakespeare and the Common Understanding* (New York, 1967) which applied the physicists' notion of 'complementariness' to the way Shakespeare's plays resist the imposition of neat critical designs, and 'Comic Structure and Tonal Manipulation in Shakespeare and Some Modern Plays' by Herbert S. Weil Jr (*Shakespeare Survey 22*, Cambridge, 1969) which represents Shakespearian comedy as having the openness of Genet and Albee:

Because affirmation in comedy has received the most intelligent and stimulating criticism – as for example in the well-known works of Frye, Barber and Gardner – I feel that possible alternative perspectives now need more of our attention. It is important that we should

be able to understand how *Much Ado About Nothing* can succeed for the spectator who does *not* believe in Claudio's transformation.

This perhaps overlooks the recognition of comedy's being a communal and hence not totally unanimous event which (I have tried to suggest) was frequently indicated by the archetypal school of critics. Writers of the present decade tend, however, to make a dialectical link between thematic and archetypal criticism. Alexander Leggatt sums up the new approach in 'Shakespeare and the Borderlines of Comedy' (*Mosaic*, 5, 1971).

After the play is over, we may want to look back and sort it out into some kind of pattern, around a theme – identity, order and disorder, or our old friend appearance and reality; or in a series of archetypes – the green world, the blocking character, the new society. But I suspect we may learn more about these plays by submitting to their very instability, watching carefully as one kind of experience or set of values is tested against another, and being prepared to find that the testing itself, more than the nature of the result, provides the common factor.

This testing has been carried out in the theatre by Brown, whose 1961 'Directions for *Twelfth Night*, or What You Will' (subsequently in *Shakespeare's Plays in Performance*, 1966) departs from his previous thematic criticism by emphasising a further variable in Shakespeare's comedy, the casting of the plays. Close textual study aimed not at an infallible interpretation but at the full range of possibilities, the 'theatrical life implicit in the printed words', is his method in *Shakespeare's Dramatic Style* (1970) which gives much attention to *As You Like It* and *Twelfth Night*. It is a compliment to call this an unreadable book; it requires to be argued out by a congenial group with ample acting space. An interest parallel to Brown's, the directions implicit in Shakespeare's text, has been pursued with great subtlety by Jörg Hasler in *Shakespeare's Theatrical Notation: The Comedies* (Bern, 1974).

To say that the approach to Shakespeare's plays in the fifties was thematic, taking a birdseye view, that in the sixties it was archetypal, taking a telstar view, and that in the seventies it is experimental, taking (Patrick Swinden's word) a kaleidoscopic view, would be in itself to impose an over-rigid pattern. The best of contemporary criticism avoids the categorised approach. This is true of the exploratory richness of Alexander Leggatt's *Shakespeare's Comedy of Love* (1974) and of Brown's wise reconciliation of Shakespeare's 'wide focus' with the underlying governing idea in 'The Presentation of Comedy: The First Ten Plays' (*Shakespearean Comedy* edited by David Palmer and Malcolm Bradbury, 1972). The book which is likely to give the most complete account of our enjoyment of a Shakespearian comedy, as we anticipate the play's archetypal form, share in its many-faceted theatrical experience and reflect on the ideas it has embodied, has yet to appear, but is on the stocks. Leo Salingar has chosen to make it the second volume of his *Shakespeare and the Tradition of Comedy* (Cambridge, 1974). His first volume is an erudite study of Shakespeare's inheritance from the comic traditions of the Middle Ages, and from the Roman and Italian stages. A little slow to ignite, the book catches fire when its author comes to deal with the historical circumstances that led Shakespeare, as a pioneer professional actor–dramatist, to reshape these multiple traditions into new forms of comedy of which our three plays are the leading examples.

III

Salingar views these three plays as each belonging to a distinct group of comedies: those concerned with escape into the green wood, those about deceptions in an urban setting, and those more sombre ones that are about broken nuptials. Sherman Hawkins too ('The Two Worlds of Shakespearean Comedy' in *Shake-speare Studies*, 3, 1967) sees only *As You Like It* as a play of Frye's green world and assigns the other two to an archetype 'in which intruders force their way into a closed world and draw its thwarted or random emotional forces to themselves'. But for most critics the three comedies with the oddly throwaway titles constitute a 'set' by virtue of the fact that they are courtly and concerned with courtship; whereas the contemporary *Merry Wives of Windsor* deals with bourgeois marriages and the nearly contemporary *The Merchant of Venice*, set in a merchant society, portrays love in terms of a fairy story rather than of *Il Corteggio*.

Few of them, however, join with John Vyvyan (*Shakespeare and the Rose of Love*, 1960; *Shakespeare and Platonic Beauty*, 1961) in finding Shakespeare's courtly comedies neo-Platonic. There is a general feeling that Shakespeare and his audience shared a more Anglo-Saxon attitude. Salingar is aware of a tension between exalted 'romantic 'notions of love and the mockery inherited from the English humanists. M. A. Shaaber believes that 'Shakespeare's characters are Laodiceans in the religion of love' ('The Comic View of Life in Shakespeare's Comedies', *The Drama of the Renaissance*, edited by E. M. Blistein, Providence, R.I, 1969) and for H. M. Richmond (*Shakespeare's Sexual Comedy*, New York, 1971) Shakespeare's view of sex is 'a wise hypocrisy'. These views are most applicable to the scenes between Beatrice and Benedick, and between Orlando and Rosalind, on which there have been many illuminating commentaries.

Another common feature of the three plays is a stylistic one. They are all, even *Twelfth Night*, predominantly in prose, and hence figure large in Brian Vickers's *The Artistry of Shakespeare's Prose* (1968). Vickers's knowledge of Elizabethan rhetoric, though it results in a brilliant exposé of Rosalind's 'pair of stairs to marriage' speech, is not the sharpest instrument for dissecting Shakespeare's style, and Ludwig Borinski, in a somewhat breathless article in *Shakespeare Survey 8* (Cambridge, 1955) on 'Shakespeare's Comic Prose', could only hint at the greater cutting edge of modern stylistics. A few critics have analysed particular linguistic features of the separate plays: the outstanding articles are Francis Fergusson's analysis of the final exchange between Beatrice and Benedick (1954 and subsequently in *The Human Image in Dramatic Literature*, New York, 1957); William G. McCollom's 'The Role of Wit in *Much Ado About Nothing*' (*Shakespeare Quarterly*, 19, 1968); Jonas Barish's 'Pattern and Purpose in the Prose of *Much Ado About Nothing*' (*Rice University Studies*, 60, 1974); another syntactical study, this time of *As You Like It* and *Twelfth Night*, 'Much Virtue in "If"' by Peter B. Murray (*University of Pennsylvania Library Chronicle*, 32, 1966); and Angus McIntosh's discussion of the use of 'thou' and 'you' between Rosalind and Celia (1963 and subsequently in *Patterns of Language*, 1966). The plays do, however, have certain stylistic qualities in common, not least their marvellously refreshing lucidity. Yet no one has yet followed the inviting clue held out by F. P. Wilson when he wrote that in these three plays 'the satisfaction of mind and sense given to us in verse and prose which it is a pleasure to speak or hear or read radiates an extraordinary happiness'.

By contrast, a great deal has been said in the last twenty-five years about another feature common to the three comedies, the importance of the 'Clown' parts. Much of it has been concerned with who acted whom. Dogberry, we know, was played by Kempe and, after he left the company in 1599, by Armin, whom John H. Long (*Shakespeare's Use of Music*, Gainesville, Florida 1955) thinks joined the Chamberlain's Men early enough to have played Balthasar. Feste was indisputably a role created for Armin. Touchstone, however, has the critics divided, and Latham fancies he had Shakespeare divided as well: 'An uncertainty on Shakespeare's part as to what actor he was

writing for may go some way towards explaining inconsistencies.' Charles Felver, in *Robert Armin* (Kent, Ohio, 1961), speculates that Armin, a good singer, could either have played Amiens to Kempe's Touchstone or used his skill as a quick-change artist to double Touchstone with Amiens. In 'Shakespeare's Fools: The Shadow and the Substance of Drama' (*Shakespearean Comedy*, 1972) G. L. Evans views Armin as virtually Shakespeare's collaborator, and Muriel Bradbrook (*Shakespeare the Craftsman*, Cambridge, 1969) attributes to his involvement the full embodiment of Shakespeare's comic vision in *Twelfth Night*.

The difference between Touchstone's 'undaunted cooperative jollity' and Feste's 'controlled, critical derision' (a neat distinction from Nevill Coghill's 'Wags, Clowns and Jesters' in *More Talking of Shakespeare* edited by John Garrett, 1959) could have offered Armin an interesting challenge; the fact that Feste, around 1601 or 1602, is a very wise fool is no argument against this gifted actor having played Touchstone as a less than wise fool in 1599. That Touchstone is not and should not be all-wise is a point made from different angles by Dean Frye ('The Question of Shakespearean Parody,' *Essays in Criticism*, 15, 1965) and Richard Levin ('Elizabethan "Clown" Subplots', *Essays in Criticism*, 16, 1966). Both professional Fools are thoroughly discussed by R. H. Goldsmith in *Wise Fools in Shakespeare* (East Lansing, Mich., 1955) and figure in William Willeford's *The Fool and his Sceptre* (Nebraska and London, 1969).

One regrettable result of our present interest in Armin is that we tend to think of the change from a simpleton to a wise fool as all gain and no loss. F. P. Wilson is even glad to see the back of Dogberry. But in either of his two gowns, what a back it is! That magnificent exit-speech has inspired Brown to an excellent commentary ('Mr Pinter's Shakespeare', *Critical Quarterly*, 5, 1963) and Rossiter has also given Dogberry his due as a great comic figure. In 'Comic Constables – Fictional and Historical' (*Shakespeare Quarterly*, 20, 1969), Hugh C. Evans reminds us that Elizabethan constables really were like Dogberry: a fact that might escape us in this Z-car age.

IV

In my review of the criticism of the three separate plays I am reversing their chronological order in the hope of avoiding an anticlimax. There have been many lively discussions of *Much Ado About Nothing* and comparatively few about *Twelfth Night*. Critics often appear to be flagging a little when they reach the last of Shakespeare's run of ten comedies. Sometimes they overwhelm it in a highly schematic attempt to relate it to all that has gone before (Brown, *Shakespeare and his Comedies*) and at other times they retreat abashed before its elusive grace. Some are left with an uneasy feeling of having strayed beyond the frontiers of comedy. For G. K. Hunter even Viola is the plaything of chance and the end is escape, not reconciliation: 'the happiness has no inevitability, and the final song sounds perilously like a tune whistled through the surrounding darkness'. Anne Barton ('*As You Like It* and *Twelfth Night*: Shakespeare's Sense of an Ending' in *Shakespearean Comedy*, ed. D. Palmer and M. Bradbury) reads the last scene as one in which the world of revelry seems to be fighting desperately against the cold light of day. Clifford Leech, in *Twelfth Night and Shakespearean Comedy* (1965) discovers discordant elements which suggest that Shakespeare had outgrown the 'delight' of festive comedy and was ready to seek out other forms of comedy in which to confront and explore the fragility of life. Patrick Swinden, in *An Introduction to Shakespeare's Comedies* (1973) feels the play's language to have become exploratory rather than eloquent: the explanation lies through an awareness of time and mortality afforded only to Feste.

The most interesting of these sombre readings is that of Leggatt. For him, the characters of *Twelfth Night* are isolated individuals adrift in a fragmented world. Malvolio in the dark house is the image of that isolation; his mirror opposite is Sebastian in the sun and air, liberating the characters of the love plot by his arrival in Illyria. Leggatt does not overlook the explosively funny effect of such a scene as the eavesdropping in the box tree (well expounded in theatrical terms by B. Evans and by Hasler) but true to his refusal to cage the living play within the archetype, or to render it down to its governing idea, he emphasises the diversity of moods in the separate plots and their respective outcomes.

Earlier critics were frequently disturbed by the cruelty of the trick played on Malvolio, and within our period the older critics have continued to express this uneasiness. J. D. Wilson thought Malvolio a man of spirit and self-respect, and found the mad scene painful, while F. P. Wilson made the excuse that Shakespeare must have felt an actor's natural hostility for any kind of gentleman usher. Leech replied to similar arguments in the critics' own terms when he pointed out that Malvolio has, for his part, had the unfortunate and presumably innocent Captain thrown into prison. Since 1957 most readers have been sufficiently persuaded by Barber's ideas about the festive exorcism of unwelcome spirits for them not to be troubled by the baiting of Malvolio. Their view is well represented by M. Seiden writing in *The University of Kansas City Review*, 28 (1961) on 'Malvolio Reconsidered'. The same journal earlier published 'The Masks of *Twelfth Night*' (no. 22, 1955), an influential essay by Joseph Summers who relates the play's visible deceptions and disguises to the self-deceptions of its characters. A recognition of the play's affinity with 'masques and revels' has led recent critics such as Porter Williams Jnr ('Mistakes in *Twelfth Night* and their Resolution', *PMLA*, 6, 1961), F. B. Tromly ('*Twelfth Night*: Folly's Talents and the Ethics of Shakespearian Comedy', *Mosaic*, 7, 1974), and Richard Henze ('*Twelfth Night*: Free Disposition on the Sea of Love', *Sewanee Review*, 83, 1975) to underline the play's celebration of such festive virtues as generosity and the readiness to take a risk.

The festive virtue of outgoing and generous natures is the theme of Harold Jenkins's essay, 'Shakespeare's *Twelfth Night*' (*Rice Institute Pamphlet*, 45, 1959) which concentrates upon Orsino and Olivia – two characters who have been rather roughly handled by critics anxious to show that they are not to be taken in by a pair of romantic poseurs. Thus, while not following W. I. D. Scott (*Shakespeare's Melancholics*, 1962), into the intricacies of Orsino's relation with his mother and Olivia's with her brother, Leech ('Shakespeare's Comic Dukes', *Review of English Literature*, 5, 1964) confidently speaks of Orsino's 'insufficiency as an adult being'. Jenkins, like Shakespeare, is gentle: he shows the process by which Olivia and Orsino, persisting in their folly, become wise, whereas the no less deceived Malvolio ends up a 'poor fool'. The development is signposted in the differing responses of Olivia and Malvolio to Feste in I, iii:

What the comedy *may* suggest is that he who in his egotism seeks to fit the world to the procrustean bed of his own reason deserves his own discomfiture. But Olivia, who self-confessedly abandons reason, and Orsino, who avidly gives his mind to all the shapes of fancy, are permitted to pass through whatever folly there may be in this to a greater illumination.

The only objection one might make to this admirable reading is that it upstages Viola. But William Bache's essay on her redemptive role ('Levels of Perception in *Twelfth Night*', *Forum*, 5, 1964) fully reinstates her at the play's centre. The relation of her role to Olivia's is defined by Nevill Coghill when he says that the effect of the juxtapositions in the first three scenes of the play is that we take only one grief seriously, Viola's. Feste's joke about the departed soul could never have been made to Viola about her brother. Made almost in passing, in *Shakespeare's Professional Skills* (Cambridge, 1964), this is the kind of observation which outweighs many a boiled-down thesis.

V

As You Like It was just the play for the fifties. Its air of liberation, its informality of style, its delight in 'happenings' and eccentricity, above all its 'image of life triumphing over chance' which Suzanne Langer dubbed the essence of comedy, all chimed in with the mood of the 1951 Festival of Britain. The decade produced some splendid essays on the play. John Shaw, in 'Fortune and Nature in *As You Like It*' (*Shakespeare Quarterly*, 6, 1955) demonstrates persuasively that Shakespeare's handling of his source reveals that this thematic contrast was uppermost in his own mind. Jenkins, in an essay on the play in *Shakespeare Survey 8* (Cambridge, 1955) shows that Shakespeare clears his stage of conventional action in order to make room for many contrasting elements in human nature to comment on one another by their juxtaposition. This creation of 'a space to work things out' is Helen Gardner's starting point (in *More Talking of Shakespeare*) for an essay in which she deftly characterises the space, Arden, and defines the nature of the 'working out' as a discovery of where true happiness is to be found.

As B. Evans points out, Arden is a very still world after the bustle of Messina. 'No Clock in the Forest' gives Jay L. Halio the title for a telling study of time in the play (*Studies in English Literature*, 2, 1962) which suggests that in this timeless world, which is yet haunted by Jaques's and Touchstone's sense of riping and rotting, it is the role of Rosalind to lead Orlando towards 'a proper balance of unharried awareness'. One wishes Halio had himself had more time to develop this complex and thought-provoking theme; Frederick Turner is able to treat the subject more expansively, and with a pleasing lucidity, in *Shakespeare and the Nature of Time* (Oxford, 1971).

The charm of Arden for all these critics is that the forest – as shown in Mary Lascelles' 'Shakespeare's Pastoral Comedy' (*More Talking of Shakespeare*) – is a place where no one has the last word and no one wants it. This was no country for the rebellious sixties, and it is fascinating to see how the mood of the decade entered into even the most sober and scholarly articles. In "Strange Events": Improbability in *As You Like It*' Sylvan Barnet, in 1968 (*Shakespeare Studies*, 4), maintained that the play's characters act strangely, not because of any romance convention but because Shakespeare wanted to draw attention to their metamorphoses – mythical representations of the sudden changes that in real life are accomplished by suicide, psychosis or conversion. D. J. Palmer ('Art and Nature in *As You Like It*', *Philological Quarterly*, 49, 1970) views the encounters in the forest not as juxtapositions but as confrontations which bring the inhabitants face to face with themselves. Most challenging of all is Ralph Berry's 'No Exit from Arden' (1971 and subsequently in his *Shakespeare's Comedies*, Princeton, N.J., 1972) for whom these encounters are not debates so much as power struggles; virtually all the relationships manifest a sense of latent or open hostility: 'There is little true accord in Arden, prior to the final scene: and the audience is entitled, if it wishes, to its reservations even then'.

Although Berry's Rosalind, 'motivated above all by a will to dominate' might be more at home on the Paris barricades of 1968 than in the Globe Theatre, she is a refreshing change from the winsome Rosalinds invented by critics earlier in this century. Michael Jamieson too avoids the trite by dealing with Rosalind in theatrical terms; for him the part is 'Shakespeare's gesture of faith in the boy-actress'. ('Shakespeare's Celibate Stage', *Papers Mainly Shakespearian* edited by G. I. Duthie, 1964). Recently interest has shifted from the heroine to the hero and his brother. Francis Berry has given us an acute analysis of the dramaturgical skill with which Shakespeare persuades his audience of Oliver's conversion. The brief and sensible comments of Gardner and Latham on Orlando's merits as a hero, together with the fuller discussion by Thomas Kelly ('Shakespeare's Romantic Heroes: Orlando Reconsidered' in *Shakespeare Quarterly*, 24, 1973) perhaps do more to rehabilitate him than does J. Doebler's exaltation of him into 'Orlando: Athlete of Virtue' (*Shakespeare Survey 26*, Cambridge, 1973).

The one person of the play who never ceases to fascinate critics is Jaques. Peter G. Phialas's presentation of him in *Shakespeare's Romantic Comedies* (Chapel Hill, N. Carolina, 1966) is representative of the complexity which most observant critics find in the character: Jaques is 'the most vulnerable pseudo-idealist in the play', for while he is altogether opposed to romantic love he outdoes every other character in his commitment to an extreme form of pastoralism. True to the spirit of the seventies, subsequent critics have delighted in Jaques's enigmatic personality, and he figures prominently in three essays in *Shakespearean Comedy* (1972). In 'Two Unassimilable Men', A. D. Nuttall himself uses a wide lens to explore Jaques's libertine past, satiric present and anchorite future, against the background of pastoral's paradoxical blend of innocence and experience. R. A. Foakes also stresses the ambiguity of Jaques, though his prime purpose is with him as one of the 'Voices of Maturity in Shakespeare's Comedies'. Anne Barton, in the essay already alluded to, focuses upon Jaques's last speech, in which his pessimism is no longer set aside and he is allowed a sudden dignity:

This new attitude towards Jaques is important in determining the character of *As You Like It* at its ending. It represents, in Focillon's terms, that 'slight, inappreciable tremor' within the immobility of the classical moment.... Jaques' unwillingness to be part of this world shows that there are certain kinds of experience, certain questions, which lie outside the scope of the happy ending.

Though few critics of this generation have concerned themselves with the possibility that Jaques is a portrait of Jonson or Marston, many have viewed *As You Like It* in association with literary fashions of its age, notably for satire, pastoral and masque. The most original essay on the play's relation to satire is that of Herbert Howarth ('Shakespeare in 1599: The Event and the Art' in *University of Pennsylvania Library Chronicle*, 30, 1964). This argues that Shakespeare's response to the bishops' bonfire of satires was not Jaques's defence of polemics, but the play itself as a whole of sweetness and light intended to demonstrate that satire did not need to be 'snarling'.

Since parody and burlesque are forms of satire, the question of Shakespeare's satiric intentions merges with the problem of his attitude to pastoral. For the more perceptive critics, that attitude is decidedly ambivalent. Shakespeare may challenge the convention, says Lascelles, but he gets the right reply and can say 'Pass, friend, and all's well.' Madeleine Doran ('Yet am I inland bred', *Shakespeare 400* edited by James McManaway, New York, 1964) locates the ambiguity in incompatible myths: that of rudeness tamed into civility and that of a paradisial golden world; Shakespeare, for her, resolves the contradiction by making the one reality, the other a necessary dream. Hasler explores the extent to which these ambiguities of pastoral affect the verbal mise-en-scène of Arden. Two particularly thorough investigations of Shakespeare's use of the pastoral mode in this play occur in David Young's *The Heart's Forest* (New Haven, 1972) and Rosalie A. Colie's *Shakespeare's*

Living Art (Princeton, N.J., 1974). Resonant voices have however been raised against this kind of genre study: Marco Mincoff concludes from his study of 'What Shakespeare Did to *Rosalynde*' (*Shakespeare Jahrbuch*, 96, 1960) that Shakespeare's parody of pastoral is mere makeweight to his interest in the comedy of courtship, and F. P. Wilson says firmly that there are few traces of pastoral left in the play.

If the pastoral mode has been over-emphasised, too little has been said about the masque in the last scene. G. K. Hunter has to compress into a page or two some arresting ideas about the masque as summation. V. Y. Kantak, as constricted in 'An Approach to Shakespearian Comedy' (*Shakespeare Survey 22*, Cambridge, 1969), well sums up the effect of Rosalind's stage-management:

It is as though she were to possess a double identity as ritual prototype and naturalistic character, presenting a kind of fusion of the ceremonial and the historical in an easy combination. With one part of her mind she gives way to the saturnalian release and holds it in check with the other.

To Marilyn L. Williamson, writing in *Comparative Drama*, 2, 1968 ('The Masque of Hymen in *As You Like It*'), the important point is that the masque is, as it were, a play *outside* the play, offering a generalised perspective which includes ourselves. Once again, the recent trend towards multi-consciousness is felt; and perhaps only an awareness of the multiplicity of responses in the 'house' and in each succeeding house, can resolve the question of whether Hymen is the god himself or a handy shepherd acting in Rosalind's charade. Our individual answer will depend on our total and personal experience of the play; as Gardner says, this too must be taken as you like it.

VI

This is the place to refer to another kind of personal experience. Whereas the better essays on *Twelfth Night* and *As You Like It* have given a form and language to my own rather ill-defined enjoyment of these plays, the better essays on *Much Ado About Nothing* have made it possible for me thoroughly to enjoy a play I once thought a failure. This they have done by genuinely elucidating, rather than seeking to explain away, those features of plot and structure I once found so unsatisfactory.

The role of Margaret is one such stumbling-block. Rossiter smartly demolishes the common notion that Margaret could not have called Borachio 'Claudio' from Hero's window. But the ambiguity of her part in the whole play causes John Wain, in 'The Shakespearean Lie-Detector: Thoughts on *Much Ado About Nothing*' (*Critical Quarterly*, 9, 1969), to describe her as 'one of those characters on whom Shakespeare has simply given up' while Allan Gilbert ('Two Margarets: The Composition of *Much Ado About Nothing*', *Philological Quarterly*, 41, 1962) is driven to conclude that Shakespeare first wrote the play without Margaret's disguise and subsequently revised it. There is an edge of desperate ingenuity about various attempts to explain away the play's apparent false start, usually by connecting the characters' 'alacrity to deceive and be deceived' with the broken nuptials. James A. S. MacPeek's article 'The Thief "Deformed" and Much Ado About "Noting" ', in *Boston University Studies in English*, 4, 1960, is worth mention here for the skill with which it attempts neatly to tie in one of the more trailing loose ends. But critics are so hard put to it to make *Much Ado About Nothing* a well-made play in the conventional sense that one welcomes the candour of Swinden's assertion that its *non sequiturs* and confusions add up to undeniable clumsiness.

The culprit, for both Wain and Swinden, is Claudio. His behaviour has amassed a whole thesaurus of abuse. Critics find him unattractive, unpleasant, despicable, insufferable; he is self-indulgent, mentally undeveloped, stupid, morally blind, inflexible, insensitive, unimaginative, suspicious, jealous, faithless, hypo-critical, shallow, trivial, petty, volatile, verbose, ungenerous, conventional, ill-tempered, smug, selfish, callow, and cruel. A spoilt whipper-snapper, with no more spirit than a dabchick, he is outwardly polished but inwardly tarnished: a sadistic prig. With this bad report in our hands it is difficult to listen to the gentle protests made on his behalf by Mulryne for whom he is young, insecure, and vulnerable; or by Brown who sees him as tongue-tied at the obligation to denounce Hero; or by Fredson Bowers who points out that that obligation would be regarded as a public duty ('Shakespeare's Art: The Point of View' in *Literary Views* edited by Carroll Camden, Chicago, 1964); or by J. D. Wilson who argues that because Count Claudio marries beneath him his acceptance of the substitute bride is a gracious reparation for the damage done to Leonato.

Wain, for whom 'Which is the lady I must seize upon?' has a claim to be called the worst line in Shakespeare, is among those who feel that Claudio is a 'miscalculation' on Shakespeare's part. Others believe that in making Claudio the man he is Shakespeare knew exactly what he was about. In the mid-sixties (when else?) both Walter N. King ('Much Ado About *Something*', *Shakespeare Quarterly*, 15, 1964) and John Crick, contributing to *The Use of English*, 17, 1965, read the play as in large measure the denunciation of a corrupt society. The objection to such an interpretation is that it forces us to separate Beatrice and Benedick from Claudio and Hero in a way that the play's diversity of interest, marked as it is, does not really justify; in the end the bickering lovers are content to go the way of their world.

This diversity of the double plots ('involved, not integrated' says Gilbert) has proved painful to the thematic critics in their search for a governing idea. The play *must*, they insist, be about something. So the Nothing of the title is promoted to a philosophical abstraction, the abyss of creativity (Paul Jorgensen 1954 and subsequently in *Redeeming Shakespeare's Words*, Berkeley, 1962). Or it is a pun on Noting, and the dominant theme is observation (Dorothy C. Hockey, 'Notes, Notes, Forsooth', in *Shakespeare Quarterly*, 8, 1957). Others have struggled on, searching for the key to Deformed's lock – love and self-love, faith and fashion, wit and wisdom.

But who wants to take a map into a maze? The pleasure of a maze lies in thinking we know the way and finding we do not; running down blind alleys; hearing voices through the hedge; meeting people as lost as ourselves. That the play is maze-like in its wrong turnings, whether these were designed or spontaneous, is implicit in its title. In speaking of 'an almost Shandean muddle in which no expectation is ever gratified in the anticipated manner' Bowers crosses the carpet to join the genuine explainers of the play as distinct from the excusers or attackers.

Of course Claudio is insufferable. 'It is unnecessary', writes Frye, 'to change our attitude to Claudio, by historical or other arguments, in order to make the play a comedy for us.' The comic drive is to the altar. Francis G. Schoff, in 'Claudio, Bertram, and a Note on Interpretation' (*Shakespeare Quarterly*, 10, 1959), is more persuasive when he stresses the Friar's assumption that Hero still wants to marry the man who has publicly called her a rotten orange, than when he tries to whitewash Claudio. We share and are meant to share, claims R. G. Hunter, Beatrice's wish to eat Claudio's heart in the marketplace; yet in the end, because the genre has absorbed the medieval miracle play as well as the love-chases of the New Comedy and the *commedia erudita*, we see cause to become an actor too in the play, and to bestow a god-like forgiveness on the bridegroom. Such an audience-involvement, the total comprehension required for a total forgiveness, is beautifully analysed in Jörg Hasler's detailed discussion of the church scene.

Like the meanders of the plot and like our dissatisfaction with Claudio, the play's disunity, once it is confronted rather than evaded, becomes an essential part of this full and varied theatrical experience. Critics who listen attentively to the play's tone are struck by its unique naturalism. In so convincing an atmosphere of 'ennobled domesticity' (as Barbara Everett calls it in *Critical Quarterly*, 3, 1961) Dogberry is right to claim that 'All men are not alike.' In an essay in *More Talking of Shakespeare* which is somewhat hampered by the compulsion to discover a central theme – he finds it in 'giddiness', which sounds more centrifugal than central – Graham Storey maintains that to worry about the play's lack of structural unity is to underrate the comic capacity of both Shakespeare and his audience 'to create, and to respond to, varying and often contradictory experiences'. When we have entrusted ourselves to these varying experiences, and stopped worrying about the structural or thematic relationship between the various parts of the play we can, with Rossiter, enjoy the displacement of the main plot by the subplot, as in a Mannerist painting; or with Everett enjoy the movements between a man's world and a woman's world; or with Leggatt enjoy the reversal of the audience's expectations in the resolution of each part of the intrigue:

The action of the Claudio plot, by its very formality, is seen as connected with the basic, familiar rhythms of life. And the love-affair of Beatrice and Benedick – so naturalistically conceived, so determined by individual character – is seen, at bottom, as a matter of convention.

Recent criticism, then, has helped us to enjoy *Much Ado About Nothing*. This is what matters. Shakespeare was the dramatic master of the catchphrase, so this survey of a generation of criticism can well end with a catchphrase of twenty-five years ago: what's it all in aid of? The Ph.D., the *curriculum vitae*, the *Who's Who* entry? Or Shakespeare? I have named several critics whose approach to the middle comedies seems to me wrong-headed and no doubt, in another catchphrase of the fifties, the feeling is mutual. But most of the articles and books mentioned here could, I believe, send the reader to the theatre with a heightened capacity to enjoy one of these three comedies. And that is what they are in aid of.

'PERFECT TYPES OF WOMANHOOD': ROSALIND, BEATRICE AND VIOLA IN VICTORIAN CRITICISM AND PERFORMANCE

RUSSELL JACKSON

George Bernard Shaw, writing to *The Daily News* in 1905 to make clear his position on Shakespeare, claimed that the playwright had attempted 'to make the public accept real studies of life and character in – for instance – Measure for Measure and All's Well That Ends Well' but had failed to overcome the public's philistine preference for 'a fantastic sugar doll, like Rosalind'. The eighth point of his polemic was 'That people who spoil paper and waste ink by describing Rosalind as a perfect type of womanhood are the descendants of the same blockheads whom Shakespear, with the coat of arms and the lands in Warwickshire in view, had to please when he wrote plays as they liked them.'[1]

Shaw was attacking not a handful of eccentrics, but the main body of Victorian critical opinion in the theatre and out of it. It is the intention of this article to describe the principal features of this orthodoxy, and to examine some of its theatrical manifestations.[2]

I

In an age of general enthusiasm for Shakespeare's heroines as examples of womanhood at its finest, the heroines of the three 'mature comedies', Rosalind, Beatrice and Viola, were outclassed only by Imogen – and that principally because she suffered more than they. Ruskin in 'Of Queens' Gardens' (1865) and Swinburne in *A Study of Shakespeare* (1880) joined a chorus of editors and critics when they proclaimed their admiration for Shakespeare's

noble ladies. The most influential work of this kind was Anna Jameson's *Shakespeare's Heroines – Characteristics of Women, Moral, Poetical and Historical*, first published in 1832. Here the female characters served as examples for a study of their sex's psychology, sparing the author any hazards that might arise from the use of living subjects, 'modified by particular customs, by fashion, by situation'. Shakespeare's characters are such that 'the virtuous and calm affections predominate, and triumph over shame, fear, pride, resentment, vanity, jealousy' and they are 'perfect in their kind, because so quiet in their effect'.[3] For the same reasons Mary Cowden Clarke commended the study of Shakespeare to girls, giving a forbidding account of the lessons to be learned:

[1] Edwin Wilson, ed., *Shaw on Shakespeare* (Harmondsworth, 1969), p. 26.

[2] Most of my examples of stage-business are drawn from promptbooks: in identifying these, reference is made to Charles H. Shattuck's *The Shakespeare Promptbooks: A Descriptive Catalogue* (Urbana, 1965). The spelling and abbreviations of the originals have been retained: in some cases punctuation has been added. I am grateful to the curators of the following collections for permission to quote from unpublished material: The Folger Shakespeare Library; Harvard Theatre Collection; New York Public Library; The Shakespeare Centre Library, Stratford-upon-Avon and the Governors of the Royal Shakespeare Theatre. This article is based on research supported by a grant from the British Academy.

[3] Anna Jameson, *Characteristics of Women, Moral, Poetical and Historical*, 2 vols. (3rd edition, 1835), I, 53.

From his youthful women [the girl] can gain lessons in artlessness, guilelessness, modesty, sweetness, ingenuousness and the most winning candour; from his wives and matrons she can derive instructions in moral courage, meekness, magnanimity, firmness, devoted tenderness, high principle, noble conduct, loftiest speech and sentiment.[1]

In *The Girlhood of Shakespeare's Heroines* (1850–5) she produced further instances of these qualities in characters of whom Shakespeare himself had given all too brief a glance. There the reader might encounter 'the opening buds of the future "bright consummate flowers" which Shakespeare has given us in immortal bloom'.[2]

Whereas Cordelia, Miranda, Imogen and Perdita were easily accepted as exemplary women, Rosalind, Beatrice and Viola, for all the affection they attracted, could not be accepted without some special pleading. They enjoyed a freedom of speech and mind beyond what was proper in a well-brought-up Victorian girl. Two of them dress as men and, unlike Imogen, seem at times to enjoy the disguise. Ellen Terry, a freer spirit than most of her contemporaries, welcomed this 'vindication of woman' in Shakespeare's 'fearless, high-spirited, resolute and intelligent heroines', but others were more cautious.[3] The author of *Shakespeare's Garden of Girls* (1885), after some discussion of Rosalind's 'philosophy', insists that for all her acuteness 'she surrenders herself to the mastery of love with a self-abandonment that never oversteps the modesty of maidenhood'. She assures us that Rosalind finds it 'positively painful' to be seen in man's attire.[4] The problem drew some stern writing from Henry Hudson, an altogether more important critic. He claimed that Rosalind's superficial 'frolicsomeness' covered 'a firm basis of thought and womanly dignity', so that 'she never laughs away our respect'. Hudson was able to assure his readers that Rosalind's dreams were 'made up of cunning, quirkish fancies; her wits being in a frolic even

when she is asleep'. Her seeming so well at ease in doublet and hose shows her enjoyment of an innocent deception, rather than any relish for the clothing.[5] Helen Faucit, considered by many to be the century's finest interpreter of the part, suggested that an ordinary comic actress could not do justice even to 'the joyous, buoyant side of her nature', mingled as it was with 'deep womanly tenderness' and showing 'an active intellect disciplined by fine culture, as well as tempered by a certain native distinction'.[6] Dowden, in an 1885 essay on 'Shakespeare's Portraiture of Women', insisted that Rosalind's wit was not hard or cold, but 'A cascade of sparkling speech...it is sun-illumined as it falls, and over it hangs the iris of a lover's hope'.[7] Mrs Jameson distinguished between Rosalind's wit, which 'bubbles up and sparkles like the living fountain, refreshing all around', and that of Beatrice, which 'plays about us like the lightning, dazzling but also alarming'. Even in Rosalind's 'most petulant raillery' is a redeeming 'touch of

[1] Mary Cowden Clarke, 'Shakespeare as the Girl's Friend', *The Girl's Own Paper*, VIII (1887), quoted by Richard D. Altick, *The Cowden Clarkes* (1948), p. 232.

[2] Mary Cowden Clarke, *The Girlhood of Shakespeare's Heroines*, 3 vols. (Everyman's Library, 1906), I, xii.

[3] Ellen Terry, *Four Lectures on Shakespeare*, edited with an introduction by Christopher St John (1932), p. 81. The lectures were delivered in the period 1911–1925.

[4] [Mrs M. L. Eliott], *Shakespeare's Garden of Girls* (1885), pp. 98, 94.

[5] H. N. Hudson, *Shakespeare: His Life, Art and Characters*, 2 vols. (4th edition, revised, Boston, Mass., 1898), I, 345 and 346. Hudson's book was first published in 1872.

[6] Helen Faucit, Lady Martin, *On Some of Shakespeare's Female Characters* (2nd edition, 1891), p. 236.

[7] Edward Dowden, 'Shakespere's Portraiture of Women', *The Contemporary Review*, 47 (April 1885), 517–35; p. 531. In *Shakespere* (Literature Primers series, 1877), Dowden commented that 'Rosalind's bright, tender womanhood seems but to grow more exquisitely feminine in the male attire which she has assumed in self-defence' (p. 110).

softness'. Mrs Jameson even congratulated Shakespeare on the success with which he has brought so forthright a character as Beatrice 'within the pale of our sympathy'.[1] That this might be a problem for Victorian readers is suggested by Thomas Campbell's description of Beatrice as an 'odious woman', but commentators usually found in her the virtues that would make a good wife for Benedick. One anonymous author offered a picture of the couple at home, which Furness included in his note on the notion of 'Benedick the married man':

her voice will often be 'gentle and low, an excellent thing in woman' as on flaky feet she comes stealthily behind her husband reading in his easy-chair, (for he goes no more to the wars), and lays on his shoulder her hand of light, or, as she drops a kiss on his cheek, insinuates into his ear a wicked whisper.[2]

George Fletcher, in his *Studies in Shakespeare*, argued that both Rosalind and Beatrice had been ill served by giving the parts to actresses whose talents lay in comedy. In Rosalind they had missed the 'strong feeling of earnest purpose' and in Beatrice the 'profound seriousness' which could only be expressed by 'an artist capable of embodying the still higher ideals of Shakespearean womanhood'.[3] As for Viola, critics agreed that her pathetic bereavement and the strength of her love for Orsino redeemed her. Mrs Jameson pointed out that, unlike Rosalind, Viola gets no pleasure from her disguise and bears within her an 'inward and spiritual grace of modesty'. Charles Knight found difficulties in Olivia's outspoken wooing of Cesario, but conceded that the dramatist had managed to make her 'not in the slightest degree repulsive'. Given the 'old stories' as his raw material, 'nothing but the refined delicacy of Shakespeare's conception of female character could have redeemed him from approaching the anti-feminine'.[4]

Insistence that these comic heroines were, for all their wit, devoted and modest was regularly accompanied by reminders that the plays were written in a spirit of holiday. Even before Dowden's systematic discussion of the canon in terms of periods in the author's spiritual life, it was generally agreed that Shakespeare wrote *As You Like It*, *Twelfth Night* and *Much Ado About Nothing* when he was at the height of his powers and, to say the least, happy to be so. John Barton's 1969 production of *Twelfth Night* for the Royal Shakespeare Company, with its pervasive melancholy, and the remark of a reviewer that the same company's 1974 production missed the play's 'inherent ambiguity and sadness' would have been puzzling to a Victorian playgoer or reader.[5] Hazlitt had wondered whether *Twelfth Night* might not be 'too good-natured for a comedy' and Charles Knight described its geniality in terms that are representative of those applied commonly to all three plays: 'The "sunshine of the breast" spreads its rich purple light over the whole champaign, and penetrates into every thicket and every dingle.'[6] Hazlitt considered *Much Ado About Nothing* to have hit 'that middle point of comedy...in which the ludicrous blends with the tender, and

[1] Jameson, *Characteristics*, I, 147 (Beatrice and Rosalind) and 129 (Beatrice).

[2] Thomas Campbell (1838) cited by Furness, New Variorum *Much Ado* (Philadelphia, 1899), p. 289. The anonymous article is one of a series by John Wilson, reviewing Anna Jameson's *Characteristics*: *Blackwood's Magazine*, 33 (April 1833), 539–60; p. 546 (attribution in *The Wellesley Index to Victorian Periodicals*, I (1966), 43).

[3] George Fletcher, *Studies of Shakespeare* (1847), pp. 226, 282 and 234.

[4] Charles Knight, *The Pictorial Shakespeare*, 8 vols (1865–6), II, 185. Charles Cowden Clarke, in *Shakespeare–Characters* (1863), observed that Shakespeare had redeemed Olivia 'from the charge of violating the principles of delicacy in women; for, instead of being the retiring and attracting, she is the seeking party' (p. 196).

[5] *The Observer*, 25 August 1974.

[6] William Hazlitt, *Characters of Shakespeare's Plays* in *Works*, ed. P. P. Howe, 21 vols. (1930–4), IV, 165–361; p. 313. Charles Knight, *The Pictorial Shakespeare*, II, 185.

our follies, turning round against themselves in support of our affections, retain nothing but their humanity'.[1] Edward R. Russell, expressing the wish that Irving would turn his hand to a production of *As You Like It*, gives an orthodox summary of its appeal:

As You Like It, sunny and shady in sylvan beauty, decked with all the sprightly guise of poetic masquerade, ravishing with the infinite charm of fair, frolicsome pure womanhood, solemnised with the tender gravity of exile, sententious with the quaint wit of wise folly and the delicate communings of ruminant philosophy.

After reading such eulogies, one appreciates the full iconoclastic force of Shaw's contempt for Duke Senior, the 'unvenerable imposter, expanding on his mixed diet of pious twaddle and venison'.[2]

II

The theatre responded fully to the demands of critical opinion for 'depth' in the characterisation of the heroines and serenity in the pictures within which they were to be set (See plates IA, B and C). The resources of scenic artists and stage-management afforded ways of placing on stage the 'sunshine of the breast'. As, towards the end of the century, methods of staging grew more and more sophisticated, and designers moved away from painting to 'building-out' sets, effects became more elaborate. Henry Irving's *Twelfth Night*, in 1884, had lighting effects that impressed William Archer:

There is even in some scenes, such as that in Orsino's palace, an apparently intentional effort to indicate a semi-magic light, neither that of common day nor of any visible lamp, torch or candle, but a suffused rich radiance contrasting exquisitely with the blue moonlight in the background.[3]

Augustin Daly's efforts in this direction were not always successful, as Shaw's exasperated reviews of his productions suggest. For the opening of his *Much Ado About Nothing* (New York, 1896) he provided a set of the interior of Leonato's house, with a view of Messina 'now in the sunset glow: and later illuminated, when night comes on'.[4] In the course of the first act the change from evening to night takes place, the curtain falling on a 'picture' of Claudio and Hero together at the balustrade overlooking the city. A quartet sings offstage. When Beatrice overhears Hero and Ursula talking of Benedick's love, it is by moonlight ('Blue Calcium from flies R. on Beatrice') and the mimed episode of Claudio's deception by Borachio and Don John is seen by the same light. Daly's final act begins with a slow curtain to reveal Hero, alone in the garden:

Blue Borders, Strips & Footlights. Red Footlights 1/2 up. Hero discovered on seat C. Sings to harp accompaniment. After song, rises & exits back of C. and off R.U.E., back of House. Then enter Leonato & Antonio. Red lights slowly up – Foot, borders & strips.

The New York Times valued highly this 'exquisitely beautiful pictorial realisation of the poet's Messina' and 'the atmosphere of romance imparted by the music, the songs, the hymn, and the antique dances' (Daly, ever anxious to give value for money, had 'Sigh no more, ladies' accompanied by a dance of gypsies). There was also praise for 'the play of light and shadow, the tasteful combination of rich colors, the delightful fantasies of sight and sound'. Daly chose to omit the tomb scene

---

[1] Hazlitt, *Works*, IV, 338.
[2] Edward R. Russell, 'Mr Irving's Work', *The Fortnightly Review*, n.s. 36 (September 1884), 401–10; p. 410. Shaw, reviewing Daly's *AYLI* (1896), in *Shaw on Shakespeare*, p. 48.
[3] William Archer, '*Twelfth Night* at the Lyceum', *Macmillan's Magazine*, 50 (August 1884), 271–9; p. 277.
[4] Promptbook of Daly's *Much Ado* (New York, 1896–7), New York Public Library at the Lincoln Center, *NCP 1897 – Shattuck, *Much Ado* 51. This was the ninth Shakespearian revival at Daly's Theatre.

(v, iii), despite Irving's having shown in 1882 how effective it could be.[1]

Arden presented more of a problem: the simpler painted flats and cut cloths were capable of a lightness that built-up, three dimensional settings could not manage. An actor–manager might easily be betrayed into fussiness and claustrophobic detail. Oscar Asche's 1907 *As You Like It* is the most famous of such productions, loaded with potted plants ('two thousand...besides large clumps of bamboo'). The stage floor of the Haymarket was covered with 'cartloads of last autumn's leaves' and logs on which moss still grew. Replacements were provided for the ferns as they were trodden down, and the whole plantation was kept on the roof of the theatre during the day. A note in the stage-manager's book asks 'When are we going to have new oak-leaves?'. This is not simply set-dressing: the leaves served as hand-props. When Orlando meets Jaques in the forest, he has been busy carving 'ROS' on a tree, and he wipes his dagger on a handful of leaves.[2] Much ingenuity was devoted to stage Ardens: Daly claimed to have based his on a photograph of the remaining corner of the Warwickshire forest, sent him by an enthusiast in Birmingham; for the Kendals in 1885 Wingfield designed a glade with real water and grass made from dyed feathers; E. W. Godwin, Gordon Craig's father, took the logical step of producing the 'pastoral scenes' outdoors.[3] Winter and rough weather did not appeal to the Victorians as they have done to some recent directors. Much was made of the travellers' tiredness when they reach the forest, but the life of the exiled court was always jolly. Winthrop Ames, the diligent Bostonian producer of Shakespeare, noted in his copy of Asche's acting edition that the London manager had provided a cauldron of soup for the forest banquet: 'At back a kettle steaming with a stew, which is given to various in Earthenware bowls, & this avoids *cold* look. Black bread. Gourdlike fruits.'[4]

Against such pleasing backgrounds were set the various pieces of elaborate business designed to bring out Rosalind's passionate devotion to Orlando, Viola's feelings for Orsino and Beatrice's fundamental seriousness of character. Ames, in his own production of *As You Like It*, took care that no one missed the depth of Rosalind's love. His third scene begins with Rosalind alone on the lawn before the palace at night:

Enter Rosalind, in happy meditation, from L.U.E. on terrace. Comes to where Orlando wrestled, and stands a moment as if imagining the scene again in fancy; sees wreath which he has thrown there, and picks it up, looks at it fondly, and taking it with her, with a happy little sigh, comes slowly down steps and stands R. of C., as if thinking of her parting with Orlando.[5]

Rosalind's first meeting with Orlando in the forest showed both her lack of ease in male

[1] *The New York Times*, 27 December 1896. For an illustration of the tomb scene in Irving's 1882 *Much Ado*, cf. George Rowell, 'A Lyceum Sketchbook', *Nineteenth Century Theatre Research*, 6 (Spring 1978), 1–23; p. 21.

[2] *Oscar Asche, His Life, By Himself* (n.d.), p. 120. Promptbook for this production in the Shakespeare Centre Library, Stratford-upon-Avon, 72.903 ASC – Shattuck, *AYLI*, 86. cf. Max Beerbohm's review in *Around Theatres* (1953), pp. 477–80, where the production is described as 'an awfully jolly affair'.

[3] On Daly and the photograph, William Winter, *Shakespeare on the Stage, Second Series* (New York, 1915), p. 275. On Wingfield's staging, R. Jackson, 'The Shakespeare Productions of Lewis Wingfield, 1883–1890', *Theatre Notebook*, 31 (January 1977), 28–41. On Godwin's *AYLI*, John Stokes, *Resistible Theatres* (1971) pp. 47–50 and plates 6 and 7.

[4] Copy of Asche's 1907 acting edition, annotated by Winthrop Ames, New York Public Library at the Lincoln Center, *NCP + 1907 (not in Shattuck). The business recorded corresponds to that in the Shakespeare Centre promptbook of Asche's production. After noting the business at the end of act II, Ames adds 'My end better'.

[5] Winthrop Ames, promptbook for *AYLI*, New York Public Library *NCP – Shattuck, *AYLI*, 80. Ames managed the Castle Square Theatre in Boston, Massachusetts for five years from 1904, before moving to New York.

attire and her love for him. Viola Allen's business would make it hard for Orlando not to think that something peculiar was going on:

Rosalind slaps Orlando on the shoulder. He takes no notice of it. Then she coughs and he does not notice that either. Then she speaks in as loud & rough a manner as she can – he answers very quietly. She is at a loss for words when she says 'What is't a'clock?' Orlando looks at her all over as if she reminded him of his Rosalind then falls back as if it couldn't be possible.[1]

(There is a good deal more of this including a 'love gesture' mimed towards Orlando behind his back: Celia frowns at her cousin's recklessness). This is surely making too much of Orlando's remark in v, iv,

My Lord, the first time that I ever saw him,
Methought he was the brother to your daughter,

(ll. 29–30)

and Miss Allen might well have heeded Helen Faucit's advice that 'once fairly launched on her delicate venture, Rosalind does not give Orlando time to examine her appearance too closely, or to question himself on wherein this attraction lies'. It was difficult, she admitted 'while carrying it off with a vivacity and dash that shall avert from Orlando's mind every suspicion of her sex, to preserve a refinement of tone and manner suitable to a woman of Rosalind's high station and cultured intellect'. Charles and Mary Lamb painstakingly explained that Orlando thought he detected a likeness, but then perceived that Ganymede 'had none of the dignified deportment of that noble lady'.[2] The combined demands of propriety and probability made this a difficult passage.

The parting from Orlando at the end of IV, i served to show just how near the surface Rosalind's feminine instinct is. In Asche's production Lily Brayton crossed slowly up towards her cottage with 'Ay, go your ways, go your ways' (l. 162), and was 'pretending to cry' at 'that flattering tongue of yours won me' (l. 164):

Orl. follows, stands above her when she hides her face in her hands. Orl. loks at Cel. who laughs & shakes her head. Orl. then places his hand on her shoulder saying 'Ganymede'. She looks up and laughs – Runs L.

Then, on 'so come, death', she 'weeps – both laugh'. Orlando's exit is delayed: Rosalind calls him back and holds out her hand. He looks at it, and makes off with an 'exclamation of disgust'. He is called back again, and this time shakes her hand. Finally 'he comes with mock gallantry, kisses her hand, smacks it & runs off L1E'[3] Winthrop Ames had devised a more sentimental version of this exit:

Orlando starts off. She checks him with a little exclamation. He has forgotten something. Orlando turns inquiringly. She holds out her hand to him reprovingly. He recollects, and laughingly kisses her hand, and then gaily waving adieu, exit Orlando L2E Rosalind stands at L2E gazing after him, and as soon as his back is turned, kisses her hands after him passionately.[4]

The episode of the bloody napkin served to show Rosalind's loving concern for Orlando and her womanly shrinking from the sight of blood. Any comedy in the scene must have been lost in a treatment as melodramatic as that found in Fanny Davenport's promptbook. There 'Calcium, green, from flies R2E on Rosalind' is indicated for Oliver's narration, with a powerful effect for the curtain: 'Ros. faints on bank C. Oliver on R. & Celia on L. of bank. Flash Calcium to White. *Picture.* Ring as Ros. falls.' Not all actresses could rise to this scene's demands. A critic recalled in 1883 that the last Rosalind he saw (probably Mrs Langtry) 'behaved much as if Oliver had shown her a beetle, which she feared might fly

[1] Promptbook of Viola Allen's *AYLI* (New York, 1904), Harvard Theatre Collection, uncatalogued – Shattuck, *AYLI*, 55.
[2] Faucit, *On Some of Shakespeare's Female Characters*, p. 258. Charles and Mary Lamb, *Tales from Shakespeare* (Everyman's Library, 1906), p. 69.
[3] Asche's promptbook – Shattuck, *AYLI*, 86.
[4] Ames's promptbook – Shattuck, *AYLI*, 80.

upon her, and in the end she turned and clung to Celia's shoulder'.[1]

In *Much Ado About Nothing* the church scene, IV, i, was the principal occasion for bringing out the 'profound seriousness' of Beatrice and Benedick. Clement Scott described Ellen Terry's 'sudden passionate sob of suppressed emotion' on 'O God, that I were a man! I would eat his heart in the market-place' (ll. 303–4).[2] Irving, as Benedick, lightened the declaration of love by interjecting 'oh' and 'ah' at strategic moments, and by comic bashfulness in 'I do love nothing in the world so well as you', after which he paused, 'bus. of ogling – hat in hand – he then takes her hand'. His promptbook shows how efficiently he cleared the stage after the disruption of the wedding. Daly, characteristically, had the organist remain behind to accompany the dialogue, and kept the entire wedding party on stage until Don John's 'Come let us go' (l. 110). Ada Rehan, Daly's Beatrice, threw herself on the altar steps, weeping.[3]

The printed promptbook of Winthrop Ames's production has a powerful curtain for the end of the act. Benedick, about to leave the church, finds Beatrice standing at the altar steps, her arms stretched out towards him. He rushes to her, she to him, and they meet, centre-stage. She falls into his arms, sobbing, and buries her face on his breast. 'PICTURE'.[4] It was clear that something needed to be done with the end of the scene, but the traditional way was to add a 'gag' of some half-dozen lines. It was this additional material that Hazlitt complained of when he wrote that Miss Brunton, 'when grief should have full possession of her mind,...flippantly, and in a transport of joy...calls [Benedick] back to kiss her hand again'.[5] In Daly's production, a change in mood was prepared for by the ceasing of organ music on Beatrice's 'Yea, and I will weep a little while longer', accompanied by the direction 'White footlights up a little'. This detaches the end of the scene from the

crisis of the accusation and its aftermath. After 'Claudio shall render me a dear account' Daly's version is as follows:

Beatrice. You will challenge him!
Benedick. By these bright eyes I will.
Beatrice. Kiss my hand again! [*He does so*]
Benedick. As you hear of me, so think of me; and so, farewell. [*going, R.*]
Beatrice. Kill him! Kill Claudio! [*L.H.*]
Benedick. As sure as he is alive, I will. [*Organ Music*]
Exeunt, Benedick R1E, Beatrice L1E. Quick Drop.[6]

Macready's version ends with Benedick's triumph:

Going with Beat. to R. – still kissᵍ her hand, – when she is off, he puts on his hat, – arranges his costume, &c – and, drawing on his glove, walks off, very self-satisfiedly, L.

This promptbook allows Beatrice's grief full expression (she 'bursts into tears, & fall[s] on his shoulder' at 'Kill Claudio') but shifts our attention to comedy in the last moments of the scene. Ellen Terry remembered pleading with Irving to discard the 'gag': Irving 'said that it was necessary: otherwise the "curtain" would be received in dead silence'.[7]

[1] Fanny Davenport, *AYLI* promptbook (*c.* 1885), Harvard Theatre Collection, TS.3059.500 – Shattuck, *AYLI*, 57. R. G. White, 'Stage Rosalinds', *The Atlantic Monthly*, 51 (February 1883), 248–59; p. 258.

[2] Clement Scott, *From 'The Bells' to 'King Arthur'* (1896), p. 253.

[3] George Becks, promptbook of Irving's *Much Ado*, New York Public Library at the Lincoln Center, *NCP 1848 – Shattuck, *Much Ado*, 47. Promptbook of Daly's *Much Ado* – Shattuck, *Much Ado*, 51.

[4] *Much Ado About Nothing* (William Warren Edition, Boston, Mass., 1916), p. 78. Based on Ames's promptbook, this edition includes copious notes on business, lighting, sets, etc. Ames produced the play at the Castle Square Theatre on 30 October 1905.

[5] Hazlitt, *Works*, XVIII, 263–5; p. 264.

[6] Daly's promptbook – Shattuck, *Much Ado*, 51.

[7] George Ellis's transcript of Macready's *Much Ado* promptbook (1843), Harvard Theatre Collection, 13486.69.13*/TS M82A – Shattuck, *Much Ado*, 16. Ellen Terry, *The Story of My Life* (1908), pp. 162–3. Irving's acting edition (1883) omits the 'gag' but both Folger promptbooks include it (Folger Shakespeare

A similar alteration was customary in the final lines of the play. Shakespeare ends with the news of Don John's arrest and return to Messina, allowing Benedick to set this in its proper perspective:

> Think not on him till tomorrow. I'll devise thee brave punishments for him. Strike up, pipers.
>
> (v, v, 122–4)

French's edition gives the traditional ending:

> *Benedick.* Come, come, we are friends. Prince, thou art sad.
> *Don Pedro.* Yes, I've got the tooth-ache.
> *Benedick.* Got the tooth-ache! Get thee a wife; and all will be well. [*all laugh*] Nay, laugh not, laugh not.
> Your gibes and mockeries I laugh to scorn:
> No staff more rev'rend than one tipt with horn.[1]

The intention here, as in the church scene, is to redress the balance of the play.

In 1820 a critic advised Miss Marion Tree to 'infuse more tenderness into her recitation' as Viola.[2] Some later performances gave more than an infusion. Viola Allen inserted a mimed finale, ending the second act of her version with Viola's exclamation 'O if it prove/Tempests are kind and salt waves fresh in love!' (III, iv, 367–8). Viola then falls asleep on a bench:

> Spot light on Viola – full moon light. Song 'Who is Silvia?' Singing off stage L. Olivia comes from house, sees some one on bench, turns to Maria who is following her with a lantern, sees Viola, gives lantern back to Maria who returns up steps & waits for Olivia. She kisses Viola on cheek, rises as singers come on and goes up steps. *Duke* enters, sees Olivia and in pantomime implores her to speak. She turns coldly and enters house. Duke wakes Viola, who does not recognize him for a second. He goes C., holds out hand to her. She goes to him and kneels and kisses his hand – *Curtain* (The singers, lords and ladies and musicians have crossed the stage from L. to R.)

The prompter notes that this will stand 'three curtains of moonlight' and 'at least three more with calls for the comedy people & one for Viola and Olivia – Viola and Duke – Then Viola alone'.[3] Julia Marlowe collapsed in tears

after Orsino's exit at the end of II, iv. H. M. Walbrook, reviewing her performance in London in 1907, considered this 'a legitimate illumination of the text'.[4] Winthrop Ames shows what could be done with the lines themselves. He gives Viola a tearful exit at the end of I, iv:

> I'll do my best
> To woo your lady [*go slowly up to door L.C.*]
> [*As Duke goes up, you look after him, then wistfully down at ring, which you slowly fit on your finger, and then withdraw with a sigh, that is almost tearful*]
> Yet a baleful strife!
> Whoe'er I woo, myself would be his wife.
> [*During the first line or two of Song, you stand in doorway, regarding ring, then hastily dashing away a tear and with a gesture of despair, exit, door up L.C.*]

Viola's interview with Olivia in III, i moves her so much that she is obliged to make a 'strong exit' ('quickly, as if to conceal your emotion, through gate up L. and off L3E, not looking back'). The effect is reinforced by the omission of Olivia's concluding couplet.[5] Ellen Terry gave Viola a womanly sympathy for the feelings of her own sex in her reactions to Olivia's speech earlier in the scene,

> Give me leave, beseech you. I did send, After the last enchantment you did here, A ring in chase of you;...
>
> (III, i, 108–10)

Library, Mu Ad 8 and Com Err 11 – Shattuck, *Much Ado*, 45 and 46). For a fuller discussion of the various treatments of this scene, see J. F. Cox's article on pp. 27 to 36 of the present volume.

[1] *Much Ado About Nothing*, French's Acting Edition no. 512 (n.d.), p. 61.

[2] Leigh Hunt, review in *The Examiner*, 3 March 1820, reprinted by Gāmini Salgādo, *Eyewitnesses of Shakespeare* (Sussex, 1975), pp. 205–7; p. 206.

[3] Viola Allen's promptbook – Shattuck, *TN*, 55.

[4] H. M. Walbrook, *Nights at the Play* (1911), pp. 188–9.

[5] Ames, partbooks for *TN* (1907), New York Public Library at the Lincoln Center, *NCP 1907 – Shattuck, *TN*, 73.

The actress 'managed to convey, by the wistful expression of her face...how much she longed to sympathize with the woman who was the victim of a mistake brought about by Viola's assumption of a character and sex other than her own...With all the loving sympathy of her tender-hearted nature, she utters the words "I pity you"; and then, when she sees that even this amount of sympathy encourages Olivia's delusion, with a gentle sternness she shatters that illusion....'[1]

By contrast the duel between Viola and Andrew Aguecheek was often made too farcical. William Winter considered Adelaide Neilson to have achieved a 'deliciously droll' portrait of 'feminine cowardice – commingled of amazement, consternation, fear, weakness and dread of the disclosure of her sex'. Miss Neilson was a Viola 'affluent in petty bravado and demonstrative glee'.[2] Winthrop Ames instructed his Viola to remember Spedding's observation that 'The inward sinking of the heart may be made visible without any display of unseemly terror', and the business he proposes for the scene is correspondingly restrained. Viola Allen's promptbook has elaborate slapstick, of which one point will be sufficient example: Fabian offers Viola a choice of swords, but she refuses to take one. He chooses for her, and hands it to her, but she drops it on his foot when he turns to look at the others. A mid-century promptbook gives the outline of 'a very comical kind of combat' in which Viola and Sir Andrew chase each other round the stage until she 'accidentally strikes Sir A. who bellows out and Viola shrieks and turns to Fabian'. To Cumberland's direction 'Sir Andrew hides himself behind the trees' is added 'up the tree so that when he's called he shows himself thro tree at top'.[3]

In this scene it was hard to resist the temptation of broad farce, and of making Viola as big a coward as Sir Andrew to lessen her claims to courage and strength of mind. Shakespeare's Viola confesses in one aside that a little thing would make her tell them how much she lacks of a man (ll. 286–7) but there is no warrant in the text for business that will make the matter plain. The Victorian insistence on Viola's timidity is part of that 'common practice' complained of by Granville Barker, whereby actresses would 'seize upon every chance of reminding the audience that they are girls dressed up' and 'impress on one moreover, by childish by-play as to legs and petticoats or the absence of them, that this is the play's supreme joke'.[4] At Rosalind's 'Alas the day! what shall I do with my doublet and hose?' (III, ii, 204–5) Mrs Kendal put her hands over her face, exclaimed 'Alas the day', paused, crossed to Celia and whispered in her ear 'what shall I do with my doublet and hose?' Ada Rehan was 'at first startled and ashamed at being caught out of her petticoats', then laid hold of Celia's skirt and tried to wrap it round her legs. Julia Marlowe uttered a little cry of dismay, pulled forward her large cloak and 'let it fall about her from shoulder to heel like a domino'. Winthrop Ames devised the following variation:

[*After a little pause of dismay*] 'Alas the day! what shall I do with my doublet and hose?' [*Quickly pulls her cloak about her; and then as quickly forgetting her attire in her eagerness runs to L. of Celia and sitting on stage cuddles close beside her in delighted amazement*][5]

[1] F. M. Marshall, review of *TN* in *The Theatre*, n.s. 4 (August 1884), 86–90; pp. 87–8.

[2] Winter, *Shakespeare on the Stage, Second Series*, p. 44.

[3] Ames's and Viola Allen's promptbooks – Shattuck, *TN* 73, 75. The mid-century promptbook is Eliza Hamblin's: Harvard Theatre Collection, TS.2678.50.2 – Shattuck, *TN*, 13. On the combat, cf. A. C. Sprague, *Shakespeare and the Actors*, (Cambridge, Mass., 1944), pp. 8–9.

[4] *Shakespeare's Comedy of Twelfth Night, with a producer's preface by Granville Barker* (1912), p. vii.

[5] Mrs Kendal described by Harry Quilter, *The Dramatic Review*, 1 February 1885. Ada Rehan's business in a promptbook of Daly's production, Folger Shakespeare Library, *AYLI*, 16 – Shattuck *AYLI*, 58. Julia Marlowe's noted by Ames in the

Before we dismiss these absurdities as products of the Victorian appetite for coyness, it is worth considering William Winter's remarks on the business used by Ada Rehan. For Winter, the point was of the gravest importance: it made the spectator 'aware of contact with a nature radically good, – a nature of which sincerity was a cardinal virtue and to which meanness was impossible'.[1] Elsewhere the same critic is at pains to praise Julia Marlowe's Viola as a powerful force for good, claiming that 'such an ideal, suitably presented on stage..., sinks into the mind, remains in the memory, and beneficently influences the conduct of life'. When Viola Allen devised a dress for Viola that made her disguise too convincing (see plate IA) Winter complained that she had made the character unpoetical, and reminded his readers that a woman who succeeds in passing herself off as a man is 'abnormal, unfeminine'.[2]

Clearly this was dangerous ground. The various costumes adopted by actresses playing Viola and Rosalind compromised uneasily between the demands of historical consistency and feminine modesty. It was important, above all, not to remind the audience of the displays of leg that were customary in burlesque and pantomime. Although Elizabethan dress would make the disguises easier, too many Rosalinds persisted in wearing silk tights that would soon be torn by the brambles of Arden, and tunics that were long enough to pass for skirts. One commentator suggested that Rosalinds should besmirch their faces (none did) and forgo the 'low-crowned, broad-brimmed something, more like what is known to ladies of late years as a Gainsborough than anything else that has been named by milliners'.[3] Although gaiters were adopted by some actresses (Mrs Kendal and Helena Modjeska, for example) thigh-length boots, with doublet and trunk-hose were established as the proper wear by the end of the century. Mary Anderson, Lily Brayton (plates IB and C) and Ada Rehan

appeared in some approximation of this dress. For Viola, some quasi-Greek (Illyrian) national dress was popular: a skirted robe, with a sash and a jaunty cap. The danger here was of making Sebastian look effeminate in order to allow for the modesty of the leading lady.

III

Little of the business described in this article would be acceptable on today's stage. We have abandoned the polarity of farce and powerful emotion that gave the Victorian theatre its vitality and, frequently, crudity and we respect intellectual values that few nineteenth-century critics could have imagined to exist in Shakespeare's plays. If we alter the text, it is likely to be because we see the dramatist struggling towards expression of his thoughts on appearance and reality, or the structure of Illyrian society, and wish to offer him the benefit of our experience. When a Victorian Rosalind takes Celia's exit-lines from her ('Now go we in content/To liberty, and not to banishment'), or a manager follows tradition in playing the first scene of *Twelfth Night* after the second, we usually ascribe the change to a simple desire for theatrical effect. Sometimes the effect is not so simple: giving the First Lord's description of Jaques and the deer (II, i, 25 etc.), with suitable alterations, to Jaques himself appears at first sight a device only to build up the part. But another consequence of the change is to make Jaques more sympathetic, with a pleasant sense of his own humour – whimsical rather than melancholic. In the case of the transposition at the beginning of *Twelfth Night*, the Victorian distrust of Orsino (whose repining at Olivia's rejection of him was considered unmanly) may

promptbook from which his own business is taken (Shattuck, *AYLI*, 80).

[1] Winter, *Shakespeare on the Stage*, 2nd series, p. 272.

[2] *Ibid.*, pp. 81–2 (Viola Allen) and 90 (Julia Marlowe).

[3] White, 'Stage Rosalinds', pp. 252–3.

have helped perpetuate a change that does not necessarily benefit the actress of Viola – after all, a delayed entrance was considered a strong one.[1]

In these comedies Victorian critics and performers established a subtext in which virtuous, modest and loving women, endowed with uncommon resources of wit and tact, found happiness through marriage. Their success was achieved despite disguise (in the case of Rosalind and Viola) and independence of mind (in the case of Beatrice). This is an interpretation we find difficult to accept, principally because we have different ideas about women. We would not all agree unreservedly with Beerbohm Tree's assertion that Viola 'throws herself with a gay spirit into the masquerading adventures through which she passes to Comedy's inevitable goal – the bridal chamber',[2] nor would we share the misgivings of a number of critics concerning the propriety of the male disguise. It is not only a differing estimate of woman's place in society that alienates us from the Victorian view of these comedies. The Victorian theatre, as the century drew to its close, was better and better equipped to imitate life – to present quasi-photographic images of everyday reality. Outside pantomime and burlesque, there was little place for theatrical self-consciousness, or for ironic effect. The methods of earlier modes of theatre were considered makeshifts – the Elizabethans had simply been putting up with what they had, and Shakespeare's remarks in the choruses of *Henry V* were cited as evidence. By the same token, Shakespeare was assumed to have wished above all to hold the mirror up to nature: his efforts as an artist being devoted to doing so without our being conscious of his technique. To Charles Cowden Clarke, the dramatist's 'ample wisdom and bland morality' consisted in his mind being 'a transmission in daguerrotype of the created world, animate and inanimate'.[3] It followed that he would have embraced with gratitude the technical accomplishments of the Victorian theatre, and would also have welcomed the opportunity to have his heroines impersonated by women. That the formal arrangements of his scenes and the choruses of *Henry V* might be anything other than signs of the immaturity of dramatic art in his time was not considered. That there might be advantages in the use of boy-actors did not appear any more likely.

The insistence of performers on the womanliness of Rosalind, Beatrice and Viola, and on their fundamental seriousness of mind, was in the main a response to the kind of critical attitude outlined at the beginning of this article. It was also a function of the ambiguous social position of the Victorian actress. Michael Baker, in *The Rise of the Victorian Actor*, has commented on this connection between sentimental interpretations and the problem of a class of women whose independent careers and public appearances set them apart from most of their sex – prostitutes excepted.[4] It is because of this that the memoirs of many actresses are full of reminders that they managed to combine virtue and domesticity with membership of the theatrical profession. The objection was not simply that the stage world was immoral, but that it treated the emotions lightly. Wilde plays on this attitude to emphasise his hero's perversity when he has Dorian Gray exclaim, in telling Lord Henry Wotton of his passion for Sybil Vane,

Night after night I go to see her play. One evening she is Rosalind, and the next evening she is Imogen. I have seen her die in the gloom of an Italian tomb, sucking the poison from her lover's lips. I have watched her wandering through the forest of Arden, disguised as a

---

[1] In Daly's *TN*, Viola's entrance is preceded by an elaborate storm and the dialogue of Antonio and Sebastian from II, i. Cf. Marvin Felheim, *The Theater of Augustin Daly* (Cambridge, Mass., 1956), pp. 252–3.

[2] *Souvenir* of Tree's *Twelfth Night* (Her Majesty's, 5 February 1901).

[3] Cowden Clarke, *Shakespeare-Characters*, p. 215.

[4] Michael Baker, *The Rise of the Victorian Actor* (1978), p. 101.

pretty boy in hose and doublet and dainty cap...I have seen her in every age and in every costume. Ordinary women never appeal to one's imagination. They are limited to their century...But an actress! How different an actress is! Harry! Why didn't you tell me that the only thing worth loving is an actress?[1]

One consequence of the fear of insincerity was the belief that there must be some correspondence between the personality of the actress and the parts she played. A characteristically extreme statement of it comes from William Winter:

The reason why Rosalind is not more often embodied in a competent and enthralling manner is that her enchanting quality is something that cannot be assumed – it must be possessed; it must exist in the fibre of the individual, and its expression will then be spontaneous.[2]

The unwillingness of actresses to play unchaste or even merely unsympathetic women was a serious limitation – a self-censorship in the theatre that Shaw, among others, fought to overcome.

The limitations of interpretations influenced by such inhibitions are self-evident. It seems better to conclude with a reminder of the power that could be achieved by an actress notable for her 'emotional' approach to her characters. When Joseph Knight, reviewing an 1875 performance of *As You Like It*, wanted an example of what was missing in the new Rosalind, he turned to his memories of Helen Faucit. He recalled the 'rapture of tenderness with which she asked Orlando if he had written the verses and the manner in which they were 'hugged to her heart and then furtively pressed to her lips'. Helen Faucit's own account of the scene, like many similar passages in her book on Shakespeare's heroines, gives a sense of her passionate involvement. First, when she read the verses,

Think of the throb at her heart, as she reads her own name running through every couplet! Still there are many Rosalinds in the world; and how should he, of whom she has been dreaming, even know her name, – or how should he, of all men, be there in Arden? No, no, it must be mere coincidence; and yet the pulse is quickened, the heartthrob felt...

Then, when Celia confirmed that this was Orlando:

Oh happiness beyond belief, oh rapture irrepressible! The tears at this point always welled up to my eyes, and my whole body trembled...[3]

[1] Oscar Wilde, *The Picture of Dorian Gray* (ed. Isobel Murray, Oxford English Novels, 1974), pp. 50–51.
[2] William Winter, *Shadows of the Stage, Second Series* (Edinburgh, 1893), p. 168.
[3] Joseph Knight, *Theatrical Notes* (1893), p. 16 (on Mrs Kendal's performance as Rosalind). Helen Faucit, *On Some of Shakespeare's Female Characters*, pp. 255–6.

© RUSSELL JACKSON 1979

THE STAGE REPRESENTATION OF THE 'KILL CLAUDIO' SEQUENCE IN 'MUCH ADO ABOUT NOTHING'

J. F. COX

In the stage production of *Much Ado About Nothing* the subtle interplay of emotions, and the delicate tonal balance in the dialogue between Benedick and Beatrice at the end of the church scene, have always proved testing to the players. An examination of a range of English productions of *Much Ado* between Garrick and the mid-1950s highlights some of the principles of the dramatic organisation of this sequence, illustrating both the variety of legitimate interpretation which it admits, and the extent to which it has sometimes been falsified in the theatre.

The first point to emerge in the study is that the plausibility of the sequence depends to a large extent on the players' success in establishing a sense of continuity between the emotions aroused in the first part of the church scene, and the reactions of Benedick and Beatrice in their concluding dialogue. In the more sensitive performances, Beatrice and Benedick have shown in their solicitude for Hero at the altar[1] a depth of sympathy sufficient to give their later confessions of love the degree of inevitability and seriousness which the text (despite its latent comic undertones) demands. Players such as Helen Faucit and Ellen Terry have shown, furthermore, that by conveying in the first part of the church scene a sense of the passionate resentment that Claudio's behaviour arouses within Beatrice,[2] an actress can help avoid the situation in which the shock of her 'Kill Claudio' may seem so incongruous as to raise unwanted laughter, or in which her

subsequent storm of indignation may seem out of character. On the other hand, some late nineteenth- and early twentieth-century managers impaired the dramatic logic of the scene by deliberately breaking the continuity between the Benedick–Beatrice dialogue and the events on which it depends. In three such cases, the break was made merely to introduce additional spectacle. Edward Saker (Alexandra Theatre, Liverpool, 1878) destroyed the momentum of the scene by interpolating an elaborate recessional at the end of the denunciation sequence.[3] Richard Flanagan (Queen's Theatre, Manchester, 1900, 1901, 1917) stopped the action at the same point to make room for a tableau representing high mass in a separate cathedral setting, where a choir rendered the Kyrie from Palestrina's *Missa assumptu est Maria* while the play waited.[4] Sir Herbert Beerbohm Tree (His Majesty's, 1905) introduced a change of scene from the church to

---

[1] e.g. Irving and Ellen Terry. See *Liverpool Courier*, 27 Sept. 1883; *New York Mirror*, 22 Nov. 1884; and Irving promptbook in the Folger Shakespeare Library, Washington.

[2] Helen Faucit, 'On Some of Shakespeare's Female Characters,' *Blackwood's Magazine*, 137 (1885), 221–2; J. E. Agate, *My Theatre Talks* (1933), p. 44. Helen Faucit played Beatrice between 1836 and 1879, Ellen Terry between 1882 and 1903.

[3] *William Shakespeare's Much Ado About Nothing Produced at The Alexandra Theatre, Liverpool, on Monday, April 22nd, 1878. Arranged for Representation by Edward Saker* (Liverpool, 1878).

[4] *Manchester Guardian*, 22 Jan. 1900; *Stage*, 22 Feb. 1917.

the cloisters before the final Benedick–Beatrice dialogue;[1] and Fred Terry (King's, Hammersmith, 1920) lowered a curtain between the two parts of the scene.[2] The disjunction caused by such breaks in the action may be gauged from reviews of Tree's production which pointed out that his change of location destroyed the climaxing tension of Shakespeare's scene, and reduced the impact of the Benedick–Beatrice dialogue by divorcing it from its motivating circumstances.[3]

One of the hallmarks of the finest performances in the 'Kill Claudio' sequence has always been an appreciation of the extreme tentativeness with which Benedick and Beatrice feel their way towards mutuality in the thirty lines culminating in Beatrice's confession of her love. It requires a good deal of tact and sensitivity for the players to register in these lines the subtle fluctuations of feeling as the rising desires of Benedick and Beatrice to admit affection for each other are restrained by a very natural embarrassment, and checked to some extent by Beatrice's urgent impulse to have Hero's cause avenged. Mrs Abington in the late eighteenth century seems to have caught something of the reticence of Beatrice in this section of the dialogue.[4] So did Fanny Kemble in the 1830s – especially in her half-willing, half-evasive reply to Benedick's declaration of his love ('It were as possible for me to say I loved nothing so well as you; but believe me not, and yet I lie not'). These words Miss Kemble spoke 'half good-humouredly, half peevishly', following them with an embarrassed attempt at disguise which came too late ('I confess nothing, nor I deny nothing'), and concluding with an evasion, uttered abruptly and tearfully: 'I am sorry for my cousin.'[5] But she somewhat marred the general delicacy of her performance when later in the scene she threw herself too precipitately into Benedick's arms at the words 'I love you with so much of my heart, that none is left to protest.'[6] There were no lapses of tact in

Helen Faucit's rendering of this passage. Miss Faucit spoke the words 'It is a man's office, but not yours', not sarcastically, as some other mid-Victorian actresses had done; instead she placed a pause, 'full of exquisite humour', in the centre of the line, then spoke the rest in a tone that merely signified Benedick's unfitness on account of his being unconnected with Hero's family. As Benedick removed that difficulty by declaring his love, she smiled in remembrance of what she had overheard in the garden, but found it hard to confess her own affection. She twice half-yielded, and withdrew, in a speech which Sir Edward Russell described as 'a series of little speeches, each like a pretty bon-bon, with a dramatic surprise ready to leap out with the detonation' – and then tried to escape her embarrassment by turning away from the subject with the words, 'spoken with tremulous emotion', 'I am sorry for my cousin.' As Benedick pressed her to declare her affection she kept him in suspense for a few lines, her emotions see-sawing between him and Hero, and then half-wittily, half-earnestly, made her confession.[7] Violet Vanbrugh (Shakespeare Memorial Theatre, Stratford, 1911, 1913)[8] and Sybil Thorndike (Lyric, Hammersmith, 1927) also caught sensitively the hesitation in Beatrice's surrender to Benedick, Gordon Crosse noting especially the way in which Sybil Thorndike spoke the last three words of the line, 'It is a man's office, but not yours,' not as a taunt, or to raise a laugh, but 'as if checking herself in

---

[1] Promptbooks of Tree's production, University of Bristol Theatre Collection.

[2] Programme, 12 May 1920 (Enthoven Collection, Victoria and Albert Museum, London).

[3] *Daily Telegraph*, 25 Jan. 1905; *Westminster Gazette*, 25 Jan. 1905; *Sketch*, 1 Feb. 1905; *Modern Society*, 4 Feb. 1905; *Sphere*, 4 Feb. 1905.

[4] *Public Advertiser*, 22 Jan. 1785, 3 Nov. 1785.

[5] *Tatler*, 18 Feb. 1831; *Observer*, 20 Feb. 1831.

[6] *Times*, 18 Feb. 1831.

[7] *Liverpool Daily Post*, 16 Dec. 1870; Faucit, p. 224.

[8] *Evesham Journal*, 3 May 1913.

an appeal for Benedick's help'.[1] The hesitancy was also well caught in the Stratford productions of W. Bridges-Adams.[2]

During the nineteenth century, however, some actors of Benedick had marred the tentativeness of their opening lines in this sequence by too deliberate an approach to Beatrice. Frederick Vining (Haymarket, 1833, 1836) went intentionally to Beatrice as she was filing out of the church with the other guests and handed her down to the front of the stage in readiness for the succeeding dialogue[3] – an action which must have robbed the situation of some of the piquancy which it has when Benedick and Beatrice are left together more or less by chance, and Benedick has to search a little for his opening words. Charles Kean's failure here was much more conspicuous. As soon as he found himself alone with Beatrice he rushed into hearty love-making, with evident delight at feeling at last 'relieved from a state of ignorance as to what he was to do next', and at 'finding himself once more at liberty to speak as plainly as in the days when he vowed he would never become "Benedick, the married man"'.[4] Irving and Ellen Terry (Lyceum, 1882–95) preserved a better sense than the Keans of the exploratory quality of the initial exchanges in this sequence[5] – though it will be shown that their performance of the dialogue was not in all respects ideal.

Sir John Gielgud gave a most delicate interpretation of the whole passage in 1952, when he played to Diana Wynyard's Beatrice, and also in 1950 and 1955, when in partnership with Peggy Ashcroft. In Gielgud's 1955 production, the opening tentativeness of the situation was well caught as Beatrice and Benedick, at first seeming inclined to leave the church with the rest of the wedding party, stopped independently of each other, Benedick returning to the centre of the stage, Beatrice remaining hesitantly at one side.[6] In 1952 Gielgud and Miss Wynyard played the succeeding interchanges with exquisite grace.

At 'Lady Beatrice, have you wept all this while?' a long look of sympathy passed between them,[7] and as the scene progressed 'the intensity of their love mute[d] their voices almost to a whisper' – a quietness which, after the bolder drama of the denunciation sequence, came with great effect. Gielgud put 'all the wonderment and earnestness imaginable' into his confession of love; Miss Wynyard responding in turn with a 'breathless ardour'.[8] 'Their scene of confessed love is all in prose,' wrote Ivor Brown: 'yet to hear this Benedick say "I do love nothing in the world so well as you. Is not that strange?" and Beatrice "You have stayed me in a happy hour" is to be a listener on the foothills, almost the peaks, of Parnassus, where words are raised to a higher power and simplest speech is magical.'[9]

But the dialogue has not always been rendered with such tact. Some of the more waspish actresses of the mid-Victorian period misrepresented Beatrice as a character devoid of generous, sympathetic feelings.[10] Some of them played Beatrice's confession of love mainly as a feigned declaration intended to secure

---

[1] 'Shakespearean Performances Which I Have Seen' (MS. in Shakespeare Memorial Library, Birmingham), XI, 35; *Shakespearean Playgoing* (1953), p. 52.

[2] Bridges-Adams promptbooks, Shakespeare Centre Library, Stratford; *Birmingham Mail*, 18 April 1925.

[3] Vining promptbook, dated at the Haymarket, May 1833 (Harvard Theatre Collection).

[4] *Times*, 30 Jan. 1861. Charles and Ellen Kean played *Much Ado* in London at the Haymarket (1850), Princess's (1852, 1858), and Drury Lane (1861).

[5] Irving promptbooks in the Folger Shakespeare Library and the New York Public Library; George Foss, *What the Author Meant* (1932), p. 113; *Saturday Review*, 21 Oct. 1882; *Times*, 24 Oct. 1882; *Boston Daily Advertiser*, 28 Feb. 1884.

[6] Promptbook of Gielgud's 1955 touring production (Shakespeare Centre Library, Stratford).

[7] *Drama*, no. 25 (Summer 1952), 14.

[8] *Punch*, 23 Jan. 1952; *Morning Advertiser*, 23 Jan. 1952.

[9] *Observer*, 13 Jan. 1952.

[10] e.g. Miss Reynolds, Haymarket, 1853 (*Morning Advertiser*, 29 Nov. 1853).

Benedick's agreement to avenge Hero,[1] turned Beatrice's outrage at Claudio's behaviour into a mere fit of petulant vexation, and interpreted her amenability at the end of the scene (see Kemble's interpolated dialogue, reproduced below) largely as an expression of satisfaction at the prospect of the impending duel.[2]

Players have also at times blurred and cheapened the delicate interplay of sensibilities in this passage by over-demonstrative external displays of emotion. Julia Neilson (St James's, 1898) and Margaret Chatwin (Birmingham Repertory Theatre, 1919–20) marred the transition to the sequence by stagey outbursts of sobbing as Hero was led offstage.[3] Fanny Kemble (Covent Garden, 1831–2) threw herself impulsively into Benedick's arms after confessing her love[4] – a piece of business which was also current at the Haymarket in the 1850s.[5] Irving and Ellen Terry likewise broke the delicate emotional balance of this moment by a passionate embrace, excessive kissing, and a sigh of delight from Beatrice[6] – business which made the emerging mutuality of Benedick and Beatrice seem a more finally settled thing than it is at this point. Worse still was the way Mrs Nisbett (Drury Lane, 1843) impulsively clasped Benedick about the neck, fell on his shoulder, and burst out sobbing at the words 'Kill Claudio'.[7] In Tree's production (His Majesty's, 1905), the feelings evoked in the scene were cheapened by sentimentally indulgent love-play, Beatrice even speaking her 'Kill Claudio' while clasped in Benedick's arms.[8] It should not be thought, however, that the tactful expression of affection is totally out of place in this sequence. A note in Walter Lacy's transcription of one of the Kemble promptbooks records a piece of business (whether Kemble's or Lacy's is uncertain) in which Benedick, watching Beatrice's face, 'gently and very gradually' took her hand in his, raised it 'slowly and cautiously until near his lips', snatched a kiss of it, and then, looking 'full in her face', said, 'I do love nothing in the world so well as you.'[9] The delicacy and restraint of this business seems entirely consistent with the tentativeness of Benedick's emerging feelings for Beatrice at this point.

One of the most difficult matters for players in the 'Kill Claudio' sequence to judge to a nicety has been the subtle balance of serious and comic elements in the dialogue. Many actors have made the mistake of over-exaggerating the comic potentialities of the passage, some playing deliberately for laughs, others simply misjudging the tone of some of the lines. Garrick (Drury Lane, 1748–76) seems to have allowed the comic spirit a good deal of licence throughout his performance of this sequence, *The London Chronicle* (19–22 March 1757) reporting that his rendering of the passage was one of the most entertaining parts of the whole play. Miss Brunton (Covent Garden, 1817) intruded repeated giggles into her outburst of indignation.[10] Charles Kemble (Covent Garden, 1824) marred a generally tactful rendering by raising a laugh at Beatrice's confession of her love, tittering and touching her arm for an embarrassed moment before kissing her.[11] At

[1] *Observer*, 28 Feb. 1858.

[2] *Weekly Dispatch*, 13 Sept. 1857.

[3] *Morning Post*, 17 Feb. 1898; *Birmingham Post*, 5 May 1919.

[4] *Times*, 18 Feb. 1831.

[5] Note added by Walter Lacy to his transcription of the Kemble promptbook in the Garrick Club, London. Lacy's transcription is in the Folger Shakespeare Library.

[6] Irving promptbooks in the Folger Shakespeare Library and the New York Public Library; [Glasgow] *Evening Citizen*, 28 Aug. 1883.

[7] Promptbooks relating to Macready's production (Drury Lane, 1843) in the University of Illinois Library and the New York Public Library; *Morning Post*, 25 Feb. 1843.

[8] Tree promptbook (University of Bristol Theatre Collection); *Standard*, 25 Jan. 1905.

[9] Lacy's transcript of the Kemble promptbook in the Garrick Club (Folger).

[10] *Times*, 29 Nov. 1817.

[11] *Morning Herald*, 28 Jan. 1824. Charles Kemble also played Benedick at Drury Lane in 1803, and many times at Covent Garden between 1811 and 1840.

the Haymarket in the 1850s, Benedick's response to Beatrice's confession was badly falsified by a piece of interpolated comic business in which Benedick strutted about the stage, presumably in self-congratulation at having won her.[1] Henry Irving played perilously close to overt comedy during the first fifteen lines or so of the sequence, producing laughter in at least three places. The first was when he limped across to Beatrice 'in unusually grotesque fashion' to ask if there was 'any way to show such friendship'.[2] Later, on the point of confessing his love, he paused, ogled at Beatrice, his hand delicately approaching hers and touching it as it hung by her side, and then abruptly and clumsily said, 'I do love nothing in the world so well as you', raising laughter as he added with altered intonation, 'Is not that strange?'[3] The Glasgow News (28 August 1883) described his stance towards Beatrice in the early part of the sequence as one of 'wittily glossed sympathy' – though the element of balance which this description implies was badly upset in the course of Beatrice's next reply ('As strange as the thing I know not . . .'), during which the two moved hither and thither awkwardly, Irving interpolating interjections of 'Ah' and 'Eh' in a different tone after each phrase,[4] raising laughter which one critic found most tasteless.[5] In Tree's production of 1905 Winifred Emery invited laughter at this speech by making as if to nestle into Benedick's arms, and then moving coyly away.[6] At Stratford in 1929 Wilfrid Walter raised mirth at the end of the scene by a deliberate pause at 'I will kiss – your hand';[7] while in Robert Atkins's Stratford production of 1945, the comic element was tactlessly exaggerated through much of the later part of the sequence.[8]

Perhaps the most difficult moment for players to judge is the 'Kill Claudio' speech itself, where the balance between the serious and the comic becomes very precarious indeed. There is something potentially comic in the sheer extravagance of Beatrice's demand – something comically satisfying, too, in the swift literalness with which it takes up Benedick's equally extravagant invitation, 'Come bid me do anything for thee', and exposes its unguarded romantic breadth with an irony whose justice is obvious. But on the other hand, Beatrice's demand registers a sense of genuine outrage, which the audience must grasp if it is to respond with very much more than mild amusement to her ensuing outburst of indignation, or to appreciate fully the dramatic logic of Benedick's ultimate agreement to challenge Claudio. Altogether it would seem best for the players to guard against too overt a comic response at 'Kill Claudio' – although at times even the most accomplished artists, such as Gielgud and Peggy Ashcroft, have not been able to avoid it. When the laugh comes, there is a danger that too sudden a release of the dramatic tension will leave the audience unprepared for the tautness of Beatrice's next response ('You kill me to deny it, farewell'), and insufficiently poised to hold in focus the significance of the whole passage as an expression of the deeper sensibility which the events in the church have brought to the surface in Beatrice. Sprague and Trewin have noted, furthermore, that when the audience laughs at this point (as often happened in Bridges-Adams's Stratford productions in the

[1] Note added by Walter Lacy to his transcription of the Kemble promptbook in the Garrick Club.

[2] [Chicago] Morning News, 21 Jan. 1885.

[3] Irving promptbooks in the Folger Shakespeare Library and the New York Public Library; Saturday Review, 21 Oct. 1882; [Glasgow] Evening News, 28 Aug. 1883.

[4] Irving promptbooks (Folger; New York Public Library).

[5] Knowledge, 10 Nov. 1882.

[6] Tree promptbook (University of Bristol Theatre Collection).

[7] Stratford Herald, 26 April 1929.

[8] Promptbook (Shakespeare Centre Library, Stratford); Times, 2 April 1945; Stratford Herald, 6 April 1945.

1920s and early 1930s), Beatrice has to fight to win back the house for the speech, 'Is he not approved in the height a villain. . . .'[1]

Stage history demonstrates, however, the variety of ways in which Beatrice's 'Kill Claudio', and Benedick's reply, can be successfully rendered. Helen Faucit spoke the words half-appealingly, half-commandingly, in a voice earnest, yet startling in its bitterness and force.[2] Mrs Kean was spirited, though with a fire not inconsistent with the heat of her indignation against Claudio.[3] Sybil Thorndike's 'Kill Claudio' was 'quiet but intensely strong';[4] while Marie Ney once spoke the words in 'a voice as sharp, as clear, as cold as an icicle'.[5] Charles Kemble, Macready and Irving had all hesitated before replying, their features showing the conflict between Benedick's impulse to oblige Beatrice, and his wish to spare Claudio.[6] James Dale, who with Florence Saunders (Stratford, 1925) had negotiated 'the thin ice' of this dialogue 'with exquisite delicacy',[7] in 1936 spoke his 'not for the wide world' 'quietly with a slight smile, as who should say, "No; I can't do that, even for you." '[8] Ellen Terry spoke her 'Kill Claudio' with swift impulsiveness, turning with sudden, almost fierce eagerness on Benedick.[9] While she was less intense than some actresses,[10] on her best nights she delivered the words with 'concentrated energy', 'like an arrow from a full-drawn bow', emphasising them with 'a gesture like that of a thrusting lance'.[11] The control with which she and Irving played at this critical moment may be gauged from the fact that only one report[12] has been found of their raising laughter at 'Kill Claudio'.

At the Phoenix Theatre in 1952, Gielgud and Diana Wynyard avoided the laugh by structuring their approach to this point with a mutual finesse[13] described by Harold Hobson as 'perfection of a thrilling and difficult kind'.[14] Their method was to subdue 'the humour of the love declaration so that Beatrice's sudden murderous entreaty [could] be received not as a climax threatening anticlimax but as a deepening of the lovers' new-found seriousness'.[15]

Their sudden discovery of love [cast] over them, hitherto so gay and irresponsible, a sense of awe; and, in the dim and solemn light of the church, they [spoke] to each other in a sort of tranced whisper, as though in the presence of ineffable things, of which Beatrice's unexpected injunction, and Benedick's scarcely breathed, horrified refusal, seem[ed] the perfect, the inevitable completion.[16]

The words 'Kill Claudio' were 'hummed low', with a 'deadly calm', 'sounding a note of unease rather than of sudden hysteria', and Gielgud's reply came in a 'quick, startled undertone'.[17] 'The passage,' wrote Trewin, was lifted gradually to 'Bid me do anything for thee', spoken by a loyal lover;. . .Beatrice paused for a

[1] A. C. Sprague and J. C. Trewin, *Shakespeare's Plays Today* (1970), p. 75.

[2] *Manchester Courier*, 11 April 1866; *Liverpool Daily Post*, 16 Dec. 1870.

[3] *Sunday Times*, 17 March 1850, 28 Nov. 1858.

[4] Crosse, *Shakespearean Playgoing*, p. 52.

[5] *Sunday Times*, 20 Oct. 1946. Marie Ney played Beatrice at the Old Vic in 1925. The reference cited is Harold Hobson's recollection of her performance in an unidentified radio broadcast.

[6] *John Bull*, 12 April 1840; transcription, dated 1845, of Macready's *Much Ado* promptbook (Harvard Theatre Collection); *Lloyd's Weekly London Newspaper*, 26 Jan. 1851; *Bell's Weekly Messenger*, 16 Oct. 1882.

[7] *Birmingham Mail*, 18 April 1925.

[8] Crosse, *Shakespearean Playgoing*, p. 73. That Crosse is referring to Dale's Stratford performance of 1936 is evident from Crosse's MS account in 'Shakespearean Performances', XV, 151.

[9] *The Theatre* (1 Nov. 1882), p. 298; *Philadelphia Inquirer*, 19 March 1884.

[10] *Athenaeum*, 7 June 1884.

[11] *Philadelphia Inquirer*, 19 March 1884; *Boston Daily Advertiser*, 28 Feb. 1884.

[12] *St James's Gazette*, 6 Jan. 1891.

[13] *Illustrated London News*, 2 Feb. 1952.

[14] *The Theatre Now* (1953), p. 135.

[15] *Times*, 22 July 1955.

[16] *Sunday Times*, 13 Jan. 1952.

[17] *Sunday Graphic*, 13 Jan. 1952; *Truth*, 18 Jan. 1952; *Sunday Times*, 24 July 1955; *Sketch*, 30 Jan. 1952.

moment in a charged silence;...the actress held this before she replied 'Kill Claudio!' (words forced from her); and...Benedick's 'Not for the wide world' was quick, low-toned, the almost incredulous exclamation of a man who had not realized how friendship must struggle with love and honour.[1]

The passionate outburst of indignation with which Beatrice reacts to Benedick's refusal of her command is the climax of the conflicting emotions that have been welling up within her throughout the scene. It is important that the actress playing Beatrice should beware lest the intensity of her outrage should seem incompatible with the womanly sensibilities that Beatrice has already revealed. Mrs H. Johnston (Covent Garden, 1807, 1811, 1812) made Beatrice's indignation seem almost malevolent.[2] Florence Buckton (Old Vic, 1921), who had shown a touch of the shrew throughout, cheapened her indignation by 'click-click[ing] about the stage in a pettish temper'.[3] On the other hand Mrs Jordan (Drury Lane, 1798–1808), Louisa Angel (Haymarket, 1863) and Julia Neilson (St James's, 1898) rather underplayed the intensity of Beatrice's outburst.[4] More satisfactory were the performances of those actresses who managed, in various ways, to convey a sense of the fusion of emotional elements in Beatrice's passion. In Mrs Abington's interpretation a turmoil of disdain, rage and pity agitated a mind shown to be essentially generous.[5] The 'sudden impetuousness' of Mrs Kean's reaction seemed quite 'consistent with the ardent character' of a Beatrice 'who, in the heat of her indignation against the villain that had slandered...her cousin, thinks no punishment too great for the offense'.[6] This was also true of Helen Faucit's outburst, conceived as a release of 'all the pent-up passion that has shaken [Beatrice] during the previous scene'.[7] Kate Terry's indignation (Adelphi, 1867) was alternately coaxing, petulant, fierce and menacing, though without seeming unfeminine.[8] Violet Vanbrugh's was neither turbulent nor combative,

but rather the controlled outrage of a wounded sensibility.[9]

Ellen Terry's outburst, though coloured somewhat by her natural lightness,[10] was very powerful when she performed it at her best. 'None who have ever seen...it,' wrote Bram Stoker, 'can forget her futile helpless anger, the surging, choking passion in her voice, as striding to and fro with long paces, her whirling words won Benedick to her.'[11] But even here there was moderation. Her cry 'O God that I were a man' was

not the scornful rage of a vixen, or the scream of a vulgar shrew, but a sudden, passionate sob of suppressed emotion. 'O! God, that I were a man! I would –' and then there [was] a long pause, as if the woman were too passionately indignant to give her thoughts utterance, but soon, with a wounded cry, and with rage expressed in the scarcely suppressed tears, [came] the words, 'I would eat his heart in the market-place.'[12]

Then again she paced up and down 'in magnificent anger', giving 'the full measure of sarcastic bitterness' to her second 'O that I were a man for his sake...'[13] Sometimes, especially

---

[1] Sprague and Trewin, *Shakespeare's Plays Today*, p. 75.

[2] *Examiner*, 3 Jan. 1808.

[3] *New Age*, 29 Sept. 1921.

[4] *Courier*, 16 Nov. 1807; *Morning Post*, 7 April 1863; Crosse, 'Shakespearean Performances', I, 158.

[5] Poem 'To Mrs Abington', cut from *European Magazine* (c. 1780), in scrapbook entitled 'David Garrick. A Memorial' (Garrick Club, London), IV, 92; *Morning Post*, 3 Nov. 1785.

[6] *Daily Telegraph*, 22 Nov. 1858; *Sunday Times*, 17 March 1850.

[7] Faucit, 'On Some of Shakespeare's Female Characters', p. 224.

[8] *Times*, 26 July 1867; *Sunday Times*, 28 July 1867.

[9] *Stratford Herald*, 21 April 1911.

[10] *Daily Telegraph*, 2 June 1884.

[11] *Personal Reminiscences of Henry Irving* (1906), I, 101.

[12] Clement Scott, *The Theatre* (1 Nov. 1882), p. 300.

[13] [Chicago] *Morning News*, 16 Jan. 1885; *Era*, 7 June 1884.

in her earlier years as Beatrice, she misjudged the tone, and rendered the passage more lightly than these descriptions indicate.[1] But as her performance matured, the indignation gained a somewhat deeper resonance.[2] That she intended it this way is suggested by a marginal notation on this passage in the manuscript of her *Four Lectures on Shakespeare* (1932): 'Not *emotion*. A *passion*'.[3] Her intention may also be inferred from the disparagement with which she observed that, in the mid-Victorian theatre, it had been common practice to make Beatrice's indignation 'rather comic'.[4]

One of the most persistent falsifications in the stage history of the 'Kill Claudio' sequence was the alternative ending devised by J. P. Kemble, and perpetuated in the English theatre throughout the nineteenth century. In the original text, the scene finishes quietly, on a note of gradually falling intensity, which is dramatically right after the passionate climax of Beatrice's indignation. Shakespeare's ending is tactfully inconclusive, implying the still-tentative quality of the understanding between Beatrice and Benedick, and pointing forward to the challenge in the final act as the pre-condition for a mutuality yet to be fully established. But Kemble and his successors, influenced perhaps by the demands of the picture-frame theatre, looked for a more climactic curtain-line than Shakespeare had provided. The effect was to sentimentalise the end of the scene, and to make the Beatrice–Benedick relationship seem at this point a little more firmly crystallised than it is in the original text:

Benedick. Enough, I am engag'd; I will challenge him.
Beatrice. Will you?
Benedick. Upon my soul I will. I'll kiss your hand, and so leave you. By this hand, Claudio shall render me a dear account.
Beatrice. You'll be sure to challenge him.
Benedick. By those bright eyes, I will.
Beatrice. My dear friend, kiss my hand again.
Benedick. As you hear of me so think of me. Go,

comfort your cousin – I must say she is dead & so farewell. [*both going*]
Beatrice. Benedick, kill him, kill him if you can –
Benedick. As sure as he is alive, I will. *Exeunt*.[5]

The earliest extant record of the interpolation is probably that in Kemble's manuscript partbook for Benedick (Folger Shakespeare Library). The manuscript is dated 30 April 1788 – though this is probably a reference to Kemble's first performance of Benedick at Drury Lane, rather than to the date of writing. The interpolation is recorded in all the extant *Much Ado* promptbooks relating to John and Charles Kemble, but not in Kemble's printed acting versions of the play.

During the Victorian period several variant forms of the interpolation emerged, Macready's version sentimentalising the ending even more than Kemble's had done:

Benedick. Think you in your soul the Count Claudio hath wronged Hero?
Beatrice. Yea, as sure as I have a thought or a soul.
Benedick. You do? –
Beatrice. I do! –
Benedick. You? – / Beat assents. / Enough! – I am engaged – I'll challenge him! – I will! / Beat with her hand resting on his shoulder is now in front of Ben and looks up in his face delightedly, – their eyes meet – he smiles – and takes her hand / – I will kiss your hand, and so leave you: By this hand, Claudio shall render me a dear account.
Beatrice. – Kiss my hand again! / he does so. /
Benedick. As you hear of me, so think of me. Go, comfort your cousin: I must say, she is dead; and so, farewell [*sic*].[6]

[1] See, e.g., *Spectator*, 14 Oct. 1882; *New York Commercial Advertiser*, 14 Nov. 1884.
[2] *Daily Telegraph*, 14 June 1887; *Illustrated Sporting and Dramatic News*, 18 June 1887; *Observer*, 19 June 1887.
[3] Editorial note to p. 90 of the published work.
[4] *Four Lectures on Shakespeare*, p. 95.
[5] Partbook for Beatrice, marked by J. P. Kemble, and formerly owned by Maria Foote (Folger Shakespeare Library).
[6] Transcription of Macready's Drury Lane promptbook of 1843, made by George Ellis in 1845 (Harvard Theatre Collection).

Macready conveyed here a sense of almost smug assurance in Beatrice's love, delivering his decision to challenge Claudio with an 'exulting and important air', at the same time 'putting on his hat with a kind of comic resolution'.[1] At the end of the dialogue he accompanied Beatrice to the exit, still kissing her hand, and as soon as she had gone, replaced his hat, arranged his dress, and, drawing on his glove, strutted off in the opposite direction, with a very self-satisfied air, that bespoke 'the pride of successful love'.[2] The stage has too often cheapened the closing moments of the scene by similar expressions of self-satisfaction from Benedick, and by displays of rapturous delight from actresses intent on showing Beatrice's pleasure not only at having won Benedick, but at having secured his word to challenge Claudio.[3]

Walter Lacy, who played Benedick at the Haymarket Theatre in 1859, recorded a crass variant of Kemble's dialogue which had been used at the Haymarket earlier in the 1850s:

Benedick. I will challenge him.
Beatrice. And fight him?
Benedick. Fight him!
Beatrice. Kill him?
Benedick. Kill him!
Beatrice. Dead?
Benedick. Dead![4]

Lacy, whose own performance showed considerable tact,[5] strongly disapproved of this variant, although he accepted Kemble's interpolation itself.[6] Irving at the Lyceum spoke a slightly shortened version of Kemble's dialogue – though very much against Ellen Terry's wishes.[7] During the first decade of the twentieth century most theatres reverted to Shakespeare's ending,[8] though from time to time an occasional producer still sought by suggestive stage business to build the final moments of the scene to an artificial climax.[9]

Gielgud was truer to Shakespeare's design when in 1950, 1952 and 1955 he played the conclusion of the scene not towards a climax,

but towards a falling close – a 'grave and peaceful ending',[10] held, according to Anthony Cookman, to a 'single sustained note of glowingly romantic tenderness'.[11] Ronald Hayman has described how Gielgud retreated on

'Enough, I am engaged . . .', and then, halting, as if arrested by a premonition, . . . spoke the words, 'I will kiss your hand and so I leave you . . .' About to go, he still hesitated. 'As you hear of me, so think of me.' And then he took another lingering pause before 'Go comfort your cousin; I must say she is dead; and so farewell.'[12]

It was in fact characteristic of Gielgud's

[1] *Morning Post*, 24 Jan. 1851.
[2] *Ibid.*; promptbooks relating to Macready's *Much Ado* production in the Harvard Theatre Collection, the University of Illinois Library, and the New York Public Library.
[3] e.g. Miss Brunton (*Times*, 29 Nov. 1817); Charles and Ellen Kean (*Athenaeum*, 27 Nov. 1858); Charlotte Cushman (*Times*, 4 April 1845); Louisa Herbert (*Sunday Times*, 8 April 1866); Henry Irving (W. H. Pollock, *Impressions of Henry Irving* (1908) p. 86); Tree and Winifred Emery (Tree promptbooks, University of Bristol Theatre Collection); Iden Payne's 1936 Stratford production (promptbook, Shakespeare Centre Library, Stratford).
[4] Note by Lacy in his transcription of the Kemble promptbook in the Garrick Club.
[5] *Globe*, 6 Oct. 1859.
[6] See Lacy's promptbook transcription.
[7] Irving promptbook in the Folger Shakespeare Library; Ellen Terry, *The Story of My Life* (1908), p. 163; Ellen Terry, *Four Lectures*, p. 96.
[8] The earliest discovered instances of a return to Shakespeare's ending were in the productions of Edward Gordon Craig (Imperial, 1903) and of William Poel (Court Theatre and various London halls, 1904). See promptbooks of Craig (Ellen Terry Museum, Smallhythe, Kent, and Bibliothèque Nationale, Paris), and of Poel (Enthoven Collection, Victoria and Albert Museum, London).
[9] e.g. Tree, His Majesty's, 1905 (promptbooks in University of Bristol Theatre Collection); Iden Payne, Stratford, 1936 (promptbook, Shakespeare Centre Library, Stratford); Robert Atkins, Stratford, 1945 (promptbook, Shakespeare Centre Library).
[10] Hobson, *The Theatre Now*, p. 137.
[11] *Tatler and Bystander*, 23 Jan. 1952.
[12] *John Gielgud* (1971), p. 172.

achievement in *Much Ado* that he made the text live less by tricksy innovations on the part of the producer, than by performances attuned sensitively to the subtle organisation of the play itself.[1] His success in this respect makes his work a useful reference point by which to judge those whose lack of confidence in Shakespeare's dramatic technique may have tempted them to manipulate the 'Kill Claudio' sequence to the point of falsification, on the pretext of audience appeal.

[1] See especially *Stratford Herald*, 9 June 1950; *Tatler and Bystander*, 3 Aug. 1955. Norman Marshall (*The Producer and the Play*, (1957) pp. 201–2) makes a similar observation of Gielgud's work generally.

'AS YOU LIKE IT' ADAPTED:
CHARLES JOHNSON'S 'LOVE IN A FOREST'

EDITH HOLDING

It is remarkable that *As You Like It*, one of Shakespeare's greatest and best-loved comedies, should – as William Winter, in his history of *Shakespeare on the Stage*, put it – have 'sunk into abeyance and remained for a long time unused' after the closing of the theatres. It was not until December 1740 that it was presented at Drury Lane, the playbill for that production declaring that it had not been acted for forty years. John Genest's comment on this, that it had probably been unperformed since the Restoration, is taken by that other great stage-historian, C. B. Hogan, to be 'almost certainly correct'.[1]

Comedy never has been as popular as tragedy, it is true, and the gradual revival of interest in it amplified only after 1740 with an increased demand for the original texts. Nevertheless, many Shakespearian comedies were always available in various forms: briefly but successfully, so was *As You Like It*.

At Drury Lane nearly twenty years before the Shakespeare revival, Charles Johnson's adaptation, *Love in a Forest*, was given six performances on 9, 10, 11, 12, 14 and 15 January 1723. This reflected an average run in the eighteenth-century repertory system, when the size of the theatre-going audience was too small to permit anything more extensive. The *London Post* for 14 January testifies to its success, saying that 'there was as numerous an Audience as has for this great while been seen; not only the Boxes, Pit and Galleries, but the Stage too being crowded with Spectators'.[2]

Despite its contemporary popularity *Love in a Forest* is little known. Inaccurate descriptions of it occur frequently as it is regularly mentioned in Shakespearian stage histories. Unfortunately, statements about it generally reflect little acquaintance with the adaptation itself and seem to derive second-hand from such accounts as G. C. D. Odell's where it is called a 'pastoral intermezzo' which constituted a 'decidedly insipid' perversion. Two misrepresentations occurred fairly recently. Agnes Latham, in the Introduction to her New Arden edition of *As You Like It*, refers to Oliver and Orlando using lines from *Richard II*: in fact it is Charles and Orlando who have this conversation. Gāmini Salgādo, in his *Eyewitnesses to Shakespeare*, goes one stage further by naming the source as *Richard III*.[3]

The adaptation has been, and still is, intolerantly assessed. Genest's review began the critical tradition by calling it 'a bad alteration of Shakespeare's play', but his account is a good deal more objective than many subsequent ones. Winter, for instance, dismisses it as 'worthless', and Agnes Latham calls it a 'travesty'. Odell, however, concedes

[1] William Winter, *Shakespeare on the Stage*, 2nd Series (New York, 1915), p. 232; C. B. Hogan, *Shakespeare in the Theatre 1701–1800, A Record of Performances in London*, 2 vols (Oxford, 1952–7), I, 91.

[2] See E. L. Avery and others, *The London Stage*, 11 vols. (Carbondale, 1960–9), part 2, vol II, 704.

[3] G. C. D. Odell, *Shakespeare – From Betterton to Irving*, 2 vols. (New York, 1920; reprinted, 1963), I, 244, 247; *As You Like It*, edited by Agnes Latham (New Arden Shakespeare, 1975), p. lxxxvi; Gāmini Salgādo, *Eyewitnesses to Shakespeare* (1975), p. 16.

that *Love in a Forest* represents 'a step forward', for the 'revival showed at least a dainty side of Shakespeare's genius hitherto neglected'.[1]

The time has come to redress the balance and subject *Love in a Forest* to the sympathetic treatment which Christopher Spencer so rightly advocates for adaptations.[2] Looked at within the literary, political and theatrical context which gave it life, as one of the plays which constituted a popular and substantial part of Augustan drama, *Love in a Forest* may begin to justify itself. It deserves some attention in view of its contemporary success, its significance as the first work based on *As You Like It*, and its contribution to the gradual revival of interest in Shakespeare's comedies. For these reasons it is worth trying to understand what its author was doing to *As You Like It*, and why.

Adaptations of Shakespeare's plays became increasingly popular after the Restoration when, for various reasons, the content of certain works suggested to dramatists short of original material that, suitably modified, they would provide excellent fare for the newly reopened playhouses. Shakespeare's reputation as a dramatist of incomparable genius was recognized by seventeenth- and eighteenth-century adapters alike, as the dedicatory pieces of such as Dryden, Davenant, Tate and even Charles Johnson himself attest. Nevertheless, they undertook to adapt his achievements convinced that they suffered from the limitations of language and the faltering stagecraft of their age. Influenced by continental neo-classicism with its regard for Aristotelian canons – Shakespeare's violation of which was not to be imitated – they attempted to re-assemble his original plays so as to reflect the altered modes of expression and the changing social patterns of their own day.

Allardyce Nicoll refers to Charles Johnson as a strange figure, one of the most prolific and diversified dramatists there then were, 'ever ready to take advantage of the current fashions in the theatrical world'.[3] He is frequently mentioned in theatrical histories, especially as a versatile and prolific writer with a plagiaristic reputation, but material concerning him is widely scattered. Born in 1679, he began writing in 1701 after admittance to the Middle Temple as a law student. Between 1702 and 1733 he maintained a steady output of nineteen plays, all of which were produced and two of which were later adapted by Garrick and Kemble. His Whig farce, *The Cobler of Preston* (1716), proved to be one of the two most controversial plays at Drury Lane between 1714 and 1728. An adaptation of the Christopher Sly episode from *The Taming of the Shrew*, it satirizes the Jacobite rebels who had just been captured on Preston Heath and was instrumental in instigating theatrical rivalry from the Tory theatre of Lincoln's Inn Fields. By 1733 he was sufficiently successful to be able to retire to a Bow Street tavern which he ran till his death in 1748. His talent in serving the interests of theatrical taste, political loyalty and even masonic sympathies is all clearly exemplified in his handling of *Love in a Forest*.

Divided into five acts of sixteen scenes, *Love in a Forest* has a total of 2,026 lines (just seven hundred lines shorter than the new Arden edition of *As You Like It*). Johnson omits much of his main source but adds passages from other comedies in order to remould the characters. Thus, though Touchstone, Audrey, William, Sir Oliver Martext, Phebe and Silvius are omitted, Johnson 'supplies the deficiency' by altering those who remain, giving them lines from *Much Ado About*

[1] John Genest, *Some Account of the English Stage from the Restoration in 1660 to 1830*, 10 vols (Bath, 1832), III, 100–2; Winter, *Shakespeare on the Stage*, p. 232; Latham (ed.), *As You Like It*, p. lxxxvii; Odell, *Shakespeare – From Betterton to Irving*, I, 247.

[2] Christopher Spencer, *Five Restoration Adaptations of Shakespeare* (Urbana, 1965), pp. 7–10.

[3] Allardyce Nicoll, *A History of English Drama 1660–1900*, 6 vols (1952–9), II, 156, 242.

Nothing, Love's Labour's Lost and *Twelfth Night*.[1]

Johnson alters a few character names. The banished Duke is given the Christian name Alberto, and the third du Bois brother is renamed Robert, doubtless to avoid confusion with his namesake Jaques. Johnson's Sylvius (his spelling) is in fact Shakespeare's Corin but his role is reduced to simply accommodating the girls on their arrival in the forest; all his subsequent lines are structurally irrelevant in view of the omission of Touchstone, Phebe and Silvius and are therefore cut accordingly.

Scenes of spectacle provide a framework for the play. The contest of the Lists is introduced from *Richard II* for the combat between Orlando and Charles, and the burlesque tragedy of Pyramus and Thisbe, from *A Midsummer Night's Dream*, is performed just before the adaptation ends.

Though Johnson makes some contribution himself it is not, in Genest's words, a 'vast deal'. His hand is mainly to be seen in linking passages; even in those scenes for which he is entirely responsible, echoes of Shakespearian imagery and thought are not absent for long. For Johnson the plagiaristic impulse was strong and he appears to have acted on it compulsively.

Though both Shakespeare and Johnson begin their stories with the same conversation between Orlando and Adam, act I of *Love in a Forest* introduces several significant changes. The most striking initially is the carefully delineated motivation with which Oliver contrives the public testing of his brother; this takes place at a fencing match which replaces the original wrestling and is given all the ceremony of the Lists from *Richard II*. Johnson's selection, taken from various scenes in the history's first act, provides a suitable context for the challenge and signifies the increased formality and importance which he gives it.

Charles, 'the Duke's Fencer and Master of his Academy', is suborned by Oliver to challenge Orlando as a traitor to Duke Frederick against whom he is accused of plotting from allegiance to Alberto, the banished Duke. Oliver's resentment, originally purely personal and jealously irrational, is given clear motivation. The original fight is therefore changed from an incidental occurrence, which Orlando could have avoided, into a formal and highly dramatic event.

As Johnson contrives it, Orlando's participation in the scene is essential, particularly in terms of consistent character development. The hero stands falsely accused of attempting to poison the usurper, out of loyalty to whom Oliver justifies his own treachery. Orlando's opposition to Charles now symbolizes the conflict between the forces of good and evil – Alberto on the one hand, and Frederick on the other.

After watching the fencing Rosalind is banished, as in the original, and determines on disguised flight accompanied by Caelia (Johnson's spelling) but, of course, without Touchstone. Then Orlando himself is forced into exile, banished at the end of the second act. News of his sentence is brought just after Adam warns him of Oliver's intended fratricide; so Orlando sets off with the old man to seek his fortunes elsewhere. Before moving to the Forest of Arden Johnson concludes his court dealings: Frederick demands that Orlando be captured or, if not, that Oliver explain to him about his brother's whereabouts.

Jaques is introduced in the scene where originally he is only mentioned. Replying to Duke Alberto's reflections on the contentment of forest life and Amiens's novel account of the 'crowds' that flock to join them, Jaques admits his own misgivings about the pastoral existence. His appearance at this point, decrying the hunting of venison and describing the sobbing deer, helps to establish him as a leading character in the loyal party.

His future lover, Caelia, enters the forest

[1] Genest, *English Stage*, III, 100.

with Rosalind now, disguised respectively as Aliena, a 'Shepherdess', and Ganymede. The girls soon discover Sylvius, who helps them negotiate for the vacant sheep-cote, but he is the only forest native they meet.

Once Orlando and Adam have arrived in the forest, Johnson returns to the Duke's party: Jaques tells us that – even in Touchstone's absence – he has come upon a fool, and he describes their meeting in a carefully pruned version of the original from which all reference to his mis-spent past and desire for critical licence is excised. Amiens then announces that some 'Citizens of Liege', amateur players, intend to give a perfomance of the *Pyramus and Thisbe* play later on. News of their arrival thus gives Jaques a literal-minded excuse for deducing that 'All the World's a Stage'.

When Orlando hangs his love poems on the trees there is only Caelia to parody them, using Touchstone's lines. Johnson moves on quickly, after Rosalind has cross-examined Caelia about the unknown poet's identity, to the ladies' interruption by Orlando and Jaques. The men's conversation together lacks the perverse antagonism with which Shakespeare imbued it; instead, Jaques's cynicism is expressed in terms of Benedick's kind of verbose misogyny:

That a Woman conceiv'd me I thank her: That she brought me up I likewise give her my most hearty Thanks; but that I will have a Recheate winded in my Forehead all Women shall pardon me: Because I will not do them the wrong to mistrust any, I will trust none. (III, i, 131–6)[1]

Generous employment of *Much Ado About Nothing* prepares the way for his romantic downfall. This happens despite the reservations of Orlando, who inherits a version of Don Pedro's 'obstinate heretic' description, and against his own better judgement. Jaques becomes friendlier with Caelia by walking with her while Orlando talks with Rosalind.

Johnson's adherence to Shakespeare's text is fairly faithful at this point, though he finds no place for the heroine's discourse on the metaphysics of time. Orlando agrees to the wooing of Ganymede and then this couple leave the stage to Jaques and Caelia; to their love affair Johnson gives almost as much emphasis as to that between Orlando and Rosalind.

He creates the new lovers' conversation from an amalgam of his own prose and that of Touchstone and Audrey from III, iii of *As You Like It*. At first Caelia is unimpressed by her lover's attentions but Jaques describes her effect on his composure in a rather titillating passage:

Caelia. . . . You have some Symptoms [of love], have you not?
Jaques. I doubt so – Yet I hope not – When I lean'd my Shoulder against yours to read *Orlando*'s Verses, I caught a Tingling; aye, – here it is still; and creeps every Moment more and more into my Blood.

(III, i, 302–8)

Caelia explains that he must wait two years before winning her and during that time he should work on the galleys – an idea reminiscent of Mosca's punishment in v, xii of *Volpone*[2] – and he is then left to soliloquize on his plight. In this speech, an uneasy blend of various sources, he rationalizes both his predicament and his imminent change of character: Benedick's justifications of the 'doth not the appetite alter' kind provide some motivation for his decision to abandon bachelorhood. Johnson then carefully balances his love story by introducing a Caelia whose mind runs as freely on Jaques as Rosalind's does on Orlando.

Jacques asks Rosalind–Ganymede's permission to marry Caelia at the beginning of the fourth act. His traveller's melancholy and nihilism are replaced by a compilation of Berowne's protestations, designed to give plausibility to the Jaques-in-love character of

[1] All references are to *Love in a Forest* (1723; reprinted by the Cornmarket Press, 1969).
[2] *Ben Jonson*, edited by C. H. and E. Herford and Percy Simpson, 11 vols. (Oxford, 1925–52), v, 134.

Johnson's creation. A rearrangement of various remarks of Berowne's helps remind us of Jaques's misogynous reputation and the all-the-more astonishing character change that is taking place.

Rosalind teases him, pretending to withhold permission and trying to dissuade him. While Rosalind's lines are wholly provided by Johnson, Jaques's are redolent of Berowne at every stage of his capitulation to Rosaline. Even so, the Johnsonian technique is prevalent, re-phrasing, clarifying and compounding every-thing with his own additions:

Rosalind. Is it then possible that thy solemn Gravity shou'd relax into Wantonness at last?

Jaques. Aye! so it is, I do worship, yes I fall down, I am touch'd in the Liver Vein it seems, and have learn'd the Trick to turn a Green-Goose into a Deity – flat Idolatry! – Heaven mend me, I am much out o' the Way.   (IV, i, 37–44)

Rosalind then conducts her second interview with Orlando. The original is adhered to closely except for the introduction of a short passage from *Twelfth Night* near the end. Johnson has Orlando ask Rosalind to be his 'Voucher that she ought to give Credit to my Oaths', an idea which may have come from Shakespeare's reference to the distinction between men making vows and women's practical love. Accordingly he incorporates some of Viola's response to Orsino in Rosa-lind's reply:

Oh no – I will tell her no such Thing, too well I know what sort of Faith we Men to Women owe, my Father had a Daughter lov'd a Man; as it might be, perhaps, were I a Woman, I might love you.

Orlando. And what is her History?

Rosalind. A Blank. She never told her Love, but let Concealment, like a Worm i'th Bud, feed on her Damask Cheek; she pined in thought; and with a green and yellow Melancholly, she sat like Patience on a Monument, smiling at Grief –

Orlando. Alas, poor Maid – Well, my dear *Rosalind*, for these two Hours I will leave thee.

(IV, i, 160–72)

The superficial similarity between Rosalind and Viola – able by virtue of disguise to talk to their lovers of their loves – doubtless appealed to Johnson. Viola's poignant account reflects the apparent hopelessness of her own situation, however, and culminates in ambiguity and confusion. But Rosalind knows that Orlando returns her love: to give just some of Viola's thoughts to her negates the original intention and misplaces the lines' innate wistfulness, so the effect is really of rather gratuitous inclusion.

Caelia then suggests and conducts the mock marriage ceremony, afterwards commiserating with a Rosalind who is no longer alone in her love-plight: her cousin makes it clear that she endures similar frustrations to Rosalind's and that the sleep into which she falls is one through which thoughts of Jaques may break.

While they await Orlando's return from dining with the Duke we see Amiens (not Jaques, as in the original) hunting in the forest. Then Robert du Bois, Orlando's 'youngest' brother arrives. Playing Oliver's role he explains what has happened at court and why he has come: Charles the fencer, he tells the girls, has confessed to plotting against Orlando with Oliver; Oliver's recent suicide ensures that Orlando shall inherit the family fortune. He also describes his rescue from the lioness at Orlando's hands and after he shows them the bloody handkerchief – at which Rosalind faints – the girls take him to the Duke.

In a conversation between Orlando and Jaques (replacing that between the hero and Oliver) Orlando agrees to obtain permission for the marriage to Caelia. Then there is a condensed account of Rosalind's plan to conclude everything successfully the next day, and in the lovers' catechism Jaques and Caelia replace Silvius and Phebe.

The last act includes a performance of *Pyramus and Thisbe* before Hymen blesses the two pairs of lovers. This little burlesque 'proved a regular Robin Goodfellow to so many perverters of Shakespeare', as Odell points out. In using it to his own ends Johnson followed the example of Richard Leveridge who was the first to extract it from *A Midsummer Night's Dream* in 1716. His *Comick Masque of Pyramus and Thisbe* was itself later amplified by J. F. Lampe in 1745, but not nearly so successfully. Both of these were mock operas, but for his purposes Johnson keeps it strictly non-musical.[1]

He sets his amateur play at the point in *As You Like It* where Touchstone originally gave his encore on the causes of a quarrel. The performance provides a sufficient interval for Rosalind and Caelia to change their clothes for the wedding scene. Johnson shortens the text slightly, omitting occasional remarks of both the players and the on-stage audience, whose speeches are redistributed from the Athens gentry to the inhabitants of Arden. After the players 'vanish', *As You Like It* is resumed with the arrival of Hymen and the wedding masque.

Just before the end Robert du Bois re-enters, bringing news of Duke Frederick's conversion and the restoration of Alberto's lands. After a celebratory dance Rosalind is denied her original epilogue, and Alberto is given the final couplet.

Several of the outstanding theatrical personalities of the time were in the cast. Barton Booth and his second wife, Hester Santlow, played Duke Alberto and Rosalind. Mrs Booth's beauty and dancing talents as well as her husband's reputation as a fine tragedian of perfect articulation, deportment and dignity are all recorded by Benjamin Victor in his *History*.[2] However, Colley Cibber, who played Jaques, sneered at Booth for professional reasons.

Cibber himself dominated Drury Lane for over forty years as actor, playwright, manager and, eventually, Poet Laureate. Not surprisingly his Jaques role is suitably enlarged to fulfil the requirements of this extraordinary man who, in Odell's opinion, ' "padded" it for his own

glorification'. In their own way both Cibber and Booth 'brought glory...to the English stage' and so did Robert Wilks, who played Orlando.[3] This Irish actor's ease, sprightliness and distinguished manner came to be thought the model of behaviour in fashionable society: even Cibber admired his diligence. Wilks appears to have been influential in Johnson's life and encouraged him to write in the first place. Once Wilks became joint-manager of Drury Lane in 1712 Johnson found their friendship a useful spur in the production of his later plays, nearly all of which were presented in this Whig theatre.

This political connection was not accidental. Johnson was himself a Whig whose persistent attendance at Button's Coffee House in Covent Garden – a stronghold of Whig wits since its founding – was satirized by Pope in *Umbra*.[4] The Drury Lane management retained a close allegiance to the Whig party, and particularly Walpole's ministry, the theatre itself being considered a 'loyal' house.[5] It is not surprising then that Johnson associated closely with Drury Lane, nor that in a politically sensitive climate *Love in a Forest*'s epilogue should display some Whig affinity.

Uncertainty continues concerning the consistency with which the rival theatres, Drury Lane and Lincoln's Inn Fields, intentionally used their stages as political platforms. Nevertheless, literary opposition became increasingly organized in the 1720s and politics did become

---

[1] Odell, *Shakespeare – From Betterton to Irving*, I, 244.

[2] Benjamin Victor, *The History of the Theatres of London and Dublin*, and *An Annual Register of all the Plays Performed at the Theatres-Royal, London* (1761, 1771; reissued 3 vols in one, 1969), II, 10–13.

[3] Odell, *Shakespeare – From Betterton to Irving*, I, 246; Cecil Price, *Theatre in the Age of Garrick* (Oxford, 1973), p. 3.

[4] Alexander Pope, *The Poems of Alexander Pope*, VI, *Minor Poems*, edited by Norman Ault (1964), 140.

[5] John Loftis, *The Politics of Drama in Augustan England* (Oxford, 1963), pp. 65–72.

an important issue in itself so far as theatrical rivalry was concerned. By the mid 1720s the significant political distinction was that between the Walpole Whigs and the opposition – in contemporary terms, the Court and Country parties. Thus we find that the gist of Johnson's epilogue seems to question the commendation of country life that *Love in a Forest* might be thought to imply. The contrast between court and country – a theme of *As You Like It* and to a lesser extent *Love in a Forest* – had long been the matter of comedies: most dramatists' evaluations implied a preference for the town, but Johnson was an exception in this work. So to clarify any possible misunderstandings Johnson's epilogue confidently associates the cultured pleasures of an educated mind with residence in the town; in comparison, the 'dull Souls' of the country only 'Vegetate away'. Perhaps this glance at contemporary politics would have redressed any political imbalance with which Drury Lane may have been charged for presenting the unconventional attitude expressed in *Love in a Forest*.

Freemasonry also has some bearing on Johnson's adaptation. He dedicated *Love in a Forest* to the Freemasons, to which Society it is almost certain he belonged: indeed the performance for the 15 January was advertised in the *Daily Courant* as being 'For the Benefit of the Author, a Free Mason'. The dedication itself is of obvious relevance to the Fraternity and is written in deferential praise of their 'social Virtues', philosophy of universal brotherhood and benevolence. Johnson addresses his 'Brethren' in a characteristically masonic way, invoking their 'Protection' for the play in a passage of sustained admiration.

Whether this implies that freemasons attended a specific performance, either officially or unofficially, is uncertain, as is the question of whether *Love in a Forest* was bespoken by the Society itself. There is evidence that plays were requested on occasion – commemorative prologues, epilogues and songs being written especially. *Love in a Forest* does have two passages of masonic significance both of which refer to 'Mechanicks' who have joined the exiled Duke in the forest. The term 'Labourers in Handicraft' occurs in one of them, a phrase which specifically refers to the original medieval craftsmen in whom freemasonry's history is founded. These superficial glances at esoteric particulars suggest they were aimed at Brothers in the audience who would appreciate their inclusion. *Love in a Forest*'s dedication was felt significant enough in Fraternity terms to find a place for itself in a work on *Early Masonic Pamphlets*.[1]

In its refinement of Shakespeare's language and its attempt at observing some element of the unity of place, *Love in a Forest* certainly shows the influence of the adapting tradition. Johnson openly acknowledged, however, that he was willing to sacrifice style to the plot and adhered to the unities only when expedient to do so.[2]

The absence of supernumeraries such as Touchstone, Audrey, Phebe and Silvius is in accordance with neo-classical concerns. In other respects, however, the alterations point to the influence of sentimental comedy, in the campaign for which Colley Cibber himself played such an important role. Cibber's career forms a convenient link between the contrasting dramatic ideologies of the Restoration and eighteenth-century stages. The comedy of the theatres in which his own Shakespearian adaptations had been produced generally reflected the moral disorder and indelicacy of its audience. A break in the tradition of profligate heroes and amusement in illicit love affairs occurred when an increasingly vocal campaign for theatrical reform came to a head; a campaign which sought to arrest the decline into which drama had fallen

[1] Douglas Knoop, Gwilym P. Jones and Douglas Hamer, *Early Masonic Pamphlets* (Manchester, 1945), pp. 18–20.
[2] Nicoll, *English Drama*, II, 51.

by insisting on its purpose as a corrective agent. Shakespeare was again invoked as an archetypal imitator of nature, from whose works instruction as well as delight could be gained.

The theories of such writers as Richard Steele provided the framework against which the reformed comedy developed: comedy should represent the success of wholly admirable heroes and their progress towards finding faithful wives and happy marriages – the 'just state' applauded by Cibber in *Love's Last Shift*, the seminal comedy from which eighteenth-century sentimental drama partly stems. A definition of this rather 'unclassifiable type' of drama is, as Nicoll points out, notoriously difficult to find; it is certainly characterized by the employment of conventions such as the separation of families, reconciliation and reunion.[1] It is understandable that dramatists, finding that Shakespeare's plays use similar conventions, should have turned to them in their search for new material, as Johnson did when he saw the themes he wanted united in *As You Like It*.

Johnson saw the possibilities of drastically altering Jaques's character to make him an unwilling but fated victim of wedlock – an object lesson in the moral value of the man with a reflective turn of mind finding happiness in yielding to his emotions. He could no longer be the cynical Shakespearian original, the satirist with the dubious past. But, with a little help from Benedick and Berowne, Johnson saw in him the makings of a redeemable leading character whose prevarications and wit would provide amusement as well as sentiment.

Orlando constituted the ideal victim of another sort, for a certain amount of restructuring enabled Johnson to translate him into the perfect sentimental hero. Shakespeare had already made him handsome, kind, loving and unjustly dispossessed of his inheritance. In sentimental terms this was ideal. Johnson had only to exaggerate the injustice and blacken the villains to point the contrast with Orlando's

virtue still further, thus generalizing the character to serve the interests of moral clarity.

To this end his initial meeting with Rosalind occurs within a less ambiguous context than in the original: Johnson ensures that the hero's and heroine's similarity of circumstances is keenly emphasized, especially in view of the fate they are to share. The forces of evil opposing Orlando are augmented and stressed accordingly when news of his banishment arrives straight after he learns that Oliver means to kill him. Nevertheless, from this unfortunate slough hero and heroine eventually emerge victorious and united in love to share the material rewards to which their virtue entitles them.

Johnson shows a characteristically Augustan concern for telling his story as clearly and directly as possible. As Christopher Spencer points out, adaptations are by nature 'tightly coherent and are primarily *social*: they emphasize permanent patterns of human relationships with less attention to the depths of individual experience'.[2] For this reason Shakespeare's suggestive language has to be modified in order to communicate explicitly. Accordingly Johnson modernizes archaic expressions and syntax, substituting modern equivalents for specifically Elizabethan references. He also clarifies Shakespeare's abundance of metaphorical expressions, replacing the unusual with the commonplace, the general with the specific.

Alterations for modernization's sake range from the simple replacement of such words as 'hath' by 'has' and 'doth' by 'does' (e.g. II, vi, 25) to the substitution of an archaic construction like 'or Charles, or something weaker' with 'something weaker than Charles' (I, iii, 104) and 'on such a sudden' with 'suddenly' (I, iv, 22). Similarly, 'quintain' becomes 'Statue' (I, iii, 95), Rosalind's

---

[1] See Nicoll, I, 263–5 and II, 179–84; also Joseph Wood Krutch, *Comedy and Conscience after the Restoration* (New York, 1924; reprinted 1961).

[2] Spencer, *Five Restoration Adaptations*, p. 12.

'doublet and hose' – long out of fashion by Johnson's time – become 'Hat and Breeches' (II, iv, 6 and III, i, 74–5) and instead of Orlando's shoes not being 'untied' they are said to be not 'unbuckled' (III, i, 222).

Johnson frequently sacrifices the richness of vocabulary and variety of imaginative reference inherent in Shakespeare's figurative expressions. His literal-minded determination to avoid imprecision and wordiness, reflecting an age less linguistically refined, leads him to alter such poetic phrases as 'within this roof' to 'beneath this Roof' (II, i, 17) and 'out at the chimney' to 'up the Chimney' (IV, i, 154–5). The clarity of such expressions as 'as you say' far outweighs that of the original 'your gesture cries out' (IV, iv, 43), but as in the case of substituting 'at the height of heart-heaviness' with 'the heavier in my Heart' (IV, iv, 33) something ineffably Shakespearian is lost in translation. It is easy to recognize Johnson's preference for the concrete to the metaphorical phrase but the extent to which this continual process diminishes the evocative power of Shakespeare's original is inescapable. It is practical enough on Johnson's terms to use the colourful epithet 'birds' in place of 'cattle' and 'accord' for 'atone' (III, i, 257 and V, i, 230). However, it is this sort of persistent alteration which has such an impoverishing effect on the overall beauty of Shakespeare's lines.

The poetically reductive effect of such changes – as well as those omissions made in the cause of the new decorum – is undoubtedly cumulative. When the texts of *As You Like It* and *Love in a Forest* are considered side by side there is no doubting that Johnson's adaptation is inevitably inferior in many ways. His aims and intentions, not to mention his abilities, differed greatly from Shakespeare's and his resulting adaptation of *As You Like It* accordingly reflects the dramatic principles of another theatrical age; one with which it is less easy to find a natural sympathy. Nevertheless, an attempt to compare *Love in a Forest* with its main source would provide an appropriate conclusion.

As You Like It has been described as an organized 'dance' wherein the contrasting elements of human nature are left, 'by their juxtaposition or interaction', to comment on one another in a series – not of events linked by cause and effect – but encounters.[1] In his version of Arden, Shakespeare has several lovers of differing degrees of sensitivity, sufficiently perceptive and intelligent to reflect on their romantic plight, the imposition of worldly on natural values and the resulting disturbance this makes in their normal routine. Against the background of the pastoral tradition the debate between court and country is continued, a subtle and delicate conflict of values whose reality and significance obtains in virtue of the very characters who give them depth, and by means of whom the contrast is explored.

This more serious element would in itself have attracted a playwright like Charles Johnson whose work was influenced by the requirements of the sentimental school. The campaign to replace the immoral perversity and cynicism of the Restoration stage with a reformed drama which would teach the principle of virtue would have found the play's serious discussion of love and marriage outstanding commendations indeed. The reward of the hero's virtuous defiance of tyranny with material success, in contrast with Duke Frederick's material failure, would be highly appropriate for presentation on a stage whose purpose is counsel and reproof.[2] Johnson is pragmatic enough to recognize that those other aspects of Shakespeare's play which do not conform to his own view of Arden can be deleted during the adapting process. In making his selection and retexturing what remains he is forced to distinguish the

[1] Harold Jenkins, '*As You Like It*' in *Shakespeare Survey* 8 (Cambridge, 1955), pp. 40–51 (pp. 42, 50).
[2] Krutch, *Comedy and Conscience*, pp. 208–11,

intricate relationship of its 'encounters' and in so doing he undermines the delicate balance on which *As You Like It*'s greatness rests.

Unlike many other of his comedies, Shakespeare's *As You Like It* has no complicated story line. Helen Gardner points out that 'the soul' of the play is not to be looked for in its plot; that its essence lies in a presentation 'of an image of the flow of human life'.[1] Just how real that image is becomes increasingly obvious as the comparison with Johnson is made.

Shakespeare's Rosalind and Celia, accompanied by Touchstone, exchange liberty for banishment in a forest where Corin is as much a victim of society as his more civilized counterparts and where his own problems prevent him from remedying others' misfortunes. These woods are by no means devoid of peril or discomfort; apart from the snakes, the lioness, the deer's anguish and Corin's churlish master, there is the dubious integrity of Sir Oliver, Phebe's cruel perversity, Audrey's grossness and William's utter dullness. All these exist and impinge upon the possibility of another paradise. This is a new sort of 'golden world', where the weather is inclement and a living hard to come by – 'a miserable world'. Yet each of the aspects of the country life affects one or other of the visitors, and their interaction is fruitful and important to the image of human life which Shakespeare is exploring. It is an image not without its unfortunate occurrences – though these are carefully prevented from obtruding. Brutality, hatred and death exist somewhere; shadowy human functions undirected by motivation and ultimately dominated by repentance and forgiveness.

This motivation Johnson provides for himself in an adaptation which reflects a characteristically Restoration concern for simplifying and regularizing the existing structure. Using the context of the original political framework he sharpens the definition of those features Shakespeare leaves too vague.

Such 'loyal' themes as heroic Orlando's banishment at a tyrant's hands were popular at the time anyway. Whig dramatists attempted to iterate 'the apostrophes to liberty and freedom in times and places fictionally remote' in order to illustrate the immutability of their constitutional principles.[2] From this Johnson goes on to distinguish carefully between the models of good and evil. He emphasizes Orlando's patient endurance while his so-called treachery is tested at the Lists. News of Oliver's determination to murder him comes simultaneously with the order for his banishment – at which point the wronged hero flees. Poetic justice demands that the evil Oliver be punished, and accordingly he dies, offstage and by his own hand, betrayed by his repentant accomplice, Charles.

Orlando's original moral dilemma is thus dismissed from Johnson's Arden and it is his good brother, Robert, whose life he is required to save. By the end the contrast between hero's virtue and villain's vice has been truly emphasized and their ensuing apportionment of reward and punishment – expressed in sentimental terms by material success and failure – richly deserved accordingly.

Orlando and Rosalind represent ideal models for lovers' conduct, avoiding as they do the profligacy and smut of Restoration types. Their witty discussion of love and marriage commends itself to the sentimentalist and is thus retained for the most part uncut. But what deletions there are contribute to the narrowing of the perspective from which Johnson insists on viewing love, refusing as he does to permit the admissible reality of those human aspects of it which appear either vulgar or indecorous.

Consequently the original variety of love's expressions is sacrificed while Johnson concen-

[1] Helen Gardner, '*As You Like It*' in *More Talking of Shakespeare*, edited by John Garrett (1959), pp. 17–32 (p. 21).
[2] Loftis, *Politics of Drama*, pp. 82–3.

trates on the more romantic relationship between hero and heroine and the added sentimentalism of that between Jaques and Caelia. This additional love story seriously rivals the theatrical dominance of that between Rosalind and Orlando: Jaques's role becomes a lead of which only Mr Cibber had probably dreamed before, and the augmented part of Caelia displays an awareness of the Restoration habit of exploiting women players' charms. The development of their affair becomes central to the play's career, their sentimentality contaminating Rosalind's relationship with Orlando. Shakespeare's Rosalind, with her combination of 'whole-hearted feeling and undistorted judgement',[1] derives her strength of character from her relationship with the Forest's other inhabitants. Touchstone, Audrey, Silvius and Phebe enhance her love for Orlando by facilitating her awareness of its reality as well as the illusions love creates and by means of which it is expressed. She can therefore evaluate her own sentiments, sensible of the conventions she uses. Consequently, her love for Orlando is made independent of those illusions whose incongruity with life is recognized and then laughed off.

Johnson's Rosalind, however, is denied the comprehensive outlook on love from which her original benefited. Her conversations with Orlando and Caelia are censored of the worldlier observations which added such maturity to her character, and her practical wit goes unchallenged by either Jaques' nihilistic antagonism or Phebe's trying infatuation. Gone is the poignancy of her solitary love-sickness with which the detached and slightly bored Celia found nothing to sympathize. But for Rosalind the humanity of Touchstone's personal recollections of Jane Smile and Silvius's love-agony had a special relevance; each facet of love is a reflection of a common nature which Shakespeare intentionally explores. His creation is an enigmatical world of human beings who can employ their natural intelligence in re-assessing the effects of Fortune, reinterpreting adversity if necessary; in other words, 'translating' it into a system of values to which they can be reconciled.

Those aspects of *As You Like It* which probe the metaphysics of existence do little but obscure the already cluttered plot so far as Johnson is concerned. Corin's sound bucolic philosophy – as true in its unequivocal way as Touchstone's paradoxes – is as dispensable in plot terms as the irrelevant bombast of the clown himself. However, it is the comprehensive quality of experience in Arden that is lost by such omissions and by Johnson's fundamental alteration of Jaques's character. Both Jaques and Touchstone enunciate and develop the deeper themes of the play, providing in their opposing natures a richer framework of wisdom and experience which reaches beyond the romance world of pastoralism into the controversial world of reality. They represent a dichotomy in philosophies of life: the one pragmatic, accommodating and optimistic; the other cynical, detached and pessimistic. Together they combine to provide a three-dimensional context within which the philosophical questions raised by the play find their significance; a context which, compounded by their roles at the end of the play, ensures that *As You Like It* ultimately asks more questions than its happy ending might superficially appear to answer.

The variety of intellectual and emotional life which Shakespeare offers is, however, more than Johnson wants. Nowhere is the enormous reduction of Shakespeare's breadth of vision which *Love in a Forest* represents clearer than in the ending.

For Shakespeare's lovers Jaques remains an unassimilable character at the wedding celebration; a living reminder of their journeys of self-discovery to which development his

---

[1] C. L. Barber, 'The Use of Comedy in *As You Like It*', *Philological Quarterly*, 21, no. 4 (October, 1942), 353–67 (p. 362).

relationships with them throughout owe much. The individuality of love is represented in the less-than-romantic choice of Touchstone for Audrey, their imperfections attesting the measure of reality which Shakespeare's view of love embraces and which Jaques's estimation of their future corroborates.

It is an ending which expresses in terms of union in love that the true liberty in Arden – the fundamental one at the heart of the play – is the liberty begotten of self-discovery in the awareness of others. It is a liberty derived from a tolerant appreciation of a broad perspective of experience, of which love is but one fact.

Viewed superficially though, the end of *As You Like It* provides Johnson with the ideal conclusion to his sentimental love story. It has the reunion of separated father and daughter, the hero's reward for virtue and the final destruction of evil in the repentant conversion of Duke Frederick whose redemption brings Duke Alberto back to repossess his own lands. All were recurrent motifs in sentimental plays of the time.

Jaques and the other lovers are dismissed by Johnson into an unqualified happiness which is nothing more than what Anne Barton called an ' "improbable fiction" ',[1] his characters confined within the limits of the sentimental world to which they have been made to conform. Nevertheless, Shakespeare serves Johnson's purpose well, providing him with no less than six sources for a concoction vastly different from any of them. The resulting adaptation is ingenious; even innovatory. Curious and eclectic as *Love in a Forest* may seem, with its conventionalized characters and laboured moral, it represents the undoubted preference of eighteenth-century audiences for whom *As You Like It* itself was as yet unacceptably complex.

[1] Anne Barton, '*As You Like It* and *Twelfth Night*: Shakespeare's Sense of an Ending', in *Shakespearian Comedy*, edited by Malcolm Bradbury and David Palmer, Stratford-upon-Avon Studies, 14 (1972), 160–80 (p. 169).

SOCIAL RELATIONS AND THE SOCIAL ORDER IN 'MUCH ADO ABOUT NOTHING'

ELLIOT KRIEGER

The distinction between appearance and reality is articulated as a theme in Shakespeare's comedies in two distinct ways: (1) fortune, or some other external force, imposes on the characters some incorrect perception of reality, and, as the plot proceeds, that misperception rectifies itself (e.g. *Comedy of Errors, Twelfth Night, Midsummer Night's Dream*); or (2) some characters voluntarily create deceptions that impel the plot, initially by deceiving other characters about reality and ultimately by demonstrating the necessity of distinguishing appearance from and achieving useful knowledge about reality (e.g. *Love's Labour's Lost, As You Like It, Measure for Measure, The Tempest*). *Much Ado About Nothing* fits neither pattern, for the series of deceptions that compose the plot, although created by the characters, are lived through *en route* to other deceptions, and are not overcome; false perception characterizes rather than disrupts the norm of the society depicted in the play. The characters adopt superficial attitudes toward what, in *other* dramas, might have been metaphysical crises; their overt considerations never become epistemological, as will those of Hamlet, Troilus, and Othello – the latter two at least involved in similar plots but in radically different societies. In short, although philosophic problems of 'noting' and 'knowing' can be abstracted from the plot of *Much Ado About Nothing*, the characters, when viewed in relation to the plot, are marked by their exceptional lack of concern with the philosophic implications of their series of deceptions.[1]

The crucial question about *Much Ado*, then concerns not how the characters learn to perceive reality and to see *beyond* deception,[2]

[1] The suggestion was first made in R. G. White's first edition of Shakespeare's works (1858) that 'Shakespeare and his contemporaries called [the play] "Much Ado About Noting"'. The importance of the pun, as White explained in his second edition (1883), was that it signified that 'the play is made up of much ado about noting, that is, watching, observing. All the personages are constantly engaged in noting or watching each other', reprinted in *A New Variorum Edition of Shakespeare: 'Much Ado About Nothing'*, ed. Horace Howard Furness, (1899, reprinted New York, 1964), p. 6. White's suggestion led, almost exactly a century later, to Dorothy C. Hockey's analysis of noting and mis-noting or poor judgement as *the* unifying device of *Much Ado*'s seemingly disjointed plot, *Shakespeare Quarterly*, 8 (1957), 353–8. Although her article, as a response to H. B. Charlton, *Shakespearian Comedy* (1938), who saw *Much Ado*'s plot as largely informal, and to E. K. Chambers, *Shakespeare: A Survey* (1925), who saw the plot as set up on two separate tiers, has been helpful, her failure to clarify what the characters 'misjudge' sharply limits the importance of her work. As Walter N. King rightly asks in his article 'Much Ado About *Something*', *SQ*, 15 (1964): 'What do the key characters misjudge? Simply themselves, others, events as they occur, as Miss Hockey suggests? Or more fundamentally, do they misjudge all these things by preferring poor values to better ones?...With respect to values, Miss Hockey is not very explicit' (p. 144).

[2] B. K. Lewalski, 'Love, Appearance, and Reality: Much Ado About Something', *Studies in English Literature* (1968), 235–51, emphasizes the difficulty Claudio has in learning to ascertain the validity of appearance, and Lewalski argues that he learns, via the neo-Platonic Friar, that the inner form, accurately *represented* by appearance, is what is most meaningful (*passim*).

for it is not at all clear that they can do so even at the play's 'festive' conclusion,[1] but what about the society of Messina both allows its inhabitants to create deception as a continual menace and at the same time leaves them unable to recognize and to forestall the deceptions with which they are confronted.[2]

The significant aspect of deception in Messina is its casual mundanity, its normalcy. The catastrophes of *Much Ado* differ in degree but not in kind from its society's accepted social diversion; in fact, the kind of crises in which the characters find themselves are not the totally fantastic and unique confusions such as in *Comedy of Errors* or *Twelfth Night*, but are only exaggerations of the way the social relations of this play's world are normally developed. For example, the central crisis of the play is that which concerns Hero's chastity (IV, i ff), but the audience is forestalled from seeing it *as* a crisis because it follows on the heels of a similar disaster that had merely concerned her fidelity. In addition, there follows the double-trap set for Beatrice and Benedick, and the trick of Hero's 'death' set to win back Claudio, both deceptions that, through their supposedly benevolent plotting, help to frame – and thus to distract apprehension from – the play's central misperceptions.[3]

The incorporation of all kinds of deception into the everyday life of *Much Ado* emphasizes the way in which the social relations of Messina can 'naturally' lead to crises, and explains the failure of the characters to consider the most serious personal accusations and disasters as anything more than factors that will alter their social relations. The society of *Much Ado* is prevented from becoming philosophically absorbed in the epistemological problems raised by the denunciation of Hero because this exact sort of event has been quite typical of its daily life. Characters shift loyalties and relations throughout *Much Ado* with a fluid ease, quite different from the radical

[1] Among those who find *Much Ado* a festive play see C. L. Barber, who deftly side-steps discussion of *Much Ado* by claiming that his treatment of it would have been much like his 'of the other festive plays', *Shakespeare's Festive Comedy* (1959, reprinted Cleveland, 1963), p. 222 and *passim*, and Francis Fergusson, *Shakespeare: The Pattern in His Carpet* (New York, 1971), who writes that '*Much Ado* is a holiday from the cares of the world; an entertainment in which humour of several kinds is delicately mingled with real music and the magic of verse' (p. 133). T. W. Craik, '*Much Ado About Nothing*', *Scrutiny*, 19 (1952), 297–316, also argues that *Much Ado* was never intended as a tragicomedy, but only as a 'subtle comedy' of 'sympathetic irony' (p. 316).

[2] For pioneering work in the discussion of the qualities of the society in *Much Ado*, see James Smith, '*Much Ado About Nothing:* Notes from a Book in Preparation', *Scrutiny*, 13 (1963); John Crick, '*Much Ado About Nothing*', *The Use of English*, 17 (1965), 223–7; and Walter R. Davis, ed., *Twentieth-Century Interpretations of 'Much Ado About Nothing'* (Englewood Cliffs, New Jersey, (1969)), Introduction.

John Dover Wilson, *Shakespeare's Happy Comedies* (Evanston, Illinois, 1962), writes that *Much Ado*'s 'atmosphere' is produced by 'disguise and deceit – sometimes for evil ends, but generally in fun and with a comic up-shot' (pp. 129–30). Wilson, more than any other critic, acknowledges the deceptive qualities of the play's society in order to transform the deceptive into an atmosphere of festivity.

[3] Smith disagrees with the generally held view that Hero and Claudio are the protagonists and Don John the antagonist of *Much Ado*. He develops an elaborate argument to show that Beatrice and Benedick are at the center of the plot, and that they are the play's most interesting characters. Smith tries, above all, to counter Coleridge's argument, *Notes and Lectures* (1849), that in Shakespeare's plays, 'the interest in the plot is always, in fact, on account of the characters, and not *vice versa*' (reprinted in *Variorum*, p. 5), by showing that in *Much Ado* the main plot and the play's most interesting characters *are* united. The more sensible counter-argument to Coleridge's seems to be that of A. P. Rossiter, who, in *Angel With Horns* (1961) argued that the play's 'main' plot is indeed the 'too obvious' one of Hero and Claudio, but that 'much of the play's total effect hangs on the structural mainness of the plot being displaced' (pp. 79–80). This effectively counters Coleridge, without denying Coleridge's accurate observations on the structure of the plot and on the *relative* interest of the characters.

The characters in what all (but Smith) would agree is the 'main' plot are of course distressingly un-

jolts of alignment or rigid loyalties that typify characters in other Shakespearian comedies. The difference is that here the characters are attentive to the surface of their situations, and do not care much about the deeper ramifications of feeling. Claudio falls in love quickly but not deeply;[1] Beatrice and Benedick can easily have their strongly held attitudes modified when they are made to perceive slight changes in the matrix of attitudes in their society; Leonato is ready to denounce very quickly his own daughter; and so on. Messina is a world in which 'appearances...are necessary to the social solidarity'.[2]

In a world so dependent on appearance, and on conformity, it is small wonder that the determining and most significant relation for the inhabitants is not that between appearance and reality, but between different appearances. The continual deceptions of Messina have a social explanation – appearance can continually deceive only in a society that does not question the worth and the validity of appearances. To achieve their social ends the Messinians do not search behind appearances for a 'truth', but attack and manipulate appearances, attempt to get their society into new configurations.

Claudio, in his denunciation of Hero at the altar, *could* be cited as the exception to this behavioral dictum, for he does launch out on two supposedly powerful declarations against the dependence upon appearance (IV, i, 55–60, 99–107).[3] But both of these 'outbursts' are almost painfully conventional, the first with its arch classical references:

> You seem to me as Dian in her orb,
> As chaste as is the bud ere it be blown;
> But you are more intemperate in your blood
> Than Venus...

the second with its precious quibbling and outrageous farewell to love:

> O Hero! What a Hero hadst thou been,
> If half thy outward graces had been placed
> About thy thoughts and counsels of thy heart!
> But fare thee well, most foul, most fair! Farewell,

> Thou pure impiety, and impious purity!
> For thee I'll lock up all the gates of love....

The whole denunciation scene, especially when one considers Don Pedro's cueing line (28), has about it the air of a set-up. Moreover, there is something more than a little grating about a denunciation of observation that results from a completely superficial and distanced observation of an event. It is not that Claudio's outrage is implausible; it is only that he adopts the argument to make his own appearance look good – he has not achieved any knowledge, as

interesting. Don John, in direct contrast to Iago and Edmund, for both of whom he is often considered the prototype, makes the point that he *is* just as he appears: 'I can not hide what I am' (I, iii, 10). As Coleridge points out, although he is the 'main spring' of the plot, he is merely 'shown and then withdrawn'. Hero's most notable traits are the thoroughly unengaging ones of obedience and silence (e.g., her silent betrothal to Claudio, II, i; her utterly dependent way of accepting the arranged match, and of agreeing to participate in the plot against Beatrice and Benedick, II, i, 339–40; her near silence upon accusation, IV, i). Claudio alone among these three might be considered interesting, for the ambiguity in his delineation has led to a major critical debate concerning what our attitude toward him is expected to be. Yet none I think have called his character complex, have claimed that the divergent interpretations of Claudio could co-exist in the same reading of *Much Ado*. The problem of understanding Claudio is not a problem caused by Claudio's innate complexity; it is rather a problem of examining this complex play to see what kind of *simple* character Claudio is.

[1] Whether he is mercenary in his love for Hero is another matter, but he never is devoted to her, as would be other lovers in Shakespeare – he is more devoted to her effect on his image. Perhaps she is too easily his? His inquiries into others' opinions on her worth and beauty *may* indicate a pre-disposition to jealousy, almost a desire to be jealous. Perhaps he merely falls in love 'with love', but not with Hero, as W. H. Auden suggests, *The Dyer's Hand and Other Essays* (New York, 1962), p. 518.

[2] Davis, Introduction, p. 5; Smith also talks of Messina as a society that is charming on the surface, 'for appearances lie on the surface' (p. 295).

[3] All citations are from Peter Alexander, ed., *William Shakespeare: The Complete Works* (New York, 1952).

his continuing superficial behavior throughout the rest of the play testifies.[1]

Appearances in *Much Ado* are measured for their 'correctness' against two separate social standards or codes of decorum: the domestic and the military codes. The domestic code is concerned with demonstrations of social status, and is represented in the play by the natives of Messina – Leonato, Antonio, and their households – who take pains to appear 'in great haste' (I, ii; III, v) and who delight in contriving masked entertainments or formal ceremonies (II, i; v, iii).[2] The military code, represented by the returned soldiers whose 'war thoughts have left their places vacant', becomes exaggerated by its contrast with the predominantly domestic concerns of Messina. Whereas the domestic code is concerned with social status, the military code is concerned with personal status, with honor as manifested in loyalty and in fidelity. Occasionally the military code is asserted in jocular good humor, as when Benedick asks to be commanded:

Don Pedro. What secret hath held you here, that you followed not to Leonato's?
Benedick. I would your Grace would constrain me to tell.
Don Pedro. I charge thee on thy allegiance.
Benedick. You hear, Count Claudio; I can be secret as a dumb man, I would have you think so; but on my allegiance, mark you this, on my allegiance, he is in love. (I, i, 176–82; see also II, i, 34–42)

but also, especially later in the play, in harmful configurations, as when Don Pedro, Don John, and Claudio ally themselves in a dubious camaraderie (in IV, i), or when Claudio and Don Pedro consider so carefully their own reputations upon discovering that their accusations of Hero were unjustified:

Claudio.
I know not how to pray your patience,
Yet I must speak. Choose your revenge yourself;
Impose me to what penance your invention

Can lay upon my sin; yet sinn'd I not
But in mistaking.
Don Pedro.   By my soul, nor I....
                                   (v, i, 257–61)

The potential for the military code to dominate the domestic code is diminished, however, as the military standards are abused by one of the play's excluded characters, Don John. The easily enough threatened system of loyalty among the soldiers is shown by juxtaposition to be only a step away from the service that Don John exacts from his men for a fee (II, ii, 48).[3]

The two social codes remain separate, and one of the primary motivations in *Much Ado* is to combine the two codes into a more comprehensive aristocratic ideal, not to test either code, or to measure one code against the other. The need to combine the two codes without ethical exploration of either, symbolized and actualized in the play by the marriages between members of the two separate aristocratic groups whom the two codes represent, further distinguishes *Much Ado* from Shakespeare's other comedies: whereas most of Shakespeare's

[1] M. C. Bradbrook, *Shakespeare and Elizabethan Poetry* (1951), feels otherwise, as she interprets the scene at the altar as the one moment in *Much Ado* when 'Masks' are abandoned and 'deeper issues' emerge. After Claudio has 'spoken out', she writes, 'there is no further role for him, or for Hero, save to make a pair in the final dance. They each sink into the kind of formality which the plot allowed...' (pp. 179–88).

[2] This domestic code is prevented from feeling ethically trivial by its being measured against a character, Dogberry, for whom the virtues of decorum and hospitality are desirable but unattainable. Smith discusses how Dogberry reduces the more central – that is the more privileged – characters to smaller proportionate size (pp. 242–4).

[3] Although King does not talk about military codes of honor *per se*, he makes the important point that 'the aristocrats of Messina have canalized natural instinct...according to a prescriptive code which almost everyone takes for granted' (p. 146). The point is that both military and domestic life here exist by codes that, in prescribing certain ethical decisions, obviate the need for the individual to find for himself a humane and ethical course of action.

comedies are initiated by an enforced separation of subject from object (lover from beloved, as in *A Midsummer Night's Dream*; heir from inheritance, as in *Twelfth Night*; ruler from domain, as in *Love's Labour's Lost, Measure for Measure*, or *The Tempest*; or all three separations, as in *As You Like It*), in *Much Ado* the separated groups form naturally complementary parts, and the separation of the two, at least until well into the play, is presented as an etiology, but not as a problem. The initial assumption seems to be that since the two groups form sexual complements[1] – the one group being eligible bachelors and the other fathers and their eligible daughters – separation will be overcome through the natural process of sexual attraction and its ritual acceptance in matrimony.

The sexual attraction is, however, subsumed by a more general social attraction between the soldiers and the Messinians. Both see in each other a perfected and ennobling reflection of themselves. The Messinians feel graced and honored by a visit from the brave warriors; the soldiers feel graced and honored to be treated with such respect and deference. They write a mutual fiction by which either group finds its own value – reflected in the opinions of its counterpart – caught in a spiralling inflation. The egotism of the soldiers derives from the superficiality of the Messinians – the offer of the luxury of absorption in games of courtship and domestic intrigue is a great compliment to the soldiers. The two conclusions that they can draw from their heroic reception are that their martial labors were great enough to earn them the leisure of 'at the least a month' (I, i, 127) in which they might fleet the time carelessly, and that the role of soldier does not have military victory as its only, or even as its primary, end. The impression given in this play is that war is fought entirely to increase one's honor,[2] and thus to increase one's eventual standing in domestic society; war is fought for domestic ends.

The love and eventual marriages that might result from this reflective egotism could have drastic consequences (cf. *Othello*), for the love is narcissistic, is based on concern for the self rather than for the beloved. As the two groups unify in their plans for marriage, there develops an increasing isolation of both groups from any ethical standards or even value-judgments that might be shared by any or all excluded groups, classes, or individuals. The aristocracy creates within itself its own standards of decorum and desire. The aristocrats find it more and more impossible to believe that any, particularly any of their cohorts, could dissent from their code of behavior. Their egotistical blindness can thus leave them wide open to attacks of villainy and, as we see very early in this play, usually deaf to villainy's exposure.

Formal and elegant marriage becomes the pinnacle of achievement for both the domestic and the military sections of society. For the former it incorporates a semblance of military dynamism into their otherwise relatively static society. (The sense of a leisure class springing into activity upon the arrival of guests is very precise in act I.[3]) For the soldiers, use of military 'honor' in amorous pursuits gives them the illusion of having a goal that derives from but transcends their 'everyday' existence. By devoting themselves to thoughts of marriage, they give their mundane society what appears to be a teleology – they simultaneously apotheosize themselves and make a heaven of hell, for, as Don Pedro wistfully

[1] Barbara Everett, '*Much Ado About Nothing*', *Critical Quarterly*, 3 (1961), 319–35, suggests that the world of Messina is 'a world largely feminine in character' whereas the soldiers who enter Messina form a group held together by 'masculine solidarity' (pp. 323–4).

[2] Crick, p. 34.

[3] As Clifford Leech, '*Twelfth Night*' *and Shakespearian Comedy* (Toronto, 1965), writes, a 'new arrival' can bring the sense of a 'new locality' in Shakespeare (p. 6).

declares, 'we are the only love-gods' (II, i, 349).

Playing 'love-god' becomes the only respectable occupation in Messina, as the equilibrium of the society begins to depend on the successful matches being achieved and consummated. The characters pretend to be diverting themselves – with dances, songs, jests, and plots – whereas in fact they are openly courting. In this respect *Much Ado About Nothing* is again quite different from such comedies as *A Midsummer Night's Dream* and *As You Like It*, for here the society demands marriage among its youth as an emblem of its stability. The initial problem is how to bring the two aspects of the aristocracy together most publicly, not the escape by the young lovers from public ritual.[1] In *Much Ado* the disguises are really revelations, and the intrigues are really declarations of intent. The whole society pretends to be working in secret, but its true goal is public manifestation of love – and concurrently of the aristocracy's lavish wealth and power.

In *Much Ado* we are faced with the familiar illusion of the double-plot as analysed by William Empson,[2] although here we do not see two 'levels' of society and thus suspect that we have seen the 'entire' society; rather, we see a social class divided into two sections, and thus we have the illusion that the one class composes the entire society. The more public demonstrations the aristocracy gives of its wealth and wit, the more secure – to them *and* to us – does its domination of society appear. The appearance of course is what the Messinians want, for theirs is a society where the ocular proof is all that is necessary – no one cares to go much deeper.

Messina is the aristocracy's ultimate vision of the second world, the forest brought home. The escape to the forest has never been an escape to *nature* – the penalty of Adam has been one of the hardships willingly *endured* by noble exiles. The attraction of the forest has been its (supposed) freedom from conflict and care. Yet none would doubt that, could the same freedom be achieved by the aristocracy in its native society, the opportunity would have been seized – the ultimate goal of the 'golden world' comedies has been to return 'restored' to the society with which the play began. *Much Ado About Nothing*, with its dramatic focus on the public occasions during which the reconciliation of the separated components of the ruling class occurs, is a play about exactly the kind of problems by which the aristocracy enjoys being confronted – the problems of arranging entertainments and marriages, of assuring chastity and penance, all of which confirm rather than challenge the power and authority of those whom the problems involve.

This sense of control and of domination – of equanimity – pervades the mood of the play: the sense of having built an ideal from one's own society is different from that of having left home to find an ideal. The latter situation, that of the exiles in *As You Like It*, for example, creates a mood of tenuous poise. Here the society, although less fantastic, is also less threatening, and the aristocratic poise becomes consequently more secure. Action is cushioned not with the desperate antinomies of verse – as in *Love's Labour's Lost* and *A Midsummer Night's Dream* – but in the easy repartee, as A. P. Rossiter says, of equivocation.[3]

Equivocation is a further way of solidifying the aristocracy, for it gives all of its participants

[1] In direct contrast to what Northrop Frye, *A Natural Perspective* (New York, 1965), describes as the 'formula' at the 'core' of most Shakespearian comedies: 'The normal action is the effort of a young man to get possession of a young woman who is kept from him by various social barriers: her low birth, his minority or shortage of funds, parental opposition, the prior claims of a rival. These are eventually circumvented, and the comedy ends at a point when a new society is crystallized, usually by the marriage or betrothal of hero and heroine' (p. 72).

[2] *Some Versions of Pastoral* (New York, 1950), chapter 2, 'Double Plots'.

[3] pp. 80–1.

'equal voice', while completely excluding those who will not or cannot join in the 'skirmish of wit'. The language of *Much Ado* is marked particularly by the in-joke and double-entendre, never by raucous humor or outright bawdy punning. It is a language that has been appropriated by a privileged group of people, so that they can demonstrate to each other their confederacy – that they can understand each other across great distances.[1] As it is used here, 'wit', as G. K. Hunter writes, 'is a weapon for the strong', only those with the 'poise to remain balanced and adaptive' can have the privilege of the comic vision.[2]

Of course since the ability to talk naturally in equivocations is a way of demarcating the ruling class, the inability to do so is a way of isolating those who are not members of this privileged group. The classic instance is the riotously malapropriate language spoken by Dogberry, who, in aspiring to emulate the gentry in their speech as in other things (IV, ii, 74–80)[3] over-reaches his own vocabulary. Dogberry speaks with just the opposite of the aristocratic use of double-entendres – his roughshod use of fancy speech cramps completely unrelated or only phonetically related words into the *same* meaning. Dogberry seems to enjoy his own speech, but of course its humor escapes him. Even if he were 'as pretty a piece of flesh as any is in Messina... and a rich fellow enough', his failure to use language dextrously would exclude him from the Messinian aristocracy.[4]

In fact, for several characters in *Much Ado* the use of language determines their degree of proximity to the aristocracy. Don John, who is excluded above all because of his dubious lineage, and who additionally excludes himself by his anti-social actions throughout the play,[5] is, in the first scene, marked as different from his companions by his refusal to engage in artful use of language: 'I thank you; I am not of many words,/But I thank you' (lines 134–5), his response to Leonato's welcome, are his

significant first words. In a play in which words are such an important method of social discrimination, his cursory attitude immediately sets him off as aberrant.

Hero's attendant Margaret does quite well at imitating her 'betters' with language. Both Beatrice and Benedick are surprised at the arrival of this newcomer to the aristocracy's formerly exclusive domain of wit:

Beatrice. O, God help me! God help me! How long have you profess'd apprehension?
Margaret. Ever since you left it....

(III, iv, 59–61; see also V, ii, 10–11)

They react as though their personal, or at least their class, privileges had been encroached upon. It is probably the general respect Margaret has earned through her wit that allows the aristocracy to accept her as sort of an equal and to think the best of her, insofar as they allow her to escape the whipping that she thoroughly deserves. Another minor character, the Messenger of the first scene, also makes a good impression by his elegant use of aristo-

[1] More even than *LL Lost* and the Falstaff plays. Everett accurately describes 'the easy, humorous, and conversational manner, that refers to a past and a future governed by customary event and behavior, and that carries a sense of habitual reality in a familiar social group' (pp. 323–4).

[2] G. K. Hunter, *William Shakespeare: The Late Comedies* (1962), p. 31. Rossiter, more than any other critic, stresses the use of language as the delineator of class boundaries, and he has strongly influenced my thinking on this matter.

[3] A speech quoted by Christopher Hill, *Society and Puritanism in Pre-Revolutionary England* (1964), in his complex discussion of the importance to the Puritans of being a 'householder' (pp. 460–5).

[4] Smith compares Dogberry to both Bottom and Falstaff, in that Dogberry 'has perfectly accommodated himself to those on whom he attends, making their ideals his own' (p. 244).

[5] The degree of voluntarism in his exclusion is of course an important question. Hunter describes Don Pedro as 'unpleasingly self-satisfied with a power to deceive and manipulate which is chiefly notable as providing the breeding-ground for his brother's evil' (p. 23).

cratic language; his speech gives the opening moments a serene quality rather than the mechanical fumbling by which Shakespeare's typical messenger-setting-the-scene passages are usually beset.[1] That this Messenger cannot keep pace with Beatrice's wit is surely no strike against *him*.

Yet for all the talk of those who disqualify themselves from being Messina's 'leading lights' by their insufficiently witty language, and, conversely, for all the praise of the wit that exists in *Much Ado*,[2] I am sure that I am not alone in finding the brilliant language spoken for the large portion of the play not particularly useful as a source for illustrative quotation. It may be a rash generalization, but it seems to me that those who write on *Much Ado* quote from the text less than do those writing on other Shakespearian dramas. What's more, a large percentage of passages cited from the text are selections from Claudio's outbursts against Hero, moments whose linguistic tone is really at odds with the tone of the balance of the play. Claudio, at the altar, is striking out against the integration of his society, and his denunciation speeches, in their derivative way, are exceptional – but they are so particularly as set *against* the integrated aristocratic language of the rest of the play. As much as the subtleties of wit on display here help to define subtle differences and distinctions between characters, seldom does any one bit of dialogue, when lifted out of dramatic and placed into a 'critical' context, seem any more important than the next. The wit and intelligence for which the characters of *Much Ado* are so well known are not traits that they employ to help them think.

This is not meant to *detract* from the intelligence made manifest in the aristocratic speech, but to indicate that the intelligence is operating on only one level of concern. The speech of *Much Ado About Nothing* is used neither for discussion nor for the exploration of ideas; rather, it centers upon the two related fixed ideas of proving self- (and social class-) value and of courtship – wit makes one more desirable and hence more eligible.[3] Even the soliloquies – such as Benedick's in II, iii:

...but til all graces be in one woman, one woman shall not come in my grace. Rich she shall be, that's certain; wise, or I'll none; virtuous, or I'll never cheapen her   (and so on, ll. 8–32),

or:

I hear how I am censured: they say I will bear myself proudly if I perceive the love come from her; they say, too, that she will rather die than give any sign of affection. I did never think to marry. I must not seem proud;...   (an excerpt from ll. 201–23)

are concerned with self-image and with courtship in a most pragmatic way, and are not at all probing or metaphysical. The aristocracy, in its achieved complacency, does not need or wish to use its hair-splitting linguistic abilities to explore the moral antitheses of situations, but only to arrange for its youth suitable marriages with all of the attendant rituals and public displays of wealth.[4]

---

[1] *Cf.*, *AYLI*, I, i.; *Macbeth* I, ii.

[2] Especially William G. McCollum, 'The Role of Wit in *Much Ado About Nothing*', *SQ*, 19 (1968), 165–74, who suggests that *Much Ado* itself is a kind of witticism 'in the tripartite form often taken by jests.'

[3] G. Wilson Knight, *The Shakespearian Tempest* (1932) sees wit as it 'gives place to love' as the central opposition of *Much Ado*, similar to the Tempest/Music opposition that he finds throughout Shakespeare's work (p. 76). He does not consider the narcissism that supersedes the supposedly separate categories of 'wit' and 'love' here.

[4] See Smith, who talks of the great although not important activity of Messinian society (p. 245). The importance of the marriageable daughter's market value has been thoroughly discussed by Nadine Page, 'The Public Repudiation of Hero', *PMLA*, 50 (1935), 339–44, and by Kerby Neill, 'More Ado About Claudio: An Acquittal for the Slandered Groom', *SQ*, 3 (1952), 91–107. Walter King, in his excellent article, has adopted much from the analyses of social conventions done by Page and Neill, but has *not* adopted their completely uncritical attitude toward the social conventions. Rather than 'acquit' Claudio because he is behaving as his society expects him to do,

The actions of the play, of course, do not afford the characters opportunity for moral exploration until quite late, until Claudio rejects Hero at the altar. It is only then that the separation of the two social groups and their attitudes – one world of military decorum and masculine loyalties and the other of domestic merriment and warmth – is presented as an opposition instead of as a symbiosis. The whole play had been moving toward unification of the two groups, symbolized by the marriage ceremony, for which the differences between the groups and their codes presented a necessary and a positive set of counterpoised elements. When Hero is rejected and the two groups separate, each exaggerates its differences from the other so that what had seemed complementary now becomes irreconcilable. Don Pedro and Claudio assume and assert an implicit military loyalty and jovial masculine camaraderie. They take their leave of Leonato, fully expecting him to treat them with all due courtesy, even to acknowledge that they had acted honorably in denouncing his daughter (v, i, 45–109). (Don John, who had none of their illusions about class solidarity, had by that time already fled from Messina.) Moreover, they find it nearly impossible to believe that one of their own fellow-soldiers could hold their 'honorable' actions against them on any moral grounds, as Claudio jokingly dismisses Benedick's challenge of him, and as he and Don Pedro try to bring Benedick into their coterie again, prodding him for a misogamist response with their barracks humor (v, i, 155–177), while letting him know that he has them to thank for his recent success in love (ll. 172–173).[1] They suspect, in short, that Benedick is being so sullen with them not out of any positive moral principle, but entirely 'for the love of Beatrice' (l. 188).[2]

At the same time Leonato, whose original instinct was to take the masculine side and to join with the soldiers in denunciation of his daughter:

Hath no man's dagger here a point for me?
. . . .
O Fate, take not away thy heavy hand!
Death is the fairest cover for her shame
That may be wish'd for
(IV, i, 108, 114–16; see also ll. 120–43)

shifts back to the domestic world and becomes a strong advocate of reputation and family honor. I think that we are meant to feel that his unconsolable grief (v, i, 3–32) and his challenge of Claudio (l. 66) are excessive under the circumstances; he knows that Hero is still alive, and that he and Antonio are seeking revenge for their family's scandalized reputation, not for Hero's life.[3] (By the same score, Claudio's rejection of the challenge, 'Away! I will not have to do with you', is haughty and presumptuous, as he thinks that his denunciation of Hero was fatal.)

Both aristocratic groups react to the crisis

King explores the values, or lack of values, in Claudio's society, *passim*, in an approach that I find of considerable use for discussion of all social comedies, or, as King would have it, 'comedies of manners'.

[1] Claudio's eagerness to return to familiar patterns of social behavior, and his later willingness to accept readily whatever new marriage partner Leonato imposes, makes him a perfect instance of 'passive hybris', 'the bourgeois hero', as defined by Albert Cook, *The Dark Voyage and the Golden Mean* (Cambridge, Mass., 1949), who does not 'venture' but 'trembles passively and maneuvers industriously in the probable', whose 'flaw' is 'the denial of the problem of pain' (pp. 88–90).

[2] Indeed, Benedick's mood in this scene of confrontation is an echo of one of his earlier moods (in III, ii) in which he pretended to be sullen because of a toothache (line 19). Ironically, had it been presented at that time, Don Pedro and Claudio's analysis of the egotistical basis, i.e. his wounded pride and his confusion about love, as explanation for Benedick's strange behavior, *would* have been correct.

[3] Ursula's silence is not easily explained. Maybe silence is a virtue encouraged of women in this supposedly feminine world, as it is in *Lear*? If that is so, maybe productions would benefit from having a mute character cast as 'Innogen – Wife to Leonato' as listed in the opening scene direction of the Folio text, *Variorum*, p. 7.

by assertion of their social codes, their separate ideals, but each assertion is mechanistic, the two reactions are purely reflexive. The comedy here approaches a comedy of humors and of received ideas, although Shakespeare's *treatment* of the situation is decisively non-Jonsonian, in that the mechanistic actions of the characters are not given sufficient play to lead them into folly – or into anything else. Within the same enormously active scene Claudio is twice challenged, the plot against Hero is discovered and she is vindicated, Claudio and Don Pedro are reconciled with Leonato, a final deception is devised against Claudio, and once again plans are established for a wedding. It is in part this curtailment of the severance of the ruling-class components and of the hostilities and misunderstandings that suddenly surface among the characters that gives the drama its insulation from 'inquisitions into values,' which Rossiter first observed. But I think that Rossiter was wrong in his explanation of this insulation; it does not occur because 'serious...situations' are 'handled "lightly" '.[1] Serious matters in *Much Ado* are handled seriously and realistically – but by Shakespeare, not by his characters. We can rectify Rossiter's observation if we keep this distinction in mind. The play is an inquisition into the values of a society that refuses to question its values.

The mechanistic refusal to question convention that dominates the action of the play is counterpoised by two reactions to the play's scandalous catastrophe that are separated from the society's usual concern for appearances and for decorum, and that, by contrast, emphasize the lack of perception that characterizes the aristocratic society in Messina. The Friar – an outsider, neither soldier nor family – calms the hysteria after Hero is rejected. He does so, as he says, by observing Hero in order to comprehend the deeper significance of her appearances; he uses appearance as a way to attain knowledge about reality (IV, i, 157–72).

As it happens, his empirical 'observations' of Hero correctly discern her innocence; his psychological observations and speculations, however, are not proven accurate, for his plan to win Claudio back to Hero through her feigned death goes completely by the board:

> She dying, as it must be so maintained,
> Upon the instant that she was accused,
> Shall be lamented, pitied, and excused
> Of every hearer. For it so falls out,
> That what we have we prize not to the worth
> Whiles we enjoy it; but being lacked and lost,
> Why, then we rack the value, then we find
> The virtue that possession would not show us
> Whiles it was ours. So will it fare with Claudio.
>
> (ll. 216–24)

There the Friar is completely wrong; Claudio loves Hero (and even then not convincingly) when she is proven innocent, not before.[2] The Friar's separation from the ultimate aristocratic realignment emphasizes the difference between simple deception, the manipulation of appearances, and perception, examining appearances for a deeper psychological understanding of reality.

The other counterpoised non-conventional reaction to the wedding crisis is that of the society's licensed non-conformists, Beatrice and Benedick. Although their outward scorn of the society's obsession with marriage might lead us to expect they would adopt a fashionably cynical attitude toward chastity and fidelity – *così fan tutte* – nothing prepares us for the force with which they go directly against the moral codes of their society. Barbara Everett may be right in singling out Benedick's 'How doth the lady?' (IV, i, 112) as

---

[1] pp. 80–1.
[2] Unless of course we are to take Claudio's refusal to mourn as an indication that he *never* truly loved Hero – thus vindicating the Friar, but damning Claudio. If that were so, one would hope that the Friar, citing the test he had devised to determine the validity of Claudio's professed love, would refuse to perform the final wedding ceremony, and a new plot might be under way. Out of the Friar's plan....

the most important line of the play;[1] his turning toward the woman instead of with his cohorts indicates his willingness to challenge society's standards and expectations (to the point of incredulity: see Don Pedro and Claudio's jovial reaction to Benedick's 'earnest' challenge, v, i, 197–206), in an attempt to act upon what he believes to *be*, rather than to *appear* to be, right. Similarly, Beatrice's call for revenge against Claudio does not come from a predetermined convention (literary or social) but from her revulsion against the trivial attitudes and the social codes in her society:

Manhood is melted into curtsies, valor into compliment, and men are only turn'd into tongue, and trim ones too. (from ll. 312–20)

But this incipient moral inquisition, like the Friar's rudimentary psychological exploration, is never resolved, it is dis-solved by the chain reaction of discoveries and events that abruptly brings the play to its conclusion.

Several readers have pointed out that the trivial vulgarity and sexual snobbery with which Claudio finally accepts marriage:

I'll hold my mind were she an Ethiope.

. . . .

Which is the lady I must seize upon?

. . . .

Why, then she's mine. Sweet, let me see your face. (v, iv, 38, 53, 55)

undermine the expected harmony of the comedy's conclusion.[2] I think it is important to realize that it does so not because of a moral deficiency in Claudio's character, but because it deflects the two moral inquisitions that the crisis had initiated. The Friar, despite his final protestations, is directly shown to have been quite ignorant of Claudio's character:

Friar.
Did not I tell you she was innocent?
Leonato.
So are the Prince and Claudio, who accused her
Upon the error that you heard debated.
(v, ii, 1–3)

Claudio's arrogant hostility toward Hero's 'memory' before her restoration to grace does not matter. Similarly, Benedick's challenge of Claudio, initiated by Beatrice's will, is transformed from a challenge of the social standards on which Claudio bases his honor into a challenge merely caused by a circumstantial event; the circumstances having changed, the challenge fades into subject for boisterous jocularity:

For thy part, Claudio, I did think to have beaten thee, but in that thou art like to be my kinsman, live unbruised and love my cousin. (ll. 115–18)

Further, Benedick relinquishes his unconventionally hostile attitude toward marriage, and, now that they are to be a respectably married couple, he (symbolically, I assume) 'stops' Beatrice's mouth with a kiss (l. 98).[3]

It is usually out of place to speculate

---

[1] p. 325.

[2] Even his song of penance has been shown to be entirely superficial, as it is a literary set-piece — devoted to the 'goddess of the night' — rather than a prayer devoted to any God in whom Claudio might place his faith, Richmond Noble, *Shakespeare's Use of Song* (1923), p. 67.

Robert Grams Hunter, *Shakespeare and the Comedy of Forgiveness* (New York, 1965), in contrast, believes that Claudio should be forgiven, as his failure was only in his being 'human' — was simply a 'mistaking' caused by Don John, whose sole function is to destroy love — and because Claudio does take on penance (pp. 94–5). G. Wilson Knight, *Shakespeare and Religion* (1967), who believes that Claudio attempts and fails at repentance, explains Claudio's failure as an instance of Shakespeare's 'serene' admission that 'our committed sin...was a part of ourselves and our destiny', and of Shakespeare's 'earthly, humanly warm, approach to the spiritualistic truths' (p. 15). To bring the wheel full circle, the most unforgiving attack on Claudio's 'conduct during his journey through several stages of innocence' comes from Bertrand Evans, *Shakespeare's Comedies* (1960), who finds the 'comic spirit...sustained' here only by Beatrice and Benedick and by the masterful way in which Shakespeare uses Dogberry to heighten the play's suspense (pp. 86, 79).

[3] The comparison of their behavior with the absurdly predictable conventionality of Claudio and Hero upon their betrothal, which so amused Beatrice:

subjunctively about the plots of Shakespeare's comedies, but I cannot help wondering what *Much Ado* would be about if Hero were slandered much earlier in the play instead of well into the fourth act. We might, in such a play, expect a drama with a specifically moral component – moral in the Bradleyian (via Hegelian) sense. Surely the germ of a moral tragedy is evident in Benedick's challenge of Claudio – the 'good' in a society (compassion and love) challenging the 'evil' (egotism) that is produced by the same society, yet in the process of the challenge threatening certain associated aspects of the 'good' (the standards of brotherly loyalty, or the wit and chiding on which this society thrives).[1] No such dialectic develops in *Much Ado*; the challenge, which at first isolates the moral vacuum of the society, is later itself reabsorbed into the society once the counterpoised parts of the society's codes are re-balanced. In addition, since the catastrophe of misperception is preceded by the lengthy series of voluntary and relatively inconsequential deceptions, we are made to feel that the crisis at the altar differs only in degree from the normal social behavior in the world of the play. Consequently, Benedick's challenge of Claudio, as a reaction to an event that exaggerates without distorting the social norm, is portrayed as itself abnormal; Benedick's perception and Beatrice's vengeful morality appear as socially deviant behavior, which the concluding events of the comedy must reabsorb into its appearance of harmony.

In part this interpretation implies that the behavior of the characters during the play's conclusion is superficial and that *Much Ado* raises more problems than it can resolve save on the level of plot, an interpretation that incorporates both Rossiter's theory about the play's insulation and similar theories that emphasize the superficial devotion to appearances characteristic of life in Messina. The play itself, however, is not 'insulated' from inquisitions into values, for it is designed so as to off-set and defuse the epistemological inquiries that develop directly from the dramatic events. Moreover, having taken the important step beyond Rossiter's theory and determined that the insulation is within and not around *Much Ado*, and is self-imposed, I still find it inadequate to conclude that therefore *Much Ado* is a play about trivial and egotistical people whose concerns will remain superficial because of the quality of their personalities.[2] In *Much Ado About Nothing*, as throughout

'Speak, cousin; or if you cannot, stop his mouth with a kiss, and let not him speak neither' (II, i, 279–80), is both obvious and telling.

[1] See A. C. Bradley, *Shakespearean Tragedy* (1904) in Lecture 1, 'The Substance of Shakespearean Tragedy', pp. 24–8, for the Hegelian description of the 'moral order' of tragedy, upon which I base these remarks.

[2] I hope that I have made both the importance and the limitations of Rossiter's chapter on *Much Ado* clear: he was the first to suggest the ties in this play among the social status of a leisure class, the devotion to appearance, and the tendency toward amoral behavior. Unfortunately, Rossiter's need to ' "place" the play in the course of Shakespeare's writing' (p. 81) blinds him to Shakespeare's use of the insulated society as a means to inquire into values, social status, and the process of idealization.

Among those who have followed Rossiter's lead, different sets of problems and limitations occur. Crick, and especially King, made promising beginnings with their rudimentary Marxist analyses of the social relations in *Much Ado*. But both of their articles are seriously limited by their haughty judgmental tendencies; Crick sounds like Jahweh judging Sodom, King like a severe super-ego judging the individual characters' behavior patterns. I am exaggerating; but it is important to note that both articles, although useful for the strength of the preliminary observations, are weak on analysis – neither explores why the society causes the characters to act the way they do, nor how the characters' actions constitute or delineate the corrupt society.

Davis's Introduction, which isolates the conflict between appearance and reality, remedies some of the faults of both Crick and King, especially in his interesting analytic suggestion that Shakespearian comedy 'celebrates the triumph...of reality, with all its unidealistic concessions to practicality, over illusion' (p. 14). But Davis, perhaps because he is

Shakespeare, personality is a function of social status, and the emptiness of the aristocratic personality in *Much Ado* is a function of the lack of opposition that the aristocracy faces as a class, the absence of difficulty in delineation of social boundaries. The triumph over deception that marks the harmonic conclusions of Shakespeare's other comedies is simultaneously a triumph over a challenge to the social order; similarly, epistemology becomes thematically paramount in Shakespeare's tragedies because the protagonist's knowledge about his situation within society is severely challenged by the social and political circumstances within that dramatized society.

In *Much Ado* the challenges to the social order – Dogberry's and Don John's – are deliberately excluded, as buffoonery and cardboard villainy, in the terms of the dramatic action, for no social superiors accept the 'honor' of Don John in place of the deposed family honor of Leonato, nor do they accept Dogberry's perceptions as competent in place of their own failures at apprehension. Dogberry and Don John propel the plot, but their actions do not affect the qualities of the protagonists' characters. The oppositions through which character is forged in *Much Ado* are neither the social order and its antithesis, nor reality and mere appearances, but are those between the two distinct socially accepted aristocratic standards against which appearances are measured and whose reconciliation in marriage is the play's final assertion of aristocratic hegemony. In this idealized version of what constitutes a dramatic problem or conflict (could this, after all, be what Rossiter meant in calling *Much Ado* 'a *fantasy* of equivocal appearances'?) Shakespeare presents his clearest dramatic statement of the difficulty a ruling class faces in its attempt to isolate itself from inquiry into the traditions and appearances on which it has constructed its scale of values, and of the qualitative loss – on the level of morality and of character – that such an isolation entails. Perhaps this sense of loss is the 'nothing' of the play's title.

writing an introduction to a collection, errs on the side of caution and tradition, as he emphasizes the *triumph* rather than the *reality* that Shakespeare dramatizes in the conclusion of *Much Ado*.

SEXUAL DISGUISE IN 'AS YOU LIKE IT'
AND 'TWELFTH NIGHT'

NANCY K. HAYLES

In dealing with the female page disguise in Renaissance drama, one is invariably struck by the complexity of the double sex reversal implied by the presence of the boy actor. Lamb's remarks are typical: 'What an odd double confusion it must have made, to see a boy play a woman playing a man: one cannot disentangle the perplexity without some violence to the imagination.'[1] Perhaps because most of us share Lamb's perplexity, not much work has been done on the subject[2] other than a general acknowledgement that the device is both interesting and complex. Recently, however, sexual disguise has begun to attract attention from feminist critics because it seems to offer a way to combine Shakespearian criticism with contemporary social concerns.[3] Although more work is needed, and welcome, on this complex dramatic device, the tendency to regard it solely in terms of social and sexual roles seems to me misguided. While some aspects of the disguise are common to all the plays in which it appears, its dramatic function is shaped by the particular design of each play; and the differences are fully as important as the similarities in understanding the complexity of the device in Shakespeare's hands. In fact, Shakespeare's use of sexual disguise shows a definite progression: whereas in the early plays he uses it to explore the implications of sexual role-playing, in the later plays he seems increasingly interested in the metaphysical implications of the disguise, using it as a means to investigate, and eventually resolve, the disparity between appearance and essence.

[1] Charles Lamb in remarks on *Philaster*, quoted in V. O. Freeburg, *Disguise Plots in Elizabethan Drama* (New York, 1915), p. 22.

[2] The principle book length study is V. O. Freeburg's *Disguise Plots in Elizabethan Drama*, in which he undertakes an anatomy of disguise plots, classifying them according to kinds of disguises. M. C. Bradbrook in 'Shakespeare and the Use of Disguise in Elizabethan Drama', *Essays in Criticism*, 2 (1962), 159–68, after taking exception to Freeburg's definition of disguise as a change in physical appearance, considers psychological poses as well as physical masking. In trying to cover the whole range of possible disguises, Bradbrook is forced to be suggestive rather than comprehensive, and although she comments perceptively on the interconnections between disguise and identity – the area Freeburg most neglects – her conclusions remain interesting but vague. F. H. Mares in 'Viola and Other Transvestist Heroines in Shakespeare's Comedies', *Stratford Papers, 1965–1967*, ed. B. A. W. Jackson (McMaster Univ. Library Press, 1969), pp. 96–109 gives an urbane and sensible, if not deeply reasoned, perspective on the disguised heroine in four plays. Mares considers *Twelfth Night* and *As You Like It* to be the most dramatically economical uses of the disguise, *Two Gentlemen of Verona* simplistic in its responses, and *Cymbeline* complex but not integrally related to the theme. Two dissertations have appeared on the subject. Doris Feil in 'The Female Page in Renaissance Drama' (Arizona State University, 1971) gives a statistical overview of the female page in Renaissance drama from 1592–1642. In 'The Disguised Heroine in Six Shakespearean Comedies' (Univ. of Connecticut, 1970), James P. O'Sullivan discusses *Merchant of Venice, As You Like It, Twelfth Night, Two Gentlemen of Verona, All's Well* and *Cymbeline*. His analysis is not concerned specifically with sexual disguise.

[3] Examples are Carolyn Heilbrun, *Toward a Recognition of Androgyny* (New York, 1973), and *Shakespeare and the Nature of Women*, Juliet Dusinberre (New York, 1975).

Although a study of all five plays that use sexual disguise is outside the scope of this essay, I hope to demonstrate the nature of the progression by comparing the use of the sexual disguise in *As You Like It* with its use in *Twelfth Night*.[1] The purpose of this essay is therefore not only to draw general conclusions about the nature of Shakespearian sexual disguise, but to do so in a way that does justice to the uniqueness of each play. For that we turn now to the plays themselves.

As You Like It opens with scenes that emphasize rivalry and competition. Orlando has been mistreated by his brother Oliver, and Oliver in turn feels that Orlando has caused him to be 'altogether misprised' and undervalued by his own people. The rivalry that Duke Frederick still feels with the rightful Duke is also apparent. Moreover, the chief event of the opening scenes, the wrestling match between Charles and Orlando, is a formalized and ritualistic expression of male rivalry.[2] Against the backdrop of male rivalry, the female intimacy between Celia and Rosalind makes a striking contrast. It is an intimacy, however, maintained at some cost. When Duke Frederick peremptorily orders Rosalind into banishment, Celia's protest is countered by her father's attempt to transform intimacy into rivalry between the two girls, too:

> Thou art a fool; she robs thee of thy name,
> And thou wilt show more bright and seem more
>   virtuous
> When she is gone. Then open not thy lips.[3]
>
> (I, iii, 76–8)

The opening scenes of the play, then, draw a society where intimacy among women is implicitly contrasted with the rivalry among men. When the scene changes to the forest, several incidents seem designed as signals that the forest is a world where co-operation rather than competition prevails. Orlando meets with civility instead of hostility when he seeks meat for the fainting Adam; Rosalind and Celia find

the natives to be kind shepherds rather than would-be rapists; and the exiled Duke hails his followers as 'Co-mates and brothers'. But we soon discover that competition is not altogether absent from the Forest of Arden. Jaques accuses the Duke of himself usurping the forest from its rightful owners, the deer; Touchstone confronts and bests his country rival, William; and Silvius discovers that his beloved Phebe has fallen in love with a courtly newcomer. The situation is thus more complicated than a simple contrast between court competition and pastoral co-operation, or between female intimacy and male rivalry. The sexual disguise of Rosalind mirrors the complexities of these tensions.

We can consider the disguise as proceeding in two separate movements. First, the layers of

[1] The other plays using female sexual disguise are *Two Gentlemen of Verona*, *Merchant of Venice*, and *Cymbeline*. *Two Gentlemen of Verona* shows in rudimentary form what the later plays show more fully (see Harold Jenkins, 'Shakespeare's *Twelfth Night*', *Rice Institute Pamphlet*, 45, No. 4 (1959), 19–42 for a discussion of *Two Gentlemen of Verona* as an anticipation of *Twelfth Night*). In *Merchant of Venice*, the disguise is more obviously functional and less explored in itself than in either *As You Like It* or *Twelfth Night*. The case of *Cymbeline* is complex, and is the subject of an article in preparation. Two plays contain instances of male sexual disguise, the Induction to *Taming of the Shrew* and *Merry Wives of Windsor*, both of which use boy brides. Male transvestism is mentioned as well in *Antony and Cleopatra*, but not shown on stage. Male disguise is not discussed because it seems clear that Shakespeare was mainly interested in the possibilities of sexual disguise offered by the female page.

[2] Ralph Berry in *Shakespeare's Comedies: Explorations in Form* (Princeton, 1972), comments on the need to control others in *As You Like It*, and remarks in passing that the wrestling match may be symbolic of what he sees as the dominant theme (p. 177). We part company in our interpretation of the play's later scenes. Berry singles out for attention the discordant elements, even in the final scene, whereas my emphasis is on the final resolution and reconciliation.

[3] Quotations are from the New Arden: *As You Like It*, ed. Agnes Latham (1975); and *Twelfth Night*, ed. J. M. Lothian and T. W. Craik (1975).

disguise are added as Rosalind becomes Ganymede, and then as Ganymede pretends to be Orlando's Rosalind; second, the layers are removed as Ganymede abandons the play-acting of Rosalind, and then as Rosalind herself abandons the disguise of Ganymede. The layering-on movement creates conflict and the layering-off movement fosters reconciliation as the disguise confronts and then resolves the issue of competition versus co-operation.

In the most complex layering, Rosalind-as-Ganymede-as-Orlando's Rosalind, Rosalind presents Orlando with a version of his beloved very different from the one he imagines in his verses. When Rosalind-as-Ganymede insists that Orlando's Rosalind will have her own wit, her own will and her own way, implicit in the portrayal is Rosalind's insistence that Orlando recognize the discrepancy between his idealized version and the real Rosalind. In effect, Rosalind is claiming the right to be herself rather than to be Orlando's idealized version of her, as female reality is playfully set against male fantasy. In playing herself (which she can apparently do only if she first plays someone else)[1] Rosalind is able to state her own needs in a way she could not if she were simply herself. It is because she is disguised as Ganymede that she can be so free in portraying a Rosalind who is a flesh and blood woman instead of a Petrarchan abstraction. Rosalind's three-fold disguise is therefore used to accentuate the disparity between the needs of the heroine and the expectations of the hero.

Even the simpler layering of Rosalind-as-Ganymede accentuates conflict, though this time the couple being affected is Phebe and Silvius. Rosalind's guise as Ganymede causes Phebe to fall in love with her. Rosalind's on-layering, which inadvertently makes her Silvius's rival, causes Phebe's desires to be even more at variance with Silvius's hopes than before. It takes Ganymede's transformation into Rosalind to trick Phebe into accepting her swain, as the off-layering of Rosalind's

disguise reconciles these two Petrarchan lovers. The Silvius–Phebe plot thus shows in simplified form the correlation between on-layering and rivalry, and off-layering and co-operation. It also gives us a standard by which we can measure the more complicated situation between Orlando and Rosalind.

Phebe and Silvius are caricatures of courtly love, and through them we are shown female manipulation and male idealization in a way that emphasizes the less pleasant side of the courtly love tradition. But it is important to see that this rustic couple merely exaggerates tendencies also present in Rosalind and Orlando. Rosalind's disguise creates an imbalance in her relationship with Orlando because it allows Rosalind to hear Orlando's love-confession without having to take any comparable risks herself. Rosalind's self-indulgence in demanding Orlando's devoted service without admitting anything in return could become a variation of the perversity that is anatomized for us in the relationship between Phebe and Silvius. Thus the expectations of Rosalind and the desires of Orlando are not only the responses of these two characters, but are also reflections of stereotypical male and female postures, familiar through the long tradition of courtly love. The layering of the disguise has served to accentuate the conflict between men and women; now the unlayering finally resolves that traditional tension between the needs of the female and the desires of the male.

The unlayering begins when Oliver appears to explain why Orlando is late. Oliver's tale reveals, in almost allegorical fashion, the struggle within Orlando when he sees his brother in peril, and the tale has as its point that Orlando put the needs of his brother before his own natural desire for revenge. More subtly, the tale with its depiction of the twin dangers of the snake and lioness hints at

[1] A felicitous phrase supplied by a private communication with Ellen Cronan Rose.

a symbolic nexus of male and female threats. The specificity of the imagery suggests that the details are important. The first beast is described as a lioness, not a lion; moreover, she is a lioness in suck, but now with teats sucked dry, her hunger presumably made more ferocious by her condition. The description thus links a specifically female animal, and a graphically specific female condition, with the threat of being eaten. The details, taken in sum, evoke the possibility of female engulfment. The snake about to enter the sleeping man's mouth, again a very specific image, suggests even to a non-Freudian the threat of phallic invasion. But perhaps most significant is simply the twinning of the threats itself, which suggests the presence of two different but related kinds of danger.

By overcoming the twin threats, Orlando conquers in symbolic form projections of both male and female fears. Rosalind responds to Oliver's account by swooning. Her faint is a literal relinquishing of conscious control; within the conventions of the play, it is also an involuntary revelation of female gender because fainting is a 'feminine' response. It is a subtle anticipation of Rosalind's eventual relinquishing of the disguise and the control that goes with it. The action surrounding the relation of the tale parallels its moral: Orlando performs a heroic and selfless act that hints at a triumph over threatening aspects of masculinity and femininity, and Rosalind responds to the dangers that Orlando faces with an unconscious gesture of sympathy that results, for a moment, in the loss of her conscious control over the disguise and with it, the loss of her manipulative control over Orlando. Rosalind's swoon thus provides a feminine counterpart to Orlando's selflessness.

Orlando's struggle and Rosalind's swoon mark a turning point. When they meet again, Rosalind tries at first to re-establish their old relationship, but when Orlando replies, 'I can live no longer by thinking', she quickly capitulates and re-assumes control only in order to be able to relinquish it. From this point on, the removal of the disguise signals the consummation of all the relationships as all four couples are married. The play suggests that control is necessary to state the legitimate needs of the self, but also that it must eventually be relinquished to accommodate the needs of another. Consummation is paradoxically achieved through an act of renunciation.

The way that sexual disguise is used reflects the play's overall concern with the tension between rivalry and co-operation. The disguise is first used to crystallize rivalry between the woman's self-image and the man's desires; in this sense it recognizes male–female discord and implicitly validates it. But because the disguise can be removed, it prevents the discord from becoming perpetual frustration. The workings of the disguise suggest that what appears to be a generous surrendering of self-interest can in fact bring consummation both to man and woman, so that rivalry can be transcended as co-operation brings fulfilment. In *As You Like It*, fulfilment of desire, contentment and peace of mind come when the insistence on self-satisfaction ceases. Duke Senior's acceptance of his forest exile and the subsequent unlooked-for restoration of his dukedom; the reconciliation between the sons of Rowland de Boys, in which Oliver resigns his lands to Orlando and finds forgiveness and happiness in love; the miraculous conversion of Duke Frederick by the old hermit and the voluntary abdication of his dukedom – all express the same paradox of consummation through renunciation that is realized in specifically sexual terms by the disguise.

When the boy actor who plays Rosalind's part comes forward to speak the epilogue, the workings of the sexual disguise are linked with the art of the playwright. The epilogue continues the paradox of consummation through renunciation that has governed sexual disguise within the play, as the final unlayering of the disguise coincides with a plea for the audience to consummate the play by applauding:

My way is to conjure you, and I'll begin with the women. I charge you, O women, for the love you bear to men, to like as much of this play as please you. And I charge you, O men, for the love you bear to women – as I perceive by your simpering none of you hates them – that between you and the women the play may please. If I were a woman, I would kiss as many of you as had beards that pleased me, complexions that liked me, and breaths that I defied not. And I am sure, as many as have good beards, or good faces, or sweet breaths, will for my kind offer, when I make curtsy, bid me farewell.

At this moment the playwright relinquishes control of the audience. As with Rosalind and Orlando, his success is marked by a control that finally renounces itself, a control which admonishes only to release as the audience is asked to 'like as much...as please you'. Our applause is a gesture of acceptance which encompasses both the working of sexual disguise within the play, and the art whose operation parallels it as the play ends. At the same time, the boy actor alludes to the fact that he is not after all the woman he plays ('*if* I were a woman'), and so relinquishes the last level of the sexual disguise. For the last time, the unlayering of the disguise is linked with a reconciliation between the sexes as the boy actor speaking the epilogue appeals separately to the men and women in the audience. Within the play these two perspectives have been reconciled, and the joint applause of the men and women in the audience re-affirms that reconciliation and extends it to the audience.

The sexual disguise in *As You Like It* therefore succeeds in interweaving various motifs. Many of the problems considered in the play (Duke Frederick's tyranny, Oliver's unfair treatment of Orlando, Phebe's exultation over Silvius) stem from excessive control, and the heroine exercises extraordinary control over the disguise. The removal of the disguise signals a renunciation of control on her part,

and this in turn is linked with a voluntary renunciation of control by others, so that the unlayering and the resolution of problems neatly correspond. Moreover, the sexual reversal inherent in the disguise, which itself implicitly promises a reconciliation of male and female perspectives, is used to reconcile the men and women in the play. Since the key to reconciliation has been the renunciation of control, the playwright uses his relinquishing of control over the play to signal a final reconciliation between the men and women in the audience. Because of the correspondence between Rosalind as controller of the disguise, and Shakespeare as controller of the disguised boy actor who plays Rosalind's part, Rosalind's control over her disguise is paradigmatic of the playwright's control over the play. Both use their control creatively and constructively, but for both the relinquishing of control corresponds with the consummation of their art.

The means by which resolution is achieved in *As You Like It* says a great deal about the kinds of problems the play considers. By having Rosalind as surrogate playmaker, the playwright must not pose problems that are beyond her power to solve. There are a few hints that Rosalind's control exceeds the merely human; she tells Orlando she possesses magical powers, and Hymen mysteriously appears to officiate at the wedding. The playwright likewise allows himself some hints of supernatural intervention – witness Duke Frederick's miraculous conversion. But positing a human problem-solver almost necessitates limiting the problems to human scale. Moreover, because the disguise is the key to Rosalind's ability to solve problems, the emphasis on male and female perspectives inherent in the sexual disguise places the problems in the context of the social roles of each sex. The disguise thus gives the play artistic unity, but it also imposes limitations on the play's thematic scope. The brilliance of *As You Like It* is that it so perfectly matches what the play attempts to the inherent limitations of its techniques that it makes us unaware there are limitations.

In *Twelfth Night* the techniques, and the problems, are of a different order. Rather than conferring control upon the heroine, the disguise withholds it from her. Concurrently, the nature of the problems changes; in *Twelfth Night*, they cannot be solved by a renunciation of control, because part of the problem is an anxiety about who (or what) is in control. That the removal of the disguise is insufficient to achieve resolution implies an enlargement of the play's thematic scope. In *Twelfth Night* the problems – and the solution – are associated with forces more than human.

Joseph Summers has remarked that *Twelfth Night* has an unusual structure for a comedy, because there are no parents to erect obstacles for the lovers.[1] In the absence of parents, the ruling figures of the society could be expected to fill parental roles; but the Countess Olivia and the Duke Orsino are engaged in love problems themselves. As a result of the displacement of the ruling figures into the romantic plot, a vacuum exists at the top of the social hierarchy. This peculiarity of the play's structure is, I believe, related to the function of the sexual disguise in *Twelfth Night*. As we shall see, the disguise links ambiguity of sexual identity with a concern that this ambiguity can be exploited by super-human forces for evil ends. The absence of human controllers, because it creates a vacuum in which super-human forces can operate, facilitates the shift from the physical to the metaphysical implications of the disguise.

The ambiguous nature of the controlling forces arises first in the underplot. If (as Maria and her accomplices pretend) Malvolio really were possessed by devils, his acts would express not his spontaneous reactions but the desires of the controlling devils. In this sense he would be following a diabolical script, just as he earlier followed the script of the forged letter. The underplot thus introduces the idea that when Malvolio plays a role at odds with his real identity by appearing cross-gartered and smiling, he has unwittingly given diabolical forces the opportunity to usurp his identity for their own ends. Offsetting the seriousness of these implications is our knowledge that this is pretense, the festive revenge of the 'lighter folk' against Malvolio's self-righteous solemnity.[2]

The issues implicit in the playful exorcism of Malvolio are present in the main plot as well, but here the festive mockery that is the essence of the underplot is mingled with a more serious treatment. The connection between masking and the diabolical continues as a cluster of images associates the disguised Viola with the devil. For example, when Cesario first appears at Olivia's gate, Sir Toby in response to Olivia's query about the visitor replies, 'Let him be the devil and he will, I care not' (I, v, 129). Sir Toby again associates Cesario with the devil when he concocts the duel between the foolish Sir Andrew and Cesario. 'I have persuaded him the youth's a devil' (III, iv, 298) Sir Toby assures Fabian; and indeed, after Sir Andrew has his head bloodied by Sebastian, he is convinced, when he happens upon Cesario again, that 'He's the very devil incardinate' (v, i, 179–80). Along with the misapprehensions of Sir Andrew are a related set of images in a more serious vein. Sir Toby's careless intimation that Cesario might be an aspect of the devil is echoed by Olivia after she has seen the visitor for herself. 'A fiend like thee might bear my soul to hell', she tells Cesario.

[1] Joseph Summers, 'The Masks of *Twelfth Night*', in *Shakespeare: Modern Essays in Criticism*, ed. Leonard F. Dean (Oxford 1967), pp. 134–5.

[2] C. L. Barber's important book *Shakespeare's Festive Comedy: A Study in Dramatic Form and its Relation to Social Custom* (Princeton, 1959), discusses the functions of festive misrule in Shakespeare's comedies. Barber's general formula for festive comedy is a movement through release to clarification, a formulation that does much to illuminate *Twelfth Night*.

The evocation of the diabolical puts into a new context the word-play on divinity and divine texts in the initial meeting of Cesario and Olivia (I, v). If we are distracted from our delight in the wit-contest into a serious consideration, we see that the source of the wit is blasphemy. Thus our delight is being finely balanced against a suppressed recognition of moral ambiguity. Occasionally this recognition is almost allowed to surface; such a moment occurs when Olivia lifts her veil. In this moment of unmasking, the mock-adoration of Cesario's set speeches suddenly gives way to Viola's spontaneous reaction to Olivia's beauty. 'I see you what you are, you are too proud', she tells Olivia. 'But if you were the devil, you are fair' (I, v, 254–5).

The suppressed recognition of moral ambiguity is thus linked, in both main plot and underplot, with an ambiguity of identity. The two plots use different means to contain the moral ambiguities: in the underplot it is the allowed irreverence of festive mockery, while in the main plot it is our delight in the innuendoes and witty ambiguities that Viola's disguise creates. Both plots associate masking with a loss of control. In the underplot, we of course know that the controlling agents are not really devils but Sir Toby and his friends. In the main plot, however, it is not clear into whose hands control has fallen. Viola realizes in her speech near the beginning of act II (II, ii, 17–40) that the complications caused by the sexual disguise have surpassed her power to unravel them. But she cannot clearly see the end to which the disguise leads, or the nature of the controlling agents. If the agents are diabolical, then the end is evil, and wit and beauty are traps for the unwary, audience as well as character. In that case, the play's strategy of the witty containment of moral ambiguity is subverted, because wit, as the tool of diabolical agents, is itself morally ambiguous. Viola's speech is worth examining in detail, since it is the play's most explicit

statement about the effect of her disguise and deals with the implications of her loss of control. Before looking closely at the speech, however, I want to mention a contemporary document that may throw some light on the issues being raised here.[1]

A principle support for the mounting Puritan attack on the stage during the last decade of Shakespeare's career was the Biblical prohibition against cross-dressing:

The woman shall not weare that which pertaineth unto a man, neither shall a man put on a womans garment: for all that doe so, are abominations unto the Lord thy God. (Deuteronomy 22, 5)

Whether this passage applied to the transvestism of the boy actors was exhaustively debated in an exchange of letters between three Oxford dons, with Dr John Rainolds, an eminent Puritan, arguing for a literal interpretation of the passage, and William Gager and his friend Alberico Gentili attempting to defend the academic drama at Oxford. Six of these letters, two in English and four in Latin, were printed in 1599 in a volume entitled Th' Overthrow of Stage-Plays. The debate between these formidably learned men became widely known. J. W. Binns, writing on this controversy, notes that Prynne acknowledges his debt to Rainolds in Histriomastix, and Thomas Heywood praises Gager and Gentili in his Apology for Actors.[2]

In response to the claim from those defending the drama that 'abomination' was too strong a term to apply to the innocent disguises of the stage, Dr Rainolds, citing the Bishop of Paris, forcefully argues for the potential evil of sexual disguise:

[1] For much of the information that follows I am indebted to J. W. Binns's excellent article, 'Women or Transvestites on the Elizabethan Stage?: An Oxford Controversy', Sixteenth Century Journal, 2 (1974), 95–120. Besides drawing attention to the Rainolds–Gager controversy, Binns supplied translations and summaries of hitherto unpublished letters in the controversy.

[2] Binns, p. 119.

For the apparell of women (saith he) is a great provocation of men to lust and leacherie: because a womans garment being put on by a man doeth vehemently touch and moue him with the remembrance and imagination of a woman; and the imagination of a thing desirable doth stirr up the desire...the law condemneth those execrable villanies, to which this change of raiment provoketh and entiseth.[1]

Sexual disguise, according to Dr Rainolds, is evil even when done in play because the semblance of a woman which the attire creates leads men to desire the boy wearing that attire; and this results in practices condemned by Biblical law, practices which Rainolds in an earlier letter calls 'beastlie filthiness, or rather more then beastlie'.[2]

Rainolds's comments on the effects of sexual disguise are especially interesting (and relevant to *Twelfth Night*) because they suggest a complex response that depends upon the apprehension of the sexual ambiguity. The male spectator, according to Rainolds, reacts erotically to the female attire of the boy actor; yet at the same time, the spectator has some apprehension that the actor is in fact a boy, and so is led by degrees into being inflamed with lust for the boy. The important point here is that both elements – the maleness of the boy actor and the femaleness of the womanly costume – are necessary to lead the spectator into abomination.

In *Twelfth Night*, the sexual ambiguity of the disguise – the male attire of Cesario and Viola's underlying femininity which both Olivia and Orsino sense – frees Orsino and Olivia from their initial rigidity. C. L. Barber's perceptive analysis of Olivia's and Orsino's reactions to the disguise demonstrates how the disguise functions to release the two.[3] Olivia has refused to admit suitors of any sort prior to Cesario's appearance; in particular, she has refused Orsino, the suitor who by her own admission is a fine specimen of upright manhood. Yet when she sees the effeminate Cesario, she immediately falls in love with 'him'. Thus she is led by degrees to be able to love Sebastian,

who is masculine in person as well as in attire. 'So comes it, lady, you have been mistook./ But nature to her bias drew in that', Sebastian tells Olivia at the end of the play. Meanwhile Orsino has been obstinately intent on pursuing a woman who rejects him. He admits Cesario into his service, and quickly prefers this girlish boy before all of his other attendants. As Cesario's patron, he comes to love 'him'; and when it is revealed that Cesario is in fact a woman, Orsino is content to claim Viola as his bride. As C. L. Barber concludes, it is the combination of masculinity and femininity in the love-object that accomplishes what neither could by itself. Thus the very sexual ambiguity which Dr Rainolds claimed would lead the spectator into abomination, releases the characters in *Twelfth Night* from frustration. Whereas Rainolds suggests that the fluidity inherent in sexual disguise will lead to moral chaos, the play shows that fluidity leading to fruition and fulfillment.

It is of course not *necessary* to suppose that the use of sexual disguise in *Twelfth Night* owes anything to the Rainolds–Gager controversy. It was commonplace in Puritan attacks on the stage to say that the theater in general, and cross-dressing in particular, was the work of the devil, so the play's association of sexual disguise with diabolical forces need not come from *Th'Over-Throw of Stage-Playes* pamphlet, even assuming it is indebted to the Puritan attacks generally.[4] The principal new element in the Rainolds–Gager controversy is the dynamic of sexual disguise, the suggestion that the spectator apprehends the sexual ambiguity of the actor, and that this appre-

---

[1] Binns, p. 103.
[2] Binns, p. 102.
[3] See 'You are betroth'd both to a maid and man', *Shakespeare's Festive Comedies*, pp. 245–7.
[4] For an overview of Puritan rhetoric against the stage, see Elbert Nevius Sebring Thompson, *The Controversy Between the Puritans and the Stage*, Yale Studies in English, 20 (New York, 1903), especially pp. 102–9 for theaters as purveyors of sin.

hension affects the moral state of the spectator. But it is just this dynamic which illuminates the complex effects created by the disguise, as an analysis of Viola's speech shows.

Let us turn now to that speech (II, ii, 17–40). Viola prays, 'Fortune forbid my outside have not charm'd her!' invoking the goddess of chance to intervene so that her appearance is not mistaken for her essence. As she thinks over Olivia's response, Viola convinces herself that the lady does indeed love Cesario, and concludes:

> Disguise, I see thou art a wickedness,
> Wherein the pregnant enemy does much.
>
> (II, ii, 26–7)

'Pregnant enemy' is invariably glossed as the devil, the 'dextrous fiend', as Dr Johnson called him, who uses any disruption of the established order to wreak havoc on man. Viola then imagines the matter that the 'pregnant enemy' forms to his ends:

> How easy is it for the proper false
> In women's waxen hearts to set their forms!
> Alas, our frailty is the cause, not we,
> For such as we are made of, such we be.
>
> (II, ii, 28–31)

The plasticity of the female heart, inherent in woman's flawed nature, allows a 'form' to be set there, and the form evokes love, even when the essence may be at odds with the form. So far the progression Viola describes is similar to that in Dr Rainold's letter, and, like his prediction, carries the sense of a sequence of association exploited by a diabolical agent to lead fallible mankind into damnation. Viola ends the speech by resigning the complexity of the situation to time:

> O time, thou must untangle this, not I
> It is too hard a knot for me t' untie.
>
> (II, ii, 39–40)

Ultimately, the sexual disguise in *Twelfth Night* leads to happiness rather than abomination because the metaphysical entities being invoked – fortune, nature and time – are benign. The plasticity of Olivia's female

nature allows her heart to receive Cesario's form. When she sees Cesario again and is refused by 'him', she despairs; but the disguise has already begun to release Olivia from frustration by impressing on her heart the twin's form. Fortune lends its aid by arranging events so that Sebastian is there to take Cesario's place with Olivia when the proper time comes and, by becoming Sebastian's wife, Olivia 'reaps a proper man' she never could have had in Cesario. The discrepancy between appearance and essence, which could have been exploited by diabolical agents for evil ends, has instead allowed Olivia to find fulfillment.

The claim for the beneficial effects of the disguise thus rests on the assumption that the control has been put into the hands of benign entities (fortune, nature, time) rather than diabolical agents. Such a disposition of control still does not resolve all the ambiguities, however, because these entities, although not evil, can nevertheless be ambiguous. For Malvolio, for example, time brings in its revenges. Antonio too is disillusioned rather than freed by disguise. When Cesario is confused with Sebastian, Antonio feels the confluence of this unknown element with his beloved Sebastian as a betrayal. For Antonio, the proper love-object *is* Sebastian, so the ambiguities introduced by Viola's disguise cannot lead him to a more appropriate choice; they only cause him pain. When Cesario denies Antonio his purse, Antonio uses imagery which again sets into opposition the diabolical and the divine, but now there is no redeeming potential in the confusion. Instead Antonio reacts to the ambiguity as if a true god had been transformed into an idol:

> O how vile an idol proves this god!
> Thou hast, Sebastian, done good feature shame.
> In nature there's no blemish but the mind:
> None can be call'd deform'd but the unkind.
> Virtue is beauty, but the beauteous evil
> Are empty trunks, o'er-flourish'd by the devil.
>
> (III, iv, 374–9)

Antonio sees the discrepancy between appearance and essence, which allowed Orsino and Olivia to be freed, as a diabolical trap designed to lure the unwary into worship. The ambiguity of the disguise, helpless to release Antonio from the anguish of his love, can at most restore the loved one to him, as it does when he meets Sebastian again at the end of the play.[1]

Perhaps Antonio's worship explains why Sebastian at the end uses language which denies the claim of godhood and places him firmly in the world of the flesh. When he first sees Cesario, Sebastian says,

> Do I stand here? I never had a brother;
> Nor can there be that deity in my nature
> Of here and everywhere.   (v, i, 224–6)

And then, when Viola takes him for a spirit, he replies,

> A spirit I am indeed,
> But am in that dimension grossly clad
> Which from the womb I did participate.
>   (v, i, 234–6)

Sebastian's statements imply a reintegration of form and essence when he presents himself not as a god (or a devil) but as a man, a spirit in a corporeal body. There is indeed an ambiguity in this union of spirit with flesh, but it is an ambiguity which defines the essence of man, as Sebastian proclaims himself a man, and one which is finally cause for celebration and happiness rather than temptation. The closing scenes, which resolve some of the ambiguities, reassure us that the ambiguities which cannot be resolved will nevertheless lead to good rather than evil. Gaiety, not melancholy, is finally the appropriate response to an ambiguous world.

Sexual disguise is thus a multifaceted device in Shakespeare. The progression from *As You Like It* to *Twelfth Night* shows a shift in emphasis from a *sexual* disguise to a sexual *disguise*. In *Cymbeline*, the last play where Shakespeare uses the device, the emphasis is almost entirely metaphysical rather than social. The growing sense of wonder that accompanies the removal of the disguise in the later plays is possible only because its implications transcend the merely social, or even the human. It would be unfortunate if our modern preoccupations blind us to this sense of wonder, or to an appreciation of the rich diversity with which Shakespeare uses the device. In Shakespeare's hands, sexual disguise illuminates not only the relationship of woman to man, but also the relation of appearance to reality and human beings to forces more than human. The multiplicity of meanings with which Shakespeare invests the disguise does not really 'disentangle the perplexity [of seeing] a boy play a woman playing a man', but it provides a thematic counterpart to that complexity of vision, and so orders it into one aesthetic whole.

[1] I take Antonio's dilemma in *Twelfth Night* to be another version of the dilemma of that other Antonio in *Merchant of Venice*: both Antonios love another man, and both are forced to come to some kind of accommodation when the man they love takes a wife. The pain that surrounds both Antonios seems to me an expression of the consequences of a homoerotic love in a heterosexual society. The men that the Antonio figures love (Bassanio, Sebastian) may return the love, but both ultimately marry women and give their allegiance to their wives.

'TWELFTH NIGHT' AND THE MYTH OF
ECHO AND NARCISSUS

D. J. PALMER

Orsino's attitude to love, particularly in the play's opening speech, has often provoked charges of self-indulgence and self-deception, and one critic is even driven to declare him 'a narcissistic fool'.[1] However, the association with Narcissus can be more precisely defined, since Orsino's luxuriant musing on the appetite that craves to die in its own too much, the music that cloys the sense so that it seems no longer sweet and the capacious spirit of love in which anything of value 'falls into abatement and low price' (I, i, 13)[2] plays upon the motif 'inopem me copia fecit', the complaint of Ovid's Narcissus translated by Golding as 'my plentie makes me poore' (l. 587).[3] In its original context, 'inopem me copia fecit' expresses the paradoxical realisation of Narcissus that he himself is the unattainable object of his insatiable desire, but the Elizabethan poets appropriated the tag as a paradigm of unrequited love.[4] Spenser, for instance, constructs the thirty-fifth sonnet of *Amoretti* around it:

My hungry eyes through greedy covetize,
   still to behold the object of their paine,
   with no contentment can themselves suffize:
   but having pine and having not complaine.
For lacking it they cannot lyfe sustayne,
   and having it they gaze on it the more:
   in their amazement lyke Narcissus vaine
   whose eyes him starv'd: so plenty makes me
     poore.
Yet are mine eyes so filled with the store
   of that faire sight, that nothing else they brooke,
   but loth the things which they did like before,
   and can no more endure on them to looke.

All this world's glory seemeth vayne to me,
   and all their showes but shadowes, saving she.[5]

Orsino's opening speech is not only full of similar languishing, but it also expresses the restlessness of the affections that come to 'loth the things which they did like before'. In the poems written early in his career Shakespeare himself plays some less neo-Platonised variations on the motif of 'inopem me copia fecit'. At the beginning of *Venus and Adonis*, for instance, Venus promises the reluctant youth that her kisses will 'not cloy thy lips with loath'd satiety,/But rather famish them amid thy plenty', (ll. 19–20) although later in the poem, when she tries to embrace Adonis by force, it is her own lips that 'surfeit, yet complain on drouth./He with her plenty press'd, she faint with dearth '(ll. 544–5). Similarly, in *The Rape of Lucrece*, Tarquin's lust is apparent in his 'still-gazing eyes',

Which, having all, all could not satisfy;
   But, poorly rich, so wanteth in his store
   That cloy'd with much he pineth still for more.

               (ll. 96–8)

[1] Herschel Baker, Introduction to *Twelfth Night*, The Signet Classic Shakespeare (1965), p. xxviii.
[2] Quotations of Shakespeare's plays and poems are from *The Complete Works*, ed. Peter Alexander (1951).
[3] Quotations of Arthur Golding's translation of *Metamorphoses* (1567) are from *Shakespeare's Ovid*, ed. W. H. D. Rouse (1961). All line references are to The Third Booke.
[4] L. Rick, 'Shakespeare und Ovid', *Shakespeare Jahrbuch*, LV (1919), 50–1.
[5] *The Poetical Works of Edmund Spenser*, ed. J. C. Smith and E. De Selincourt (1912), p. 568.

When Orsino calls for music as 'the food of love',

> Give me excess of it, that surfeiting,
> The appetite may sicken and so die,　　(I, i, 2–3)

Shakespeare is adapting Barnabe Riche's reflection on the foolish lover, 'onely led by the apetite of his owne affections',[1] to a conventional and perhaps slightly old-fashioned literary trope. Orsino loves by the book; at a further remove from his beloved than Spenser's tormented lover or the predatory Venus, Orsino's passion is fed neither by eyes nor by kisses, but by imagination:

> 　　　　So full of shapes is fancy
> That it alone is high fantastical.　　(I, i, 14–15)

Orsino recalls, not only the Narcissus of 'inopem me copia fecit', mediated through the tradition of Elizabethan love poetry, but also the Narcissus whose plight is somewhat unfeelingly described by Golding:

> He feedes a hope without cause why. For like a
> 　　foolishe noddie
> He thinkes the shadow that he sees, to be a lively
> 　　boddie.　　(ll. 521–2)

Orsino too pursues an illusion; the fact that during the course of the play he does not encounter Olivia until the final scene reinforces this sense of an infatuation with an image rather than love for a real person. His attitude can indeed be described as 'narcissistic', though it is defined in relation to other allusions to Ovid's fable and its later recensions in the pattern of the play as a whole.

Malvolio, for instance, is also initially identified with Narcissus when Olivia rebukes him on his first appearance for being 'sick of self-love' (I, v, 85). This Narcissus is the allegorised figure of Philautia, a diagnosis later confirmed by Maria's description of the self-conceit that she will exploit in her plot against him: 'the best persuaded of himself, so cramm'd, as he thinks, with excellencies that it is his grounds of faith that all that look on him love

him' (II, iii, 140–2). Malvolio, like Orsino, is self-deceived, but to an opposite effect. The Duke plays the long-suffering unrequited lover of poetic tradition, while the steward, 'practising behaviour to his own shadow' (II, v, 14–15), a very narcissistic pastime, imagines that his lady dotes on him.

Olivia herself is the subject of another sequence of allusions to Narcissus in Viola's criticism of her refusal of love. Again, some of these are mediated through poetic tradition, while some more directly recall the Ovidian tale. Viola's tribute to Olivia's beauty, for instance, is often compared to the opening theme of Shakespeare's own Sonnets:

> Lady, you are the cruell'st she alive,
> If you will lead these graces to the grave,
> And leave the world no copy.　　(I, v, 225–7)

The youth addressed in the Sonnets is reproached in several references to the beauty, vanity and eventual fate of Narcissus, including the following quatrain from the first sonnet, with its adroit play upon 'inopem me copia fecit' in the third line:

> But thou, contracted to thine own bright eyes,
> Feed'st thy light's flame with self-substantial fuel,
> Making a famine where abundance lies,
> Thy self thy foe, to thy sweet self too cruel.
> 　　　　　　　　(ll. 5–8)

The vanity of the mythical youth who scorned all his suitors is also paralleled by Viola's accusation that Olivia is 'too proud' (I, v, 234), while Viola's imprecation on this 'fair cruelty',

> Love make his heart of flint that you shall love;
> And let your fervour, like my master's, be
> Plac'd in contempt!　　(I, v, 270–2)

corresponds to the prayer of the rejected suitor in Ovid (Golding's version is cited again):

> I pray to God he may once feele fierce Cupids
> 　　fire,

---

[1] *Riche his Farewell to Militarie Profession* (1581) as cited in the New Arden edition of *Twelfth Night*, ed. J. M. Lothian and T. W. Craik (1975), Appendix 1, p. 158.

As I doe now, and yet not joy the things he doth
desire.   (ll. 505–6)

The wish is fulfilled upon Olivia no less ironically than it is in the myth: 'poor lady, she were better love a dream' (II, ii, 24).

More incidental to the dramatic design, but indicative of the associations at work in Shakespeare's mind, is Malvolio's description of Viola, 'yond young fellow' demanding admission at Olivia's gate, as 'in standing water, between boy and man' (I, v, 150). The New Arden edition of the play notes that the line is reminiscent of Golding's account of the adolescent Narcissus:

> For when yeares three times five and one he fully
> lyved had,
> So that he seemde to stande betweene the state
> of man and Lad,
> The hearts of divers trim yong men his beautie
> gan to move,
> And many a Ladie fresh and fair was taken in his
> love.   (ll. 437–40)

The verbal recollection brings with it the context of sexual ambivalence, appropriate to Viola's disguise and to the ironic outcome of the following interview with Olivia, while Shakespeare's improvement upon the neutral expression 'stande betweene' in the metaphoric phrase 'in standing water' is also fitting for this lady from the sea.

Viola's role, however, has more in common with Echo, the nymph deprived of her own speech by Juno and compelled to express her feelings in borrowed terms. Ovid's Echo falls in love with Narcissus, but is spurned by him and hides away until she fades into a disembodied voice. It is tempting to believe that the poignancy of Viola's secret love for Orsino is indebted to Echo's plight, particularly in the device by which Viola preserves her secrecy yet reveals to Orsino 'what love women to men may owe' in the fiction of a sister who 'never told her love' (II, iv, 109). This tale of melancholy concealment and pining love certainly corresponds in feeling to

Ovid's description of Echo (here given in the words of a literal modern translation in preference to Golding):

> Thus spurned, she lurks in the woods, hides her shamed face among the foliage, and lives from that time on in lonely caves. But still, though spurned, her love remains and grows on grief; her sleepless cares waste away her wretched form; she becomes gaunt and wrinkled and all moisture fades from her body into the air. Only her voice and her bones remain: then, only voice; for they say that her bones were turned to stone. She hides in woods and is seen no more upon the mountain-sides; but all may hear her, for voice, and voice alone, still lives in her.[1]

Viola's skill in attuning her speech to the occasion is an important feature of her use of disguise. In resolving to serve Orsino she refers to her ability to speak 'in many sorts of music' (I, ii, 58), and this claim is first tested when Orsino sends her to court Olivia on his behalf, assuring her that 'It shall become thee well to act my woes' (I, iv, 25). In her encounter with Olivia, she proves herself versatile in adopting different voices, playing in turn the impertinent youth (Orsino has instructed her to 'Be clamorous and leap all civil bounds', I, iv, 20), the flattering courtier ('Most radiant, exquisite, and unmatchable beauty', I, v, 160), the candid moralist ('What is yours to bestow is not yours to reserve', I, v, 177) and, at the climactic point of the interview, the ardent lover who would, 'If I did love you in my master's flame',

> Halloo your name to the reverberate hills
> And make the babbling gossip of the air
> Cry out 'Olivia'. O, you should not rest
> Between the elements of air and earth,
> But you should pity me!   (I, v, 256–60)

Golding describes Echo as 'a babling Nymph', but Viola is no gossip, although she voices Orsino's suit: 'what I am and what I would are as secret as maidenhead' (I, v, 203).

[1] *Ovid: Metamorphoses. With an English Translation by Frank Justus Miller.* The Loeb Classical Library. 2 vols. (1916), I, 153.

The matching response which Viola's impersonated passion so inadvertently elicits from Olivia suggests another variation on the Echo theme, as fable fades into metaphor. Echo is that reciprocation of feeling so eloquently expressed by Viola as she and Orsino listen to music:

Duke. How dost thou like this tune?
Viola.
　It gives a very echo to the seat
　Where Love is thron'd.
Duke. Thou dost speak masterly.

(II, iv, 19–21)

Orsino's praise of her response also acknowledges that her 'masterly' reply echoes and articulates his own feeling. It is a moment of true emotional consonance, and as Orsino recognises by Viola's answer that his page knows what it is to be in love, the two are drawn closer together. The irony and pathos of Viola's secret plight lend emotional conviction to her repetition of his poetic cliché:

Duke.
　For women are as roses, whose fair flower
　Being once display'd doth fall that very hour.
Viola.
　And so they are; alas, that they are so!
　To die, even when they to perfection grow!

(II, iv, 37–40)

Viola, like Feste, is a realist, and she tries to make Orsino see the truth of his fruitless pursuit of Olivia:

Viola.
　But if she cannot love you, sir?
Duke.
　I cannot so be answer'd.
Viola. Sooth, but you must.

(II, iv, 86–7)

That is the crux of the matter: love that lacks a responding echo is in vain.

Concealment and reciprocation, which I have associated with the Echo motif of the love plot, are concerns that extend into other areas of the play. 'Is it a world to hide virtues in?' asks Sir Toby (I, iii, 123), and certainly Viola's enforced secrecy and self-restraint contrast with the generally unrestrained and uninhibited temper of life in Illyria. Orsino's ready trust in his new servant, 'I have unclasp'd/To thee the book even of my secret soul' (I, iv, 12–13), is paralleled by Sebastian's unfolding to Antonio:

But I perceive in you so excellent a touch of modesty that you will not extort from me what I am willing to keep in; therefore it charges me in manners the rather to express myself.   (II, i, 10–12)

Viola persuades Olivia to unveil and withhold herself no longer, but she must in turn ungraciously refuse Olivia's offer of love (and money), while in a later scene Sebastian accepts Antonio's unsolicited gift of love (and money):

　　My kind Antonio,
　I can no other answer make but thanks,
　And thanks, and ever thanks; and oft good turns
　Are shuffl'd off with such uncurrent pay.

(III, iii, 13–16)

Requiting what is freely given is the essence of civility and proper relationship throughout the play, epitomised in Feste's thanks for the sixpence sent by Sir Andrew: 'I did impeticos thy gratillity' (II, iii, 25).

A less civil form of requital is the revenge upon Malvolio, and the great gulling scene also turns on concealment and exposure. Before he finds Maria's letter, Malvolio unwittingly betrays his secret fantasies to his enemies concealed behind the box-hedge, and then, with tantalising obtuseness, Malvolio discovers, opens and eventually deciphers the letter with its hidden message: 'daylight and champain discovers not more. This is open' (II, v, 141–2). Hilarity is tinged with a more ominous hint when Sir Toby says to Maria at the end of the scene: 'Why, thou hast put him in such a dream that when the image of it leaves him he must run mad' (ll. 173–4).

Malvolio's painful awakening from fantasy

suggests how much happiness seems to depend on deception and illusion in this play. As Sebastian says, when Olivia, a perfect stranger to him, invites him inside her house,

> Or I am mad, or else this is a dream.
> Let fancy still my sense in Lethe steep,
> If it be thus to dream, still let me sleep!
>
> (IV, i, 60–2)

Perhaps this is why the final clarifications, which depend on the recognitions of Viola and Sebastian, are deferred for as long as possible. Viola has no cause to wish for delay in resolving the various predicaments she is in, yet in the final scene, when she has more clues than anyone else to the source of the mounting confusion, she preserves a curious secrecy.

From the beginning of the play Viola has been aware of the possibility of Sebastian's survival: 'Perchance he is not drown'd' (I, ii, 5). The audience knows of Sebastian's presence in Illyria from the opening of act II, when he declares his belief that his sister is drowned. We are again reminded of Viola's tentative hope that her brother lives when she says to Orsino, almost giving herself away,

> I am all the daughters of my father's house,
> And all the brothers too – and yet I know not.
>
> (II, iv, 119–20)

But when Antonio claims his purse from her at his arrest, and actually calls her Sebastian, Viola cautiously speculates on his error without jumping to conclusions:

> He nam'd Sebastian. I my brother know
> Yet living in my glass; even such and so
> In favour was my brother; and he went
> Still in this fashion, colour, ornament,
> For him I imitate. O, if it prove,
> Tempests are kind, and salt waves fresh in love!
>
> (III, iv, 363–8)

In the final scene, as Antonio is brought before Orsino for fighting in the streets, Viola testifies on his behalf, but surely pretends to less understanding than she has:

> He did me kindness, sir; drew on my side;
> But in conclusion put strange speech on me.

I know not what 'twas but distraction.

> (V, i, 60–2)

Antonio's account to Orsino of all that he has done for 'that most ingrateful boy there by your side' (l. 71) merely draws from Viola the blank incomprehension of 'How can this be?' (l. 86). Before Antonio's grievance can be settled, Olivia appears and immediately reproaches Viola with breaking the vow which we know was sworn by Sebastian. Again Viola's response is evasive: 'my lord would speak; my duty hushes me' (l. 101). Her declaration that she loves Orsino 'More, by all mores, than e'er I shall love wife' (l. 130) provokes Olivia to protest that she is beguiled, but still Viola is seemingly as perplexed as the others: 'Who does beguile you? Who does do you wrong?' (l. 134). When Olivia directly claims Viola as 'husband: can he that deny?' (l. 138), the denial, 'No, my lord, not I' (l. 140), might be construed as arch rather than bewildered, and similarly her feigned ignorance is wearing thin when Sir Andrew enters to accuse her of wounding himself and Sir Toby: 'Why do you speak to me? I never hurt you' (l. 179).

All this is comically effective in arousing the audience's anticipation of Sebastian's own climactic entrance, and it teases us in its disingenuous use of the stock device of mistaken identity. But Viola is not obtuse, and she is in a better position than the other characters to realise that Sebastian must be the key to these apparent contradictions. Secrecy and patience are hers to the end, in contrast to Olivia's o'erhasty marriage and her summoning of the priest,

> Here to unfold – though lately we intended
> To keep in darkness what occasion now
> Reveals before 'tis ripe – what thou dost know.
>
> (ll. 146–8)

With Sebastian's eventual entrance, the twins are together on stage for the first time, but for twenty-four lines Viola remains silent, while her brother, not noticing her, greets his bride and then his friend Antonio. At last it is Antonio's astonishment that draws Sebastian's attention to his other self. The moment of recognition that will disperse error and confusion is now at hand, but still tantalisingly delayed, as brother and sister speak the antiphonal exchanges that bring them with unhurried and almost ritual solemnity to the point of mutual identification.

Even at this point, however, Viola's reticence permits only a provisional declaration of herself, drawing back from the embrace that would finally reunite her with her brother:

> *Viola.*
>
> If nothing lets to make us happy both
> But this my masculine usurp'd attire,
> Do not embrace me till each circumstance
> Of place, time, fortune, do cohere and jump
> That I am Viola. (ll. 241–5)

This protracted and deferred reunion can be explained as Viola's distrust of appearances in the uncertain and unstable world of Illyria, where, as Feste says, 'nothing that is so is so' (IV, i, 8). But from the moment of Sebastian's amazed 'Do I stand there?' (l. 218), it is Viola's identity that has to be proved. Moreover, her first reaction to Sebastian's presence as that of a spirit 'come to fright us' (l. 228), while referring to his supposed death, also has something in common with that aura of the uncanny and unearthly associated with the confusion and eventual coming together of the twins in *The Comedy of Errors*. As the Duke of Ephesus exclaims in the recognition scene of that play, 'Which is the natural man/And which the spirit?' (V, i, 332–3). In this early comedy, the identical twins pose a threat to each other's sense of self and separate identity; to find his brother, Antipholus of Syracuse must 'lose myself' (I, ii, 40). In *Twelfth Night*, 'drowned Viola' (recalling the plea of Narcissus to his own image in the water: 'It is a trifle in respect that lettes us of our love', l. 568) will not embrace Sebastian in her 'masculine usurp'd attire': according to several Elizabethan versions of the myth, Narcissus drowned endeavouring to embrace his own reflection.[1] In both plays, however, the true union of two-in-one is achieved in marriage, and the motif of the lost twin embodies that quest for the other self.

[1] T. W. Baldwin, *On the Literary Genetics of Shakespere's Poems & Sonnets* (Urbana, 1950), pp. 18–21.

© D. J. PALMER 1979

'SMILING AT GRIEF': SOME TECHNIQUES OF COMEDY IN 'TWELFTH NIGHT' AND 'COSÌ FAN TUTTE'

ROGER WARREN

In the introduction to the 1966 Folio Society edition of *Twelfth Night*, Peter Hall claims that 'the comedy is rich, *because* there is darkness and disturbance',[1] and his 1958–60 Stratford production with Dorothy Tutin as Viola was outstandingly good because it was so bitter-sweet, fully bringing out the sad, sombre aspects without sacrificing the gaiety and humour: it struck, in short, a balance between extremes of experience. This, it seems to me, is what true comedy always achieves. Its laughter does not exclude the darker sides of life: it is so inclusive because it is aware of the tragic, aware of heartbreak and intensity, but is able to absorb these elements and move beyond them to its reconciliations. These, in their turn, are richer, more complete, more satisfying, *because* the comedy has not evaded or attempted to ignore these darker elements. It is easier to feel this complexity in performance than to describe it; but the technique of another master of comedy, Mozart, especially in *Così fan Tutte*, helps to clarify Shakespeare's achievement in *Twelfth Night*.

Both works present, essentially, a survey of lovers' behaviour – their extravagances, delusions, eventually their discovery of the strength and limitations of their emotions – and they strike a humane balance between witty gaiety and emotional intensity, a balance between a clear recognition of the frailty of human beings and an awareness of their positive qualities. If these protesting lovers are frail, then the subtle power of the poetry in the one work, and of the music in the other, suggests a whole extra dimension. This can be most clearly demonstrated by considering the initial presentation of Orsino in *Twelfth Night* and of Fiordiligi and Dorabella in *Così fan Tutte*.

Much critical commentary has found the presentation of Orsino satirical and that of Fiordiligi and Dorabella parodistic. Undoubtedly these elements are there, but to select *one* element and to make it, as it were, stand for the scene at the expense of the others is surely to throw away the special potential of comedy, which is that it is able to present, not just *one* aspect of a situation, but several. It is because both Shakespeare and Mozart present this multiple view that they seem to me to have more in common with each other than, say, Shakespeare has with Jonson or other comedies of the period, or than Mozart has with *opera buffa*, or even with the operas of Haydn, a composer with whom he has so much in common in other respects. It is a commonplace that Jonson presents not characters but caricatures: his characters certainly are satirised; but if anyone in *Twelfth Night* is satirised, it is not Orsino, but Malvolio, whom more than one critic has likened to Jonson's figures. By the side of Malvolio's extravagances and extremities as a fashionable lover, Orsino's excesses may seem aberrations merely, understandably human, and so curable in a way that Malvolio's are not, because his whole life is based on fantasy. I think this contrast between the two is deliberate. Besides, in the theatre the

[1] p. 3, italics mine. Quotations from *Twelfth Night* are from the New Penguin edition (1968).

sheer *beauty* of Orsino's first scene, like that of the opening duet of Fiordiligi and Dorabella, is unmissable: it is as much a part of the audience's experience of the scene as satire or parody, and probably a greater part; it should therefore be allowed full weight.

Many recent critics, failing to make such allowance, find absurdities in Orsino's opening speech. But is it *so* absurd? It is quite true, of course, that Orsino's elaborate verse establishes a mood of relaxed, self-sufficient revelling in the expression of his situation: the language shifts quickly from one elaborate comparison to the next, rather than suggesting any real involvement with Olivia. The basic situation may be that Orsino is following 'Petrarchan' convention, and to this extent the satirical critics are right. But this is fairly obviously not the whole picture, and while the language suggests this, it also suggests much more than this, and so complicates any simplified definition – like 'Petrarchan'. However conventional Orsino's behaviour, such images as the bank of violets have a freshness and beauty which suggest the important point that Orsino is, at the very least, capable of feeling, and so of development. The language does not *only* indicate limitation or absurdity.

Orsino's hyperbolical comparison of the spirit of love to the sea is not *simply* extravagant. Harold Jenkins remarks that if love is as 'unstable as the sea, it is also as living and capacious'.[1] The image, that is, has a vigorous life as well as extravagance. And so, to an even greater extent, has Orsino's later comparison of himself to Acteon, torn apart by his hounds. This speech perfectly demonstrates the double effect: the presentation of Olivia as a purifying goddess is extravagant, no doubt, and Orsino's use of Acteon at all might be thought 'conventional'; but the *use* to which it is put is not conventional at all: the powerful, immediate image of the 'fell and cruel hounds' helps to make real and immediate the pangs of frustrated desire:

O, when mine eyes did see Olivia first,
Methought she purged the air of pestilence.
That instant was I turned into a hart,
And my desires, like fell and cruel hounds,
E'er since pursue me.   (I, i, 20–4)

From the start, the language makes the effect of the play two-edged: it is satirical in that it draws upon a poetical fashion, but the fashionable is tempered by an immediacy and vigour which suggest that Orsino is a human being capable of strong feeling, not just a caricature.

An exactly equivalent combination of the fashionable and the immediate characterises the first entry of Fiordiligi and Dorabella in *Così fan Tutte*. Admiring the portraits of their perfect lovers, they call upon the God of Love to take revenge upon them if they prove untrue. For this moment of supreme sensuous beauty, Mozart has kept his clarinets in reserve. They are neither given prominence in the overture, nor used at all in the first scene. Then, when the ladies arrive, the clarinets play in octaves with the bassoons to give a gorgeous effect of mellow sweetness; and both pairs of instruments move in the thirds and sixths of the 'style galant' that was as much a fashion of musical idiom in Mozart's day as languishing Petrarchanism was in Shakespeare's. Both dramatists are drawing upon a contemporary fashion in order to suggest excessive idealism, a following of fashions and conventions. But that is not *all* that they are doing. The power of Orsino's imagery, the sensuous beauty of the ladies' accompaniment, has an immediate impact upon us, so that we do not – or should not – write them off. They are people, not puppets. A double response is required: we are asked to smile and sympathise at the same time. The music of Fiordiligi and Dorabella is no less of, *and no more of*, a musical cliché than Orsino's imagery is a poetical one.

What applies to Orsino applies as much to Olivia and to her scenes with Viola. Just as the

[1] *Shakespeare: the Comedies*, ed. Kenneth Muir (1965), p. 78.

violets of Orsino's opening speech are not simply part of the equipment of the Petrarchan lover, so Olivia is more than the self-deluding caricature that some critics have presented. It is perfectly true that there is more than a touch of the affected, the conventional, in Olivia's mourning for her brother, as Feste adroitly brings out; and there is certainly delightful humour in the situation where the Countess throws herself upon her knees before the apparent page-boy, an oncoming wooer. But Shakespeare has surely guarded against excessive or unsympathetic laughter as Olivia falls rapidly in love, by making Olivia *herself* surprised by the suddenness and speed of the process: 'How now? Even so quickly may one catch the plague?' And he has given her a valuable sense of self-mockery when it is she herself, and not Viola, who mocks conventional love-praises and compliments when she says that she will give out 'divers schedules' of her beauty, listing the 'items'.

Also, as Orsino's image of the fell and cruel hounds suggests an emotional impulse more powerful than simple following of conventions, Olivia's language, particularly the imagery, has a solemnity and directness which makes her situation sympathetic as well as humorous:

> Be not afraid, good youth; I will not have you.
> And yet, when wit and youth is come to harvest,
> Your wife is like to reap a proper man.
>
> (III, i, 128–30)

And at the very moment when, *in terms of situation*, she might be thought at her most absurd ('Stay. I prithee, tell me what thou think'st of me') there is a potential explosiveness of emotion, a near-desperation in her utterance:

> Cesario, by the roses of the spring,
> By maidhood, honour, truth and everything,
> I love thee so that, maugre all thy pride,
> Nor wit nor reason can my passion hide.
>
> (III, i, 146–9)

Beneath the mistakings and disguises, the striking images and the direct urgency of the statement communicate an emotional intensity that takes the character far beyond mere confusion of situation. Olivia's emotions have become roused and fired, and what is more she is half-aware of the situation. That is why even the most adroit performances of a satirically-interpreted, feather-brained Olivia only fit some parts of the scenes: they cannot match the potential explosiveness of emotion here.

As Shakespeare makes his characters more complex by means of language, especially imagery, Mozart achieves the same complexity through the orchestral pointing. I mentioned the importance of the clarinets, heralding the ladies' first appearance; Mozart strategically employs clarinets throughout *Così*, and for a revealing reason; for the characteristic sound of the clarinet is not only one of sensuous beauty, but ambiguous, bitter-sweet, a timbre 'as sweet as it is sour, whose line can soothe or pungently stimulate'.[1] This bitter-sweet quality is conveyed most strongly in the Adagio of the Clarinet Concerto, Mozart's penultimate work, in which, as H. C. Robbins Landon puts it, 'an unbearable sadness seems to linger in the music, the more profound...because it smilingly emerges from the serenity of a bright major key'.[2] Even in a purely orchestral work, Mozart can be two-edged. He certainly achieves that effect at the emotional crises of *Così*.

In her first aria, Fiordiligi's statement of her never-failing fidelity, with its enormous vocal range and switch-back vocal leaps, is certainly a parody of *opera seria*, as it were a musical equivalent of the exaggerated hyperboles of Elizabethan love poetry in Orsino's Petrarchan devotion. But in her second aria, *Per pietà*, Mozart uses a wide vocal range for quite a different effect. Now, Fiordiligi's faith has been shaken: she finds that she loves, not just one man, but two at once. Her new passion

[1] Donald Mitchell, *The Mozart Companion* (1956), p. xii.
[2] *Ibid.*, p. 279.

does not mean that she has suddenly stopped loving the absent Guglielmo, and indeed she asks his forgiveness. The sudden low notes are no longer parodistic in effect: they are now an expression of remorse, horror and shame at her infidelity. But the exact nature of her problem is not that she has replaced one lover with another, but that she feels equally strongly for both, and Mozart has to find a way of expressing exactly this. He uses two horns to suggest her divided heart, but he also reinforces her pleas with clarinets again, suggesting by their sweet/sour tone her two-edged emotion, the double pull of the attraction she feels – a passion for a new lover which does not banish a sense of betrayal of the old.

If Fiordiligi's style, and her accompaniment, starts from parody and then transcends it, Viola's 'willow cabin' speech is the perfect example of a passage which starts off from a basis of fashion and convention yet goes far beyond the merely extravagant. Harold Jenkins comments:

This famous willow-cabin speech...is of course...a parody of romantic love.... The willow is the emblem of forsaken love and those songs...are easily recognizable as the traditional love-laments.[1]

Yet, as he goes on to say, 'the parody...is of the kind that does not belittle but transforms its original'. The speech in fact takes on an impassioned, erotic charge which immediately makes Olivia start to listen. Simon Gray has said of it that

it is not a classic of romantic persuasiveness for nothing. If it is ironic in its exaggerations, it is also insidiously enticing in its rhythms...and consequently the comedy in [Viola's] relationship with Olivia is both...intensely erotic and dangerous.[2]

The situation is again two-edged: part of the reason that Olivia starts to listen is that she is susceptible to this kind of language delivered with this power; but an atmosphere of erotic ambiguity is established which dominates all the Olivia/Viola/Orsino scenes. The tone is constantly shifting: no sooner has Viola expressed criticism of Olivia ('I see you what you are, you are too proud') than she has switched, between line one and the next, to the admission 'But if you were the devil, you are fair' (I, v, 239–40). What is at the very least an honest statement of fact of course seems to Olivia a compliment, or at least a sign of interest. Then again, after her wittily critical 'Excellently done – if God did all', and after Olivia has countered it with the unperturbed, equally witty reply ''Tis in grain, sir, 'twill endure wind and weather', Viola's next speech goes beyond a plain statement of fact in its eloquence, and again suggests to Olivia a measure of interest – as indeed it may be, Viola's reaction to a rival of powerful charm: but it's a sympathetic reaction too:

'Tis beauty truly blent, whose red and white
Nature's own sweet and cunning hand laid on.

(I, v, 228–9)

The complexities increase in the central Viola/Orsino scene. Viola uses her disguise to attempt to express what she feels for Orsino in the allegory of her sister: here the phrasing is crucial. She starts off from conventions and completely transforms them, as in the 'willow cabin' speech:

She never told her love,
But let concealment, like a worm i' the bud,
Feed on her damask cheek. (II, iv, 109–11)

The language here gives reality to an otherwise conventional image: the commonplace comparison of ladies' skin to damask roses becomes the startlingly sinister image of the worm eating away at the budding rose; it perfectly expresses the hidden grief eating away at Viola's heart. Then she takes the traditional idea of the pining, melancholy lover and transforms *that*, too:

[1] *Ibid.*, p. 77.
[2] *New Statesman*, 28 August 1969.

> She pined in thought,
> And with a green and yellow melancholy,
> She sat like Patience on a monument,
> Smiling at grief. (II, iv, 111–14)

That last phrase – 'smiling at grief' – sums up so much of the double vision of the play, with smiles and tears inseparable. But Viola earlier on stressed that true devotion lies, not merely in protesting and pining but, however hard it may be, smiling and accepting things, even seeing the humorous side of one's situation as well as the sad side:

> As I am man,
> My state is desperate for my master's love.
> As I am woman – now, alas the day,
> What thriftless sighs shall poor Olivia breathe! (II, ii, 36–9)

That last line is surely another example of that inseparable combination of humour and sadness, that 'smiling at grief'; she is sorry for Olivia, but can see the humour of the situation as well. And though she may be 'desperate' for her master's love, she does not in fact mope or despair, but simply gets on with the task in hand.

We also see Orsino himself develop in response to Viola; as early as their first scene together, he has clearly used a very different kind of approach to her from that used to Olivia; without fuss or affection, he has simply opened his heart to his 'page':

> Thou knowest no less but all. I have unclasped
> To thee the book even of my secret soul. (I, iv, 13–14)

And now, in response to her story, he develops further: by the end of the scene he has completely forgotten about himself, absorbed in Viola's story and, by implication, in Viola: 'But died thy sister of her love, my boy?' The scene now becomes very charged, and Viola's reply is filled with many varied emotional implications:

> I am all the daughters of my father's house,
> And all the brothers too; and yet, I know not. (II, iv, 119–20)

G. K. Hunter points out how

the doubleness of expression involves more than a pattern of wit; it evokes Viola's complex relationship of frustration and fulfilment, which is what the page's role allows to her, at the same time as it reminds us of her brother, and her aloneness in the world. . . . Viola says, 'a woman may die of love', 'I may die of love for you', 'I am alone in the world – but I am not even sure of that', and no doubt other things as well.[1]

Characteristically, Viola then shatters the atmosphere of ambiguous emotional and sexual tension, and sets off to woo Olivia again. The most characteristic technique of comedy seems to me embodied in this scene: it explores the complexities and tensions of human relationships, but keeps emotional intensity this side of explosion point.

The climax of Così fan Tutte, the duet in which Fiordiligi yields to Ferrando, sails much closer to the wind. Fiordiligi only gives in after a tremendous struggle with herself, reflected in the gasping, broken phrases with which she yields. But equally clear from Ferrando's ardent, passionate vocal line with which he finally wins her over is that he is unleashing emotions which show him as susceptible to her as she is to him. The situation has gone quite beyond the sphere of intrigue with which it all began; it is more potentially explosive even than the Twelfth Night scene since it emphasises the frailty, the waywardness and unpredictability of human impulses. This is, I think, the great advantage of the techniques of comedy – they can express areas of emotion too complex and elusive to be accounted for by conventional definitions and formulae.

Harold Jenkins calls Orsino and Olivia characters 'full of devotion to an ideal of love while mistaking the direction in which it should

[1] *John Lyly: the Humanist as Courtier* (1962), p. 366.

be sought';[1] and the emotional confusions of the lovers in *Così* are very similar: the musical treatment enables the apparently simple story of intrigue to suggest human truths and realities. While the motto of the opera may be Alfonso's cynical 'così fan tutte' – a shrugging, dismissive 'all women behave like that' – Alfonso's viewpoint is clearly inadequate to summarise the human experiences explored in the opera. The thin accompaniment of strings with which this man of reason attempts to pigeon-hole human beings with definitions and neat clichés is quite clearly meant, in terms of Mozart's musical structure, to show that Alfonso actually knows less, not more, than the lovers about human experience, as the complexities of the orchestral writing have suggested such experience. He has no idea of the turmoil that goes on inside Ferrando and (especially) Fiordiligi.

Andrew Porter says that the real moral 'is sounded by Mozart in his garlands of thirds' as the ladies beg forgiveness and the men forgive them, Mozart's 'tender benediction on human nature'.[2] It *is* tender, but it is also open-eyed and aware, carefully avoiding any glibness in the reconciliation. Mozart remains absolutely true to the characters and to the comic balance which he has established; for that plea for forgiveness does not sound with unequivocal ease: there is literally a combination, a fusion, of different attitudes. For as the lovers are reconciled, Despina's practical patter about deception and discovery is allowed to intrude upon their ensemble, to provide in fact a perspective on the reconciliation.

Such a perspective, from a more satirical viewpoint, does not invalidate the reconciliation. The orchestral commentary has enabled us to feel with, to sympathise with and understand Fiordiligi and the others. It isn't a question of Alfonso and Despina being right and the others wrong, or vice-versa, but of creating an impression of complexity and reality by balancing one attitude against another. Similarly, the final scene of *Twelfth Night*, with Feste set apart from the others to comment on the harshness of life and even of love, provides a perspective on the happiness achieved by the lovers, on their 'golden time', without invalidating the golden time itself. Rather the contrary: the play's recognition of harsher aspects makes its world seem that much more inclusive. Speaking of another Mozart work, *Die Entführung aus dem Serail*, Sir Thomas Beecham has an admirable phrase to capture the characteristically Mozartean tone of its closing quintet, 'half gay, half sad, like the smile on the face of a departing friend';[3] and it could equally well capture the effect of the finale of *Twelfth Night* or of so characteristic a sweet/sad moment as Viola's image of her sister 'smiling at grief'.

[1] p. 76.
[2] *Financial Times*, 15 July 1968.
[3] *A Mingled Chime*, paperback edn. (1961), p. 225.

© ROGER WARREN 1979

'MY LADY'S A *CATAYAN*, WE ARE POLITICIANS, *MALUOLIOS* A PEG-A-RAMSIE'

GUSTAV UNGERER

I

The last of Shakespeare's romantic comedies contains a good many quibbles and enigmatic passages that up to now have defied explanation. The midnight scene in which Sir Toby Belch, Sir Andrew Aguecheek, and Feste indulge in revelling and carousing, for instance, presents a number of unsolved textual problems. Sir Toby proposes to his boon companions to rouse Malvolio in a catch. They accept and together they intone 'Hold thy peace'. The rioting alarms Maria who hastens to warn the unruly company to put an end to their disorder (II, iii, 74–80):

Maria. What a catterwalling doe you keepe heere? If my Ladie haue not call'd vp her Steward *Maluolio*, and bid him turne you out of doores, neuer trust me.
Toby. My Lady's a *Catayan*, we are politicians, *Maluolios* a Peg-a-ramsie, and *Three merry men be wee.* Am not I consanguinious? Am I not of her blood: tilly vally. Ladie, *There dwelt a man in Babylon, Lady, Lady.*[1]

Sir Toby has invested with a special meaning the terms '*Catayan*', 'politicians', and 'Peg-a-ramsie'. The object of this paper is to question the conventional readings of these terms and to propose new interpretations.

Judging from the editions available to me, the prevailing opinion is that '*Catayan*' is a term of abuse, meaning 'sharper', 'rogue', 'cheat', 'thief', and 'liar'.[2] This reading can be traced back to George Steevens. In his edition of *The Merry Wives* (1766) Steevens suggested that Mr Page, who weighs up the rascally Nym

as a 'Cataian' (II, i, 130), likens Nym to a Cathayan or Chinese 'sharper', a term derived from 'the dexterous thieving of those people'. Robert Nares followed suit in his *Glossary* (1822), and from Nares the derogatory sense of the word found its way into the *OED*. It was as late as 1936 that Y. Z. Chang made a half-hearted attempt to debunk the assumption that Sir Toby, 'though somewhat intoxicated', styled his wealthy niece 'a sharper or crook', but his effort fell short of attracting due attention probably because most of his evidence was based on seventeenth-century foreign sources.[3]

Before looking into what the terms 'Cathay' and 'Cathayan' conveyed to the Elizabethans, we should dispose of a misapprehension about Sir Toby's drunkenness. It is generally believed that Sir Toby has fallen a victim to alcohol and that the excessive consumption of spirits has become a serious danger to his health. It is true that Olivia thinks him an incurable addict, 'in the third degree of drinke' and therefore

---

[1] All the quotations from *Twelfth Night* are made from the New Variorum edition by Horace Howard Furness (New York, 1901, repr. NY, 1964); the other plays by Shakespeare are quoted from the New Cambridge edition.

[2] The New Arden edition (1975) favours the pejorative meaning, and the New Penguin edition (1968) suggests that Sir Toby does not quite know what he is saying. Nicholas Brimble in *Notes on Twelfth Night* (Edinburgh, 1971) comments that it 'was a byword for a cheat' and paraphrases 'Your talk of *My Lady* is just a trick to try and intimidate us'.

[3] Y. Z. Chang, 'Who and What Were the Cathayans?', *Studies in Philology*, 33 (1936), 203–21.

'drown'd' (I, v, 134–5), i.e. dead. Feste, who is for 'all waters' (IV, ii, 65), however, assures Olivia that Sir Toby is drunk only in the second degree. 'He is but mad yet Madona, and the foole shall looke to the madman' (I, v, 136–7). Obviously Feste is not only confident that he can save Sir Toby from his vice, but he also acknowledges that Sir Toby's madness is akin to his own folly.[1]

For Sir Toby alcohol does not seem to be a narcotic but rather a stimulant and a source of his verbal aggressiveness. When he counters Maria's warning of a possible eviction, he is not befogged. It seems idle to maintain, as Furness does, and in his wake Chang and the New Penguin editor, that Sir Toby 'was in that stage of drunkenness when mere sounds connect words having no relationship to each other; he had heard Maria accuse the whole party of "caterwauling", and straightway the sequence was clear to him that if he was a "*cater*wauler", his niece was a "*Cat*aian" '.[2] Sir Toby may well have been sensitive to alliteration, but in this case he does not seem to react to sounds. Mere euphony misses the gyrations of Sir Toby's mischievous mind and his stupendous command of double-entendres.

Sir Toby's dramatic function in the play alone would seem to preclude any misunderstanding about the meaning of 'Catayan'. Nowhere in the play does the knight criticize Olivia in a contemptible way or level his satire against her authority, though we might expect him to do so in a period of licensed frolicking. His dramatic role is limited to deflating Sir Andrew and Malvolio, on the one hand, and to protecting Olivia against the advances of her steward Malvolio, on the other. The role of holding a mirror up to Olivia is Feste's, not Sir Toby's. Olivia does not realize that Sir Toby is concerned about her future. His concern finds expression in the very first words he utters in the play: 'What a plague meanes my Neece to take the death of her brother thus? I am sure care's an enemie to life' (I, iii, 3–5).

Indeed Olivia's vow to mourn her brother's death for seven years does go against her nature. An explanation why Sir Toby calls Olivia a 'Catayan', himself and his fellow rioters 'politicians', and Malvolio a 'Peg-a-ramsie' cannot disregard Olivia's vow of celibacy, Sir Toby's anxiety, and Malvolio's designs.

Another argument that can be adduced against seeing in 'Catayan' a term of abuse is the naval background of the comedy. The play catches the spirit of expansion overseas, native and foreign. For instance it alludes to the achievements of an English cartographer, Edward Wright: Malvolio 'does smile his face into more lynes, then is in the new Mappe, with the augmentation of the Indies' (III, ii, 78–80);[3] to the exploration of the North-West Passage by William Barentz, a Dutchman, in 1596: Sir Andrew is 'now sayld into the North of' Olivia's 'opinion, where' he 'will hang like an ysickle on a Dutchmans beard' (III, ii, 26–8); to the voyages of the English merchant Ralph Fitch: 'he that did the *Tiger* boord' (V, i, 61);[4] to the adventures of Sir Anthony and Robert Shirley in Persia: Fabian does not want to give his 'part of this sport for a pension of thousands to be paid from the Sophy' (II, v, 168–9) and

[1] John W. Draper holds the same view in *The Twelfth Night of Shakespeare's Audience* (Stanford and London, 1950). Toby's system, Draper comments, has been so used to alcohol that his puns and his 'use of non sequitur savours of clever evasion rather than drunken torpor' (p. 30).

[2] Furness, p. 119.

[3] This map was the result of the terrestrial globe (1592) of Emeric Molineux of Lambeth, of its reduction or projection to a plane by Edward Wright, and of the possible advice given by John Davies and Richard Hakluyt. It was ready for the second edition of Hakluyt's *Principal Navigations* (1598–1600). See George Bruner Parks, *Richard Hakluyt and the English Voyages*, second edition (New York, 1961), p. 186.

[4] Marion A. Taylor, 'He That Did the Tiger Board', *Shakespeare Quarterly*, 15 (1964), 110–13. The identification has not found unanimous acceptance probably because the Tiger was a current name for a vessel.

Cesario is alleged to have been 'Fencer to the Sophy' (III, iv, 278).[1] Sir Toby pays Maria the compliment of being his 'Mettle of India' (II, v, 16).

These pioneers, seamen and adventurers help to bring one of the major themes of the play into focus: the voyage to Illyria of the sea-borne twins destined to ennoble the power of love.[2] The shipwrecked Viola, disguised as Cesario, is to cure Duke Orsino of inconstancy and the 'Catayan' Lady of the illusions of spinsterhood. Moreover two of the historic figures afford a link with Cathay. Both Barentz and Fitch endeavoured to find a passage to India and Cathay, Barentz through the North-West and Fitch through the Mediterranean and the Persian Gulf. The explorations of Barentz were recorded by Gerrit de Veer in a book entered in the Stationers' Register, in 1598,[3] under the title *A true description of Three voyages by sea...by north Norwaye, Muscouya, and Tartaria to the kyngdome of Cattay and Chyna.*[4] The travels of Ralph Fitch by sea and land to the Far East were undertaken to open up new trade in the interest of the common-wealth and were promoted by the English government.[5] In February 1583, Fitch and his three companions set sail on their way to Tripoli and on to Aleppo.[6] They took with them two letters of Queen Elizabeth, one addressed to the Great Mogul Jalaluddin Akbar, King of Cambay, and the other to the emperor of China. The second letter never reached its destination, for none of the Englishmen got as far as Peking. Fitch was alone when, on 8 February 1587, he landed at the Portuguese port of Malacca. It is not known why he did not undertake the last stage of his journey to Macao, the Portuguese town, established by arrangement with the Chinese authorities on a peninsula in the estuary of the Canton river. Fitch was no sooner back in London, in April 1591, than the governors of the Levant Company availed themselves of the experiences of the first Englishman to reach the gateway

to China. An 'ample relation of his wonderful travailes' was submitted for examination to Lord Burghley, and Richard Hakluyt published what appears to be a shortened account of Fitch's relation in the *Principal Navigations*.

A further argument against the old reading of '*Catayan*' as a derogatory term can be taken from the history of the Cathay venture and its relations with the Middle Temple. Richard Hakluyt the elder, lawyer and geographer, and known as promoter of his cousin Richard Hakluyt the younger, the historian of the English maritime achievements, had studied law at the Middle Temple and remained a Templarian in good standing until his death in 1591.[7] It was in his chambers in Middle Temple Lane that he initiated his younger cousin into the secrets of cosmography and it was there, too, that the younger Hakluyt 'resolved', as he tells the reader in the preface to the *Principal Navigations* (1598), that he 'would by God's

[1] John W. Draper, 'Shakespeare and Abbas the Great', *Philological Quarterly*, 30 (1951), 419–25. Draper makes the point that Shakespeare took a risk in alluding to the fortunes of the Shirley brothers whose unofficial mission to the Persian court was sponsored by the disgraced Earl of Essex. Sir Anthony, who married Elizabeth Vernon, the Earl's cousin, was forbidden to return to England in 1600. He is believed to have met William Kempe, Shakespeare's fellow actor, in Venice about 1601 (*DNB*).

[2] For the theme of the 'sea-associated virtues' see Jon S. Lawry, '*Twelfth Night* and "Salt Waves Fresh in Love"', *Shakespeare Studies*, 6 (1970), 89–108.

[3] The first known edition of de Veer's book is dated 1609.

[4] Most contemporary reports made no distinction between Cathay and China. Cathay was simply another name for China. Thus Batman (see below) stated that it 'is also called *Sinarum regio*'.

[5] The following information has been taken from Michael Edwardes, *Ralph Fitch, Elizabethan in the Indies* (1972), particularly chapter viii: 'Gateway to Cathay'.

[6] The first Witch in *Macbeth* promises to thwart the voyage of the 'master o'th' *Tiger*' who has gone 'to Aleppo' (I, iii, 8). Is this an allusion to Ralph Fitch, too?

[7] G. B. Parks, p. 27.

assistance prosecute that knowledge and kind of literature, the doors whereof (after a sort) were so happily opened before' him. The scene of initiation, then, took place in the precincts of the Middle Temple, about 1568, in the immediate neighbourhood of Middle Temple Hall where the first known perfomance of *Twelfth Night* was staged on 2 February 1602.[1]

The importance of Richard Hakluyt the elder lies in the fact that as a Templarian he became a consultant of the Cathay Company. His advice was needed for the third voyage (1578) Sir Martin Frobisher planned in search of a North-West Passage to Cathay. Thus he drew up the 'Notes framed by M. Richard Hakluyt of the Middle Temple Esquire, given to certaine Gentlemen that went with M. Frobisher in his Northwest discoverye, for their directions', which his cousin was to edit in the second volume of the *Principal Navigations* (1599).[2] The 'directions' propounded a programme for a self-supporting colony.[3]

The Cathay venture, which was launched with a view to finding a short cut to Asia, was an enterprise drawing on the experience and resources of the whole nation. It rallied the efforts of the country's best forces: statesmen, courtiers, merchants, navigators, cosmographers, and the Queen herself.[4] A well-known lawyer of one of the Inns-of-Court was asked for advice, and his merits as an engineer of English exploration and colonization in America were kept alive and duly recorded in the annals of overseas expansion. Bearing the historical context in mind, would '*Catayan*' as a term of abuse really have made sense to a select English audience in 1602?

As it is Olivia who is styled a '*Catayan*', it is legitimate to dwell in some length on the part played by Elizabethan women as shareholders and members of the Cathay Company. Among the women who invested money in the first voyage (1576) figure the Queen (£500), the Countess of Pembroke, Lady Anne Talbot and Lady Mary Sidney, the mother of the Countess

of Pembroke. The same women, with the exception of Mary Sidney, are listed as investors of the second voyage (1577), the Queen committing herself with £1,000. A new investor was the Countess of Warwick. The Countess of Sussex was the only female subscriber to the third voyage (1578). Many were in arrears with their payments as late as 1579, among them one Mrs Anne Kyndersley.[5] As the three voyages proved a failure, the women got nothing in return save the honour of perpetuating their names on the maps of the expeditions. Thus one island was called after the Countess of Sussex[6] and another after the Countess of Warwick.[7]

The Cathay venture turned out to be a failure, because its original object to find a North-West Passage to Asia was abandoned in favour of prospecting for gold.[8] The women, too, had their share in the gold fever that seized all the company members as well as the

[1] There are a good many reasons to consider *Twelfth Night* as a play written for the entertainment of the Inns-of-Court students. The subject deserves special treatment. See below, part III.

[2] Edition made for the Hakluyt Society (Glasgow, 1904), VII, 244–50.

[3] G. B. Parks, pp. 50–1.

[4] For the Queen's interest in everything that concerned the voyages of discovery, the projects of colonization, the people and products of the new-discovered territories, see A. L. Rowse, *The Elizabethans and America* (1959), pp. 16 ff.

[5] The documents of the Cathay Company have been preserved and have been edited by Richard Collinson, *The Three Voyages of Martin Frobisher, In Search of a Passage to Cathaia and India by the North-West, A.D. 1576–78*, Hakluyt Society Publication (1867, repr. New York, 1963), pp. 107–9, 164, 321, 322, 346, 347.

[6] Report of the third voyage written by Thomas Ellis and edited by Hakluyt in the *Principal Navigations*, III, (1600), Hakluyt Society Publication (Glasgow, 1904), VII, 239.

[7] George Beste, *A True Discourse of the Late Discoverie for Finding a Passage to Cathaya, By the North-Weast* (1578); ed. Hakluyt, *Principal Navigations*, III (1600, repr. 1904), vol. VII; Collinson, pp. 137, 213.

[8] *Ibid.*, p. 19.

IA   *Twelfth Night*, New York, 1904. Viola Allen and
     James Young as Viola and Sebastian

B   *As You Like It*, Stratford-upon-Avon and New York,
     1885. Mary Anderson as Rosalind

C   *As You Like It*, produced by Oscar Asche at His
     Majesty's Theatre, London, 1907. Lily Brayton as
     Rosalind and Henry Ainley as Orlando

der Stadthoff.

IIA   Engraving by Peter Willer showing the south-western corner of the Main City in Gdansk, with a public theatre on the right

B   An enlarged detail of IIA showing the Fencing School in Gdansk, i.e., the actual theatre

III *The Taming of the Shrew*, Royal Shakespeare Theatre, 1978. Directed by Michael Bogdanov, designed by Chris Dyer. The final scene, with Paola Dionisotti as Kate (standing, left) and Jonathan Pryce as Petruchio (seated, right)

IV *The Tempest*, Royal Shakespeare Theatre, 1978. Directed by Clifford Williams, designed by Ralph Koltai. Michael Hordern as Prospero, Ian Charleson as Ariel

V *The Tempest*, Royal Shakespeare Theatre, 1978. David Suchet as Caliban

VI *The Merchant of Venice*, The Other Place, Stratford, 1978. Directed by John Barton, designed by Christopher Morley. Patrick Stewart as Shylock

VII *Measure for Measure*, Royal Shakespeare Theatre, 1978. Directed by Barry Kyle, designed by Christopher Morley. Michael Pennington as the Duke and Paola Dionisotti as Isabella at the Moated Grange

VIII *Love's Labour's Lost*, Royal Shakespeare Theatre, 1978. Directed by John Barton, designed by Ralph Koltai. From left to right: Michael Pennington as Berowne, Paul Whitworth as Dumaine, Richard Griffiths as the King, Carmen du Sautoy as the Princess, Jane Lapotaire as Rosaline, Sheridan Fitzgerald as Maria, Avril Carson as Katherine

jewellers and bankers of the City of London. On the second expedition (1577), 'good store of ore was found' on the Countess of Warwick's Island 'which in the washing helde golde plainly to be seen'.[1] The ore was shipped home and examined by a number of native and foreign experts, after the wife of one of the adventurers had melted some of the ore by accident.[2] When the London experts confirmed that the ore held gold, furnaces were built for processing the metal and shareholders did not hesitate to finance the third expedition (1578). Frobisher was commissioned to fetch two thousand tons of the promising ore and to keep a hundred men in *Terra Incognita* for the space of ten months.[3] The Countess of Pembroke was charged £28. 15s. for the transport expenses of the ore. The Countess of Sussex contributed £10 to the building of the furnaces at Dartford and £67. 10s. to the outward and £57. 10s. to the homeward journey; the Countess of Warwick £57. 10s. to the transport of the ore; Lady Anne Talbot £5 each to the building of the furnaces and the outward voyage; and Mrs Anne Kyndersley £86. 5s. to the transport costs of the ore.[4]

At least three of the Elizabethan ladies who had sponsored the Cathay Company were still alive in 1602 when *Twelfth Night* was performed at the Middle Temple: The Queen, Anne Countess of Warwick, third wife of Ambrose Dudley, and Mary Countess of Pembroke, third wife of Henry Herbert. The Countess of Pembroke was the celebrated Mary Sidney, remembered as the sister of Sir Philip Sidney and mother of William Herbert, third Earl of Pembroke and possible addressee of Shakespeare's sonnets. In the light of this illustrious sponsorship of a national enterprise, it seems reasonable to disqualify the old reading of 'Catayan' as a derogatory term and in its stead to venture the first version of a new tentative reading.

As Sir Toby is worried about the future of Olivia – and incidentally about his own future

should Malvolio marry her – it is quite reasonable to argue that he is voicing his concern by reminding Maria that their Lady is a 'Catayan' ordained to run the affairs of her court and not made to withdraw into a cloister and let Malvolio usurp her position.

This reading of 'Catayan' as a complimentary term is further supported by the descriptions of Cathay and its inhabitants which were available to the Elizabethans.[5] What may be regarded as the standard account of Cathay was the entry made by Thomas Cooper in his famous dictionary, the *Thesaurus linguae romanae et britannicae ... Accessit dictionarium historicum et poeticum propria vocabula virorum, mulierum ... urbium, montium . . .* (1565, 1573). Cooper's account was borrowed verbatim by Stephan Batman in his manual *Batman vppon Bartholome, His Booke de proprietatibus rerum ... Taken out of the most approved Authors* (1582).[6] The account in the 1584 edition of the *Thesaurus* reads as follows:

[1] *Ibid.*, p. 137.

[2] *Ibid.*, pp. 75–6, 171–206.

[3] George Beste, *A True Discourse*, ed. Collinson, p. 209.

[4] *Ibid.*, p. 348.

[5] The following contemporary evidence has been neglected by Chang in his paper on the Cathayans (above p. 85, n. 3). He was mistaken in asserting that, besides the accounts given by Polo, Mandeville, and Johannes de Plano Carpini, it was hard for the Elizabethans to tell who and what the Cathayans were (pp. 204–5).

[6] The account in Batman is headed 'Of Cathay', lib. 15, chap. 86, fol. 232 v. A facsimile reprint has been edited by Jürgen Schäfer in the series Anglistica and Americana 161 (Hildesheim, 1976). Batman added the following sentence to Cooper's text:
'As concerning further discourse of *Cathai*, or *Cataia*, read the booke tituled, A discourse of a discouery for a new passage to *Cataia*, written by Sir Humphrey Gilbert, Knight. *Anno.* 1576. wherein thou shalt finde many learned and commendable notes'. Gilbert's *Discourse*, written as early as 1566, was published in 1576 to back Frobisher's enterprise in public and was reissued by Hakluyt in the *Principal Navigations*, III (1600) (repr. Glasgow, 1904), VII, 158–90.

Cathay, A great region in the East parte of the worlde, extending to the Easte Occean sea: on the south to the ouer India: and is also called *Sinarum regio*. It is diuided into nine realmes: all be vnder the great Cham. This countrey is wonderfull rich in golde and silke, abounding in grayne, wines, and al other things necessarie for mans sustenance. The people for the more parte, honour Christe as God, but they are not baptized. They are curteous and reasonable, & very cunning artificers.

This account of Cathay diffused by two English clergymen – both Batman and Cooper were Anglican dignitaries – reflects the intellectual endeavour made by the Europeans to integrate other civilizations, the countries and peoples of the New World, into the traditional framework of their thought. The criteria of classification were supplied by both the Christian and the classical inheritance of humanism. Non-Europeans were judged, as J. H. Elliott has demonstrated, according to their 'religious affiliation' and their 'degree of civility'.[1] Thus the Cathayans were presented to the Elizabethans as belonging to the highest category of heathens or barbarians. In religious terms, they were true men, potential Christians, capable of conversion and susceptible to divine grace; in social and cultural terms, they had achieved an advanced degree of government, administration, philosophy, architecture and craftsmanship.

In addition to the textbook definition of Cathay as spread by Batman and Cooper, the historians of the discoveries supplied ample material with which the Elizabethans could make up their own minds about the humanity and nature of Cathayan civilization.[2] The chroniclers were in agreement upon the high standard of cultural achievements. The opening lines of Thamara's chapter on Cathay are worth quoting in this respect:

Beyond the riuer Ganges towards the East, is the land and part of India, that standeth on the other side of the same riuer, and therfore is called the other side of

Ganges. This is the greatest, the best, & the rychest

[1] J. H. Elliott, *The Old World and the New 1492–1650* (Cambridge, 1972), pp. 39ff.

[2] (a) The most important chronicle happens to have been ignored. It is Francisco Thamara's *A Discouerie of the countries of Tartaria, Scithia, & Cataya, by the North-East: With the maners, fashions, and orders which are vsed in those countries* (1580). It was translated by John Frampton from Thamara's treatise *De las costumbres de todas las gentes del mundo de Juan Boemo* (Antwerp, 1556). The only extant copy is in Lambeth Palace Library, shelf-mark 1576. 5.6. Frampton's translation is dedicated to Sir Rowland Hayward and to master George Barne, elderman of the City of London, the two being governors of the worshipful company of the Merchant Adventurers, as well as to 'the assistants and generalities of all the said worshipful fellowship'. The dedication is signed from London, 15 July 1580. John Dee, mathematician and cosmographer, an ardent exponent of Elizabethan expansion overseas, supported the Cathay venture. He wrote, most likely inspired by Frampton's translation, what seems to be a ruttier entitled 'Navigationis ad Cathayam per septentrionalia Cythiae et Tartariae littera delineatio Hydrographica' (1580). See *DNB*.

(b) Bernardino de Escalante, *A discourse of the nauigation which the Portugales doe make to the Realmes and Prouinces of the East partes of the worlde, and of the knowledge that growes by them of the great thinges, which are in the Dominions of China* (1579) was translated again by John Frampton from the *Discurso de la navegación que los Portugueses hazen a los reinos y provincias de Oriente y de la noticia que se tiene de las grandezas del Reino de la China* (Seville, 1577); facs. repr. in The English Experience, 593 (Amsterdam, 1973). Ralegh may have owned a copy of the Spanish original (Walter Oakeshott, 'Sir Walter Ralegh's Library', *The Library*, fifth series, 23 (1968), 315) and John Dee kept a copy of the English version in his library at Mortlake (Ungerer, 'The Printing of Spanish Books in Elizabethan England', *The Library*, fifth series, 20 (1965), 221). Escalante did not distinguish between Cathay and China. Frampton's translation was dedicated to Sir Edward Dyer who had helped to raise funds for Frobisher's first Cathay voyage (1576) in court circles.

(c) Juan González de Mendoza, *The Historie of the great and mightie kingdome of China, and the situation thereof: Togither with the great riches, huge Cities, politike gouernement, and rare inuentions in the same* (1588) was translated by Robert Parke from the *Historia de las cosas más notables...del gran Reyno de la China* (Valencia, 1585), facs. repr. in The English

countrey of all India, which is towards the East partes, where the Sunne riseth, and is now called *Cataya*, and it appertaineth to the great *Cham*, who is lorde of *Tartaria*. In old time it was saide, that it belonged to *Prester Iohn*. The countrey of *Cataya* is greate, and hath in it many kingdomes, and the buyldings like to *Europe*. There is in it great policie of al things. It is a riche countrey of Gold, spices, and precious stones, whereof there is great aboundance. The people are of great reason, and liue in better order than we do. There are among them Philosophers, who are much esteemed: The seconde sort are husbandmen: The third Shepheards: The fourth, handicraftes men: The fifth, men of warre to defende the countrey: The sixt, the presidents and gouernours, that gouerne the country: The seuenth, are the counsellors to the king. And these are cheefest, and haue charge ouer all the rest, and will not consent that any one should leane[1] his owne office or science, and take an other, and therefore they are better gouerned then we are. The great *Cham* deuyded this prouince into nine kingdomes, in the which are two thousande great cities, or thereabouts...The principall citie in *Cataya* is *Cambula*, contayning xxiiii myles in compasse (pp. 21v–23r).

Also Escalante attests in his treatise that the Chinese were 'wise in their gouernement of theyr common weales' (p. 41v). González de Mendoza, who is heavily indebted to Escalante, voices the same opinion in practically the same terms (pp. 26, 92, 93).

Now Shakespeare's *Twelfth Night* raises the very same issues of rule and misrule, order and disorder, good and bad government of a noble household. Sir Toby, by way of irony, seems to take the opposite attitude of most historians in assessing the merits of peoples overseas: for him the Cathayans are superior to the Illyrians as regards rule and order of the commonwealth. He facetiously admits that he is a caterwauling politician given to wenching and roistering,[2] whereas Olivia as a 'Catayan' lives 'in better order than' he does. Apparently he intimates that a 'barbarian' has reversed the orthodox scale of values. A female 'Catayan', in Sir Toby's topsy-turvy perspective, would seem

to assume a higher degree of civility than a revelling Illyrian who has degenerated into disorder and misrule and therefore lapsed into a more primitive form of life.[3] Sir Toby's degree of degeneration is brought home to the so-called Cathayan lady when she surprises the knight embroiled in a fight with Sebastian. In her wrath she accuses Sir Toby of being a savage who has forfeited the right to live among civilized people (IV, i, 48–50):

> Will it be euer thus? Vngracious wretch,
> Fit for the Mountaines, and the barbarous Caues,
> Where manners nere were preach'd: out of my
>   sight.

As already stated, the Cathayans were also portrayed as idolaters with a capacity for conversion to the Christian faith. Thamara reported on this aspect (pp. 22r–22v):

The *Catayans* are idolaters...There are among them many religious houses of Idolaters, which leade a straight life. They haue among them there Uniuersities and studies of learning, and the scripture of the old and newe Testament, wherof it commeth to passe

Experience 522 (Amsterdam, 1973). The translation was dedicated to the navigator Thomas Cavendish on 1 January 1589 (n.s.). John Wolfe had printed a surreptitious Italian edition in 1587 (*STC* 12004). Lord Burghley owned a Spanish edition (Ungerer, p. 226) and Ralegh a Spanish or Italian one (Oakeshott, p. 300). For Parke Cathay was part of China (see his Dedication).

[1] Read 'leaue'.

[2] See below, part II.

[3] The pattern of degeneration also applies to Sir Toby's fellow reveller, Sir Andrew Aguecheek, who 'thinkes sometimes' he has 'no more wit then a Christian, or an ordinary man ha's' (I, iii, 81–2). Critics have focused their attention on the pattern of regeneration to the exclusion of the equally important complementary pattern of degeneration. Malvolio, who declines the sportive invitation to partake in a regenerative Christmas game, lapses into the category of the barbarians. Maria comments on his fall as follows: 'yond gull *Maluolio* is turned Heathen, a verie Renegatho; for there is no christian that meanes to be saued by beleeuing rightly, can euer beleeue such impossible passages of grossenesse' (III, ii, 69–72).

that they honor God, and beleeue in the euerlasting life, but are not baptized. They loue the Christians and giue almes, with a good will...There are many Christians in *Cataya*.

Escalante in his *Discourse* harped upon the same subject. He was struck by the fact that the Chinese, despite their political maturity, were 'so false of vnderstanding, and so barbarous and blinde in the worshipping of their false vaine idolatrie. For they haue no manner of knowledge of the true God' (p. 41v). Escalante's opinion was also shared by González de Mendoza who called the Chinese 'Idolaters and blind people' (p. 26). However, the redeeming quality of the Cathayans and, by implication, of the Chinese, was their docility, their readiness to conversion and willingness to reform. As Escalante put it in chapter 16 of his history:

Of some religious men called *Jesuites*, it hath beene vnderstoode that they beganne too preache the Gospell too these people, but by reason that it is not permitted vntoo strangers too stay manie dayes in this Countrey, they were compelled too returne foorthwith without yelding that fruite whiche they desired, notwithstanding they found them very apt to be taught and willing to learne, and easie to be reformed of theyr false Idolatrie, and with al humilitie they receiue it, and acknowledged the correction of their filthines. (p. 47).

González de Mendoza followed suit in almost identical words (pp. 31–2):

They are people very ducible and apt to bee taught, and easie to bee turned from their idolatrie, super-stition & false gods: the which they haue in smal veneration as aforesaid. With great humility they do receiue & approoue corrections of their weaknes, & do know the vauntage that is betwixt the gospell and their rites and vanities, and do receiue the same with a verie good will.

The alleged virtue of the Cathayans and Chinese 'to be reformed of theyr false Idolatrie' and to 'receiue & approoue correction of their weaknes' corresponds to the comedy's pattern

of correction and regeneration. All the Illyrians, Feste excepted, can be understood in terms of their moral strength to recognize their weaknesses, relinquish their vanities and, freed from the weight or 'slough' (II, v, 140) of their old imperfections, attain to a higher degree of humanity. Some have enough strength, others have not. Those who have, benefit from the blessings of regeneration; those who have not, are caught up in the process of degeneration. Olivia recants after having gone through the humiliating ritual of being catechized and proved 'a foole' by the Fool (I, v, 55ff). In the light of the Cathayans' potential virtue of recovery and reform it is hardly possible to accept the view that the play's '*Catayan*' lady is a 'thief' or a 'cheat'. The play's pattern of regeneration and its historical background turn the scales in favour of a new reading. Sir Toby, to be sure, does not criticize Olivia, but expresses his wish that she will be awakened to her social responsibilities as head and ruler of her small court.

The new reading may be objected to on the ground that Shakespeare used 'Catayan' as a term of abuse in *The Merry Wives*. But we have it only on the authority of George Steevens, an authority that can no longer be trusted, that it is an abusive term. Indeed an examination of the relevant passages discloses that Steevens also misread the term in *The Merry Wives*. Corporal Nym is trying to hoodwink George Page into believing that Sir John Falstaff has set his eye on Mistress Page. In an aside Master Page reasons with himself (II, i, 130–1):

I will not believe such a Cataian, though the priest o'th'town commended him for a true man.

Steevens overlooked that for Master Page 'a true man' is the opposite of 'Cataian'. In canon law, 'a true man' was not only an 'honest' fellow but also a human being capable of receiving and practising the true faith. This means that 'a true man' is synonymous with 'a Christian'.[1] It follows that as 'a true man' is opposed to 'Cataian', the latter term is bound to have the same meaning as in *Twelfth Night*: a barbarian with a capacity for conversion and reception of divine grace. Hence Master Page's aside means that even though the priest commended Nym as a Christian, doing penance for his former wicked life, he would still take him for an unregenerate barbarian or heathen. Master Page therefore would rather trust his wife than Nym.

What comes as a surprise is that Steevens should have ignored contemporary evidence. He overlooked that Shakespeare's application of the term was not unique but quite in line with the acceptation of 'Cathay' and 'Cathayan', both noun and adjective, in the works of contemporary dramatists.[2] In Thomas Dekker's *The Honest Whore of Babylon* (c. 1604), the rascally Matheo tells his wife Bellafront that he is going to reform Lodovico Sforza, a knight, and turn him into a Cathayan. If his work of reform is to succeed, Matheo intimates ironically, Lodovico need not always be sober:[3]

Bellafront. Is this the suite the Knight bestowed vpon you?
Matheo.   This is the suite, and I need not shame to weare it, for better men then I would be glad to haue suites bestowed on them. It's a generous fellow, – but-pox on him – we whose Pericranions are the very Limbecks and Stillitories of good wit, and flie hie, must driue liquor out of stale gaping Oysters. Shallow Knight, poore Squire *Tinacheo*: Ile make a wild Cataine of forty such: hang him, he's an Asse, he's alwaies sober.[4]

In Sir William Davenant's most popular tragicomedy *Love and Honor* (acted 1634), Prince Leonell of Parma, the refined captive destined to marry the heroine of the play, is addressed as 'bold Catian' (II, i) by the jealous Colonel Vasco, a figure of the underplot.[5]

The regenerative qualities of Cathay's climate and products were noted in a number of plays. Maria in Fletcher's *Woman's Prize*

(1611) hopes that the climate of Cathay will change Petruchio from a monster into a man.[6] One of the ingredients of Maquerelle's restorative posset-recipe in *The Malcontent* (1603), written by John Marston at the Middle Temple shortly after the performance of *Twelfth Night*, is 'amber of Cataia'.[7] Bilbo and Tormiella in Dekker's *Match mee in London* (1611) are selling King Philip and the bawd Dildoman a pair of gloves whose 'muske' scent 'is perfect *Cathayne*'.[8]

The fascination of travel and the thrill of exoticism conjured by the name of Cathay is working in Fletcher and Massinger's *The Spanish Curate* (1622)[9] and Richard Brome's

[1] Pope Paul III proclaimed in the bull *Sublimis Deus*, issued on 9 June 1537, that the 'Indians and other peoples' were 'true men' capable of receiving the Christian faith. See Lewis Hanke, 'Pope Paul III and the American Indians', *Harvard Theological Review*, 30 (1937), 65–102; Elliott, p. 43.

[2] For the following instances I am indebted to Edward H. Sugden's *A Topographical Dictionary to the Works of Shakespeare and His Fellow Dramatists* (Manchester, 1925, repr. Hildesheim and New York, 1969).

[3] Sugden comments that 'Cathayan' means 'clever sharper', but Chang (p. 217) rejects this reading. The usual antithesis to 'true man' is 'thief', see *Measure for Measure*, IV, ii, 42–6; *Much Ado*, III, iii, 49; *Love's Labour's Lost*, IV, iii, 185; *1 Henry IV*, II, i, 91–3; II, ii, 91; *Cymbeline*, II, iii, 71–2; *Venus*, 724; in *Richard II* it is opposed to 'traitor', v, iii, 73; in *1 Henry IV* to 'villain', I, ii, 107, and to 'rogue', II, ii, 22; in *3 Henry VI* to 'robbers', I, iv, 64. This pattern does not justify equating 'Catian' with 'thief' and 'rogue'.

[4] *The Honest Whore*, part II, ed. Fredson Bowers in *The Dramatic Works*, II (1964), 181 (IV, i, 14ff).

[5] The conventional reading is 'sharper', but this does not make sense as Chang has pointed out (p. 217). *Love and Honour* is the only play not listed by Sugden.

[6] *The Works of Francis Beaumont and John Fletcher*, ed. A. R. Waller, VIII (Cambridge, 1910), 76 (IV, iv).

[7] Edited George K. Hunter in The Revels Plays series (1975), II, iv, 14.

[8] *The Dramatic Works*, ed. Fredson Bowers, III (1966), 284 (II, i, 157–60).

[9] *The Works of Francis Beaumont and John Fletcher*, ed. A. R. Waller, II (Cambridge, 1906), 79, 96 (II, i and III, ii).

The Antipodes (1638).[1] In Lodovic Barry's *Ram Alley: Or Merrie Tricks* (1608), written as it seems for the entertainment of the Inns-of-Court students, the profligate William Small-Shanks forces the thrasonical Captain Face to perform a lamentable exhibition of his professional skill on the table of a tavern, denouncing him as 'an outlandish beast,.../ Lately brought from the land of Cataia'.[2]

In conclusion it may be stated that the standard reading of *Catayan* does not take account of the play's historical background, ignores the reports of Cathay known to the Elizabethans and overlooks the use of the term in contemporary drama. What weighs heavily against the standard reading is the fact that, first, it does not suit the pattern of regeneration and, second, it disregards Sir Toby's dramatic function of protecting Olivia from Malvolio's attempt to usurp her position and thus to upset the natural order.[3] The new reading considers both the historical context and the thematic patterns of the play and does justice to Sir Toby's self-appointed function as a 'politician' of preserving the hierarchical order.

II

When Sir Toby pretends to take the part of a 'politician' to protect Olivia, he must be thinking in terms of Elizabethan social structure. He seems to view Olivia's court as a commonwealth which unites men of different degrees and vocations for their well-being and which guarantees the hierarchy of degree. The overthrow of this social hierarchy appears imminent to Sir Toby because its head is liable to shy from her responsibilities.[4] Olivia is clearly struggling to face the new facts caused by the death of both father and brother and aggravated by the untimely advances of three suitors, a noble (Orsino), a time-server (Malvolio), and a gull (Sir Andrew). This explains why Olivia, without the 'protection' of father and brother, has 'abiur'd the sight/ of

And company of men' (I, ii, 38–43) and vowed to dedicate her life to the service of the Church (I, i, 31–7).

Olivia's threat of seclusion must be seen as a symptom of her struggle to come to terms with the new realities. Admittedly, she has not yet neglected her social duties, she is still the uncontested ruler of her universe; yet her inner turmoil manifests itself in the governance of her commonwealth. The misrule of Sir Toby can be interpreted as a reflection of her own spiritual and emotional upheaval. As soon as Olivia masters her crisis, order returns to her household and Sir Toby's disorder comes to an end.[5] When the noble Cathayan 'savage' has found her real identity through trial and error, the degenerate Illyrian 'politician' is ripe for domestication.

As a member in Olivia's state, Sir Toby

[1] Edited Ann Haaker in the Regents Renaissance Drama series (1967), I, iii, 17.

[2] Robert Dodsley, *A Select Collection of Old English Plays*, fourth edn (1744, repr. N.Y., 1964), X, 348–50 (IV, i). The identification of a human being with an exotic animal from Cathay was an international stock-in-trade. Thus John Oberndorff gave vent to his contempt of quacks and credulous fashion-conscious patients in *The Anatomyes of the True Physition, and Counterfeit Monte-banke* (1602): 'For they delighting altogether in Noueltie, and loathing their old accustomed Physitions, though neuer so learned, if there come any straunge Beast, or Monster, out of Barbary, or Iacke an Apes from *Cataia*, they doo gaze vpon him with Admiration' (p. 13).

[3] D. J. Palmer comments that 'Malvolio's influence over his young mistress at the beginning of the play is a kind of usurpation, an upsetting of the natural order' ('Art and Nature in *Twelfth Night*' in *Twelfth Night: A Casebook*, ed. D. J. Palmer (1972), p. 206).

[4] John W. Draper in *The Twelfth Night of Shakespeare's Audience* (Stanford and London, 1950) describes Olivia's court as an Elizabethan household in transition. He holds that the play brings Sir Toby and Malvolio into focus and that its main theme is about social security attained through marriage.

[5] Faith Wotton Cartwright has examined the hierarchical order with particular attention to Olivia in her paper '*Twelfth Night*, An Elizabethan Commonwealth-in-Miniature', *Revista de la Universidad de Costa Rica*. 39 (1974), 59–70.

assumes the questionable duty of thwarting the marriage plans of the ambitious steward. It is obvious that in this context the traditional reading of 'we are politicians' as a derogatory term meaning 'Machiavellian intriguers' does not quite make sense. If Sir Andrew can be trusted, he would have objected to being identified as 'a political intriguer or conspirator',[1] for he hates 'policie' and 'had as liefe be a Brownist, as a Politician' (III, ii, 32–3). But Sir Andrew, who relishes listening to love songs and who, with Sir Toby, indulges in singing catches and spicy ballads, does not object to being identified as a politician who is 'catterwalling' at midnight.

The selfsame expression occurs in *Titus Andronicus*. Aaron upbraids the lamenting nurse by saying: 'what a caterwauling dost thou keep!' (IV, ii, 57). According to the entry in *OED*, Aaron is finding fault with the nurse for making a 'hideous, discordant howling noise'. So is Maria in *Twelfth Night*, yet she takes the love-sick revellers to task not only for the offending noise but also for behaving like cats in heat at rutting time. Tudor drama affords enough evidence to bear out this reading. John John in Heywood's *A Merry Play* (c. 1520) makes up his mind to 'order' his wife 'for all her brawling,/That she shall repent to go a catterwauling'.[2] The swaggering Codrus in *Misogonus* (c. 1570) boasts that he never 'left' his 'book till' he 'came to the hour a catawauling',[3] and the dissolute young Chartley insults the wise-woman of Hogsdon by branding her whores as 'Shee-Catterwaullers'.[4]

In the light of these precedents it seems safe to consider Sir Toby as 'a caterwauling politician' or would-be procurer who is pandering to the debaucheries of the impotent Sir Andrew and exalting him as a rival of Malvolio. He is giving himself the airs, on behalf of Olivia's commonwealth, of a Machiavellian lover. Needless to say, he is wrong in assuming that his dubious services rendered to the body politic will prove a blessing.

The comparison of a commonwealth to a body whose functioning required members of different degrees was a commonplace which easily lent itself to satirical treatment. The dramatists readily turned to analogies between the bodies politic and human, foremost among them Dekker, Marston, and Shakespeare.[5] Thus one of the points made in Marston's *Malcontent* (1603) is that a successful politician must be something of a bawd. Malevole manipulates political fortunes in the same way as the bawd Maquerelle manipulates maidenheads.[6] Edward Sharpham has worked out the analogy in *Cupids Whirligig* (1606), a play that seems to have been written for the entertainment of the Inns-of-Court.[7] Wages, servant to the jealous Sir Timothy Troublesome, who suspects his wife to be a punk, holds his master up to ridicule: 'Why ye cannot keepe more Gentleman like company: besides, your puncke: is like your pollitition, for they both consume themselues, for the common people. And your punck of the two, is the better member, for she like a candell to light others's, burns hir selfe.'[8]

---

[1] This is W. A. Wright's paraphrase of 'we are politicians'; quoted from Furness.

[2] *A Merry Play Between Johan Johan, the husband, Tyb, his wife, and Sir John, the priest,* ed. John S. Farmer, *The Dramatic Writings of John Heywood* (1905, repr. Guildford, 1966), p. 70.

[3] *Misogonus*, ed. John S. Farmer (1906, repr. Guildford, 1966), in *Six Anonymous Plays, Second Series*, p. 232, IV, i. Note the pun on hour/whore.

[4] Thomas Heywood, *The Wise-woman of Hogsdon*, ed. R. H. Shepherd, in *The Dramatic Works*, V (1874, repr. N.Y., 1964), 295 (II, i). The play was acted about 1604.

[5] David George Hale, *The Body Politic: A Political Metaphor in Renaissance English Literature* (The Hague, 1971); Philip Styles, 'The Commonwealth', *Shakespeare Survey*, 17 (1964), pp. 103–19.

[6] Philip J. Finkelpearl, *John Marston of the Middle Temple: An Elizabethan Dramatist in His Social Setting* (Cambridge, Mass., 1969), p. 190.

[7] Sharpham was admitted a member of the Middle Temple on 9 October 1594 (*DNB*).

[8] Sharpham, *Cupids Whirligig. As it hath bene sundry times Acted by the Children of the Kings Majesties*

The analogy is paramount in the blacklisted *The Whores Rhetorick* (1683), a textbook for professionals, in which an old bawd introduces her daughter Dorothea into the stratagems of prostitution. A whore 'moves in a higher sphere', the old bawd is lecturing to her daughter, 'than the rest of Women; and her actions ought to seem publick-spirited; though statesmanlike, she should contrive them all to meet in the centre of her own particular advantage'.[1] Such an organic analogy lies behind Sir Toby's self-appointment as a politician of mercenary love.

Sir Toby's immorality must be set in a wider context. Illyria is not a model state peopled by ideal members. Many of its inhabitants live on the lower fringes of society; and if those Illyrians do not actually appear on the stage, their mention nevertheless reminds us of the harsh realities. Profane love exists along with romantic love, vice with virtue, pestilence with health, corruption with chastity, dishonesty with honesty. Other low-life characters, apart from the pandering knight, are Mistress Mall[2] and Feste's leman. These two Illyrian prostitutes complement the pattern of degeneration, providing a contrast to Olivia's awakening love.[3] There are also a good many allusions and references to women of disreputable character.[4]

III

As a politician of love, Sir Toby devotes much of his boundless energy to unmasking Malvolio as a 'Peg-a-ramsie'. The precise meaning of this derogatory term has remained something of a mystery. Critics have seen in it an allusion to two Elizabethan dance tunes, one called 'Little Pegge of Ramsie' and the other 'Peg-a-Ramsey', but they have been hesitant to relate it to the two ballads with the same titles. However, the text of these two ballads offers the most plausible line of approach to this problem. If these ballads can be related to the

structure, the imagery, and the themes of the play, they may come to be regarded as holding the key to the meaning of 'Peg-a-ramsie'.

The better known of the two ballads is headed 'To the tune of Pegge of Ramsey' and records 'A merry Iest of John Tomson and Jakaman his wife,/Whose jealousie was justly

Reuels (1607), sig. E 2 v. Mind that 'to burn' can mean to be infected with a venereal disease.

[1] Philo-Puttanus, *The Whores Rhetorick, Calculated to the Meridian of London; And conformed to the Rules of Art. In two Dialogues* (1683), p. 42. For a discussion of this work see David Foxon, *Libertine Literature in England 1600–1745* (New York, 1965), p. 10.

[2] Steevens has identified Mistress Mall with Moll Cutpurse (alias Mary Frith), Leslie Hotson with Mary Fitton (see *The First Night of Twelfth Night* (1954, repr. 1961)), and Dover Wilson has suggested 'a certain Mall Newberry' (Cambridge 1930, repr., 1971, p. 114). Mary Newborough was indeed a notorious prostitute who caused a scandal in 1599/1600, as appears from the unpublished records of Bridewell Royal Hospital. That she fits in with the pattern of degeneration and regeneration (repentance) and the imagery of 'curtain', 'veil' and 'picture' will be shown in another paper.

[3] Juliet Dusinberre in *Shakespeare and the Nature of Women* (1975), p. 63, has pointed out that Olivia disclaims the art of a whore when she is ready to 'draw the Curtain, and shew...the picture' (I, v, 230ff), but has overlooked that Sir Toby uses the same terms when referring to 'mistris *Mals*' curtained 'picture' taking 'dust' (I, iii, 117–19).

The fact that Feste's 'Lemon' has 'a white hand' (II, iii, 28, 30) suggests that this 'Lady', whom he has obviously met at the 'Mermidons' (II, iii, 31), is a whore who has made public penance with a white sheet and white wand and has relapsed into her former way of life. She thus exemplifies Feste's definition of humanity: 'any thing that's mended, is but patch'd: vertu that transgresses, is but patch't with sinne, and sin that amends, is but patch't with vertue' (I, v, 45–7).

[4] Such ambiguous words which imply both a positive and negative meaning are: 'huswife' (I, iii, 98), 'Mutton' (I, iii, 114), '*Penthisilea*' (II, iii, 171), 'Spinsters' and 'Knitters' (II, iv, 52), 'free maides' (II, iv, 53), 'Iezabel' (II, v, 42), 'sister' (III, i, 18), 'wise woman' (III, iv, 106), 'Cockatrices' (III, iv, 193), 'firago' (III, IV 274), 'Neece' (II, v, 71; IV, ii, 16); and so is 'Madona', Feste's jocular address to Olivia used nine times in I. v.

the cause of all their strife'.[1] Deploring the by-gone days of a bachelor's freedom, Tomson complains of his wife wearing 'the yellow hose'. He presents his spouse as the watchful spoil-sport woman. To believe James O. Wood, Jakaman may have served as a possible model of Malvolio as 'a kill-joy spying on' Sir Toby's 'merriment'.[2] In this case, Malvolio's identification as a Jakaman or 'a Peg-a-ramsie' would have been made to expose to ridicule the steward's ungovernable jealousy rather than his narrow-minded prohibitionism.

The identification of a man with a woman inevitably raises the question of sexual and moral perversion.[3] There is no doubt that Sir Toby and his companions are bent on convicting Malvolio of lechery, one of the seven deadly sins leading the offender straight to hell. Thus the identification of Malvolio with a woman is pursued by Sir Andrew Aguecheek. He denounces Malvolio as a 'Iezabel' (II, v, 42) when his rival wallows in the prospect of becoming 'Count *Maluolio*' (II, v, 36) and 'sitting in' his 'state', 'Hauing beene three moneths married to' Olivia (II, v, 45–6). It is irrelevant to the present argument that Sir Andrew betrays his ignorance of the Bible when identifying Malvolio with Ahab's shameful wife; what matters is that he emulates Sir Toby in identifying Malvolio with a woman who happens to be a 'paragon' of wickedness and whose name has become synonymous with 'whore'.[4]

Tudor writers used to list Jezebel in their inventories of immoral women together with Eve and Herodias. So did Edward Gosynhill in the *Schole house of women* (c. 1542), Abraham Vele in *The deceyte of women, to the instruction and ensample of all men* (1560), and Thomas Bentley in *The Monument of Matrones: conteining seuen seuerall Lamps of Virginitie* (1582).[5] Bentley provided a converse 'Mirrour for all sorts of wicked women, as in a cleere glasse with Athalia, Jezabell, Herodias and such like, perfectlie to see their shameless pride,

cdrueltie, idolatrie, and contempt of religion.'[6] Another instance may be adduced from Simon Forman who made the ironical entry in his case book that England was free from 'any lascivious and adulterous Jezebel that, with her painted face and whoredom, enticeth men to come in to her to fulfil the lusts of the flesh, provoking the Lord to wrath and indignation'.[7]

Malvolio's identification as a 'Peg-a-ramsie' and a 'Iezabel' is obviously meant to expose the steward's jealous nature and lascivious disposition. In terms of their trade, Sir Toby, the procurer, and Sir Andrew, the impotent would-be womanizer, look upon Malvolio as a dangerous whoremaster, one of their own kind, who must be overreached. Malvolio, in point of fact, is portrayed as one of their 'element' (III, iv, 127) whatever he says to the contrary. Thus he unwittingly betrays his knowledge of a bawdy ballad. When standing cross-gartered before Olivia, he declaims: 'If it please the eye

---

[1] James O. Wood, '*Maluolios* a Peg-a-Ramsie', *English Language Notes*, 5 (1967), 11–15. The ballad was entered in the Stationers' Register in 1586, but the only extant copy is of later date.

[2] *Ibid.*, p. 14.

[3] A 'peggy' has come to denote a man of feminine habits, a molly. The first entry in *OED* dates from 1869. – In the main plot, this theme corresponds to Viola's disguise as a man. But in Viola's case the metamorphosis serves to bring out her virtuous character. Her love ennobles, whereas Malvolio's profanes. She is the picture of selfless love, he of ignoble self-love. The two offer diametrically opposed examples of repressed desire.

[4] John S. Farmer and W. E. Henley, *Slang and Its Analogues Past and Present. A Dictionary, Historical and Comparative*, VII (1904), under 'tart', p. 78; Hermann Kostial, 'Englisches erotisches und skatologisches Idiotikon', *Anthropophyteia, Jahrbücher für folkloristische Erhebungen und Forschungen zur Entwicklungsgeschichte der gesellschaftlichen Moral*, 6 (1909), 19–23.

[5] See Louis B. Wright, *Middle-Class Culture in Elizabethan England* (Chapel Hill, 1935), pp. 468, 470–1, 475, respectively.

[6] L. B. Wright p. 475.

[7] A. L. Rowse, *Simon Forman: Sex and Society in Shakespeare's Age* (1974), p. 46.

of one, it is with me as the very true Sonnet is: Please one, and please all' (III, iv, 25–6). This is an allusion to the popular ballad 'intytuled: The Crowe sits vpon the Wall,/Please one and please all'.[1] Olivia, according to the text of the ballad, is no more than one among many women Malvolio dreams of conquering and gratifying. Here follows the inventory of those women with whom Malvolio, if we take his statement literally, would go whoring:[2]

> Please one and please all,
> Be they great be they small,
> Be they little be they lowe,...
> Be they white be they black,...
> Whether they spin silke or thred,...
> Be they sluttish be they gay,...
> Drinke they Ale or drinke they beere,...
> Be they sower be they sweete,
> Be they shrewish be they meeke,...
> Be they halt be they lame,...
> Be she Lady be she dame,...
> Be they wanton be they wilde,
> Be they gentle be they milde,...
> Be she coy be she proud,...
> Is she huswife is she none,...
> Be she ritch be she poore,
> Is she honest is she whore,...

Malvolio's amorous incontinence is one of the 'elements' that most Illyrian males share. His seemingly voracious appetite for women is parallelled by Orsino's illusion that his love 'is all as hungry as the Sea,/And can digest as much' (II, iv, 106–7). Orsino, too, finds solace in music and songs. He is particularly fond of listening again to an 'Anticke song' (II, iv, 5) which dallies 'with the innocence of loue' (II, iv, 55). But the singer does not do the Duke the favour of repeating the song which 'The Spinsters and the Knitters in the Sun,/And the free maides that weaue their thred with bones' (II, iv, 52–3) used to sing. Does he refuse to comply with the wish of the languishing Orsino because it is a woman's ditty or because Feste deems it to be too indecent and licentious?[3]

A maid experienced in wanton dalliance was 'Bonny Peggy Ramsey' whose trade was praised in the ballad of the same name. Most critics have come to consider this ballad as quite irrelevant.[4] A few, however, are inclined to believe that Sir Toby is alluding to its heroine and dismissing Malvolio as 'handsome, coarse, and immoral'.[5] Though the date of this ballad is still questionable, the very ribaldry of the subject recommends 'Bonny Peggy Ramsey' for being the particular wanton 'piece of Eues flesh' in the Illyrian demimonde whom Sir Toby is likely to have in mind. It will suffice to quote the first three stanzas to demonstrate the qualities of this 'Peg-a-ramsie'.[6]

> Bonny *Peggy Ramsey* that any Man may see,
> And bonny was her Face, with a fair freckel'd Eye,
> Neat is her Body made, and she hath good Skill,
> And square is her Wethergig made like a Mill:
> With a hey trolodel, hey trolodel, hey trolodel
>   lill,
> Bonny Peggy Ramsey she gives weel her Mill.

[1] E. P. Kuhl sees in Malvolio's allusion to the ballad the author's intention to satirize the steward as a sexually incontinent Puritan ('Malvolio's "Please One, and Please All" ', *PMLA*, 47(1932), 903–4).

[2] Quoted from the broadsheet in the B.L., shelf-mark Huth 50 (31). The ballad was reprinted by Joseph Lilly in *A Collection of Seventy-Nine Ballads* (1867), pp. 255–9.

[3] Spinsters used to voice their dissatisfaction 'with the innocence of love' and chaste life in coarse terms. I intend to deal with the age-long tradition of spinning and singing in a separate paper. In any case, 'Spinsters', 'Knitters', and 'free maides' were current Elizabethan terms for unmarried women of easy virtue.

[4] Wood's intentions are restricted to revealing Malvolio as a jealous spoilsport (above p. 97, n. 1). For the New Arden editor the ballad seems to be of later date.

[5] Yale edition (1954); from Wood (p. 14). The ballad is recorded in the unpublished edition of *Twelfth Night* by Robert K. Turner and Maurice Charney. See note in the New Arden edition, p. 48.

[6] Thomas Durfey, *Wit and Mirth, or Pills to Purge Melancholy* (1719), v, 139–40. Durfey began the publication of his *Pills* as early as 1684. John Steven Farmer reprinted the ballad in *Merry Songs and Ballads*, II (1897), 151–2, from Durfey's edition of 1707, III, 219.

Peggy to the Mill is gone to grind a Bowl of
   Mault,
The Mill it wanted Water, and was not that a
   fault;
Up she pull'd her Petticoats and piss'd into the
   Dam,
For six Days and seven Nights she made the Mill
   to gang;

Some call her *Peggy*, and some call her *Jean*,
But some calls her Midsummer, but they are all
   mista'en;
For *Peggy* is a bonny Lass, and grinds well her
   Mill,
For she will be Occupied when others they lay
   still.

Some of the coarse metaphors of the ballad are
quite in line with the sexual imagery of *Twelfth
Night*. Thus the female body as a quarry for
anatomical imagery has supplied, on the one
hand, 'weathergig'[1] and, on the other, 'CUT'
(II, v, 86ff), 'cherrie-pit' (III, iv, 119),[2] and
'Sinke-a-pace' (I, iii, 122).[3] These sexual
metaphors, in the comedy, are not offensive
because they are subordinated to the dramatic
function of language and to the delineation of
character. Thus Malvolio's inadvertent, though
indecent, allusion to Olivia's vulva is worked
out by means of book and letter imagery,[4]
which derives from the religious rituals of
early civilizations.[5] The subtle piece of
unconscious self-exposure reads as follows:[6]

Malvolio. By my life this is my Ladies hand: these bee
   her very *C's*, her *U's*, and her *T's*, and thus makes
   shee her great *P's*. It is in contempt of question her
   hand.
Andrew. Her *C's*, her *U's*, and her *T's*: why that?

Malvolio's lechery has already come to the
fore in an earlier passage. His sexual ardour has
roused him to anticipate the pleasures of carnal
knowledge in 'a day bedde, where' he has 'left
Oliuia sleeping' (II, v, 49–50), pleasures he
thinks he is entitled to because his 'Fortunes'

[1] The gig or top, spinning and simultaneously
sleeping at full speed, was an old phallic symbol which
can be traced back to Greek comedy. See Jeffrey
Henderson, *The Maculate Muse: Obscene Language in
Attic Comedy* (New Haven and London, 1975), pp.
124, 170. Francis Grose in the *Classical Dictionary of
the Vulgar Tongue* (1785, repr. Menston, Scolar Press,
1968), lists under 'Gigg' the meaning of 'a woman's
privities'. There is also an association between
'weathergig' and the play's 'whirligigge of time' (v, i,
395), a dramatic symbol of mythic and philosophical
scope which deserves separate treatment.

[2] Sir Toby insinuates that Malvolio is playing 'at
cherry-pit with sathan', the prize being 'hell', i.e., in
Elizabethan slang, the pudendum of a prostitute. The
metaphorical use of 'cherry-pit' as pudendum muliebre
has inspired Herrick's small poem entitled 'Cherry-
pit':

> Julia and I did lately sit
> Playing for sport, at Cherry-pit:
> She threw; I cast, and having thrown,
> I got the Pit, and she the Stone.

Robert Herrick, *Hesperides* (1648) in *The Poetical
Works of Robert Herrick*, ed. L. C. Martin (Oxford,
1956), p. 19. This instance is listed in Farmer's
dictionary of *Slang*, v (1902), 217, under 'pit'.
Herrick's inspiration was not original, as can be
gathered from an identical poem in *Facetiae...Wits
Recreation* (1640), (repr. London, 1817), II, 449. The
first line reads: 'Nicholas and Nell did lately sit'. The
innuendo apparently was a commonplace.

[3] Sir Toby is punning on 'making water' while
dancing a 'cinquepace' and quibbling on 'pissing in a
sink or sewer'. Moreover he seems to crack a joke on
copulation. Compare the effects of wine as envisaged
by Shorthand, one of the attendants of the usurer
Quomodo in Middleton's *Michaelmas Term* (1607):
'This Rhenish wine is like the scouring stick to a gun,
it makes the barrel clear; it has an excellent virtue, it
keeps all the sinks in man and woman's body sweet in
June and July; and, to say truth, if the ditches were not
cast once a-year, and drabs once a-month, there would
be no abiding i'th'city' (Middleton, *The Works*, ed.
A. H. Bullen, vol. 1 (New York, 1885), III, i, 218ff).

[4] The book and letter imagery of the play, together
with the pen and ink imagery, as well as the letter
riddles, deserve special treatment.

[5] It may suffice to refer to the seminal study of
Ernst Robert Curtius, *Europäische Literatur und
Lateinisches Mittelalter* (Berne, 1954), ch. 16.

[6] According to Gershon Legman, *The Horn Book:
Studies in Erotic Folklore and Bibliography* (New York,
1964;), pp. 105, 256, Malvolio's blunder was first

have 'cast' him on Sir Toby's 'Neece' (II, v, 70–1).[1]

Malvolio's unwitting self-revelation as a lecher is also connected with the sea and water imagery of the play. The sea is a metaphor of destruction and renewal which serves to unfold the theme of degeneration and regeneration. All the inhabitants of Illyria, whether natives or stranded visitors, irrespective of their degree and origin, are under the spell of either the destructive or the regenerative powers of the sea. The importance of the sea and water symbolism has duly been recognized,[2] yet one aspect of the symbolism, relevant both to the main and to the sub-plot, has been overlooked. The sea and water symbolism is associated not only with regeneration and birth but, by implication, also with fertility and procreation. The play's symbols of fertility are, at one level, rain and dew, at the other, urine, all three standing for the male principle of generation.[3]

In Feste's ribald song,[4] serving as a coda to the whole play, heaven's sperms descend in the shape of rain to fertilize the face of the earth; in Orsino's love poetry, as delivered by Viola, the same concept is cast in such suggestive terms that they leave the pea-brained Sir Andrew flabbergasted (III, i, 86ff):

Viola. Most excellent accomplish'd Lady, the heauens raine Odours on you.
Andrew. That youth's a rare Courtier, raine odours, wel.
Viola. My matter hath no voice Lady, but to your owne most pregnant and vouchsafed eare.
Andrew. Odours, pregnant, and vouchsafed: Ile get 'em all three already.

'Odours', here synonymous with 'word', 'voice', 'breath', and 'wind', is a symbol of the male principle of divine generation current both in pagan and Christian mythology.[5] The striking turn in Orsino's poetry is the fusion of the pagan and Christian myth of the descending god. In classical mythology, the myth was exemplified by Jove's metamorphosis into a

shower of rain or gold to impregnate Danae detained in a tower by her father. The myth had become a stock joke already in Greek and Roman literature and remained such in Elizabethan poetry and drama. Poets and dramatists levelled their satiric guns at the divine adulterer and seducer, transmuting and degrading the golden rain or shower into the coarse spermal symbol of piss. Thus in *The Second Part of the Return From Parnassus*, acted by Cambridge students in St John's

recognized by G. B. Harrison, the editor of the Penguin Shakespeare (1937). It is now taken for what it is. See Helge Kökeritz, *Shakespeare's Pronunciation* (New Haven, 1953), p. 133; Herbert A. Ellis, *Shakespeare's Lusty Punning in Love's Labour's Lost* (The Hague, 1973), Appendix II; E. A. M. Colman, *The Dramatic Use of Bawdy in Shakespeare* (1974), pp. 85, 190.

[1] For the lewd implications of 'cast' see 'to cast, love, favour, a fancy unto' (*OED*, 1. 7. b). – There is good reason to believe that 'niece' like 'sister', 'cousin', and 'aunt', in Elizabethan parlance, meant 'a daughter of the game', 'a concubine', 'a bawd'. See also Feste's enigmatic reference to 'a Neece of King Gorbodacke' (IV, ii, 16).

[2] L. G. Salingar, 'The Design of *Twelfth Night*', *Shakespeare Quarterly*, 9 (1958), 117–39; D. J. Palmer, 'Art and Nature in *Twelfth Night*', *Critical Quarterly*, 9 (1967), 201–12, repr. in *Twelfth Night: A Casebook*, ed. D. J. Palmer (1972), pp. 204–21; Jon S. Lawry, '*Twelfth Night* and "Salt Waves Fresh in Love"', *Shakespeare Studies*, 6 (1970), 89–108; Richard Henze, '*Twelfth Night*: Free Disposition of the Sea of Love', *The Sewanee Review*, 83 (1975), 267–83.

[3] Sperm symbols in literature are of very long standing, as can be gathered from Gaston Vorberg's *Glossarium eroticum* (Hanau, 1965). Vorberg lists the following instances gleaned from classical authors: aqua venerea, imber, pluvia, sanguis, ros, sudor venereus, pix, urina.

[4] Eric Partridge in *Shakespeare's Bawdy* (1968), revised and enlarged edition, observes that the refrain in Feste's song 'may bear a sexual connotation' (p. 171).

[5] Ernest Jones, 'Die Empfängnis der Jungfrau Maria durch das Ohr: ein Beitrag zu der Beziehung zwischen Kunst und Religion', *Jahrbuch für psychoanalytische Forschungen*, 6 (1914), 135–206, part. pp. 140ff; Adolf Joseph Storfer, *Marias jungfräuliche Mutterschaft. Ein völkerpsychologisches Fragment über Sexualsymbolik* (Berlin, 1914), p. 86.

College probably during the Christmas festivities of 1601/2, Furor hurls the following volley of words at Sir Raderick:[1]

> The great proiector of the Thunderbolts,
> He that is wont to pisse whole clouds of raine
> Into the earthes vast gaping vrinall,
> Which that one ey'd subsizer of the skie,
> *Don Phoebus*, empties by caliditie:
> He and his Townesmen *Planets* bring to thee
> Most fatty lumpes of earths faelicitye.

Sir Raderick, ill-disposed to scholars, affects indifference and is made to blunder out some sort of indecency against the Queen like Malvolio against Olivia. Sir Raderick's 'Why, will this fellowes English breake the Queenes peace? I will not seeme to regard him' is reminiscent of Malvolio's mistaken recognition of Olivia's 'great *P's*'.[2] Another instance occurs in William Percy's play *The Faery Pastorall or Forrest of Elues* (1603). Hylas, a fairy elve, asks Sir David, the schoolmaster of the fairy children, for some information and is overheard by Christophel, a keeper:

> *Hylas.* What is Jupiter's pisse of?
> *David.* Of Balme I suppose him to be.
> *Christ.* Would I had of it for the Kybes.[3]
> *David.* Tis the dewe of the welkin.
> *Hylas.* Why, I pray you, drinking Nectar,
>   voydeth he but such thin geare then?
> *David. Quod supra nos nihil ad nos.*[4]

Urine as a symbol of procreation and the Elizabethan stock satire upon Jove's emission of semen in the form of piss promise to throw new light on the meaning of Sir Toby's to 'make water but in a Sinke-a-pace' (I, iii, 122), on Fabian's mocking advice to 'Carry' Malvolio's 'water to th' wise woman' (III, iv, 106), on Feste's statement that he is 'for all waters' (IV, ii, 65),[5] and on Sir Toby's identification of Malvolio as a 'Peg-a-ramsie'. Sir Toby's remark, seen in the perspective of the play's water symbolism, has to be taken for a mock encouragement of the impotent Sir Andrew to have sexual intercourse with a woman (rather than with a man).[6] Fabian's advice to take Malvolio's urine to a female

[1] James Blair Leishman (ed.), *The Three Parnassus Plays* (1949), lines 1521ff, pp. 317–18.

[2] This pun can be explained only in a much wider context, taking account of the multiple ramifications of associative imagery in Elizabethan literature, Shakespeare's works included. The imagery which is drawn from fruit, clothes, human anatomy, water, love, etc., clusters round the following terms: cod/ peascod / codling / codpiece / codpiss / piece / peace / P's / pistol / Cod's life / God's life.

[3] 'Kibe' is a 'chapped or ulcerated chilblain' (*OED*).

[4] The play was edited for the Roxburghe Club (1824), p. 168. The punctuation is mine.

[5] This is certainly a hyperbole; if not, Feste intimates that he is not afraid and does not disapprove of contaminated or diseased water as does Malvolio of 'standing water' (I, v, 158–9). As Malvolio is showering his contempt on the supposed youth Cesario for scenting a potential rival, though he has reached a stage only 'betweene boy and man' (I, v, 159), all editions at my disposal are unanimous in commenting that 'in standing water' means 'at the turn of the tide'. Yet W. Roy Mackenzie has demonstrated long ago that Malvolio's contemptuous expression is synonymous with 'standing pond' and 'standing pool', i.e. with stagnant water lacking the alternate motion of ebb and flow and therefore gathering scum on the surface ('Standing Water', *MLN*, 41 (1926), 283–93). Mackenzie has missed the association between Malvolio's comparison of Cesario with a green and immature 'pescod, or a Codling when tis almost an Apple' (I, v, 157–8) and the green colour of scummy and corrupt water. The water imagery of the play, therefore, prompts another reading: Malvolio expresses the secret wish that Cesario may never reach full sexual maturity, that he may remain for ever 'a boy' and rot in the scum of 'standing water'! A flagrant self-revelation of the steward blinded by jealousy and self-love. See also Jacqueline E. M. Latham,' "Standing Water" in *The Tempest* and Joseph Hall's "Characters",' *NQ*, 21 (1974), 136. In Cheryl Bair Lents's bibliography of *Twelfth Night* published in the *Bulletin of Bibliography and Magazine Notes*, Westwood, 31 (1974), 152–64, 180, Mackenzie's article is dated 1927.

[6] It is practically impossible to fathom the depth of Sir Toby's wanton witticism. It goes without saying that this passage allows various readings.

quack – such as the wise woman of Hogsdon, mother Nottingham or mother Bombye, notorious stage uroscopists and, not to be forgotten, procuresses[1] – seems to betray the mischievous intention of having a dabbler diagnose Malvolio's madness (self-love) or cast his lechery (abundance of semen) as well as the plan to procure 'medical' authority for the exorcism and purification of Malvolio's vices.

Malvolio's seeming sensitiveness to Olivia's 'copious' discharge of urine – her 'great *P's*' – can be understood best in terms of the inveterate popular view that has held urine to be the magical carrier of the vital power. It is also this selfsame view which accounts for the public admiration of the supernatural quality of Bonny Peggy Ramsey's water as being strong enough to generate the power required to run the mill for a week. It seems therefore justifiable to speculate that the loose heroine of this crude ballad, who fits so neatly in the water symbolism of the play, may well have inspired Sir Toby's identification of Malvolio with 'a Peg-a-ramsie'. The so-called crudities or obscenities are no longer a reason for disregarding this ballad.

Sir Toby's relegation of Malvolio to the characters of Illyrian low-life is borne out by the name of Ramsey. Place names in the comedy are mostly dubious and serve to underline the theme of degeneration and corruption. Thus Sir Toby teases Sir Andrew to set down in his challenge to Cesario 'as many Lyes, as will lye in thy sheete of paper, although the sheete were bigge enough for the bedde of *Ware* in England' (III, ii, 45–8). Sir Toby is punning on 'lye', 'sheete' and 'bedde of *Ware*' and suggesting the pleasures of dubious lovemaking in the sheets of the huge four-poster which adorned an inn of the town of Ware in Hertfordshire.[2] – The shipwrecked Sebastian and Antonio lodge 'In the South Suburbes at the Elephant' (III, iii, 44) in whose neighbourhood Antonio's eye may 'light vpon some toy'

[1] Thomas Heywood, *The Wise-woman of Hogsdon* (acted *c.* 1604), in *The Dramatic Works* (1874, repr. New York, 1964), V, 292, 306, 310. There is a long list of such irreverent matrons on p. 292. For their trade see Herbert Silvette, *The Doctor on the Stage: Medicine and Medical Men in 17th-Century England* (Knoxville, 1967), pp. 20–1.

It is worth noting that wise women were the butt of the Inns-of-Court students. Thus during the famous Middle Temple revels mounted for the Christmas season of 1597/98 one of the thirty charges brought to the attention of the Chief Justice under the rule of the Prince d'Amour was proclaimed as follows: '15. If any man seek his Mistresses Favor by promising Mountaines, uttering of great and mighty speeches, thundering out words of Conjuration, raising any unlawful spirit, or using the aide of the wise woman of Seacole-lane, or of the Bank-side, or by any artificial mean, other than by the naked Truth, he shall be punished as a Sorcerer' (Benjamin Rudyerd, *Le Prince d'Amour or the Prince of Love* (1660), p. 63). Heywood in his play (see above) has identified as 'Mother Philipps' the wise woman of 'the Banke-side, for the weaknesse of the backe', i.e. specialized in curing impotence (p. 292). Mind the innuendo in 'raising any unlawful spirit', i.e. erecting the penis.

There are many hard passages in *Twelfth Night* that savour of students' jokes, and the temptation is great to regard them as belonging to the staple of sexual, legal, and literary jokes that were current among the Inns-of-Court students, particularly the students of the Middle Temple (see Manningham's *Diary*). Would John Manningham, for instance, on watching the comedy have put down the following elusive quibble to Feste's Rabelaisian turn of mind, i.e. to his debunking of authorities, as is generally assumed, or would he rather have recognized in it an allusion to Thomas Norton's tragedy *Gorboduc* which was acted in the Inner Temple Hall in 1561? Feste, disguised as Sir Topas, addresses Sir Toby: '*Bonos dies sir Toby*: for as the old hermit of *Prage* that neuer saw pen and inke, very wittily sayd to a Neece of King *Gorbodacke*, that that is, is...' (IV, ii, 15–18). The modern editor of *The Diary of John Manningham* (Hanover, 1976), Robert Parker Sorlien, has identified Manningham as a kinsman of Thomas Norton (p. 314). The passage is loaded with sexual innuendoes: pen and ink imagery (see above) and the metaphorical use of names, such as 'niece', 'sister', 'cousin', in the sense of 'prostitute' (see above).

[2] The bed of Ware is now in the Victoria and Albert Museum. Jokes about the enormous size of this bed are quite frequent in Elizabethan drama. In the present case, Shakespeare has drawn on his own work

(III, iii, 49).[1] The London stews, many of which were the property of Philip Henslowe, the theatrical manager,[2] were situated on Bankside. The inn called the Oliphant or Elephant was in Southwark, too, i.e. in the suburbs of the City of London.[3] Another dubious tavern mentioned in the play is 'the Mermidons' (II, iii, 31). Feste pretends facetiously that he acted as brothel-keeper or petticoat-pensioner of 'the Mermidons', pocketing a whore's fee which Sir Andrew owed him (II, iii, 27ff):

Andrew. I sent thee six pence[4] for thy Lemon, hadst it?

Feste. I did impeticos[5] thy gratillity: for *Maluolio* nose is no Whip-stocke. My Lady has a white hand,[6] and the Mermidons are no bottle-ale houses.[7]

Andrew. Excellent: Why this is the best fooling, when all is done.

No London tavern called the Myrmidons is known to have existed in Shakespeare's time. The name, however, must have conveyed a special meaning to an Elizabethan audience.[8] For Feste it seems to have been a lower-class tavern providing both wine and women.

Sir Toby's characterization of Malvolio as a lecher raises the contested issue of whether the portrait of Malvolio conforms to the tradition

---

and added the pen and ink imagery which is of the same origin as the book and letter imagery. See *Much Ado About Nothing*, II, iii, 136ff:

> *Claudio.* Now you talk of sheet and paper, I remember a pretty jest your daughter told us of.
>
> *Leonato.* O, when she had writ it and was reading it over, she found 'Benedick' and 'Beatrice' between the sheet?

[1] The term 'toy' was applied to persons, particularly to females. Pistol in *The Merry Wives* calls the elves 'airy toys' (v, v, 42). In a Restoration ballad, the milk maids are styled 'female toys' (A. W. Green, *The Inns of Court and Early English Drama* (New Haven and London, 1931), pp. 61–2.

[2] F. G. Emmison, *Elizabethan Life: Morals and the Church Courts* (Chelmsford, 1973), p. 21.

[3] The owner in 1602 was one Mr Rich and the tenant John Ford (A. C. Southern, 'The Elephant Inn', *TLS*, 12 June 1953, p. 381). It catered for Italian customers (S. Schoenbaum, *William Shakespeare: A Documentary Life* (Oxford, 1975), 127. The Elephant or Oliphant was an inn-cum-brothel. In October 1505 Edward Wharton, the stewholder, was fined 8d. See E. J. Burford, *Bawds and Lodgings: A History of the London Bankside c. 100–1675* (London, 1976), pp. 115., 150–1 As for the disreputable meaning of 'suburbs', see Sugden's *Topographical Dictionary*; Colman, *The Dramatic Use of Bawdy*, pp. 65, 156, 217; Farmer, *Slang*, VII (1904), 21. One instance may serve as illustration. Portia asks her husband Brutus: 'Dwell I but in the suburbs/Of your good pleasure? If it be no more,/Portia is Brutus' harlot, not his wife' (*Julius Caesar*, II, i, 285–7).

[4] Innumerable examples in the Tudor drama bear out that the standard fee of a whore was sixpence.

[5] 'Petticoat' was a current synecdoche for 'woman' and 'whore' as well as for the 'female pudendum'. See Farmer, *Slang*, v (1902), 179; Partridge, *Shakespeare's Bawdy*, under 'placket'; Colman, *The Dramatic Use of Bawdy in Shakespeare*, under 'placket'. Compare also Gullio's railing at Ingenioso in *The First Part of the Return from Parnassus* (acted 1599/1600): 'Peace you impecunious peasant, as I am a souldier, I was neuer soe abusd since I firste bore arms. What you vassall, if a Lunaticke bawdie trull, a pocketinge queane detracte from my vertues, will thy audacious selfe dare to repeate them in the presence of this blade?' (J. B. Leishman (ed.), *The Three Parnassus Plays* (1949), lines 1422–6).

[6] A repentant, reformed, and most likely relapsed prostitute (see above).

[7] The Myrmidons were the followers of Achilles, surnamed the 'Grig' in John Eliot's *Ortho-epia Gallica* (1593), as the Arden editor has noted without however pointing out the pun on 'Greek', 'grig', and 'eel'. A grig is a young eel (*OED*) and 'eel' in Shakespeare stands for 'penis' (See Partridge and Colman). Elizabethan writers often held Greek heroes up to ridicule for their erotic adventures. Hercules was made fun of for being subjected to Omphale and Achilles for falling a victim to the charms of Polyxena. In Greene's play *Orlando Furioso* (c. 1591), Sacrepant is compared to Achilles, 'the Mirmydon Trapt in the tresses of Polixena' (Sugden, *Topographical Dictionary*, under 'Myrmidons'). John Taylor, the water poet, has written a poem on the ill-starred Achilles under the title 'A Whore': 'The mighty Captaine of the *Mermidons*,/Being captiu'd to these base passions,/Met an vntimely vnexpected slaughter,/For faire *Polixena*, King *Priams* daughter' (Taylor, *All the Workes* (1630), repr. Menston, Scolar Press, 1973), sig. Kk 2 v.).

[8] Could it have been the nickname of a tavern haunted by the students of the Inns-of-Court?

of the stage Puritan. In a way it does conform; the Puritan pattern is unmistakably there, even though Malvolio bulks too large to be contained within a conventional mould. What he shares with the stage precisian is, for instance, the imputation of sexual immorality and the repressed longings for the pleasures of the flesh.[1] Commentators have hesitated to take Malvolio for a Puritan, because Maria puts him down as being 'a kinde of Puritane' (II, iii, 136) and, on second thoughts, as 'a time-pleaser, an affection'd Asse, that cons State without booke' (II, iii, 143–4). Maria, in fact, does not say that Malvolio is a Puritan, but all the same she clearly resorts to the terminology of the stage Puritan to denounce Malvolio as a lecher and whoremaster. This is the very meaning of 'a kinde of Puritane' as is borne out by the self-same expression in *What You Will* (c. 1601/2), another play written by John Marston of the Middle Temple and best suited for entertainment at an Inns-of-Court revel.[2] Bidet, a lower-class Prince of Purpoole (Gray's Inn revels) or Prince d'Amour (Middle Temple revels), on being proclaimed 'Emperor of Crackes, Prince of Pages, Marques of Mumchance, and sole regent over a bale of false dice', divides his subjects, the pages, into three categories, the first being the 'Court pages', the second the 'Ordinary Gallants pages', and 'the third apple-squiers,[3] basket bearers, or pages of the placket'.[4] He wants to 'proceede first' with the petitions of the last. So he orders Slip, whom he addresses as 'page of the placket' to 'stand forth', asking him 'what is your mistress?'. Slip answers that she is 'A kinde of puritane'.[5] Slip, classified as a male bawd, intimates that his mistress, i.e. his punk, is 'A kinde of puritane'. It follows that the application of this expression to Malvolio is designed to deride him as a male prostitute and it corroborates his identification as a 'Peg-a-ramsie' and a 'Iezabel'.

[1] William Holden, *Anti-Puritan Satire 1572–1642* (New Haven, 1954), pp. 123–6. There are some more Puritan traits of Malvolio that have still gone unnoticed. See, for instance, Feste's ingenious exposure of the Puritan denunciation of the transmigration of souls (IV, ii, 52ff) or the Puritan disapproval of rings (II, ii, 7ff). An Inns-of-Court audience is likely to have sensed allusions to Puritan behaviour and character that remain hidden to modern theatregoers. Thus one would like to know why on 14 November 1602 Manningham recorded in his *Diary* the following saying which had been reported to him by Walter Curle, afterwards bishop of Winchester: 'An hypocrite or puritan is like a globe, that hath all *in convexo, nihil in concavo*: all without painted, nothing within included' (*The Diary*, ed. R. P. Sorlien, p. 124). Was this a common saying among law students and could Manningham have been struck by the analogy between this gibe at the Puritans and Malvolio contorting 'his face into more lynes, then is in the new Mappe' (III,ii, 78–9), which, as stated above, was projected from Molineux' globe on the advice of the Templarian Richard Hakluyt the elder?

[2] Finkelpearl, pp. 162–3.

[3] In Tudor English, an 'apple-squire' was a harlot's attendant or a male bawd. See Farmer, *Slang*, I (1890), 64; Eric Partridge, *Dictionary of Slang and Unconventional English* (1970), I, 15.

[4] For 'placket' meaning 'vulva' see above.

[5] *The Plays of John Marston*, ed. H. Harvey Wood, III (1938), 270. Finkelpearl observes that *What You Will* has 'many superficial resemblances' besides the title to *Twelfth Night* (p. 176).

THE IMPORTANCE OF BEING MARCADE

J. M. NOSWORTHY

Den Gott des Ganges und der weiten Botschaft,
die Reisehaube über hellen Augen,
den schlanken Stab hertragend vor dem Leibe
und flügelschlagend an den Fussgelenken.[1]

I

It is a disconcerting fact that what nowadays appear to be the main problems attaching to *Love's Labour's Lost* arise out of ill-advised attempts, over the past hundred years, to attribute to Shakespeare a rather uncharacteristic preoccupation with satirical allegory whose interpretation has produced a diversity of mutually antagonistic hypotheses. Once we accept that these major problems may be non-existent and the minor ones, though insoluble, negligible, the residue is a straightforward, intensely vigorous yet gently sardonic comedy; a *tour-de-force* in which Shakespeare is able, through sheer technical dexterity, to sustain a dialogue involving no less than eight characters, of whom two or three are sufficiently heightened for the initiative to shift hither and thither and from whom there emerges a comic hero, Berowne, whose vitality surpasses that of any of his successors, Benedick alone excepted. Though it would be idle to pretend that there is a Shylock, a Jaques or a Malvolio among them, the main supporting characters – Armado, Holofernes, Moth, Sir Nathaniel, Dull, Costard and Boyet – are firmly and memorably depicted and, in addition, there is Marcade, whose twenty-eight words make an impact that must be something of a record. As R. W. David perceptively remarks:

Anyone who has seen *Love's Labour's Lost* acted will admit the powerful effect of Marcade's entrance in Act V, Scene ii, not only as a superb coup de théâtre but as setting up an ever present pressure of reality throughout the rest of the play until it fades out in bird-calls. And yet this sudden enrichment of texture has been anticipated again and again in earlier scenes, as in the tale of Katherine's sister or in Berowne's set speeches. In a flash we are back to earth, and it is all the more solid and immediate for our absence and for the suddenness of our return.[2]

It remains, however, to explain how it comes about that Marcade, the *deus ex machina*, is also a *multum in parvo*, who, by the very lateness of his appearance, imposes on the play a most unusual and even daring structure in which about five per cent of near tragedy follows some ninety-five per cent of pure comedy. In effect it is the reversal precipitated by Marcade which brings with it those earnest moral issues which serve to transform a good comedy into a masterpiece.[3] Linked with this transformation, however, is the bibliographical and hermeneutic problem posed by the seemingly irrelevant and discrepant endings of the early editions.

Immediately after the two songs about spring and winter, the 1598 Quarto, which was

[1] R. M. Rilke, *Orpheus, Euridike, Hermes,* lines 42–5. 'The god of travel and of widespread tidings; the travelling hat over clear-seeing eyes; the slender staff held out before his body and wings fluttering at his ankles.'

[2] *Love's Labour's Lost* (New Arden, 1969), p. xvi.

[3] The process, though rare, is not unique. It seems to me that it is the closing chapters that transform *The Woodlanders* from a good novel into a great one.

printed by William White and claims, on its title-page, that it had been 'newly corrected and augmented', prints, in twelve point:

The vvordes of Mercurie, are harsh after the songes of Apollo

FINIS.

In the Folio, which was set up from a copy of Q that had received little or nothing in the way of correction, the reading is:

Brag. The Words of Mercurie,
Are harsh after the songs of Apollo:
You that way; we this way.

Exeunt omnes.

Four questions immediately arise:

1. Why did the Q compositor use a larger type?
2. Is F right in assigning the words to Armado?
3. Was Shakespeare the author of either sentence?
4. If he was, what do the words mean?

Dover Wilson's answer to the first (and half of the third) question was that the line was an anonymous reader's comment on the play as a whole. If the larger type had been exclusive to the Folio, this would be an acceptable explanation since one could readily believe that the unknown had scribbled the words, in no very clerkish hand, at the end of the particular quarto that served as copy for the Folio. But the large type is peculiar to the Quarto, and that was set up directly from Shakespeare's foul papers. This virtually eliminates Wilson's anonymous reader, leaving us to choose between the author and the book-holder, with the Master of Revels as a further remote possibility. Since it was not the normal practice for either prompters or censors to subscribe enigmatic comments, the odds, I think, are overwhelmingly in favour of Shakespeare. E. K. Chambers's suggestion that the line 'looks like the beginning of an epilogue or a presenter's speech for a following mask' has, understandably, been widely accepted and there is some force, at least superficially, in his

observation that 'Mercury has nothing to do with what precedes.'[1] The same might be said to apply to Apollo, save that he figures in an isolated simile. To this I shall return.

The answer to the first question is the straightforward one that no significance attaches to the compositor's use of larger type. My own impression was that there were other quartos which made occasional use of abnormal founts, though the only instance that sprang to mind was, by what will shortly emerge as an odd coincidence, Danter's 1594 quarto of *The Cobbler's Prophecy*, which prints a seven-line stage direction in quite enormous type.[2] Feeling that one example was insufficient, I referred the problem to Mr Richard Proudfoot, who generously examined five quartos printed by White between 1597 and 1600 with gratifying results. The findings germane to the present enquiry are that all these quartos reflect, in greater or lesser degree, the typographical aberrations present in *Love's Labour's Lost* and that four of them make occasional use of the larger fount. Critics who have read strange matters into the ending of Shakespeare's comedy have overlooked the fact that twelve-point type is also used at its beginning in part of the initial stage direction of I, i. Evidently the compositor's aim was to achieve a certain symmetry by the use of contrasting type.

The answers to the other questions must depend on our interpretation of the Quarto title-page's claim that its text had been 'newly corrected and augmented'. This has been widely accepted as evidence that there had been an earlier 'bad' quarto, but must perforce remain a hypothesis. The reference to augmentation suggests that Shakespeare may have made some additions to his original version for the Christmas presentation before the Queen, and this possibility led Dover Wilson to

[1] E. K. Chambers, *William Shakespeare*, (Oxford, 1930) vol. 1, p. 338.
[2] R. Wilson, *The Cobbler's Prophecy* (Malone Society Reprint, Oxford, 1914) lines 1324–30.

embark on a characteristically elaborate theory of revision. There are certainly two notable instances of duplication in Berowne's exposition of the doctrine that he derives from women's eyes (IV, iii, 293–362) and in the dialogue relating to the penance imposed upon him by Rosaline (V, ii, 807–61), but these alterations might, as Greg observes, 'have been made quite as easily, and much more probably, during the original process of composition'.[1] It seems to me, however, that the last fifty lines of the play testify to some kind of revision or augmentation, so that the 1598 Q preserves Shakespeare's original comedy of c. 1594 plus a new ending provided for the royal occasion in c. 1598. The basic evidence for this view is J. W. Lever's demonstration that, in the Cuckoo song, Shakespeare drew upon Gerard's *Herbal*, registered on 6 June 1597, and, since the Cuckoo song and the Owl song obviously go hand in hand, it follows that neither could have been written before the latter half of 1597.[2] The dialogue itself affords supporting evidence, for Armado is, in fact, brought back to offer what is almost an apologetic explanation:

But, most esteemed greatness, will you hear the dialogue that the two learned men have compiled in praise of the owl and the cuckoo? It should have followed in the end of our show.

The last ten words sound like a device for justifying augmentation, especially as owls and cuckoos have no readily perceptible connection with the Nine Worthies.

Once this possibility is admitted, two discrepancies immediately present themselves. One is that the two songs which compose the dialogue are completely out of character. The 'two learned men' can only mean Holofernes, whose poetic attainments have already been exhibited in his 'extemporal epitaph on the death of the deer', and Sir Nathaniel. Presumably the pageant was the outcome of collaboration between them. If so, they were about as capable of devising the polished bitter-sweet

'dialogue' at the end of the play as Peter Quince was of writing *Paradise Lost*. Shakespeare must have gambled on the hope that the incongruity would pass unnoticed, as it probably did. The second discrepancy is more perplexing. At V, ii, 662–72 Costard reveals that Jaquenetta is two months pregnant by Armado, who, at V, ii, 713–15, declares: 'I will right myself like a soldier', clearly implying that he will take the honourable course of marrying the woman he has wronged. At V, ii, 872–4, however, he says:

I am a votary; I have vowed to Jaquenetta to hold the plough for her sweet love three year.

Here both tone and context suggest that, instead of going through with a shotgun marriage, Armado, like Navarre and his companions, has committed himself to a period of probation. It would be entirely in character for his commitment to be three times that of anyone else and there is a pleasing irony in a situation which means that the play ends as it began, with a three-year dedication to abstinence and hard work.

I suggest, then, that the received texts of *Love's Labour's Lost* preserve alternative endings, though it would be hazardous to claim that these are more than vestigial. It is, however, credible that, in its original form, the play ended with:

King.
   Come, sir, it wants a twelvemonth and a day,
   And then 'twill end.
Berowne.   That's too long for a play.

This means that Berowne, deservedly, had the last word, but his right to this is powerfully challenged by Armado and by no other character. If I am right in believing that the two songs and a few lines of dialogue represent the postulated augmentation of c. 1597, it seems

[1] W. W. Greg, *The Shakespeare First Folio* (Oxford, 1955), p. 222.
[2] J. W. Lever, 'Three Notes on Shakespeare's Plants', *RES*, n.s. 3 (1952), 117–20.

unquestionable that Shakespeare, making a virtue of necessity, allowed Armado, who is now obviously in control, to have the final say. This indicates that the line about Mercury and Apollo is authentic and that the Folio speech-heading is correct. It may be remarked that the line:

> While greasy Joan doth keel the pot

does not provide a satisfactory ending. The only other comedy by Shakespeare that ends with the sung word is *Twelfth Night*, but Feste's song is, of course, also a supremely accomplished epilogue, which the Owl song in *Love's Labour's Lost* is not.

The brief closing sentence peculiar to F presents difficulties. Greg detects 'the editor's desperate attempt to fit the final words of Q into the structure of the play',[1] but, in my view, no such attempt was necessary. Richard David's suggestion that the addition was 'perhaps made by the stage-manager to ensure a tidy *Exeunt*'[2] leans rather heavily on the supposition that Shakespeare had been content to leave an untidy one and seems to impinge on Wilson's discredited theory that Jaggard's compositors worked from a copy of Q that had served as a prompt-book. The words are obviously a spoken stage direction in which Armado, as master of ceremonies, directs half the characters through one door and the other half through the other. One imagines that, if the stage-manager had been involved, he would have inserted a specific, and perhaps elaborate, direction and not have tampered with the dialogue. It is clear that the actual Q used at the F stage had, in Greg's words, 'received some editorial attention', albeit of an extraordinarily erratic and perfunctory nature. The possibility that Heminge or Condell or whoever provided the copy for F was able to rectify an omission cannot be ruled out. Since, in the 1598 Q, the compositor's predilection for large type apparently led him to omit both speech-heading and *Exeunt*, a third lacuna seems far from unlikely.

Hence, the provisional answers to three of the questions posed above are that the twelve-point type in Q is insignificant, that F is correct in assigning the closing lines to Armado and that it preserves those lines as Shakespeare himself wrote them. It now remains to consider what those lines mean in relation to the play as a whole and the process of interpretation will, I think, do much to validate the hypotheses so far proposed.

II

The retort courteous to Chambers's observation that Mercury has nothing to do with what has gone before is that he has, in fact, been quite heavily involved in the guise of Marcade. Of this latter character, Greg, in a rare and uncharacteristic flight of fancy, remarks: 'Monsieur Marcade, who appears... in place of the usually anonymous messenger, must certainly have had an earlier history',[3] and this offers food for thought. Shakespeare's nomenclature is unpredictable and anonymity sometimes extends to major characters. It is only from the list of characters appended at the end of *Measure for Measure* that we learn that the Duke's name was Vincentio (and even this may have been invented by Ralph Crane in 1621), while the fact that Macbeth's wife was named Gruach is something that Shakespeare was, perhaps advisedly, content to leave buried in the chronicles. In *Love's Labour's Lost*, it is the Princess herself who is left nameless, a seemingly ironic circumstance in view of the fact that the dramatist was evidently at some pains to bestow a name on her mere messenger with his twenty-eight words. It may be concluded from this, together with the impact made by Marcade in actual performance, that Shakespeare invested him with a particular significance which has been obscured by certain irregularities in transmission. The original transgression, it seems, attaches to the

[1] Greg, p. 223.
[2] David, p. 196.
[3] Greg, p. 224.

Q compositor, who, oblivious to the fact that the Princess is normally a verse speaker, set up the relevant lines as prose, thereby rendering the pronunciation of Marcade ambiguous. F followed Q and light thickened further when editors emended the name to 'Mercade' and actresses adopted the disyllabic pronunciation. What is required is a trisyllable since the correct reading of the passage must obviously be:

Marcade.
  God save you, madam.
Princess.   Welcome, Marcade,
  But that thou interrupt'st our merriment.
Marcade.
  I am sorry, madam; for the news I bring
  Is heavy in my tongue. The king, your father –
Princess.
  Dead, for my life!
Marcade.   Even so; my tale is told.

Once we accept that the pronunciation of the name was Marcaday or, in actual practice, more probably Marcady, we can affirm that the character certainly had an earlier history, though not exactly in Greg's sense. In 1594, in pursuance of an entry dated June 8th, Cuthbert Burby issued a quarto of Robert Wilson's comedy, *The Cobbler's Prophecy*, in which the name, or rather the misnomer, 'Markady' occurs. The possibility that *Love's Labour's Lost* had been completed prior to Burby's publication must be conceded but is immaterial since Shakespeare would doubtless have had a theatre-goer's knowledge of a play that is manifestly the product of an earlier period. In Wilson's pleasant but dated comedy, the assembled gods decide to frustrate the amorous endeavours of Venus by means of a prophecy which Mercury delivers to Ralph the Cobbler. But the cobbler is an ignorant man who uses words wrongly and, just as Dull and Costard make fritters of the name of Armado, so he perverts Jupiter into 'Shebiter' and Mercury into 'Markedy', using this latter form five times in all. Here, then, is the apparent source from which Shakespeare derived his name for a

human *deus ex machina* who, at the same time, transparently fulfils two of the functions of the god, Mercury – those of messenger and psychopomp.[1] Similar dovetailing occurs elsewhere in Shakespeare, and the pointed ambiguity of Seyton in *Macbeth* and Eros in *Antony and Cleopatra* springs readily to mind. Far more significant, however, is the fact that, in *The Winter's Tale*, the snapper-up of unconsidered trifles, 'litter'd under Mercury', the god of thieves, bears the name of Mercury's own son, Autolycus. This circumstance must surely establish the claim that, *pace* Chambers, Mercury, artfully but not impenetrably disguised, has appeared in *Love's Labour's Lost*.

It is, of course, a very late appearance and the momentary role of messenger and psychopomp may not amount to much. But there is the impact, already mentioned, which is, in fact, the outcome of a significant dramatic reversal through which 'the scene begins to cloud' and 'Jack hath not Jill' – a reversal which makes the overall structure of the play daringly experimental and, in my view, entirely successful. The control established by Mercury, in the shape of Marcade, is maintained throughout the remainder of the play and emerges in the probationary injunctions laid down by both the Princess and Rosaline. Navarre is dispatched to a hermitage and Berowne to a hospital. Hermits, of course, have no etymological connection with Hermes but the erroneous initial *h* testifies to that kind of false derivation which was not uncommon in the Middle Ages.[2]

[1] The conclusion that Shakespeare was indebted to *The Cobbler's Prophecy* for the name 'Marcade' has been reached independently by Dr Anne Barton in an article on the sources of *Love's Labour's Lost* published in the *T.L.S.*, 24 November 1978.

[2] The word ultimately derives from Greek *erēmitēs* I am indebted to Professor Alarik Rynell for pointing out that, despite the intrusive *h*, the false etymology connecting the word with Hermes could not have arisen until after the weakly stressed medial *ē* had disappeared. For a discussion on hermits see E. L. Cutts, *Scenes and Characters of the Middle Ages* (1872), pp. 93–119.

Hermits were thought of as recluses who, like Roger Bacon, practised hermetic philosophy. It was their special duty to assist travellers and, to this end, hermitages were normally situated in the vicinity of fords and bridges. The exemplar of the hermit-saint was St Julian and, in picture and legend, St Christopher was always assisted by a hermit in the transportation of travellers across dangerous fords – a partnership which sufficiently resembles that of Hermes and Charon in respect of the Styx. The word also acquired a pejorative sense and, as the Reformation gathered momentum, came to signify vagabond and even thief. Its capacity for wrongly accommodating several notable attributes of Hermes or Mercury must have been powerfully emphasised in the fifteen-nineties by Spenser's portrayal of Archimage as a hermit, and there can be little doubt that, in Shakespeare's mind, Navarre's penance subjected him to 'the words of Mercury'.

It looks, at first sight, as if Berowne's twelve-month sojourn in a hospital should subject him to the rule of Apollo, who, as the father of Aesculapius, is the ultimate author of the healing arts, and this would be so if the offices prescribed for Berowne were therapeutic. But his task is 'to move wild laughter in the throat of death' and we have to remember that the vast majority of the inmates of sixteenth-century hospitals were 'the speechless sick' and 'the pained impotent', who were past all cure and were merely awaiting the moment when Mercury would conduct their souls to the nether world. Berowne then, like Navarre, is doomed to submit to the yoke of Mercury and this submission is consequent upon the reversal precipitated by Marcade. The words are harsh because the romantic artifice which has been sustained for more than four acts must suddenly yield to the reality of death and to the acceptance of the fact that the path of true love never did run smooth. It is a harshness which is forcefully underlined by the two songs which, though exquisite in themselves, are essentially catalogues of transient joys and enduring miseries which equate the owl's merry note with greasy kitchen-maids and the cuckoo's song with cuckoldry.

Once 'the words of Mercury' have been accounted for, 'the songs of Apollo' are not far to seek. It is a simple fact that, from its beginning down to v, ii, 704, *Love's Labour's Lost* has been substantially controlled by the nature and functions of Apollo.[1] It is by courtesy of the sun-god that the play, with its exclusive, almost unique, outdoor setting exists at all. The court of Navarre is sunlit parkland and it is only with the entry of Marcade that the scene begins to cloud and Phoebus is eclipsed. The demands of Apollo Musagetes are more than generously fulfilled by song, sonnet, dance and pageant. It is under the aegis of the god of institutions that the academe is conceived and it is he, as the punishing god whose arrows were thought to be the cause of every sudden death, who brings the revelry to its abrupt end. Moreover, there is, throughout, a moral pattern, far more ponderable than the play's detractors have supposed, which turns on the Delphic precepts – 'Know thyself' and 'Nothing in excess'. It is a play in which the main male characters, including Armado, move from self-delusion to self-knowledge and are ultimately purged of artifice and exaggeration, so that even the Braggart ends by speaking almost, but not quite, like a man of God's making. Berowne, one of the great paradoxical figures of Shakespearian comedy, is at all times the seemingly self-knowing exponent of moderation and normality but he is also the victim of a form of self-delusion which is reflected in a distinctive language that thrives on a fascinating juxta-

[1] Professor Leslie Hotson's *Shakespeare by Hilliard* (Berkeley, 1977) affords a mass of valuable information about the Elizabethan treatment of both Apollo and Mercury. I do not, however, subscribe to either his main thesis or his views on *Love's Labour's Lost*.

position of affectation and downright home-
liness in both vocabulary and imagery. If, in the
end, he is the one upon whom the heaviest penance is imposed, it is because, though he knows
that the three years' abstinence is a sin against
nature and eloquently proclaims the fact, he
nevertheless acquiesces, only to discover that
he, who had been love's whip, is in thrall to

> A whitely wanton with a velvet brow,
> With two pitch-balls stuck in her face for eyes.

His exposition of the Delphic precepts and his
attempts to put them into practice are, however,
unequivocal and memorable but it is significant
that their cogency is reinforced by Apolline
analogy. At the outset he proclaims that

> Study is like the heaven's glorious sun,
> That will not be deep-search'd with saucy looks

and develops this into an argument against
excess:

> At Christmas I no more desire a rose
> Than wish a snow in May's new-fangled shows;
> But like of each thing that in season grows.

Later it is Rosaline who is likened to the sun:

> Who sees the heavenly Rosaline,
> That, like a rude and savage man of Inde,
> At the first opening of the gorgeous east,
> Bows not his vassal head, and strooken blind,
> Kisses the base ground with obedient breast?
> What peremptory eagle-sighted eye
> Dares look upon the heaven of her brow,
> That is not blinded by her majesty?
>
> (IV, iii, 218–25)

and the analogy is repeated, again in terms of
sun and sun-god, in:

> Vouchsafe to show the sunshine of your face,
> That we, like savages, may worship it.
>
> (V, ii, 201–2)

But love itself is a force that 'adds a precious
seeing to the eye', so that

> A lover's eyes will gaze an eagle blind,
>
> (IV, iii, 331)

and this elaboration of the Elizabethan belief
that the eagle is the only creature not blinded
by gazing directly on the sun is promptly
followed by the claim that love is

> as sweet and musical
> As bright Apollo's lute, strung with his hair.
>
> (IV, iii, 339–40)

It remains to add that the preoccupation with
black and white and light and dark, which some
critics consider a significant feature of the play,
is concordant with those aspects of the Phoebus
myth which incorporate the 'snow-white
Swan' and the 'coal-black Crow' as birds
sacred to Apollo.

It would seem that the affirmation that 'the
words of Mercury are harsh after the songs of
Apollo', together with the data so far presented,
imply that *Love's Labour's Lost* turns on direct
conflict between the two gods, but this is not
the case. In classical tradition Apollo and
Mercury were, of course, bosom friends whose
functions and attributes sometimes overlapped,
especially in artistic contexts. Apollo was the
god of song but, while one tradition credited
him with the invention of the lyre, another
affirms that the instrument was presented to
him by Mercury, whose title of King of the
Dance would also seem to be irreconcilable
with the concept of Apollo Terpsichoros. There
is the same apparent confusion in respect of
poetry but with this, as with the other arts,
the basic distinction is that Apollo was the
remote, ultimate source of that inspiration
which his friend Mercury, as messenger and
god of eloquence and communication, conveyed to man. This, however, is an academic
distinction which, in Elizabethan practice, was
often disregarded and it would be wrong to
suppose that Mercury is entirely excluded from
that extensive portion of *Love's Labour's Lost*
which is dominated by Apollo. The fact is that,
prior to Marcade's entrance, the Mercurial
elements are somewhat inconspicuous and
relate mainly to the minor characters, that is to

the professions of Holofernes and Sir Nathaniel, the rhetoric of Armado and the intermediary functions of Moth and Costard. It may, with caution, be remarked that the abundance of arithmetical and literal jokes may reflect Shakespeare's awareness that Mercury was the reputed inventor of both numbers and the alphabet. It is even possible that some of those jokes turn on the fact that seven was Apollo's number and that four was Mercury's, but, like Armado, I am ill at reckoning and am content to leave it for others to elucidate the play's more cryptic witticisms. These are, in any case, minor issues and far more significant is the subtle way in which, in the first part of act v, the initiative passes from Apollo to Mercury, who assumes complete control after his fellow-god has discharged his final function as the bringer of sudden death. The transition is achieved through the masque and the pageant, both of which may be said to be Apolline in intention but prove, in the event, to be Mercurial. The collocation of black and white is effectively conveyed by the fact that the projected dance of the 'frozen Muscovites' is preceded by a dance of blackamoors, whose pigmentation was thought by the Elizabethans to have resulted from exposure to the intense heat of the equatorial sun. Russians, on the other hand, were associated with vast regions of ice and snow, and if, in performance, Shakespeare directed that Berowne and his companions should wear white costumes, the Apolline colour symbolism would have been immediately apparent. The dances themselves, as already noted, involve both gods and, if the Russian one fails to materialise, this is presumably because Mercury surrenders one of his most joyful offices in order to fulfil his saddest one. For the ensuing pageant of the Nine Worthies he must be debited with total responsibility since the bards who devised it assuredly held nothing in fealty to Apollo. Mercury, as the god of eloquence and founder of written records, must perforce exercise a

less critical benevolence and comply with the demands of a McGonagall as readily as with those of a Milton. Undeniably the pageant affords further instance of the comparative harshness of the words of Mercury.

Love's Labour's Lost was written at a time when it was by no means uncommon for plays to complement the basic human action with varying measures of supernatural activity which can amount to a dominating force. *The Spanish Tragedy* and *Doctor Faustus* are examples that spring readily to mind and Marlowe's *Dido, Queen of Carthage* is a notable example of a play which integrates conflict between mortals with that between the immortals. This is something that *The Cobbler's Prophecy* also does in its naive, desultory way. The delicate symbolism that Shakespeare employs in *Macbeth* and *Antony and Cleopatra* has already been mentioned and to this may be added the imminent mockery of the gods which informs both *King Lear* and *Coriolanus*. Divine intervention becomes virtually a *sine qua non* in the final romances. It may well be protested that the complex significances attaching to the products of Shakespeare's full maturity do not necessarily apply to his earlier work and, if certain recent interpretations are given credence, least of all to *Love's Labour's Lost*, but the conclusive refutation of such an argument is supplied by that comedy's immediate successor, *A Midsummer Night's Dream*. It is scarcely necessary to labour the point that there, conflict at the human level is inextricably bound up with the supernatural dissension between Oberon and Titania, but it should be emphasised that what applies to the one play can obviously apply to its immediate predecessor, especially if we regard the one, a nocturnal in which the lovers' frustrations are satisfactorily resolved, as a calculated contrasting complement to the other, a sunlit comedy in which the path of true love runs a little too smoothly and culminates in frustration.

In order to establish the underlying conflict in *Love's Labour's Lost*, we have to relate the last words of the play to the first ones, namely the title. If 'Love's' is regarded purely as an abstraction, the title is somewhat indefinite and syntactically dubious: if it is seen as a personification, the result is precision and coherence. It is love personified, in other words Cupid, who supplies the *tertium quid*. He is specifically named in the play on some eight occasions and is elsewhere given implicit identity. The allusions impress, however, more by their weight than their frequency, and when, at IV, iii, 363 and again at V, ii, 87, Navarre and his companions are represented as advancing under the standard of 'Saint Cupid', the incongruous canonisation suggests that Shakespeare was at some pains to emphasise the little love-god's significance, though that significance has already been established and made memorable in Berowne's incomparable diatribe at III, i, 170–202. There can be few plays in which this 'wimpled, whining, purblind, wayward boy' is given such prominence, but it is granted, of course, strictly on merit. Four young men simultaneously fall in love at first sight, contrary to their avowed intentions, and Armado is unable to resist the charms of Jaquenetta. *Love's Labour's Lost* depicts a most notable day's thumping with Cupid's bird-bolt, but this is a flagrant intrusion into the realm of Apollo, the ultimate begetter of the Academe, and of his factor, Mercury. For the greater part of the play the conflict is mainly between Cupid and Apollo, with apparent gains and losses on either side until the Pythian god despatches the arrow which is more potent than the love-god's darts. Thereupon Mercury, who, in accordance with his traditional character as the god of prudence and subterfuge, has hitherto been making his contribution inconspicuously, assumes control as psychopomp, the necessary consequence of the King of France's death, and, in the corporeal form of Marcade, as messenger. Under his aegis the clouds gather and the strenuous, often bitter,

realities of life abruptly dispel the holiday humour of the preceding scenes. We return to the world of Jack and Jill, of Dick and Tom and Joan and Marion, of cooks and cuckolds: a world of which only Berowne has had earlier cognizance.

The embodiment of the less reputable aspects of Mercury in the character of Autolycus has already been mentioned and it remains to add that it is *The Winter's Tale* which most fully corroborates the present interpretation of *Love's Labour's Lost*. There is, of course, little or no structural similarity and the conspiracy is directed not against the god of Love but against the god of Time, whose power of destruction is frustrated by the restoration of Hermione and Perdita: but the conspirators are the same. It is Apollo who, through the oracle, the importance of which Shakespeare is at some pains to emphasise, determines the conduct of the first half of the play and who, in the face of Leontes's blasphemy, brings sudden death to Mamillius and (seemingly) to Hermione. Underlying the spoken profanation is Leontes's manifest failure to comply with the Delphic precepts relating to self-knowledge and moderation, and it is Perdita's exposition of the second precept, 'Nothing in excess', at the sheep-shearing feast which sets the key for that rectification which, in the second half of the play, is so unexpectedly effected by the Mercurial Autolycus. That there should exist such links between the two plays is not altogether strange since *Love's Labour's Lost*, with its ultimate imposition of strenuous probation, distinctively anticipates a theme which becomes a *sine qua non* in Shakespeare's final romances.

There remain the six words with which the Folio text ends. To the arguments already presented in defence of their authenticity may now be added the more pregnant consideration that, in the mouth of Armado, the 'refined traveller', they round off the Mercurial significances to perfection. Their speaker, we cannot but suppose, directs the Princess and her party through the one stage-door to begin their journey back to France, and ushers the remaining characters through the other. Mercury was the god of travellers. He was also the god of doorways.

© J. M. NOSWORTHY 1979

A HEBREW SOURCE FOR 'THE MERCHANT OF VENICE'

S. J. SCHÖNFELD

Prefatory note

The author of this essay, for all his unassuming bearing, was such an unusual and truly original personality that a few words about him may be in place. Born in Rumania in 1892, he received a traditional schooling in Biblical and Talmudic studies. Later in Vienna, he listened receptively to everything the University there had to offer. He belonged to the circle of Sigmund Freud, living on commissions from officework as a side-line. At that time he was already taking an interest in Shakespearian research. In 1938 he emigrated to Israel, where he gained a very modest living for himself and his family as an ill-paid official, devoting his nights to the study of Shakespeare, until his death in Haifa in 1951. He could never bring himself to publish this essay, as he considered it a 'preliminary communication', no more.

I had the privilege of being personally acquainted with Schönfeld, and it has also been my privilege to prepare this study for publication at the behest of his admirers. I have reduced the original text by more than half, written as it was in rather complicated German and with no little hair-splitting subtlety. I can only express the hope that in the process I have nowhere misinterpreted or misrepresented Schönfeld's thinking.

The translation from the German is the work of Mrs Daphna Allon of Jerusalem. I wish to thank her for her more than professional interest.

YEHUDA T. RADDAY

It can confidently be predicted that the hypothesis presented here will meet with considerable resistance, the hypothesis of a Jewish, Hebrew-language source for *The Merchant of Venice*. The idea runs counter to orthodox views in Shakespearian research, but the unbiased reader will not let this influence him overmuch; still less so the researcher, whose theories have to be brought into line with the facts and not the other way round.

To enumerate all the problems that *The Merchant of Venice* is burdened with would take too long, and it can moreover be assumed that these are known to the reader. It is only necessary therefore to remind ourselves that neither researchers nor spectators have ever been of one mind on what the play has to say *vis-à-vis* its central character, that is whether it is to be regarded as pro- or anti-Jewish. It will become evident in the course of what follows that neither of these views can be accepted without qualification, and at the same time the origin of the apparent contradictions will be made clear.

We start with a hitherto disregarded point, which will prove of decisive importance.

The opening statements in the judgement pronounced by Portia are greeted by Shylock with an enthusiastic exclamation, which appears natural and a matter of course, but only at first sight. The question immediately arises, 'Why does Shylock say what he does?' There is no real, obvious reason, since Portia's judgement in no way differs from what all Venice considers right and fair: in fact, appeal has been made to a renowned outside authority only because it is clear that the case is likely to go in favour of a Jew. Nevertheless, Shylock enthusiastically praises the foreign doctor of laws with the words,

A Daniel come to judgement!

(*Mer. Ven.* IV, i, 219)[1]

But why 'a Daniel'? 'A Solomon' would be the expected name here, not only from a Jew but from any Christian referring to some exceptionally wise judgement. True, the role of Daniel in a trial scene was known from the Book of Susanna, but there it applied only to confounding false witnesses by interrogation.

DANIEL

Leaving this first question aside for the moment, let us turn to another one. The Hebrew name, Daniel, can be translated, 'a God-like judge', and it looks as if Shylock must have been thinking in Hebrew in uttering this cry. Might this not signify that we have a character here who is not only a Jew but who thinks in Hebrew and is understood in Hebrew by his audience? Now, Shakespeare is hardly to be credited with any extensive knowledge of Jews and certainly with none at all of Hebrew, but it is a commonplace to say that he made use of older pieces as a framework for many of his plays, and a certain presumption, if still a weak one, begins to take shape in support of the hypothesis that *The Merchant of Venice* is based on an old Hebrew-Jewish source, which was not known to Shakespeare himself, of course, but which reached him indirectly.[2]

If this presumption can be verified, other difficulties would be resolved at the same time, including the aforementioned contradiction between the play's apparently anti-Jewish tendency and the impact of many of its most impressive and outright philo-Semitic passages.

Naturally the matter is not finished with the reference to Daniel, which we shall later revert to. Not only do many other obscure points prove to be best elucidated through the Hebrew, but far more than this – the entire plot can be shown to have its roots in the Hebrew!

Let us turn first to Portia.

PORTIA

The decision of Bassanio in favour of the leaden casket seems a matter of pure chance, for the argumentation he bases it on is clearly at fault: it is patently absurd to infer that one is more likely to find something precious in a leaden container than in one of some other metal. Thus, when Portia says,

O these deliberate fools! when they do choose,
They have the wisdom by their wit to lose,

(II, ix, 80–1)

this would apply even better to Bassanio than to the other two suitors.

The case turns out to be completely different in Hebrew. Here Bassanio's choice is seen to be the only possible correct solution to the riddle – and at the same time the wittiest one. However, to understand this properly a certain acquaintance with Hebrew is necessary, and we shall try here to impart the essential minimum required. The central point is that the Hebrew language is written only in consonants; vowels are represented, if at all, by means of sub-linear diacritical signs. These vowel signs vary and modify the basic meaning of the tri-literal root of the verb. This characteristic of Hebrew does not present any great difficulty to one who knows the language. True, it can give rise to misunderstandings, but a misreading is soon rectified by the context; on the other hand, almost endless possibilities open up for plays on words and these are widely taken advantage of even in the most serious Hebrew writings, including the Bible. It will soon appear what a

[1] Line references are to the Arden Shakespeare, 7th edition, 1955.

[2] A connection between Shakespeare's works and Hebrew writings has been surmised in the past. Schönfeld refers in a note to the monograph by Leon Kellner on the influences of the Mishna Tractate *Sayings of the Fathers* in Shakespeare. This is all that Schönfeld had to say on the subject, and unfortunately I have been unable to pin down any more details. (Y.T.R.)

large role these puns play in the Shakespeare passages before us.

From this point on, we print the Hebrew word with the decisive root consonants in capital letters and the vowels in lower case.

Now let us turn to Portia. What must her name have sounded like in our hypothetical Hebrew original? If we drop the Latin suffix, we are left with the consonants PRT, which every Bible student will instantly recognise as the word that appears in Genesis ch. XLIX, verse 22: 'Joseph is a bough (literally, a son) of PORaT, a bough of PORaT by a well', rendered by the English translators, 'a fruitful bough'. It is by no means certain what PORaT means exactly, since this is the sole occurrence of this word in the Bible, but it is clear that it was in the nature of a pet name for someone loved. This is why it fits Rachel, Joseph's mother, and why it can equally well apply to someone else beautiful and beloved. Just as Jacob sold himself into bondage for Rachel's sake, so Bassanio and his friend Antonio pledged life and limb for Portia's sake.

The meaning of the name PORaT is not however limited to a word of praise and a mark of affection. It is derived from the Hebrew root PRH, to bear fruit (from the sense: break forth from the earth or the womb) and also from the cognate root PRR, to break, destroy. It is thus Janus-faced, its meanings opposed to each other but connected, a not uncommon linguistic phenomenon. This is reflected, moreover, in Freud's interpretation of the figure of Portia as goddess of life and death.[1]

If we assume that we now have our hands on the original of Portia's name, we can see its double connection with the leaden casket. Portia herself specified the relationship when she explained, first,

> ...that wherein I am contained (II, ix, 5)

and later on,

> ...I am lock'd in one of them (III, ii, 40)

To grasp the hidden indications here, further remarks on Hebrew letters are indispensable. The Hebrew alphabet has a guttural consonant, called *ayin*, which can take various vowel sounds (like the other consonants) and for which there is no equivalent in European languages. For the sake of simplicity and for lack of a better solution, we shall indicate this letter by the sign ø. Finally, we shall represent the difference between the voiced and unvoiced forms of certain consonants by a line above the letter: thus B̄ is pronounced not /b/ but /v/; K̄ is pronounced /kh/ (the sound of *ch* in Scottish *loch*); and P̄ is pronounced /f/. Now the word lead, the metal, is *oferet* in Hebrew; if we transcribe this in the fashion explained above, we get ØPRT. Here we have the Hebrew Portia, PRT, actually 'locked in' ØPRT, which could not fail to vastly amuse Hebrew listeners. They would enjoy the joke still more when they perceived that the solution of the riddle was indicated precisely in the source: the only difference between PRT, Portia, and ØPRT, lead, is simply the first letter, ø, *ayin*, which as a word on its own means source or well! (That *ayin* may also mean eye and thus offer occasion for another pun will be seen below.) In this way the unique but supremely familiar Biblical verse gives Bassanio the solution to the riddle: 'Porat by the well' equals 'Porat (PRT) by the (letter) *ayin*'. He is being told: 'Just put "Porat" and "well" together and you've got the answer: (PRT + ø = ø + PRT = ØPRT = *oferet*, lead): You have chosen aright!'

THE CASKETS

It may be objected that Portia was supposed to be enclosed not in lead, but in a leaden casket. Not only is this not a very solid objection, but it brings to light still another play on words:

[1] For this and all further reference to Freud's comments on *The Merchant of Venice*, see his essay, *Das Motiv der Kästchenwahl*, which first appeared in 1913 and was reprinted in *Gesamte Werke* (1946), I, 24–37.

The Hebrew word that corresponds to the idea of a casket is TEVAH, but this also means, among other things, a *word*. Portia is as truly 'enclosed' in the leaden casket as her name, PORAT, is in the word ØPRT. The right lover understands exactly what Portia means when she says,

> If you do love me, you will find me out
> (III, ii, 41)

as the very name of his beloved fills his mind. The question,

> What says this leaden casket? (II, vii, 15)

is also seen to have a deeper meaning. The casket may not 'speak', but it tells all. While Morocco stumbles through his involved reasonings, incapable of 'hearing' what the casket 'says', the spectators, for their part, like those of ancient Greek drama, already know the answer and smile with relief when the unwanted suitor guesses wrong.

PLAINNESS AND ELOQUENCE

Bassanio appears to disregard the objects before him and confine himself only to the sound of the words. This itself brings out precise proof of the play's direct provenance from the original. Addressing the leaden casket, he says,

> Thy plainness moves me more than eloquence
> (III, ii, 106)

an expression called by Freud 'eigentlich so ganz unvermittelt'.[1] To be sure, not only Freud felt this line to be difficult. 'Plainness', the Quarto reading, is so far from constituting the logical opposite of 'eloquence' that it has been emended in modern editions.[2] But when the words are translated back into Hebrew, they give two technical terms commonly used in Biblical interpretation for two different methods of exegesis: *pešat*, literally 'plain' meaning, and *deraš*, the preacher's 'eloquent' reading an idea of his own into the text.[3]

TWO VARIANTS

The unknown translator from the Hebrew (and unknown of course to Shakespeare) apparently had two variants of the casket story in front of him. The one that deals with the materials and their names can be called the Material-variant. The other version, where the test proposed is to guess the import of riddling inscriptions, can be called the Verbal variant.

Both variants are made use of in the first monologue of Morocco. On the basis of the inscription,

> Who chooseth me, shall gain what many men.
> desire (II, vii, 5)

he decides on this casket, saying,

> Why that's the lady, all the world desires her.
> (II, vii, 38)

Then he begins reflecting all over again:

> One of these three contains her heavenly picture
> (II, vii, 48)

as if he had not seen the inscriptions at all. It looks very much as if the two variants are interwoven here in front of us.

In the case of Arragon, nothing remains of the Material variant except his opening words,

> ...gold, silver and base lead (II, ix, 20)

and for the rest, he restricts himself to the inscriptions.

Bassanio takes only the materials into account, except when he addresses the leaden casket:

> Which rather threaten'st than dost promise aught.
> (III, ii, 105)

The 'threat' which he says he sees here is presumably a reference to the inscription,

---

[1] *Ibid.*

[2] E.g., see the involved argumentation in the Arden edition to justify accepting the emendation, 'paleness'. *Loc. cit.*, footnote, pp. 82–3. (Translator)

[3] Accordingly, any expository sermonising is called *derašah* in Hebrew.

> Who chooseth me, must give and hazard all he
>   hath   (II, vii, 9)

but nothing in the text indicates that Bassanio has in fact read this inscription at all. This one subordinate clause, like the classical allusion,

> ...hard food for Midas   (III, ii, 102)

only serves to blur the sharp contrast between 'gaudy gold' and 'meagre lead'. They may have been inserted by the compiler who combined the two variants, as may the inconsistent reproof:

> All that glisters is not gold   (II, vii, 65)

Morocco's error was not that he preferred false glister to real gold, but real gold to lead.

The two variants utilise different means to indicate the right solution. In the one, they are objects – a portrait or the like – and in the other they are scrolls, disclosed inside the caskets. With Morocco's choice, the two are skilfully combined; with Arragon's, they are kept separate: he first finds

> ...the portrait of a blinking idiot   (II, ix, 54)

and then he quite unnecessarily has to read a scroll. The double source is even more in evidence in Bassanio's case. Already holding 'fair Portia's counterfeit' in his hands, he still reads out a supplementary confirmation. Suitors who failed were left with nothing but these objects or scrolls.[1]

Thus at some point in time before *The Merchant of Venice* was written, two versions existed with two incompatible casket-choice procedures, and these must later have been combined in the version to which Shakespeare had access.

A further example of a point that has been lost but can be retrieved by reference to the Hebrew is the inscription on the gold casket, the one that had a death's-head inside. The inscription reads:

> Who chooseth me, shall gain what many men
>   desire.   (II, vii, 5)

The Hebrew for 'desire' is again a word with a double meaning, both 'desire/lust' and 'border/end', so that a man's lust equally signifies his end or death, a double meaning that is also to be found in other times and languages. And into the bargain, this Hebrew word, таАwaн, meaning 'desire/lust', also appears only once in the Scriptures in the threatening sense of 'end/utmost bound' and then it is very close (Gen XLIX, 26) – only four verses apart! – to the similarly unique PORaT (Gen XLIX, 22).

DESERT

The original pre-Shakespearian English translator seems not only to have recognised the Hebrew play on words but, surprisingly, to have succeeded in transposing them here and there into English. He has Morocco say,

> Why, that's the lady   (II, vii, 31)

and the word 'lady' sounds not unlike 'lead'. However when Morocco asked earlier on,

> What says this leaden casket?   (II, vii, 15)

the echo of 'lady' did not occur to him, and so he kept on asking himself what each casket said. The caskets are indeed all speechless, but the leaden one alone 'says' something in the name of its material about the beautiful, beloved lady whose hand he is sueing for, and he cannot take the hint.

The translator also attempted another play on words, as good as the Hebrew ones, when he had Arragon say first,

> I will assume desert   (II, ix, 51)

only to have him exclaim bitterly soon after,

> Are my deserts no better?   (II, ix, 60)

[1] Originally the choice was not at all a harmless affair – when wrong, it meant the death of the suitor. All that remains of this in our play is the death's-head, and the fact that by chance the term 'chest' for a casket has as its Hebrew equivalent the word *aron*, which is also used for coffin.

The noun 'desert' means 'deserving/merit', while its homonym means 'wilderness'; and the verb 'to desert' means 'to leave/run away'. No wonder he is dismissed with

Be gone   (II, ix, 72)

which may even have been meant to echo 'Arragon'. Whether the word 'desert' does or does not suit Arragon's lack of deserving and his departure, Shakespeare overlooked the applicability of the pun to Morocco and so here the ironical flavour was lost.

All the foregoing implies nothing more about Shakespeare himself than that he had a piece in his hands that was itself derived from some more vigorous source. This may contradict the view that the work of his predecessors was mere raw material that Shakespeare converted into masterpieces. Perhaps in this instance the quality of genius was already in the ancient source. We shall return to the idea of an ancient source, but we still have some supplementary observations to make on the choice of caskets.

PORTIA'S SONG

While Bassanio is making his choice, Portia's maid sings a song (III, ii, 63 et seq.) at Portia's bidding:

Let music sound while he doth make his choice.
                                (III, ii, 43)

Now Portia is forbidden to give any open assistance to any suitor, so she explains her reason for calling for music:

Then if he lose he makes a swan-like end,
Fading in music.   (III, ii, 44–5)

She then proceeds to expatiate on this far-fetched notion, which is very far from her secret desires, for another seven lines, in the course of which the swan song becomes an epithalamium – again the coincidence of death and desire. The song itself, meanwhile, is in fact exactly calculated to produce the desired solution.

The opening word of the song is, 'Tell –'

Tell me, where is fancy bred? (III, ii, 63)

The Hebrew for 'tell', HAGGED, is used in the Bible as a technical term for 'solving' a riddle, mystery or dream (Jud. XIV, 12).

The word 'fancy' is explained in scholarly commentaries on *The Merchant of Venice* as 'fond affection', but this is a later meaning. 'Fancy' derives etymologically from 'fantasy', and in Hebrew both 'fancy' and 'fantasy' are DIMYON, also meaning, 'similarity likeness'. Incidentally, the closeness of the ideas involved appears in the English 'image' and 'imagination', while 'imagination' and 'fantasy' were for long linked in English poetical and critical vocabulary. In the original text the word must have been DIMYON, meaning 'similarity' and 'likeness', since the riddle is indeed based on words sounding or looking like each other.

The next line of the song,

Or in the heart, or in the head

– a Hebraism in its use of double 'or' for 'either...or' – gives an even broader hint of the solution than what went before. In Hebrew, the initial letter of a word is called 'head of the word' (hence the Hebrew for 'acronym' is 'heads-of-the-words'), and thus Bassanio's attention is directed to the fact that PRT and ØPRT differ from each other by an initial letter only.

The song now asks, 'How begot...? ...' and at the insistent demand of 'All' standing around – 'Reply, reply', the reply is forthcoming:

It is engend'red in the eyes.   (III, ii, 67)

This peculiar phrase contains two perfectly plain pointers to the solution. Something is said to have its origin in the eyes, as if it were 'begot' or 'engendered' in them or by them. Now in Hebrew one and the same verb can mean 'to be begun' or 'to be engendered'. In this instance it is not a matter of two words related to each other or derived from the same root, far less of merely similar-sounding words, but exactly the same root and the same form: YUḤAL (Ḥ sounds like *ch* in German *ich*). In Is. LXVI, 8, we find: 'Shall the earth *be made to bring forth* in one day?' The five words, be made to bring forth, translate the one Hebrew word: ha-YUḤAL (where the prefix *ha-* is merely a question marker). This half-verse could be translated: 'Shall the earth engender?' a meaning confirmed in the parallel half-verse, 'Shall a nation be born at once?' In Gen. IV, 26 we find the same verb: 'Then men began to call upon the name of the Lord.' Here the Hebrew means literally, 'It was begun...' In Portia's song, then, what was not engendered but begun 'in the eyes'? We again recall that the Hebrew words PRT and ØPRT comprise an identical series of consonants except for the one initial letter 'at the head' of the second word, and this initial is the letter called *ayin* in Hebrew, which we have already stated means 'well/source'. But it also means, 'eye' – and this meaning is even the commoner one.

In these conditions, subjected to a flood of broad hints and the clearest of clues, how could the Hebrew Bassanio conceivably have gone wrong in his choice? His attention was directed *in expressis verbis* to the metal, lead, ØPRT, with Portia, PRT, 'contained' therein; even the affix attached to the beginning of her name is plainly given: it is 'the eye' = the letter *ayin*. To make doubly sure and also to stress the witticism, her name, PORAT, is said to be 'in the *ayin*' = 'upon' or 'by a well'.

FIRE SEVEN TIMES TRIED

The first line of the scroll in the silver casket reads:

> The fire seven times tried this.   (II, ix, 63)

A conventional and formal way of praising silver, perhaps, but it is worth remarking that

the Hebrew for 'try' (BḤN), in the sense of 'test', differs by only one consonant from the word for 'choose' (BḤR), and the two consonants, *N* and *R* are often interchangeable. The form, 'chosen' (NIBḤAR, the passive past participle of BḤR) is found in a well-known verse in the Book of Proverbs as an adjective describing silver: 'The tongue of the just is as choice [lit. chosen] silver' (Prov. X, 20). The disappointed chooser learns that he and other suitors before him have made the same mistake – seven times is a conventional, poetic way of saying 'many times' in Hebrew. Moreover, the same Hebrew word means 'young man' (BAḤUR) or else 'chooser' and 'suitor' (BOḤER), according to the vocalisation.[1]

To return for the last time to 'Joseph, son of PORAT': – There are three great sages and interpreters of dreams in the Bible, Joseph, King Solomon and Daniel. Portia utilises Joseph's method of explaining dreams as bodying forth a play on words,[2] exemplified in his interpretation of Pharaoh's dream; she also plays the role of the wise judge, King Solomon; and she is hailed by the name of the third, Daniel, when she presents herself before the tribunal in Venice to unravel the riddle of Shylock's bond or pact.

DANIEL AGAIN

Even if we allow ourselves to be persuaded that the cry, 'A Daniel come to judgement!' must

---

[1] It is worth mentioning that the Mishna (*Ta'anit* 4:8) recounts that it was the custom in Jerusalem on certain holidays for the maidens to call out to the young men as they danced, 'See for yourself what you choose for yourself!' and that the refined and beautiful as well as the plain ones among them always had something to say to attract the choice to themselves.

[2] Schönfeld's manuscript does not go into what play on words he is referring to here, but I had it from him by word of mouth that he had made an extensive study of Joseph's interpretations of dreams. It is to be hoped that we shall learn more of this when his manuscripts are finally deciphered. (Y.T.R.)

originate in the literal meaning of the name, 'God-like judge', we are far from having exhausted the relationship between Daniel and *The Merchant of Venice*. Shylock compares Portia with Daniel, and a Daniel indeed appears in the apocryphal Book of Susanna, but there are numerous other and far more striking parallels between the play and the Daniel of the Bible, interpreter of dreams.

In Babylon, according to the story in the Book of Daniel, chapter 11, what was at stake was the lives of renowned 'wise men' (v. 12) – magicians, astrologers, sorcerers (v. 2); in Venice it was the life of a patrician of renown. The wise men of the Chaldeans were to be 'cut in pieces' (v. 12); Antonio was to have a pound of his flesh cut off. The King in Babylon, like the Duke of Venice, makes the rescue of those threatened depend on an exceptionally difficult intellectual feat. Both jurists have a second name, and in both cases it is Balthazar:

> ...a young doctor of Rome, his name is
> Balthazar.   (IV, i, 152–3)

In both stories, Daniel's appearance is made possible by a high-ranking personage: in the Bible he was called Ariokh, the captain of the King's guard (v. 14), in the play and its putative source, Bellario, 'a learned doctor' (IV, I, 105). They are in fact the same person: *Ario*kh/*Bell*ario. Take the name Ariokh, prefix the Babylonian god, Bel, drop the final 'kh', and the resulting name sounds perfectly Italianate, Bellario. The sound that was discarded – /kh/ – will soon be encountered elsewhere. In Gratiano, friend of Antonio and Bassanio, we recognise Daniel's friend, Hananiah: the Italian form is an exact translation of the Hebrew name, which means 'graced', 'blessèd'. All this points to only one conclusion: we are dealing with a treatment of the source-piece that displays a close acquaintance with the Biblical narrative in the original Hebrew text.

A PRELIMINARY RESUME

To sum up: What were the antecedents of Shakespeare's play? There was in all likelihood a whole series, and it looks as if Shakespeare knew only one version (A), certainly in English, of an Italian tale about a wicked Jewish usurer who is successfully bamboozled and fleeced. Whether the casket choice was also recounted in this version, or whether it came from some other Italian play, can be left open, but for the sake of simplicity let us assume that it was already a part of (A). The author of this tendentious Italian play had two variants of the casket choice in front of him, one based on the metals and the other on enigmatic inscriptions. Both variants plus the Shylock plot go back to a Hebrew-language piece (B), also tendentious but in the reverse direction: the Jews were the 'good side' as against medieval Christianity. This piece too must have had a predecessor (C), the earliest source of all, also in Hebrew, which made no distinction between 'good Jews' and 'bad Christians' or vice versa, but was played out in an entirely Jewish context. Therefore, as is normal within a homogeneous civilisation, the conflict in this piece (C) was not between the followers of different faiths but the eternal conflict between good and evil among and within men.

We are now in a position to reconstruct what must have been the oldest, still recognisable source (C).

SHYLOCK

In the oldest layer of all, then, what form does Shylock assume?

If we compare the Biblical story of Daniel with the Venetian play, we find that the two roles of the King and the captain of the guard in the former are combined in the later piece in a single personage. Nebuchadnezzar demands the death of the wise men, and Ariokh is commissioned to carry out the sentence, while in our play both the desire and the deed are allocated to Shylock – and so is the name: the /kh/ is cut off the end of Ariokh (leaving the first bit, 'ario', to be attached after the Babylonian god 'Bel-' to make the Italian form Bellario) and is transferred to Shylock, who becomes the sole embodiment of evil. If we take the first part of Shylock's name, we can find two and only two Hebrew words that fit, each written with the same consonants, Saul (ŠAUL), the name of King David's predecessor, and ŠEOL, which in Hebrew signifies the underworld and Death personified.[1]

In the original source (C) the Christians of the later versions (A, B) were still Jews; it fits in perfectly, then, that in the beginning the villain (later the Jew) was if not exactly a non-Jew, in fact an enemy of the Jews or more precisely an enemy of mankind in general. It is a significant pointer in this respect that other Jewish figures in Shakespeare's play[2] have names that are indeed Hebrew, but pre-Israelite: Jessica (=Iscah, Gen. XI, 29) and Tubal (Gen. X, 2).[3]

Shylock displays all the distinctive qualities of Pluto in Hades: he is bloodthirsty, merciless and rich, and he concludes a diabolic pact with human beings.[4]

The name of Daniel now carries its full weight of meaning for the first time. Just as in the name Israel the component EL = God is in the objective case and is explained in the Scripture as meaning 'one who prevailed over God' (Gen. XXXII, 28), so the -EL in Daniel can also be construed in the objective case, and then the name means, one who judges a god. But who is the god that is judged here?

We have already said that to the Hebrew ear the name Shylock recalls ŠEOL, the underworld, and also the name of King Saul himself. To this we now add that the Hebrew verb root ŠAL means 'to lend/borrow'. Lending is the basic motif of the whole plot of the play and it is also the means by which in all the legends the Devil lures men into his snare. Thus we see that in the original story we are concerned with

a fable or myth about a pact between man and the Devil. This accounts for the names of both the Death-God and the judge. Both are mythical, pre-Biblical figures. Besides the two Daniels of the Bible and the apocryphal Book of Susanna, we have still another obscure and even older Daniel, one whom Ezekiel (XIV, 14) names in the same breath with Noah. How right Shylock is when he says to Portia–Daniel,

How much more elder art thou than thy looks!

(IV, i, 247)

THE PACT OR BOND

The Hebrew word for pact (treaty, agreement, bond, covenant) is formed by the consonants HZH, pronounced when vocalised: ḤOZEH. The same three consonants. differently vocalised, give ḤAZEH, which means 'breast/chest'. We already suspect that we have here a play on words which conceals a characteristically 'devilish' trick: the same text, if written without vowel-points, can be read to mean, 'upon the bond' or 'upon the breast'. (The Hebrew preposition for 'upon' is used in both ways, as in English.)

Perhaps most significant of all, Isaiah (XXVIII, 15) uses the two phrases, 'a covenant with death' and 'an agreement with Hell', as if already in his day this represented a familiar, proverbial expression: 'Because ye have said, We have made a covenant with death, and with hell are we at agreement (ḤOZEH)...'.

If Antonio were to agree to the pact with Shylock, it had to be made to appear a harmless agreement, a 'merry bond' (I, iii, 169):

[1] The Septuagint translates the word ŠEOL as Hades or else Thanatos.

[2] See the list of *Dramatis Personae*.

[3] Jessica mentions another 'countryman' of her father's with a Biblical but again non-Israelite name, Chus (III, ii, 284). (Y.T.R.)

[4] Shylock is actually called 'the devil' repeatedly by the various protagonists. E.g. II, ii, 23, 25, 26; III, i, 19–20, 30, 71. He is also referred to as a 'fiend', etc.

Three thousand ducats for a pound of flesh, perhaps only the flesh of 'muttons, beef or goats' (I, iii, 163), whereby the debt was to be discharged in full, without the imposition of any further penalty for failure to repay by the day the bond expired, may indeed have looked cheap enough. It is worth mentioning that the number 3,000 also originates from an old Hebrew substratum, this many 'shekels' adding up to exactly one 'talent'.

Now that we can vaguely discern the outline of this third source, the ancient universal (not Jew-versus-Christian) theme, a lot more things are suddenly clear:

1. We understand why no one was found in the whole of Venice to obviate the consequences of the agreement, since it was not thought that there was anything serious to obviate.

2. When Shylock says,

> You'll ask me why I rather choose to have
> A weight of carrion flesh, than to receive
> Three thousand ducats...   (IV, 1, 40–3)

this only makes sense if the agreement meant that a pound of flesh discharged the entire debt, and was thus in the nature of a 'merry bond', as explained above.

3. It is now plausible that Portia should refuse Shylock even the return of his capital, with the words,

> Thou shalt have nothing but the forfeiture.
> (IV, i, 339)

4. Only of a 'merry bond' of this kind (I, iii, 169) could Shylock possibly affirm that it was a 'friendship' extended in order to buy Antonio's favour (I, iii, 164) and dissipate the Venetians' distrust. So it is not mere stupidity or naivety that makes his interlocutor Antonio assert,

> There is much kindness in this Jew
> (I, iii, 149)

and that Shylock 'grows kind' with these 'fair terms' (I, iii, 174–5). These things belong to the original source (C) and cannot have been part

of the later Jewish piece (B) where the parties were openly at enmity. It is equally implausible for them to have come from the most recent layer (A) with its anti-Jewish line.

5. There is no other explanation for Antonio's answering Portia's first question,

> You stand within his danger?

with,

> So he says,

which is a disclaimer, and then her second question,

> Do you confess the bond?

with,

> I do.   (IV, i, 176–8)

How is it that Antonio admits to the agreement but yet does not agree with Shylock? He is faced with a riddle: he has been tricked by a play on words, the substitution of ḤAZEH (breast) for ḤOZEH (bond).

6. It is now possible to understand why Portia should declare that the pound of flesh must 'be by him [Shylock] cut off nearest the merchant's heart' (IV, i, 229) and so threaten Antonio's life. This is so difficult to explain without the Hebrew that the commentators are driven to surmise that presumably Shylock made the further stipulation when the bond was prepared[1] though there is nothing of the kind anywhere in the text.

7. When Shylock overcomes the objections of the other party to his proposed bond by asking him to bear in mind that

> A pound of man's flesh... / Is not so estimable.../
> As flesh of muttons   (I, iii, 160–3)

the joke is on him and it is a devilish one. His remark is a scornful sneer, but the dramatic irony consists in his assertion's pointing to exactly what is to be his portion in the future.

[1] See e.g. Arden edition, p. 113, note to line 229. (Translator)

The same joke is concealed behind the enthusiastic, 'Most learnèd judge!', with which he ironically praises the jurist, who, he thinks, has not seen through his plot, but who is in fact about to confound him.

8. When Shylock insists over and over again, 'I will have my bond' (III, iii, 4–17), he means that he is determined to have the terms of his bond honoured. The repetition of the word 'bond' no less than six times in fourteen lines permits at least a surmise that the original text rang the changes on 'bond' and 'breast' – ḤOZEH/ḤAZEH – with deliberately comic effect, not unlike the juxtaposition of 'daughter' and 'ducats' earlier on (II, viii, 15–24).

9. When Portia recognises Shylock's right by saying,

> He shall have merely justice and his bond
> (IV, i, 335)

the 'merely' means that he is to have strict 'justice' according to the exact terms of his bond, and nothing more: no repayment of the money lent, and not a drop of blood.

BLOOD

Portia's dead father, dictating from beyond the grave how she was to live, was indeed in some sort a god of Death. (Freudian symbolism sees Death as a dead man and one dead as Death.)[1] Herself the daughter of a dead man, and very much at home with the craft of riddles – those caskets! – Portia sees through the deception when Shylock demands his 'bond' but means Antonio's 'breast', and she defeats Shylock with his own weapon, a play on words.

The comparison of money with blood, more, the congruence of the two, is an ancient affair. In Hebrew it is perfectly explicit. The same word, DAMIM, stands for both. This particular point is so decisive for the thesis presented here that it would almost suffice to clinch the argument on its own. The conditions of the original Hebrew agreement must have entitled

Shylock to a pound of flesh 'upon ḤZH', in return for which he pledged himself not to demand DAMIM = money. Portia accepts this entirely, but with a trick: 'If you, Shylock, read ḤZH not as ḤOZEH (bond) but as ḤAZEH (breast), then I construe DAMIM not as money but as blood. Hereby there is indeed due to you a pound of Antonio's flesh, but without a single drop of blood – exactly as written in the pact!'

Shylock is justifiably taken aback. The misunderstanding could easily be cleared up, but then he would risk exposing his own word-trickery. He therefore contents himself with saying,

> Give me my principal and let me go
> (IV, i, 332)

but this Portia rejects. Shylock now wants to hurry off, since his claim suddenly looks like a criminal conspiracy. But here too Portia is a match for him:

> Tarry Jew,
> ...For it appears...
> Thou hast contrived against the very life
> Of the defendant   (IV, i, 343, 354–67)

showing that she has unmasked him.

This judgement of Portia's again parallels Daniel's procedure in the case of Susanna and Solomon's judgement on the two mothers, inasmuch as all three affairs are concerned with an attempt to deceive the court.

SAUL AND DAVID

The name Shylock, we have said, reminds a Hebrew listener of the name of King Saul. If we focus on this point, some additional noteworthy elements emerge connected with the story of Saul.

The friendship between Bassanio and Antonio follows the very pattern and example of the proverbial friendship of David and Jonathan, son of King Saul. Shylock seeks the

[1] See p. 117 note 1 above.

life of Antonio, who has stood pledge for Bassanio, just as Saul sought to kill his own son when Jonathan interposed on behalf of David (1 Sam. XX, 3 *et seq.*). Moreover, the name Jonathan itself can easily be identified in Antonio: Jo-, Jeho-, -yah, -iah, the theophoric component, can appear equally well at the beginning or the end of a Hebrew name. Thus e.g., the same King of Judah is called Jehoiachin in one place (Ezek. I, 2) and Jechoniah in another (Jer. XVII, 20). J*onathan* is the same as *Nathan*iah, which is Italianised as Antonio.

Bassanio's advice to Antonio to shoot a second arrow to find the first that was lost also recalls the arrows shot by Jonathan to warn David in the Biblical story (1 Sam. XX, 18–22, 35–40).[1]

Just as the friendship motif echoes the Hebrew story of David and Jonathan, so the inexplicable melancholy of Antonio, which strikes the opening note of the play, is at least a reminder of the 'evil spirit' that troubled Saul (1 Sam. XVI, 14).

The two derivations of the name, Shylock, as given above, are not mutually exclusive. King Saul himself can if one wishes be equated with the God of Death. He can be conceived of as a bloodstained tyrant, who deserts his people in their war against the Philistines (1 Sam. XIX, 8–9), wipes out an entire city of the priests, slays the Gibeonites (2 Sam. XXXI, 1–2), persecutes David, the 'man of Israel' who defeated Goliath (1 Sam. XVII, *passim*) and almost starts a civil war. He never lets his javelin out of his hand (1 Sam. XIX, 9) and once even tries to smite his own son to the wall with it (1 Sam. XXX, 33). He is a God of Death who consumes his own children.

That Saul too is embodied in Shylock is further confirmed by other details in the play: in the original, Nerissa must have been Nerit (= of Ner) or Bat (= daughter of) Ner, and was thus the counterpart of the captain of Saul's host, Abner son of Ner (1 Sam. XXVI, 5). Abner 'made himself strong for the house of

Saul' and for the house of Saul's heir and successor, David (2 Sam. III, 6, 13). True, 'house' here means the royal dynasty, but it is another play on words to give the name to Nerissa, who serves in the house of the heiress Portia, the 'lady richly left'. Moreover, Abner, son of Ner, brings about the marriage of David to Saul's daughter (2 Sam. III, 12–16), and similarly Nerissa accomplishes the joining together of Portia and Bassanio; and both these marriages had been delayed after an earlier encounter of love at first sight!

One may still ask how Bassanio can possibly be said to correspond to King David of the Bible, the ideal figure of Jewry, when at first sight his unusual name seems to lack any particular significance, in Italian or Hebrew. Unusual it may be, but not inexplicable. Bashan (Bašan) was the only province that remained to King David in the wars of his old age, and hence it is fitting that the most favoured of the suitors should be called Prince of Bashan – Bassanio – and all the more so since all the other candidates for Portia's hand were called after their countries.

When King David had to retreat across the Jordan and take refuge in the Bashan region because of the revolt of Absalom, one of his few trusted companions was his old friend, Barzilai, the man of Gilead (2 Sam. XVII, 27). Now Barzel is Hebrew for iron, *ferrum* in Latin, and the region of Gilead in Transjordan is mountainous, and its nomenclature syn-

---

[1] Another Biblical allusion in the play, similarly an echo rather than an exact parallel, concerns a specific commandment of the Torah (Deut. XXII, 6, 7) to the effect that if a bird's nest chances to be in your way, the dam must not be taken with the young, but 'thou shalt take the young to thee'. On Jessica's elopement, Solanio comments, 'Shylock knew the bird was fledge [fledged] and then it is the complexion [nature] of them all to leave the dam.' (III, i, 26–7). The commandment is hardly known outside Jewry, and Shakespeare could not conceivably have had it in mind. It looks as if it was quoted in his source, and he made the best sense of it he could. (Y.T.R.)

onymous with Bashan. This Barzilai has a very minor role in the Book of Samuel (1 Sam. II, 114), exactly like his counterpart in *The Merchant of Venice*, for he is indeed to be found there, again as a chance companion, the Marquis of Montferrat, whose name, perhaps originally Ferratus de Monte (= Mount Gilead), corresponds exactly to that of his prototype, Barzilai.

Even Gobbo, Shylock's servant, is to be found in the oldest version (C) in the days of Saul. The Gibeonites were lowly 'hewers of wood and drawers of water' ever since the days of Joshua (Jos. IX, 4–7, 27), but they identified themselves so completely with the people of Israel that they even went with them into exile in Babylon and came back from there with the rest of the exiles who returned (Ezra II, 43–54). The name Gobbo could well come from Gibeonite: Gobbo is designated without the slightest cause as 'of Hagar's offspring' (II, v, 44). This is nothing but a misreading of the Hebrew word. HGR can be vocalised as HaGaR – or else as Ha-GeR: the latter means a convert, and the Gibeonites were indeed converts of a special kind.

The plays on words and the clues from names are even more extensive than we have seen so far. In her role of Daniel, Portia has a servant named Balthazar, a sub-form of the Belshazzar of the Book of Daniel. And she also has another servant, named Stephano, which means 'wearing a crown on one's head' in Greek; this can be linked to the Hebrew APeR, the disguise worn on a head as recounted in 1 Kings XX, 38; and if it is given a feminine ending, it vocalises as Ephrat (APRT) – behold, our well-known consonant group PRT with a different prefix. Moreover, King David himself is called the Ephrati (APRTI) in 1 Sam. XVII, 12.[1] The fact that neither Balthazar nor Stephano has anything to do in the play but that they are nevertheless entitled to have their names mentioned is another of these apparently insignificant details that can only really be explained on the assumption that they had roles in a Hebrew model.

To return at last to the main problem. The casket-choice story is generally considered by critics a heterogeneous element introduced into the play as a sub-plot for no very good reason. Now at last the casket choice and the Shylock-pact are seen to have been organically connected in the Hebrew original.[2]

CONCLUSION

At the beginning of this essay, we remarked that the hypothesis of an original Jewish-Hebrew source (C) of the Shakespearian drama can expect to meet with rejection at the start. But once the immediate objections are overcome, the question remains whether strong arguments cannot in fact be raised against our hypothesis. At bottom there is only one valid counter-argument: no documentary proof exists of either of the previous versions (A) or (B), let alone the original source (C). It can be argued against this at least by analogy that practically all modern Bible criticism is agreed that the Pentateuch was compiled from different scriptural sources – the so-called Jahvist, Elohist and Deuteronomical 'documents' and a priestly codex. The question

[1] The homiletic collection *Midrash Bereshit Rabbah* (99:13) explicitly derives Ephrat (EPRT), the other name of Bethlehem, where Rachel died and David was born, from Porat (PRT) in Gen. XLIX, 22.

[2] Schönfeld's MS. stops abruptly here, except for some brief notes on the connection between Shakespeare's play, the novella *Il Pecorone*, the *Gesta Romanorum*, the Dolopathos, and the two hypothetical Hebrew sources. That the MS. has been preserved at all is thanks to Dr Bertha Gruenspan, and all the friends of the author owe her a debt of gratitude. Schönfeld also left a card-index with 30,000 cards, written in shorthand, dealing further with this subject and also, *inter alia*, with *Hamlet*. This material is in the possession of the author's daughter, Mrs Hanna Shoham, who is at present deciphering the notes in the hope that they can eventually be edited for publication. The two paragraphs that conclude this essay were written by the editor. (Y.T.R.)

whether this documentary hypothesis holds good or not is not the issue here. We only wish to point out that not a single line of any of these hypothetical sources has ever been discovered, but modern Biblical criticism treats anyone who doubts their having existed as an obscurantist.

Our hypothesis concerning *The Merchant of Venice* rests on a much firmer foundation. A whole series of Hebrew-language secular plays written in Italy in the early Renaissance has been preserved, and these plays are themselves testimony to the fact that others like them must have existed. The greater part of this literature has been lost, understandably so, for two reasons: firstly, Jews throughout their history have concerned themselves with matters of religion, and learned Jews have strenuously resisted the production and propagation of all other literary genres; at all events, far less weight has been attached to preserving and transmitting non-religious works, something that can be substantiated by evidence from Biblical times right down to the emancipation of the Jews in the nineteenth century. Secondly, a glance at Jewish history with its endless persecutions and expulsions and the burning of Hebrew writings is enough to make one wonder how anything survived at all of medieval Jewish literature, religious and secular alike.[1]

---

[1] In the course of a preliminary, superficial review of the material left by Schönfeld, a newspaper cutting came to light, taken from the *Neue Zürcher Zeitung* of 16 May 1936, which to be sure has no direct connection with *The Merchant of Venice* but which gives sufficient

support to some of Schönfeld's conjectures to be worth reproducing here:

Susanna re-discovered

English literary historians were aware of the existence of a morality play based on the story of the apocryphal Susanna, but all trace of it had been lost since the middle of the 18th century. Prof. B. Ifor Evans has now rediscovered this old play in the Sir George Beaumont Library in Coleorton Hall. It is attributed to one Thomas Garter and was written around the year 1569. The Devil, the Clown, Sinfulness and Lust appear in the play, and there is no lack of dramatic action including a stoning, an execution and a court scene with the Prophet Daniel. The circumstances in which the old play was brought to light were unusual. Prof. Evans was starting to collect material on Wordsworth and Coleridge when he came upon a parchment tome containing thirteen old pieces bound together. Since the library of the Hall could not hold all the books there were in the place, this tome was put away in the attic and that is where its Columbus found it. Prof. Evans rightly complains of the not very obliging attitude of English Midases: 'There are many still uncatalogued literary treasures in Great Britain. If only the owners of old libraries would give scholars access to them, much more might come to light. But many collections which might fill the *lacunae* in our literary knowledge have up to now closed their doors to the experts. The curators of the Beaumont have authorized me to prepare a new edition of the *Susanna* for the Malone Society. Even if this find is in fact of interest only to the world of scholarship, the hope should nevertheless not be abandoned of one day unearthing some priceless Shakespeare document. What happened to the American Prof. Charles William Wallace should not remain a unique stroke of luck.'

It should be noted, in connection with this curious piece of news that, according to the Arden edition, the earliest text of *The Merchant of Venice* is a Quarto dated 1600, but therein the play was stated to have been 'divers times' acted before. The Susanna morality play discovered by Evans was therefore relatively recent theatrical history when Shakespeare wrote *The Merchant*. (Y.T.R.)

THE MARRIAGE CONTRACTS IN 'MEASURE FOR MEASURE': A RECONSIDERATION

KARL P. WENTERSDORF

I

To judge from the continuing spate of publications on the topic, there seems to be no end to the disagreement over the nature and dramatic significance of the marriage contracts in *Measure for Measure* – that of Claudio and Juliet, and that between the Deputy Angelo and Mariana. The action of the play is set in motion when Claudio is sentenced to death by Angelo for the crime of fornication, even though he protests his innocence on the grounds that he and Juliet were truly man and wife by a clandestine wedding contract, and that they had kept their union secret only for fear of antagonizing the friends of Juliet, who controlled her dowry (I, ii, 145–55).[1] The first problem is as to the validity of Claudio's defence. Later, when his sister Isabella appeals to the Deputy to show mercy, she is told that she can save her brother's life only by submitting to Angelo sexually. The second problem arises when the Duke assures Mariana, a lady once betrothed to Angelo and still in love with him, that she could – without sinning – take Isabella's place at the proposed assignation with Angelo. The Duke's assurance that she would not be guilty of fornication in doing so is based on the circumstance that she was formerly contracted to marry Angelo (III, i, 213–30). Why will Mariana be guiltless, if Juliet and Claudio are guilty?

It was asserted by one of the contributors to *Shakespeare's England* that the sentencing of Claudio to death for fornication was, and was

intended by Shakespeare to be, tyrannical and illegal.[2] Most of the later critics, including Harding (1950)[3] and Schanzer (1960),[4] believe the death sentence to be unmercifully severe but just, since Claudio, in their view, is guilty of violating the moral code by consummating his private betrothal before the public nuptials. Schanzer asserts in addition that, whereas Claudio's relationship with Juliet was established by a private or clandestine contract entered into at the very moment of exchanging the marital vows (known in canon law as

[1] References to Shakespeare are to the text of *The Riverside Shakespeare*, ed. G. Blakemore Evans *et al.* (Boston, 1974).

[2] Arthur Underhill, 'Law', in *Shakespeare's England* (1916), I, 408. See also Elizabeth M. Pope, 'The Renaissance Background of *Measure for Measure*', *Shakespeare Survey 2* (Cambridge, 1949), p. 76: 'Angelo's treatment of Claudio is from the first inexcusable, even by the strict standards of the Renaissance. For clemency in this particular case would certainly have had "a good foundation upon reason and equity."' Furthermore, Claudio is defended by Escalus and the Provost, both of whom are 'kind, sensible men who represent the normal point of view and whose support of Claudio is therefore significant'.

[3] Davies P. Harding, 'Elizabethan Betrothals and *Measure for Measure*', *JEGP*, 49 (1950), 156.

[4] Ernest Schanzer, 'The Marriage-Contracts in *Measure for Measure*', *Shakespeare Survey 13* (Cambridge 1960), pp. 82–7. Cf also A. P. Rossiter, *Angel with Horns* (1961), p. 161, n. 2: 'Critics who say Angelo's actions were *tyranny* depart utterly from the text. To Escalus and the Provost, Claudio is simply "a hard case" – not a case of illegality or wresting the law.'

sponsalia [spousals] *per verba de praesenti*), that of Angelo with Mariana was a contract for a future marriage (*sponsalia per verba de futuro*). For Schanzer, the dramatic problems arise because of inconsistencies inherent in the attitude of the church toward clandestine marriages like Claudio's – the view that whereas such marriages were valid, their consummation before the public solemnization was gravely sinful. As for Angelo and Mariana, Schanzer cuts the Gordian knot by denying any validity to the Duke's assurance that Mariana's pre-nuptial sexual union with Angelo would not be immoral: that assurance, he argues, is based neither on law nor custom, and it is attributable to a ducal idiosyncrasy (the Duke, in Lucio's words, 'had crotchets in him').

A somewhat different approach is made by Nagarajan (1963), who asserts that Claudio is legally guilty because his was only a *de futuro* betrothal, and that this 'did not confer the right of sexual union on the partners'; the legal authority consulted by Nagarajan persuaded him that 'only a *de praesenti* contract allowed any sexual union'. Since the description of Mariana's situation allegedly points to the existence of a *de praesenti* contract, Nagarajan argues that the Duke *was* justified in proposing the bed-trick, provided that the physical union was followed by a church ceremony (which he insists on in the fifth act).[1] Critical perplexity reaches its peak in a paper drawing attention to the dangers involved in imposing 'a thoroughly rigid framework on what in essence is a work of dramatic fiction' and in basing arguments on a 'so called marriage code whose validity must remain questionable owing to the ambivalence toward the code inherent in the contemporary ecclesiastical jurisprudence'. In spite of the dangers, however, the same writer concludes that 'the clandestine nature of Claudio's contract...makes his punishment dramatically valid in view of the fact that he is reprehensible according to the Church's edict'.[2] And in the

British Academy lecture for 1974, Maxwell reveals a similar belief in the 'paradoxical' nature of traditional Church law: 'What were known as *sponsalia de praesenti* actually made the parties man and wife, though the church regarded cohabitation after the contract, but before a church ceremony, as fornication.' As for *sponsalia de futuro*, 'if they were followed by cohabitation, though once more the church regarded this as fornication, the parties became man and wife'.[3]

In a brief examination of the controversy over the nature of the contracts in *Measure for Measure*, Harriett Hawkins recently reached the conclusion that the issue 'is of no importance whatsoever'. She doubts the value of the various discussions of Elizabethan and Jacobean betrothal laws and customs, on the ground that although they purport to shed light on the situation in the play, scholars have failed to reach anything like agreement concerning those laws and customs, and any consultation of their studies leads merely to confusion. Furthermore, 'the nature of [the scholarly] arguments raises some embarrassing questions about...appeals to the "Elizabethans" for answers to questions that Shakespeare himself may purposely have left unanswered – or left unasked'. The same critic draws attention to the diversity of opinions regarding the two contractual situations (Schanzer, for instance, argues that the contract between Claudio and Juliet was a *de praesenti* betrothal and that between Angelo and Mariana a *de futuro* betrothal, whereas Nagarajan arrives at the opposite conclusion), and she goes on to assert that the action in

[1] S. Nagarajan, '*Measure for Measure* and Elizabethan Betrothals', *SQ*, 14 (1963), 115–19. Nagarajan bases his arguments on an article on marriage in the ninth edition of the *Encyclopaedia Britannica*, 15 (1883), 567.

[2] J. Birje-Patil, 'Marriage Contracts in *Measure for Measure*', *Shakespeare Studies*, 5 (1969), 107, 111.

[3] J. C. Maxwell, '*Measure for Measure*': *The Play and the Themes* (1974), p. 4. The paper also appeared in *The Proceedings of the British Academy*, 60 (1974).

Measure for Measure was obviously designed to show Angelo committing the same offence for which he was sending Claudio to execution. She concludes: 'The dramatic irony of Angelo's situation can only be obscured by scholarly arguments that the pre-contract between Claudio and Julietta did not give them any marital rights, whereas Mariana's contract with Angelo did.'[1]

Of course, the assertion that Shakespeare thought of Claudio and Angelo as guilty of the same offence under the law presupposes some presumably scholarly interpretation of the evidence in the play regarding the existence of matrimonial contracts. Angelo certainly believes himself to be guilty of fornication (v, i, 470–7), and his situation can be considered parallel to Claudio's only on the assumption that Claudio and Juliet were *not* bound by a relationship that permitted sexual intercourse. And whatever the conclusions reached as to the guilt or innocence of Claudio and Angelo, it would still seem desirable to understand the rationale of the advice which the Duke, disguised as 'Friar Lodowick', gives to Isabella and Mariana.

The existence of present-day critical confusion regarding the significance of the two betrothal relationships does not warrant dismissal of their ambiguities as a non-problem. If one deplores the traditional attempts to understand Shakespeare better by exploring the social, political, and religious beliefs of his day, it is hardly logical to illustrate 'the essential Elizabethan requirement for a *de praesenti* betrothal contract' by citing a sixteenth-century author's definition of such betrothals (Hawkins, p. 176). Was there a clearly verifiable Elizabethan viewpoint on the subject, and is the author cited representative of that viewpoint? Does an authority writing about 1520 necessarily represent the view prevailing in the early seventeenth century, when Shakespeare was working on *Measure for Measure?* Did the Elizabethan *sensus communis* differ from that of the ecclesiastical establish-ment? And if the phrase 'Elizabethan view-point' is taken to signify the official stance of the Anglican Church around 1600, do the authorities cited by the various scholars reflect that stance, or are they Calvinistic?

The term 'Elizabethan' is, in fact, misleading if it is used in such a way as to ignore the complexity of the religious beliefs and social practices in the age of Elizabeth I and her successor. To recognize that there were widely differing viewpoints on matters of morality and that Shakespeare's work was intended to mirror the ambiguities of his time may not immediately clear up the confusion regarding the action in *Measure for Measure*. It may, however, save us from the temptation to give up on the problem.

II

The disagreement among modern critics as to the nature and social significance of Elizabethan marriage contracts is scarcely surprising in view of the differences of opinion in Shake-speare's England concerning matrimonial laws and rights, particularly with regard to clan-destine marriages. Such marriages had con-stituted a serious social abuse throughout Europe for centuries, and the abuse rose contemporaneously with the theory, crys-tallized by Church canonists between the eleventh and thirteenth centuries, that the essence of the marriage sacrament lay not in the sacerdotal blessing but in the intention of the couple entering into the marriage contract. If they solemnly took each other as man and wife with the concomitant intention of fidelity, then – unless there were nullifying impedi-ments such as consanguinity or prior contracts – a valid marriage existed at the moment of

[1] Harriett Hawkins, 'What Kind of Pre-Contract had Angelo? A Note on Some Non-Problems in Elizabethan Drama', *CE*, 36 (1974–5), 173–9. See also the same author's *Likenesses of Truth in Elizabethan and Restoration Drama* (Oxford, 1973), pp. 51–76.

speaking the words of the contract, and it could not normally be dissolved.

A distinction was made between a matrimonial contract in which the couple exchanged promises indicating their intention to become husband and wife at some future time (*sponsalia per verba de futuro*) and a contract taking effect immediately (*sponsalia per verba de praesenti*). Papal pronouncements of the thirteenth century made it clear that in the eyes of the Church, a *matrimonium per verba de praesenti* was a valid marriage even before sexual consummation (the *carnalis copula*). Furthermore, a marital contract *per verba de futuro*, when followed by sexual intercourse, was automatically transformed by that act into a valid marriage, the equivalent of spousals *de praesenti*, since the *carnalis copula* was interpreted as a legally significant sign that the parties intended to convert the earlier promise of future marriage into the reality of a present marriage. The blessing of a priest was not regarded as essential to the validity of a sacramental marriage.[1]

This theory of marriage was bound to lead to social difficulties. Marriages were frequently entered into, for a variety of reasons, in complete privacy; and the absence of any official records of such clandestine unions created problems where questions as to the legitimacy of children and the inheritance of property were involved. Worse still, those contracting marriage privately might later change their minds regarding their spouses, might separate, and then enter into other 'marriages' which, even though contracted publicly, blessed by a priest, and placed on record, would not be valid unions before God or (if the facts of the earlier unions became known) in the eyes of the Church. So the ecclesiastical authorities, while admitting the validity or at least the potential validity of secret marriages, nevertheless legislated and preached strongly against them. From the thirteenth century on, the official view of the Church was that marriage ought to be contracted only *in facie ecclesiae*, before a

priest and two witnesses, and only after prior public announcement of the couple's intention to marry, the so-called publication of the banns, so that anyone having knowledge of impediments to the union might intervene. Any marriage contracted in violation of these requirements was declared to be automatically illicit (even when it was valid); because of its illicit nature, the couple were punished by excommunication and sometimes by other punishments as well.[2]

Throughout the Middle Ages, therefore, Church councils, national synods, and local preachers militated against clandestine marriage as a serious social abuse; but though people contracting such unions were declared to be guilty of the sin of disobedience in violating Church law, they were not regarded as guilty of sexual immorality. Even during the

---

[1] The primary conciliar documents relating to marriage and clandestine marriage are available in various collections: *Acta Conciliorum*, ed. Jean Hardouin, 14 vols. (Paris, 1714); *Sacrorum Conciliorum*, ed. J. D. Mansi *et al.*, new edition 53 vols. (Paris, 1901+); *Enchiridion Symbolorum*, ed. Henricus Denzinger, 33rd edition by Adolfus Schönmetzer (Fribourg, 1965). For treatments of the subject by modern authorities, see: Emil Friedberg, *Das Recht der Eheschliessung* (Leipzig, 1885), pp. 38–45; Frederick Pollock and Frederic W. Maitland, *The History of English Civil Law Before the Time of Edward I*, 2 vols. (2nd ed. 1898), II, 367–73 *et passim*; George E. Howard, *A History of Matrimonial Institutions* (Chicago, 1904), I, 312–50, 376–86; Chilton L. Powell, *English Domestic Relations 1487–1653* (New York, 1917), pp. 1–43 *et passim*; Adhémar Esmein, *Le Mariage en droit canonique*, 2nd edition by Robert Génestal (Paris, 1929), I, 198–211; George H. Joyce, S.J., *Christian Marriage* (New York, 1933), pp. 102–145; John C. Carberry, *The Juridical Form of Marriage: An Historical Conspectus and Commentary* (Washington, D.C., 1934), pp. 11–28; Derrick S. Bailey, *The Man–Woman Relation in Christian Thought* (1959), pp. 118–39.

[2] The decree requiring publication of the banns was promulgated by Pope Innocent III at the Lateran Council in 1215: Hardouin, *Acta*, VII, 55–9. See also Pollock and Maitland, *History of English Civil Law*, II, 370–1; Joyce, *Marriage*, p. 111.

debates on marriage and its abuses at the Council of Trent, it was not concluded that clandestine marriages were fornicatory relationships rather than true marital unions; in fact, the conciliar decree on marriage (*Tametsi*), adopted in 1563 and promulgated in 1564, expressly insisted that clandestine marriages entered into before the promulgation were still to be regarded as valid.[1] Thereafter, however, validity as well as licitness was dependent on the exchange of the marriage promises before a properly authorized priest (normally the parish priest of one of the parties) and two witnesses. Any attempted marriage violating these requirements would not constitute a valid union; and so after 1564, in the Catholic parts of Europe, clandestine unions that had been consummated were *ipso facto* fornicatory relationships.

Since the edicts of the Council of Trent were not promulgated in the Protestant areas of Europe, the new theory of marriage that made clandestinity an impediment to validity did not become part of canon law in England. This is not to say that the old law was not challenged, both theoretically and in practice. Even before the Reformation swept over England, the voices of some Catholic divines as well as Wycliffite reformers were raised in denunciation of post-contractual cohabitation before the public solemnization of marriage. Thus William Harrington, a doctor of laws and rector of St Anne's, Aldersgate, who died about 1523, wrote a treatise on matrimony in which he assented to the traditional view that 'matrymony clandestinat...is valeable and holdeth afore god into so moche' that if one of the parties forsakes the other and remarries, 'they lyue in dampnable aduoutry'; yet he also maintained that even when clandestine marriage is 'laufully [that is, validly] made, yet the man maye not possesse the woman as his wyfe, nor the woman the man as her husbonde, nor inhabyte, nor flesshely meddle togyther as man and wyfe: afore suche tyme as that matrymony

be approued and solempnysed by oure mother holy chyrche, and yf they do in dede they synne deedly'.[2] At about the same time, Richard Whitforde, chaplain to Bishop Richard Foxe, complained that many couples, after making a secret marriage contract, 'suppose they may lawfully vse theyr vnclene behauyour, and somtyme the acte and dede doth folowe, vnto the grave offense of god & theyr owne soules'.[3] This attitude may have originated in the traditional teaching throughout the Middle Ages that excessive amorousness even between married persons was grievously sinful.[4] Prenuptial intercourse may have been regarded as evidence of such amorousness.

Among the authorities sometimes, though unjustifiably, cited as exemplifying the Elizabethan viewpoint on clandestine marriage is Bishop John Hooper. Hooper was a divine who fled England in 1539 to avoid prosecution for heresy and who became a close friend of Bullinger, the Swiss reformer. He returned to England in 1549 and became one of the more extreme leaders of the English Reformation. In 1551, as Bishop of Gloucester, he issued a series of injunctions to reform practices that

[1] *Enchiridion Symbolorum*, p. 417, *1813: *Tametsi dubitandum non est, clandestina matrimonia, libero contrahentium consensu facta, rata et vera esse matrimonia, quamdiu Ecclesia ea irrita non fecit...*

[2] William Harrington, *The Commendacions of Matrymony* (1528), sig. A. iv–iv[v].

[3] Richard Whitforde, *A Werke for Householders* (1530), sig. E. iii–iii[v].

[4] Cf. St Jerome, *Adversus Jovinianum* I. 49 in *PL*, 23 (1883), col. 293: *Adulter est, inquit, in suam uxorem amator ardentior.* This view is reflected in Chaucer's 'Parson's Tale' x, 938–42, in *The Works of Geoffrey Chaucer*, ed., F. N. Robinson (Boston, 2nd. ed 1957), p. 259. The Parson, after referring to three permissible reasons for sexual intercourse in marriage, condemns the practice of intercourse for pleasure: it is 'deedly synne...if they assemble oonly for amorous love and for noon of the foreseyde [three] causes, but for to accomplyce thilke brennynge delit, they rekke nevere how ofte. Soothly it is deedly synne; and yet, with sorwe, somme folk wol peynen hem moore to doon than to hire appetit suffiseth.'

had been common 'in the time of papistry and superstition'. Among other things, he instructed ministers to teach that 'all privy and secret contracts be forbidden by God's laws' as causing 'unhonest and unchaste life'; the ministers were also to see to it that 'when any persons be contracted and faithed together in matrimony,...the persons contracted [neither] cohabite nor dwell together before matrimony be solemnized'.[1] In this he followed Bullinger's injunction that 'Maried folkes [should] go to the church afore they lye together'; Bullinger decried, among many wicked practices, the custom of holding a great feast 'at the handfastynge', after which, '& euen the same night, are the two handfasted persones brought and layed together, yee certayne wekes afore they go to the church. Which is nothing els but a wicked lust'.[2] This was one point on which the post-Tridentine Roman Church and the rising Puritan movement were in agreement. English Puritans regarded unions that had not been solemnized before a minister as necessarily invalid, and therefore as fornicatory relationships; even where de futuro spousals had been contracted in the presence of parents and friends, Puritans considered sexual intercourse before the religious ceremony to be gravely sinful.[3]

The Anglican Church of Elizabeth I and James I, on the other hand, like the medieval Church of which it was the successor, continued to hold clandestine marriages to be valid, even while denouncing them as illicit. So long as the Church – whether pre-Tridentine Roman or post-Reformation Anglican – held this view, it could not with any consistency condemn them as fornicatory unions, and in fact did not do so. The argument advanced by some critics that, under medieval canon law clandestine unions were regarded as 'fornicatory marriages' (a contradiction in terms) derives from a misunderstanding of a decree, promulgated not by Rome but by an English council at Winchester in 1076:

ut nullus filiam suam, vel cognatam, det alicui absque benedictione sacerdotali: Si aliter fecerit, non ut legitimum conjugium, sed ut fornicatorium judicabitur.[4]

('Let no one give his daughter or other female relative to anyone [in marriage] without the blessing of a priest; if anyone does so, the marriage will be adjudged not as legitimate but as fornicatory.')

The intention of the Winchester decree was to distinguish between a sacerdotally blessed and therefore valid union, and a relationship which, because it had not been blessed, was invalid and therefore fornicatory.[5] It took a papal decree in the following century to clarify the situation with the judgment that validity was not dependent on the blessing or even the presence of a priest: the one essential for a valid marriage was the consent or agreement of the parties.[6]

[1] John Hooper, Injunctions (1551), repr. in Later Writings of Bishop Hooper, ed. Charles Nevinson (Cambridge, 1852), pp. 137–8. Hooper was burned for heresy under Mary I.

[2] Heinrich Bullinger, The Christen State of Matrimonye, transl. Myles Coverdale (London [?], 1541), pp. xlviij–xlviiij.

[3] See, for example, Robert Cleaver, A Godly Form of Householde Government (1598), p. 137: after the public betrothal de futuro, the parents of the couple are enjoined to set a date for the wedding, neither too near to prevent the discovery of any impediments nor so far off as 'to prouoke the parties to incontinencie. In the meane time, the parties affianced, are to bee admonished, to abstaine from the vse of marriage, and to behaue themselues wisely, chastly, louingly, and soberly, till the day appointed do come.'

[4] Hardouin, Acta, VI, i, 1562.

[5] The misleading notion that the medieval Church considered valid clandestine unions to be 'fornicatory marriages' is found, surprisingly enough, even in Pollock and Maitland, History of English Civil Law, II, 370, n. 2.

[6] Die Summa Magistri Rolandi (Alexander III), ed. Friedrich Thauer (Innsbruck, 1874), 'De Coniugio,' pp. 113–14. According to Schanzer, 'Marriage-Contracts', p. 83, the Church 'decreed that any de praesenti contract...constituted a legal marriage'. The use of the word legal here is confusing: the Church decreed such contracts to be valid (as contracts) but illicit (as acts breaking the law against clandestinity).

The principle that dominated canonical thinking and ecclesiastical court judgments right up to the time of the Council of Trent is summed up in the phrase *consensus facit matrimonium*.[1]

Naturally the Church did not wish to encourage clandestine marriages by making public declarations that they were not morally reprehensible. Hence in official and semi-official documents, the rubric dealing with clandestine marriages is restricted to a brief explanation why such unions had been declared illicit. In the widely used theological manual *Pupilla Oculi*, written about 1380 by John de Burgh, Chancellor of Cambridge University, the rubric reads as follows:

prohiben*tur* eti*am* clamdestina matrimo*n*ia dup*l*ici *r*atione: s*ci*licet ne *su*b specie mat*r*imo*n*ij fornicatio commi*t*tatur: et ne mat*r*imonia*lite*r coniuncti iniuste sepa*r*entur. sepe *en*im *i*n matri*i*mo*n*io occulte *c*ontra*c*to: alt*er* conjugu*m* mutat p*r*opositu*m* et dimi*t*tit reliquu*m* probat*i*o*n*ibus destitu*tum* et s*i*ne remedio restitu*t*io*n*is.[2] ('Clandestine marriages are prohibited for two reasons: namely, so that fornication is not committed under the appearance of marriage, and so that those joined matrimonially are not unjustly separated. For often, in a secretly contracted marriage, one of the parties changes his mind and abandons the other party, [who is left] destitute of evidence and without the remedy of restitution.')

Both of the reasons for the prohibition relate to the dangers inherent in contracting matrimony without publication of the banns. First, what appears to be a valid clandestine marriage may, because of impediments remaining undisclosed through failure to proclaim the banns, be an invalid and therefore fornicatory relationship. Second, one party to a valid clandestine marriage may be unjustly abandoned by the other party and may be unable to prove desertion because the union had not been placed on record. These reasons imply that if there were no impediments to a secret matrimonial contract, it was valid and the union was not fornicatory.[3]

It is not surprising that in the surviving records of marriage cases tried before the English ecclesiastical courts in the sixteenth century, the cases are not handled as problems in the area of sexual morality. The majority of the Christian faithful felt that clandestine marriages, while unlawful, were not objectionable in a sexual sense. The point is well illustrated in the official record of a case tried before the Archdeacon's court at Leicester in July 1598:

the comon use and custom within the countie of Leicester, speciallie in and about the townes before mentioned (Hoby and Waltham) and in other places thereunto adjoyning per spatium x, xx, xxx, xl

[1] See Joyce, *Marriage*, pp. 39–45; Bailey, *Christian Thought*, pp. 130–1.

[2] Bodleian MS. 182 (*c.* 1380–5), f 115ʳ; in seven other manuscripts I have checked, *specie* is abbreviated as *spē*. The *Pupilla Oculi* was printed at Paris in 1518 and again in 1521; both editions read *sub specie matrimonii*. This rubric on clandestine marriage was assimilated into the *Manuale ad vsum Sarum*, the official manual of the Salisbury diocese, but it is not found in any of the more than a dozen manuscripts of the *Manuale* surviving from the fourteenth and fifteenth centuries. It first appears in the printed texts of the *Manuale* published at Paris in 1498 (repr. 1500), Rouen in 1543, London in 1554, and Douai in 1604 (repr. 1610–11). The printed editions from 1498 to 1554 read *sub spe matrimonii* ('in hope of marriage'), probably in error for *sub spē*. The original reading of the *Pupilla Oculi*, namely *sub specie matrimonii*, reappears in the two editions printed at Douai.

[3] This is also the considered opinion of Joyce, *Marriage*, p. 105: 'A clandestine marriage is a grave breach of ecclesiastical law; but the union itself is not treated as immoral.' Cf. W. W. Lawrence, '*Measure for Measure* and Lucio', SQ, 9 (1958), 450: 'An Elizabethan or Jacobean audience would not have been repelled by sexual intercourse after formal betrothal but before the final religious ceremony, since this was a frequent and generally accepted occurrence.' It is true that there were at times objections to the practice. E. I. Fripp points out, *Shakespeare: Man and Artist* (1938), II, 613, that 'Puritan opinion was strong against the practice.' But then Puritans were not in the habit of frequenting the public theatres. If Lawrence is understood as referring to an audience of playgoers, his statement is valid.

annorum ultimorum hath bene and is that anie man being suter to a woman in the way of mariadge is upon the daie apointed to make a final conclusion of the marridge before treated of: if the said marridge be concluded and contracted then the man doth most comonlie remaine in the house where the woman doth abide the night next folowing after such contracte[;] otherwyse he doth departe without staying there the night.[1]

The implication is that sexual intercourse took place immediately after the contract had been concluded. As the records here and elsewhere imply, neither the Anglican authorities *in general* nor the lay members of the Anglican Church found anything morally wrong in pre-nuptial but post-contractual cohabitation.

This attitude is clearly manifested in a treatise on matrimony written about 1600 by Henry Swinburne, a canonist who was both a lawyer and, as proctor and later judge of the consistory court at York, an Anglican divine: 'albeit there be no Witnesses of the Contract, yet the Parties having verily, (though secretly) Contracted Matrimony, they are very Man and Wife before God'. Furthermore, 'Spousals *de futuro* do become Matrimony by carnal knowledge, betwixt the Parties betroathed'; and even though 'the Parties betroathed should protest before the Act done, that they did not *intend* thereby, that the Spousals should become Matrimony, yet this protestation is overthrown by the fact following; for by lying together they are presumed to have swarved from their former unhonest protestation; And so the former Spousals are now presumed honest Matrimony.'[2] And by *honest matrimony* Swinburne means 'a morally unexceptionable marital union'.

Almost a century earlier, Erasmus had added his voice to those concerned with warning betrothed couples that, under existing Church law, it was dangerously easy to slip from a *de futuro* relationship into an indissoluble marriage. One such warning appears in his manual on letterwriting. Among the letters is one penned ostensibly by a young man who, without his father's knowledge, has had intercourse with one of his mother's maidservants; she had said that she would not give in to him unless he promised to marry her (*ni pollicerer me maritum ipsi futurum*), and since Venus had taken away his reason he foolishly made the promise (*polliceor demens*); and now he has been told that what was done in that manner could not be undone.[3] Another warning occurs in the better known volume of *Colloquia*, a text used in many sixteenth-century schools in England and elsewhere. In an editorial note on clandestine marriages, added in an enlarged edition of the *Colloquia*, Schrevelius expands on the warning:

Si quis dicat puellae, *ducam te* & mox habeat rem cum illa, ratum est matrimonium, perinde, quasi dixisset, *duco te*. Hoc reti multi adolescentes capiuntur...[4]
('if anyone says to a girl "I shall take you [in marriage]," and afterwards has intercourse with her, the matrimony is [thereby] ratified, just as if he had said "I take you". Many young people are caught in this net.')

This viewpoint might seem to run counter to the basic principle that intention is of the essence in marriage (*consensus facit matrimonium*), were it not for the canonical ruling, as formulated by Swinburne in the passage quoted above, that the *carnalis copula* itself establishes a presumption of intention to transform the *de futuro* relationship into a valid marriage.

[1] A. P. Moore, 'Marriage Contracts or Espousals in the Reign of Queen Elizabeth', *Leicestershire Architectural and Archaeological Society's Reports and Papers* [later: *Associated Architectural Societies' Reports and Papers*], xxx (1909–10), Pt. 1, p. 291.
[2] Henry Swinburne, *A Treatise of Spousals or Matrimonial Contracts* (1686, repr. 1711), pp. 87, 224.
[3] *De Conscribendis Epistolis* in *Erasmi Roterodami Opera Omnia* (Lyons, 1703), I, 436.
[4] *Erasmi Roterodami Colloquia* (Amsterdam, 1693), p. 299.

III

There is ample evidence in the records and literature of the medieval and Renaissance periods for the continuing phenomenon of clandestine marriages, in spite of their illegality and the likelihood of sanctions for the breach of Church law.[1]

A pertinent instance of such a marriage in the family of the wealthy Pastons of Norfolk is provided by the touching love story of Richard Calle and Margery Paston, youngest sister of Sir John Paston. As Calle was Sir John's chief bailiff, he would have been unacceptable as Margery's suitor. Ignoring the difference in his social standing and wealth, and without the family's knowledge, Calle and Margery secretly contracted marriage, probably in 1467. Upon discovery of this fact in 1469, the Pastons were furious, forbade Margery to communicate with Calle, and tried to browbeat her into denying that she was contracted with him. In a letter written to Margery as his 'befor God very trewe wyff', Calle bitterly denounced the family's attempt to keep them apart despite 'the gret bonde of matrymonye that is made betwixt us'. He said he had heard that she had denied the existence of their marriage, and since she could have done so only under pressure, he urged her to resist and to be faithful to him: 'be pleyn to hem and telle the trouthe, ... remembryng it is in suche case as it can not be remedyed'. The family felt that the situation could be remedied: they took the matter to the diocesan court at Norwich and asked that the alleged spousals be declared null and void. There the separate testimony of the couple convinced the bishop that their matrimonial contract was a true one, whereupon Margery's infuriated mother refused to permit her daughter to return to the family home. The couple were able to find lodgings in a nunnery, and some months later the family grudgingly allowed a formal wedding ceremony to take place.[2]

It is interesting to note that shortly before Shakespeare turned to the writing of *Measure for Measure*, one of his friends, Thomas Russell (later one of the overseers of his will), wished to marry a widow who had inherited a considerable estate from her late husband. Under the terms of the will, she stood to lose the income to her eldest son if she remarried. Since the income from the estate would not be forfeited by a clandestine and therefore illicit marriage, she and Russell, in the presence of witnesses, contracted matrimony and, early in 1600, set up house together, without benefit of clergy but also without incurring the odium of immorality. In 1603, the couple reached an agreement with the lawyers representing the widow's elder son, whereby they were able to formalize their marriage ecclesiastically without being penalized under the terms of her first husband's will.[3]

In spite of the canonical sanctions against clandestine marriages, such unions were, as conciliar edicts and court records reveal, common throughout Europe; and the prevalence of the practice is abundantly reflected in Renaissance literature. For example, Boccaccio's story of Alessandro in the *Decameron* is about a secret marriage without witnesses. To

[1] For some examples, see Joyce, *Marriage*, pp. 137–138; J. W. Gray, *Shakespeare's Marriage* (1905), pp. 190–4; Moore, 'Contracts', pp. 264–98; Peter Laslett, *The World We Have Lost* (New York, 2nd ed. 1971), pp. 150–1. For original documents relative to hearings before the ecclesiastical courts, see *Depositions and Other Ecclesiastical Proceedings from the Courts of Durham*, ed. James Raines for the Surtees Society (1845), pp. 218–57; *Child-Marriages, Divorces, and Ratifications, &c. In the Diocese of Chester, A.D. 1561–1566*, ed. Frederick J. Furnivall for EETS, o.s. No. 108 (1897), pp. 56–71, 184–202; *Before the Bawdy Court: Extracts from the Church Court Records... 1300–1800*, compiled Paul Hair (New York, 1972), pp. 76–7, 218–27.

[2] H. S. Bennett, *The Pastons and Their England* (Cambridge, 2nd edn. 1951), pp. 42–6; *Paston Letters*, ed. Norman Davies (Oxford, 1958), pp. 70–6.

[3] Leslie Hotson, *I, William Shakespeare* (1937), pp. 137–40, 203–10.

avoid having to marry an old man, the King of England's daughter, disguised as an abbot, set out for Rome. On the way there, she encountered and fell in love with Alessandro, a young man of noble character but great misfortune. One night at an inn, shortage of room forced the 'abbot' to share a bed with Alessandro, and not surprisingly the young man discovered that his bedfellow was a beautiful young lady. The princess, while resisting his attempt to embrace her, explained that she had fallen deeply in love with him: 'I want you more than any other man as my husband; if you do not want me as your wife, get out of bed at once.' Alessandro replied unhesitatingly that he was ready to marry her immediately. Boccaccio continues: 'She then sat up in bed opposite a little table bearing an image of Our Lord, and, giving Alessandro a ring, made him take her as his wife. After which they kissed each other, and spent the remainder of the night with great pleasure to both parties.' After their arrival in Rome, the marriage contract, made 'in the presence of God alone', was renewed before the Pope, and a public wedding was celebrated with proper ceremony.[1]

Many examples of clandestine spousals are found in English dramas of the Renaissance. Thus in *Sir Giles Goosecap*, a play of *c.* 1602, Lord Momford urges his niece Eugenia to marry Clarence, a poor gentleman. Eugenia at first resists; but on hearing that Clarence is sick of unrequited love for her, she visits him in his bedroom and marries him by a clandestine handfasting:

> To my late written hand I giue thee this,
> See heauen, the soule thou gau'st is in this hand.
> This is the knot of our eternitie,
> Which fortune, death, nor hell, shal euer loose.
>
> (v, ii, 218–21)

She then closes the curtains, concealing Clarence, herself, and her attendants. Later, when one of the attendants informs Momford that 'the contract is knit fast betwixt them'

(v, ii, 291), he calls down a blessing on 'theis true borne nuptials' (v, ii, 292–3) and presents the couple to his friends as 'man and wife' (v, ii, 311).[2]

In *The Miseries of Enforced Marriage* (1607), George Wilkins deals with the unhappy outcome of an unconsummated *de praesenti* contract. The young hero Scarborow, not yet eighteen, secretly exchanges marriage vows with Clare: 'This hand thus takes thee as my louing wife,...till death vs depart' (242–4). Scarborow informs Clare's father of the private wedding – 'your daughters made my wife, and I your sonne' – and the father, finding them both to be in agreement, regards the marriage as settled (294–8). Later, Scarborow is forced by his guardian to marry another woman, in spite of his protest that if he abandons Clare to wed another, that marriage 'makes me an Adulterer,.../ My babes being Bastards, and a whore my wife' (429–32). When Clare hears that he has indeed entered into an enforced marriage, she laments her plight, not only in losing Scarborow but in being unable to marry anyone else, since any man 'who shall marry me:/Is like my selfe, liues in Adultery' (817–18). To avoid being compelled by her own father to marry, however invalidly, another man, she commits suicide.[3]

Perhaps the most memorable treatment of clandestine marriage in Jacobean drama is found in John Webster's *Duchess of Malfi* (1614). The young widowed Duchess defies her brothers' warnings against remarriage. She and her steward Antonio fall in love with each other; and at a private meeting, with her maid as witness, the Duchess gives him a ring

---

[1] *The Decameron of Boccaccio*, transl. Richard Aldington (1954), pp. 358–9.

[2] *Sir Giles Goosecap* (1606), Tudor Facsimile Text ed. John S. Farmer (1912; repr. New York, 1970), sig. I3ᵛ, I4ᵛ, KIʳ.

[3] *The Miseries of Enforced Marriage* (1607), facs. ed. G. H. Blayney (Oxford, 1964), sig. BIʳ–B2ʳ, B3ᵛ; C3ᵛ–DIᵛ.

and claims him as her husband. As they kneel, calling on heaven to bless their 'sacred Gordian', she observes:

I have heard lawyers say, a contract in a chamber
Per verba de presenti is absolute marriage.

(I, i, 478–89)

Then, with a comment to the effect that the Church itself could not make their union more valid ('What can the church force more?'), she invites Antonio to lead her to the 'marriage bed' (I, i, 496). In the course of the subsequent action, the Duchess bears her husband three children, and it is evident throughout that she and her husband have no doubts as to the validity and morality of their unsolemnized relationship.[1]

IV

These and numerous other English plays, from the same period as well as later,[2] make it clear that the concept of clandestine spousals as a form of marriage that could be consummated without the stigma of immoral behaviour continued to be widely if not universally acceptable, other than to those of Puritan outlook, until well on into the eighteenth century. There is therefore nothing exceptional about the introduction of the motif into *Measure for Measure*.

When Claudio makes his first entry, on his way to prison, he explains to Lucio that his plight is the result of 'too much liberty', and he continues:

As surfeit is the father of much fast,
So every scope by the immoderate use
Turns to restraint. Our natures do pursue,
Like rats that ravin down their proper bane,
A thirsty evil, and when we drink we die.

(I, ii, 126–30)

Unless these lines are spoken ironically, a possible but unlikely interpretion, Claudio seems here to regard his offence as an evil.

There is something odd about this passage,

as was noted by Knights. He admitted that he felt perplexity in considering the nature of Claudio's offence: the young man 'does not seem to have "surfeited", and he certainly was not a libertine', yet the image which he uses to express his feelings about his relationship with Juliet – that of rats swallowing poison – is 'more appropriate to lust than to love'.[3] Leavis, on the other hand, felt no such perplexity: Claudio 'has committed a serious offence, not only in the eyes of the law, but in his own eyes'; to interpret otherwise would be to create an 'emancipated' Claudio 'who took an advanced twentieth-century line in these matters' – a Claudio who 'was no part of Shakespeare's conception of his theme'. In brief, we should not be perplexed if Claudio takes 'conventional morality' seriously.[4]

The difficulty with the argument advanced by Leavis is in the assumption that there was *one* conventional morality: on the contrary, there was the pre-Reformation code, which was anything but moribund, and there was also the new code of morality adopted by the Roman Church and by the Puritans. Claudio's dilemma is that he is being judged under the new code, which he may momentarily have accepted in court in the hope of ultimate leniency if he admitted to the offence as charged. And even if the proper interpretation of I, ii, 126–30 were that Claudio does feel guilty of lustful rather than loving behaviour in getting Juliet with child, it would still be true that the consummated union would be

[1] *The Duchess of Malfi*, ed. John R. Brown (1964), pp. 34–8.
[2] Further examples from the Renaissance period are noted by William G. Meader, *Courtship in Shakespeare* (New York, 1954), pp. 186–93. For examples in Restoration drama, see Gellert S. Alleman, *Matrimonial Law and the Materials of Restoration Comedy* (Wallingford, 1942), pp. 31–105.
[3] L. C. Knights, 'The Ambiguity of *Measure for Measure*', *Scrutiny*, 10 (1942), 225–8.
[4] F. R. Leavis, 'The Greatness of *Measure for Measure*', *Scrutiny*, 10 (1942), 235–7.

regarded as a valid marital contract, and therefore not a fornicatory relationship, under traditional canon law.[1]

The critical assumption that Claudio must be expressing personal guilt feelings in his opening conversation with Lucio is, however, called in question by the subsequent dialogue. First, Lucio continues to probe into the reason for Claudio's arrest:[2]

> *Lucio.* ...What's thy offense, Claudio?
> *Claudio.* What but to speak of would offend again.
> *Lucio.* What, is't murder?
> *Claudio.* No.
> *Lucio.* Lechery?
> *Claudio.* Call it so.

Claudio's 'Call it so' implies not that he really feels guilty of lecherous behaviour but that 'Lechery is what my behaviour has been called.'

This interpretation is supported by Claudio's subsequent elaboration on his unhappy situation:

> Thus stands it with me: upon a true contract
> I got possession of Julietta's bed.
> You know the lady; she is fast my wife,
> Save that we do the denunciation lack
> Of outward order. This came we not to,
> Only for propagation of a dow'r
> Remaining in the coffer of her friends,
> From whom we thought it meet to hide our love
> Till time had made them for us. But it chances
> The stealth of our most mutual entertainment
> With character too gross is writ on Juliet.
>
> (I, ii, 145–55)

Here *true contract* can only mean 'valid spousals'; and, from the viewpoint of traditional Renaissance morality, it does not matter whether the contract was made *per verba de praesenti* or *per verba de futuro*, because the latter type of contract would have been converted into the former by the 'mutual entertainment' of the couple.

A question might be raised as to whether Claudio is speaking the truth when he alleges the existence of a matrimonial contract. In his desperate plight, it would seem all too natural for him to make such a claim, even if it was quite unwarranted, in the vain hope of persuading Angelo that his was not a case of ordinary fornication, and hence not deserving of the death penalty. It is certainly true that Juliet does not mention a contract when she is questioned by 'Friar Lodowick' about her relations with Claudio:

> *Duke.*
> Repent you, fair one, of the sin you carry?
> *Juliet.*
> I do; and bear the same most patiently.
> *Duke.*
> I'll teach you how you shall arraign your conscience,
> And try your penitence, if it be sound,
> Or hollowly put on.
> *Juliet.*   I'll gladly learn.
> *Duke.*
> Love you the man that wrong'd you?
> *Juliet.*
> Yes, as I love the woman that wrong'd him.
> *Duke.*
> So then it seems your most offenseful act
> Was mutually committed?
> *Juliet.*   Mutually.

[1] Swinburne, *Spousals*, p. 227, is quite explicit on this point: 'if the Parties having contracted Spousals *de futuro*, do afterwards know each other, but in truth not with that affection, which doth become Man and Wife, but (as Adulterers do) with a beastly purpose only to satisfie their foul Lusts, in this case it is not true Matrimony in Conscience; neither are they Man and Wife before God, though it be otherwise in Mans Judgment; because the Law presumeth, that the Parties espoused in knowing each other, had no foul intent of committing Fornication, but an honest affection as is meet for married Persons'. It should be noted that the phrase 'married Persons' refers here to 'Parties having contracted Spousals *de futuro*'.

[2] He has already been informed (I, ii, 60–76) that Claudio is to be beheaded 'for getting Madam Julietta with child'; but he has expressed a desire to 'learn the truth of it' (I, ii, 81), and now he wants to learn the details from Claudio himself.

Duke.

Then was your sin of heavier kind than his.

Juliet.

I do confess it, and repent it, father.

(II, iii, 19–29)

For Juliet, then, the 'mutual entertainment' was admittedly sinful.[1]

Some confirmation of the possibility that Claudio was lying may seem, at first sight, to come from Isabella's similarly unfavourable view of his relationship with Juliet. She, too, regards it as sinful, both in her interviews with Angelo (II, ii, iv) and in the scene in which Claudio urges her to submit to Angelo's embraces and she responds with a stinging attack on his cowardice (III, i, 135–46). In discussing the nature of Claudio's wrongdoing, Maxwell argues that it has to be 'a real moral offence'; 'If it were not, we could not enter at all into Isabella's feeling of revulsion when she has to plead with Angelo in Claudio's favour'[2] or (one might add) into her feeling of anger at Claudio's cowardice. This argument needs to be phrased more carefully: the wrongdoing has to be a real moral offence in Isabella's eyes. Now her later acceptance of the Duke's assertion that Mariana can quite properly have sexual intercourse with Angelo on the strength of their as yet unsolemnized matrimonial contract implies that she accepts the old moral code. Hence her feeling of revulsion following the revelation of Juliet's pregnancy means that nobody has mentioned to her the possibility of the existence of a clandestine marriage contract between the lovers. She takes it for granted that theirs was simply a case of fornication.

We are left, then, with Juliet's confession of sin and the question that it raises: does her feeling of guilt belie Claudio's claim that they were validly contracted?

The discrepancy between Claudio's and Juliet's statements is more apparent than real. It is not intended to cast doubt on Claudio's story or to reflect a supposed inconsistency in canon law. It reflects, quite realistically, a diversity in the attitudes and beliefs of Elizabethan and Jacobean society. The historical and literary evidence makes it clear that, for traditionalists, the enjoyment of sexual intercourse between validly contracted parties did not raise any question of morality, even though the making of the contract itself was wrong on account of the ban on clandestine marriages. On the other hand, for those influenced by the teaching of Calvinistic reformers like Bishop Hooper, consummation of the contract before the public wedding was gravely sinful.

There is therefore no dramatic inconsistency when Shakespeare implies that Juliet had at one time assented to Claudio's argument that their private contract gave them the right to sexual intercourse, and that later, when pregnant, she had succumbed to the new Calvinistic view that their exercise of marital rights had not been permissible. The laws of Shakespeare's Vienna call for the execution of fornicators; and since Angelo accepts the new moral teaching that only a public wedding ceremony guarantees marital rights, there is some foundation for the view that the merciless passing of the death sentence on Claudio is technically defensible under common law. That aspect of the dramatic situation in no way precludes acceptance both of Claudio's statement that he and Juliet were

---

[1] When, at the end of the play, the Duke orders Claudio to marry Juliet – 'She, Claudio, that you wrong'd, look you restore' (V, i, 525) – it seems at first sight as if he is aligning himself with the new moral teaching. Yet the earlier evidence, notably his belief that Mariana would not be sinning in consummating her contract with Angelo (IV, ii), indicates that he is a supporter of the traditional view of morality. The difficulty with the Duke's comment about Claudio's wrongdoing does not arise if we assume either that the Duke is still ignorant of the existence of a contract between Claudio and Juliet (an ignorance which Juliet's confession in III, i does nothing to dispel) or that he is alluding to the anguish Claudio has brought upon Juliet by failing to get the clandestine contract solemnized immediately after she had become pregnant.

[2] Maxwell, *Themes*, p. 10.

validly contracted, and of the argument that the existence of their marriage contract under canon law makes the literal application of the common law against fornication morally indefensible.

V

There can be no doubt as to the existence of a marriage contract between Angelo and Mariana, since the information comes from the Duke himself in his role as the 'Friar':

> *Duke.* [Mariana] should this Angelo have married; was affianc'd to her by oath, and the nuptial appointed; between which time of the contract and limit of the solemnity, her brother Frederick was wrack'd at sea, having in that perish'd vessel the dowry of his sister. But mark how heavily this befell to the poor gentlewoman: there she lost a noble and renown'd brother, in his love toward her ever the most kind and natural; with him, the portion and sinew of her fortune, her marriage-dowry; with both, her combinate-husband, this well-seeming Angelo.
>
> *Isabella.* Can this be so? Did Angelo so leave her?
>
> *Duke.* Left her in tears, and dried not one of them with his comfort; swallow'd his vows whole, pretending in her discoveries of dishonor; in few, bestow'd her on her own lamentation, which she yet wears for his sake; and he, a marble to her tears, is wash'd with them, but relents not.
>
> (III, i, 213–30)

The *nuptial* referred to is the appointed public wedding ceremony. The likelihood is that Angelo's was a contract *de futuro* – a contract which could be nullified by mutual consent, or broken by either party if the other proved guilty of infidelity. It is noteworthy that it was of 'dishonor' or unchastity that Angelo had accused Mariana, undoubtedly falsely, in order to justify his callous abandonment of her. And though in the last act of the play Angelo denies that there was anything more than 'some speech of marriage' between himself and Mariana (v, i, 216–24), he finally admits that he was contracted to her (v, i, 375–6).

What *is* very doubtful is the validity of the advice given by the 'Friar' to Mariana when persuading her to take Isabella's place at the secret assignation desired by Angelo:

> ...fear you not at all.
> He is your husband on a pre-contract:
> To bring you thus together 'tis no sin,
> Sith that the justice of your title to him
> Doth flourish the deceit.   (IV, ii, 70–4)

The editor of the *Riverside Shakespeare* notes somewhat ambiguously (p. 568) that 'Sexual intercourse between a bethrothed pair created a valid marriage at common law.' If that had been the case in Shakespeare's England, Thomas Russell and his troth-plighted wife would have forfeited the income from the estate of the wife's first husband by the very fact of setting up house together. Their matrimonial contract of 1600 was valid under canon law though illicit under both canon and civil law; it remained illicit until it was solemnized three years later.

More pertinent to the question of morality in *Measure for Measure* is the fact that sexual intercourse between betrothed parties did create a marriage that was valid and therefore morally unexceptionable under canon law. It must be noted, however, that the principle of canon law in question presupposes that the betrothed parties intend to have intercourse with each other. In Shakespeare's play, Angelo does not know that he is actually bedding Mariana, nor does he wish to do so; his intention is to have sexual intercourse with Isabella, and he knows that the intended act (quite apart from the element of coercion) is gravely sinful.[1] Furthermore, and again from the viewpoint of the traditional teaching,

---

[1] Cf. Schanzer, 'Marriage-Contracts,' p. 89, n. 21: 'It is doubtful, however, whether a court of law would have ruled that cohabitation with one's bride when taken for another person turned a *de futuro* contract into matrimony. Certainly *error personae*, i.e. marriage contracted with a person mistaken for someone else, was one of the recognized grounds for annulment.'

Mariana co-operates with Angelo in an act which he believes to be seriously sinful; and to that extent, contrary to the assurances given by 'Friar Lodowick', Mariana herself will be committing a serious sin.

It is unlikely that these intricate aspects of Mariana's situation under canon law would have been apparent to most of those in Shakespeare's audience. Certainly Shakespeare does not address himself to the full complexity of the moral problems involved. From a purely pragmatic angle, moreover, there is a rough-and-ready kind of justice to the perpetration of the bed-trick by which Mariana substitutes for Isabella, particularly in view of the circumstance that Mariana is now more desperately enamoured of Angelo than she had been at the time of her betrothal to him (III, i, 239–43). From the dramatic standpoint, therefore, since Angelo had promised marriage to Mariana, the 'Friar' can argue with some appearance of justice that the deceit is justifiable.

At the end of the play, after Angelo has been forced to wed Mariana and has been sentenced to die, the Duke explains to Mariana why he had ordered the wedding:

> Consenting to the safeguard of your honor,
> I thought your marriage fit; else imputation,
> For that he knew you, might reproach your life,
> And choke your good to come.   (v, i, 419–22)

According to Schanzer (p. 87), this passage indicates that the Duke 'is not unaware of the opprobrium attached to the consummation of an unsolemnized marriage-contract'. Such an interpretation would conflict with the Duke's earlier assurance to Mariana (IV, i, 71–5), that in having intercourse with Angelo she would not be sinning.[1] The most natural interpretation of v, i, 419–22 is that since the sexual union of Angelo and Mariana at the moated grange is now a matter of common knowledge, the solemnization of their marriage is intended to protect Mariana's reputation against any slander deriving from Angelo's false statements

that she was guilty of unchastity (III, i, 227) and that he had never been formally contracted to her (v, i, 216–24).

Except for the severity of its statute making fornication a capital offence, the fictional Vienna of *Measure for Measure* undoubtedly reflects the laws, customs, and thinking of Shakespeare's England. The society mirrored in the play is one in which canon law and civil law had existed side by side for centuries. In the sphere of marriage and sex, the ecclesiastical courts determined questions relating to matrimonial contracts, fornication, and slander, while the royal or civil courts dealt with questions of property, inheritance, alienation of affection, and prostitution. Hence Angelo is guilty not merely of ordering Claudio's punishment for an act which he himself subsequently intends to commit, expecting to do so with impunity. In the final analysis, he is also guilty of injustice in ordering punishment for an act which would be a crime under the 'Viennese' statute only if it were also clearly an offence under the traditional canon law; and in Claudio's case, it evidently is not. In basing his judgment on a civil statute and ignoring the ancient but still valid canon law (valid, that is, in England), Angelo grossly violates the principle of equity.

To dismiss as a non-problem the seeming inconsistencies in *Measure for Measure* would be to ignore Shakespeare's skilful implementation of his own artistic credo – that the purpose of drama is to reflect life by showing 'virtue her feature, scorn her own image, and the very age and body of the time his form and pressure'. The world of mature Shakespearian drama is always intriguing in its revelation of the complexities of the human condition. In this play, more strikingly than in any other, the dramatist comes to grips with the ambi-

---

[1] There is no merit in Schanzer's argument that the Duke's words "tis no sin' refer to the deceit practised on Angelo rather than to the sexual union to be brought about by the bed-trick.

guities and imperfections of the legal system and with the ramifications of its impact on the lives of the people. *Measure for Measure* may indeed be a flawed masterpiece, but there is no appreciable dramatic flaw in the treatment of the marriage contracts.

'RICHARD III': ANTECEDENTS OF CLARENCE'S DREAM

HAROLD F. BROOKS

Clarence's dream, like Richard's courtship of Anne, is one of the embellishments Shakespeare introduced in giving body and shape to his dramatisation of chronicle material in *Richard III*.[1] For this dream he had not, as he had for the fact though not the substance of Richard's fearful dream on the eve of Bosworth, any warrant in his historical sources. It consists of a number of distinguishable elements. First, Richard is Clarence's dream partner in his delivery from the Tower: this repeats the irony of Richard's promise to effect it (I, i, 114f), and the kind of delivery he has just despatched the murderers to effect (I, iii, 356). Further, the dream represents Richard (though innocently, in accord with Clarence's belief in his friendship) as responsible for Clarence's death by drowning – the fate he will suffer before the end of the present scene. Clarence tells how Gloucester (Richard) tempted him 'to walk/ Upon the hatches' where 'as we pac'd along'

> Upon the giddy footing of the hatches,
> Methought that Gloucester...
> Struck me...overboard. (I, iv, 12f, 16–18)

The passage is evidently indebted to Shakespeare's favourite Golding (Ovid, *Metamorphoses*, III, 792f, 797f); Acetis narrates how he 'stept Uppon the Hatches', where a ruffian gave him 'such a churlish blow' 'that over boord he had me sent'.

From that point, reached in Clarence's first eleven lines, the dream depicts the agony of drowning (ll. 21f, 36–41); the scene on the sea-floor, on his way to Hades (ll. 24–33), and what meets him in Hades itself (ll. 45–61).

It is this culmination which indicates the old and widespread tradition to which Clarence's dream belongs: the dream-vision of Hell; and I shall begin with that. The tradition has many embodiments in the literature of the Middle Ages. The classical Hades, into which Clarence's vision leads him, is the subject of the sixth book of the *Aeneid*, and the tenth of the *Odyssey*, and was familiar in many classical and Renaissance authors. Without long research, they cannot be assembled; nor is it possible to limit the number which may have played upon Shakespeare's imagination. What can be done is to look at works we know, or can reasonably believe, to have been in his mind as he wrote his play, and see where his evocation of Hades significantly resembles theirs. Major precedents are Sackville's induction to the tragedy of Buckingham in *The Mirror for Magistrates*;[2] the narrative of Andrea's ghost in the opening scene of Kyd's *Spanish Tragedy*; and in Ovid, Juno's descent into Hades to secure vengeance upon Ino and Athamas. The immediate sequel there is the attempt of her victims to flee from the 'ougly sightes' with which they are afflicted; a futile attempt, because the Fiend 'stopt their passage out'.[3] So Golding; faintly

---

[1] See my article: '*Richard III*: Unhistorical Amplifications: the Women's Scenes and Seneca', in a forthcoming issue of *MLR*.

[2] Emphasised (too exclusively) as an inspiration by Dover Wilson (ed.), *Richard III* (New Cambridge Shakespeare) pp. xxviif.

[3] Arthur Golding (transl.) Ovid, *Metamorphoses* (W. H. D. Rouse, ed., *Shakespeare's Ovid* (1961), IV, 536ff, 604f).

echoed perhaps in Clarence's phrases, 'What sights of ugly death', and 'stopp'd in my soul'. The closest parallels to Clarence's reference to Charon as 'that sour ferryman' appear to be Kyd's 'churlish Charon' the 'ferryman of Hell', and Sackville's 'grisly Charon' who 'stil ferreies ghostes'; but even these probably coalesced with reminiscences of Seneca.[1]

In Seneca, and in the *Octavia*, believed in Shakespeare's time to be his, I have noted some twenty-five descriptions of Hades, or significant allusions to it. Nine or ten are in the *Hercules Furens*, a known source for *Richard III*; the rest are in the *Octavia, Hippolytus, Medea, Hercules Oetaeus, Agamemnon* and *Thyestes*. For large general resemblances one may compare with Clarence's dream-descent into Hell the guilty dream of Poppaea in *Octavia*, where she is driven by Agrippina's ghost down through a chasm that opens in the earth.[2] After Clarence's nightmare, the Keeper to whom it will be narrated asks him why he looks so heavily; in the same way Poppaea's nurse asks her why she trembles, why her face is troubled and wet with weeping.

> O I have pass'd a miserable night,
> ...full of fearful dreams,   (ll. 2 f)

is Clarence's answer, corresponding to Poppaea's:

> Confusa tristi proximae noctis metu
> visuque...mente turbata feror.   (712f)

Still in the realm of general resemblances, there are visions or hallucinations of avenging ghosts in other Senecan plays: in the *Phoenissae* the ghost of Laius, and accompanied or associated with Furies in *Oedipus* (Laius), *Medea* (Absyrtus), *Agamemnon* (Thyestes) and *Thyestes* (Tantalus); with Agrippina in *Octavia*, Thyestes and Tantalus are actual speakers in the play, like those which appear to Richard before Bosworth. Furies are summoned by Juno in her prologue to the *Hercules Furens*, and appear to Cassandra in her trance-vision of Hades in the *Agamemnon*.[3]

A more particular significance attaches to the ghost of Agrippina, one ghost assailed by another (her husband) as in the dream Clarence becomes a ghost assailed by others; the ghost of Laius, assailing Oedipus as his murdered father, and comparable to Warwick, assailing Clarence as his wronged father-in-law;[4] and the ghost of Absyrtus, a boy, comparable to that of Prince Edward, who was little more. The Prince, 'A shadow', describes his murderer as 'fleeting Clarence'; the victim, Absyrtus, in Medea's vision, is 'incerta umbra'.[5] If 'incerta' helped to suggest 'fleeting', the transference to Clarence would come from the aptness of 'fleeting' to a double turncoat. The debt is not only probable but especially interesting, since it could not come from Studley's translation: he has 'mishapt' (mis-shaped) for 'incerta', and 'ghost', not 'shadow' for 'umbra'. The association of 'fleeting' with 'ghost' is in Golding, who uses it straightforwardly as an epithet for the departing spirit in 'yeelde hir fleeting ghost' (*Metamorphoses* VI, 368). The expression 'yield the ghost' is

---

[1] *Richard III*, I, iv, 46; *Spanish Tragedy*, I, i, 20, 27; *The Mirror for Magistrates*, ed. Lily B. Campbell (1938), p. 315. Sackville's 'Buckingham' (id., p. 330) is echoed in *Richard III*, IV, ii, 64–6: 'I am in/So far in blood that sin will pluck on sin./Tear-falling pity dwells not in this eye'; cp. '...I sawe mischiefe on mischiefe fall/So diepe in blud.../...Alas, it could not.../...make him once to rue or wet his iye.'

[2] Ll. 712ff. An earth-chasm opens also in the *Oedipus*, but there Hades, through Tiresias's necromancy, rises into sight.

[3] *Phoenissae*, 39ff; *Oedipus*, 642–5; *Medea*, 958ff; *Agamemnon*, 1ff; *Thyestes*, 1ff; *Hercules Furens*, 87ff; *Agamemnon*, 750ff.

[4] *Octavia*, 614ff; *Oedipus*, loc. cit. The association of 'father' and 'father-in-law' was stronger then than it is now, since a 'father-in-law' was referred to more often than not as 'father'. Here the full form probably betrays the influence of the *Mirror*, where Clarence also uses it of Warwick, furious at his treachery: 'This made my father in lawe to fret and fume' (p. 224); cp p. 147 below.

[5] *Medea*, 963f. See below, p. 147.

used by Clarence (l. 37), and more than once by Golding (cp. VI, 309, VII, 745).

Coming to other comparisons in point of detail, it will be convenient to tabulate these.
– 'the melancholy flood': 'tristes lacus' (Thyestes's ghost, *Agamemnon*, l. 12); 'vada tristia' (*Hercules Oetaeus*, 1,950)
– 'that sour ferryman': 'dirus...Charon', 'ipse portitor', 'aspectu horridus' (*Hercules Furens*, 771, 768, 764)
– 'the kingdom of perpetual night': 'nocte perpetua domum' (*Hippolytus*, 221; cp. 'noctis aeternae plagis', *Oedipus*, 393)[1]
– 'this dark monarchy': 'ille opaca qui regit sceptro loca' (*Hercules Furens*, 707); 'tu, nigrantis regna qui torques poli' (*Hercules Oetaeus*, 938); 'tu...domuisti.../...furva nigri sceptra gestantem poli/...dominum Stygis' (id. 558–60); 'Opaca...Ditis inferni loca' (Thyestes's ghost, *Agamemnon* 1.)
– 'my father-in-law...spake aloud': 'genitor vocat', exclaims Oedipus in *Phoenissae*, 39, referring to Laius's angry ghost; in *Oedipus*, 643, the ghost of Laius cries 'te pater...petam': cp. *The Mirror for Magistrates* (ed. Lily B. Campbell, p. 224) where Clarence declares his desertion 'made my father in lawe to.../... call me false forsworne'.
– 'what scourge for perjury': 'te pater... petam.../et mecum *Erinyn*.../traham sonantem verbera' (*Oedipus*, 643–5). Cassandra in her vision of hell (*Agamemnon*, 760) sees the Furies: 'sanguinea iactant verbera'; Juno in her prologue to *Hercules Furens*, summons them: 'viperea saevae verbera incutiant manus' (88). Medea asks (*Medea*, 959f) against whom that headlong horde of Furies is preparing their flaming blows: 'ingens anguis excusso sonat/ tortus flagello' (961f).
– 'Then came wandring by/A shadow':[2] compare Medea's vision of Absyrtus (963f):

> ...cuius umbra dispersis venit
> incerta membris? frater est, poenas petit',

– which Prince Edward's ghost proceeds to do:

> Seize on him, Furies, take him unto torment;

'fige luminibus faces;/lania, perure, pectus en Furiis patet'. (*Medea*, 965f). Juno (in the prologue to *Hercules Furens*) summons the Furies to attack Hercules: 'adsint ab imo Tartari fundo excitae/Eumenides' (86f); 'Incipite, famulae Ditis' (100); 'hoc agite, poenas petite' (104).

The way to Hades is traditionally, at a critical point, by water: the ferry over the Styx is a commonplace. Seneca has crossings also of other underworld rivers: Lethe, Cocytus, Phlegethon: Theseus in *Hercules Furens* speaks of everyone, after death, setting sail on Cocytus (869f; cp. id. 680, 686, 776.; *Hippolytus* 846f; *Hercules Oetaeus*, 1,919f, 1,963). But the Hellward journey by water does not include, as in Clarence's dream, the pain of drowning.[3] What Clarence dwells on, the impeded struggle to reach the air, is reminiscent of the wreck of Ceyx in Golding's Ovid, where alone I have found the 'tumbling billows' into which Clarence dreamed he was precipitated. Golding has 'the Billowe tumbling downe' (*Metamorphoses*, XI, 644) and the fate of the shipmen who

> ...never up too open aiër came
> But dyed strangled in the gulf.   (647f)

Clarence tells how he strove repeatedly 'to yield the ghost' (a phrase reminiscent of Golding, as we have seen),

> ...but still the envious flood
> Stopp'd in my soul and would not let it forth

[1] For this phrase and the next, cp. also Andrea's ghost, *Spanish Tragedy*, I, i, 55f '...my way to Pluto's court,/Through dreadful shades of ever-glooming night'.

[2] Reminiscences of *Medea* and *The Spanish Tragedy* here seem combined: Andrea's ghost (I, i, 35) speaks of 'my wand'ring ghost'.

[3] In the *Mirror* (p. 234), Clarence calls his drowning in the wine-butt a 'death, of deathes most straunge and hard'. Cp. in *Richard III* 'O Lord, methought what pain it was to drown' (l. 21).

To find the empty, vast, and wandring ir
But smother'd it within my panting bulk...

(ll. 34–40)

At the start of Ceyx's fatal voyage, Alcione saw him standing 'Uppon the hatches' (537f) – words which connect his story with Acetis' narrative in Golding's third Canto (ll. 792f, quoted above), and strengthen the presumption that in lines 38f Shakespeare is recalling the story of Ceyx, and in lines 12f and 17–19 (above, *loc. cit.*) that of Acetis; for the phrase appears in both places in Golding, and also in Clarence's dream.

The confinement of his soul beneath the waves, and the struggle to reach the air, seem to owe something likewise to Seneca. In the *Medea*, Pelias, seething in the pot as Clarence is to drown in the Malmsey-butt,

arsit angustas vagus inter undas. (667)

In the *Hippolytus*, Theseus, having escaped from Tartarus, cries:

...heu, labor quantus fuit
Phlegethonte ab imo petere longinquum aethera

(847f)

and in the *Hercules Furens*, Megara despairs of Hercules' return from the same underworld expedition, asking 'Demersus.../...quam viam ad superos habet?' (317f). In the *Hercules Furens* and the *Hippolytus*, where drowning is not in question, Hades is; which would link with Hades, through the struggle to reach the air, the lines in the *Medea* and Golding which are about drowning, confined 'inter undas' or 'in the gulf'.

No more usual than drowning, in dream-visions of Hell, is an undersea scene. Much the most significant precedent for Clarence's descent to Hades through the depths of the sea is in the *Hippolytus*, and in a passage expressive, like his dream, of guilt and remorse. Theseus, by his prayer to Neptune, has brought about his son Hippolytus's death. Condemning himself, he begs the sea to whelm him in its depths; and immediately before, has called on the waves of Lethe to bury him:

unda...Lethes vosque, torpentes lacus
impium abdite atque mersum premite perpetuis
    malis.
nunc adeste...nunc vastum mare,
ultimo quodcumque Proteus aequorum abscondit
    sinu,
meque ovantem scelere tanto rapite in altos
    gurgites. (1,202–6)

All the torments of hell should be transferred to him (1,229–37):

quae poena memet maneat et sedes, scio.
(1,228)

Three passages in the *Hercules Furens* might more vaguely connect descent to Hades with the sea. In that play, Theseus describes the soul's journey, and compares, in a sea-image, the downward breeze that drives them, to waves that sweep onward unwilling ships:

...ipsa deducit via.
ut saepe puppes aestus invitas rapit,
sic pronus aer urguet. (675–7)

Doubting the possibility of Hercules's return from Hades, the Chorus speak of him as 'praecipites actus ad inferos', and contrast Styx 'nigro pelagus gurgite languidum' with stormy seas in the upper world (547, 550–4). And in a phrase which, as I have already suggested, may perhaps have been recalled in the struggle of Clarence's soul to find the air, Megara asks despairingly 'Demersus.../... quam viam ad superos habet?' (317f). Amphitryon comforts her by recalling how Hercules once traversed a desert, with sands 'fluctuantes more turbati maris' (320), and another time, the sea itself (322–4).

Nowhere in Seneca, however, does there seem to be a link between Hades and the sea's sunken treasure; or even between Hades and treasure, though the underworld of Pluto is, mythically, the world of Plutus, too. These two links are supplied, I believe, by *The Faerie Queene*.

The Cave of Mammon, in Book II Canto vii[1], combines underworld riches with 'Plutoes griesly rayne' (II, vii, 21). Clarence's dream has echoes of this Canto. The cave is described (stanza 29) as 'all of gold',

> But all the grownd with sculs was scattered
> And dead mens bones.   (Stanza 30)

Clarence saw 'scatter'd' jewels, of which 'Some lay in dead men's skulls', and with them saw the 'dead bones that lay scatter'd by'. (I, iv, 27–29, 33). The

> Wedges of gold, great anchors, heaps of pearl
>   (l. 26)

which he describes, resemble Mammon's riches in Spenser:

> ...round about him lay...
> Great heapes of gold...
> ...great Ingowes and...wedges square
>   (Stanza 5)

and his 'heaps of welth' (stanza 7: 1590 – later, 'hils'). Indeed, 'anchors' is most likely a misreading of 'ingots' (borrowed by Shakespeare from Spenser's 'Ingowes').[2] There may be minor echoes of Spenser's

> ...ugly feind, more fowle then dismall day
>   (Stanza 26)

in the ugly' sights', 'sights of ugly death', 'days –/...dismal', 'foul fiends', of the dream (ll. 3, 23, 6f, 58).

The treasure of Mammon is not sea-treasure. But it would associate readily in Shakespeare's mind with the profusion of treasure on the Rich Strand (Book III, Canto iv, stanzas 18, 22, 23).[3] This is treasure which the sea had engulfed, the spoil of wrecks, cast up at Neptune's behest in answer to the prayer of Cymoent that he would endow her son Marinell.

> Eftsoones his heaped waves he did commaund
> Out of their hollow bosome forth to throw
> All the huge threasure, which the sea below
> Had in his greedy gulfe devoured deepe,
> And him enriched through the overthrow
> And wreckes of many wretches, which did weepe
> And often wayle their wealth...

> Shortly upon that shore there heaped was
> Exceeding riches and all pretious things,
> The spoyle of all the world...
> Gold, amber, yvorie, perles, owches, rings.
>   (Stanzas 22, 23)

Britomart (stanza 18) has seen the Strand

> ...bestrowed all with rich aray
> Of pearles and pretious stones of great assay,
> And all the gravell mixt with golden owre.

Here are the 'wrecks' of Clarence's dream; the 'heaped' riches – compare Shakespeare's 'heaps of pearl' and the associative link with the 'heaps of gold', 'heaps of welth' in the Cave of Mammon – and the 'pearl' and 'stones' which Shakespeare would not find in the Cave. That the precious stones were 'of great assay' may well have suggested jewels beyond assay in the dream: 'Inestimable stones, unvalued jewels' (l. 27).

This treasure, though it was once in the depths of the sea, is now on the Strand: Clarence saw treasure, and dead men's bones, on the sea-bed. There are two underwater scenes in Spenser's Book III, from which Shakespeare probably picked up a phrase or more, (though the expressions are not out of the way). Marinell's mother has

> Deepe in the bottome of the sea her bowre

which is

> built of hollow billowes   (III, iv, 43)

Proteus has

> His bowre...in the bottom of the maine.
>   (III, viii, 37)

---

[1] Dover Wilson (ed.) *Richard III*, p. 185 (n. on ll. 24–33) makes a general comparison with 'the Treasure of Mammon', but does not go into detail.

[2] So Dover Wilson, *ibid.*, (nn. on ll. 24–33, 26), accepting B. G. Kinnear's conjecture, *Cruces Shakespearianae*, 1883.

[3] J. C. Maxwell (in Dover Wilson (ed.), *Richard III*, pp. 185f, n. on l. 26) indirectly draws attention to this passage by citing 'owches' from stanza 23 as possibly supporting McKerrow's conjecture for 'anchors'.

It is 'in the bottom of the sea' that Clarence has his vision of the treasure and the bones. And probably, from the closely similar lines about the two 'bowres', 'the billows' and 'of the maine' coalesced in Shakespeare's mind with each other and with Golding's 'Billowe tumbling downe' to yield 'the tumbling billows of the main' into which Clarence falls overboard.

None of these scenes has the remains of dead men along with wrecks: the only human remains noted so far were in the Cave of Mammon. But Shakespeare is likely to have associated together all the sea-scenes of *The Faerie Queene* Books II and III (I–III, as has been observed, having reached print in 1590). Guyon's fearsome voyage to the Bower of Bliss has much of the terror of Clarence's dream. There is an impressive link between its sea-terrors and the horrors of Hades and its avenging ghosts. And it has wrecks with dead men who are preyed upon – like those Clarence saw. Spenser models on Scylla and Charybdis his 'Rocke of vile Reproch' and 'Gulf of Greediness'. The 'Gulfe' is

> ...that griesly mouth...
> That seem'd more horrible then hell to bee,
> Or that darke dreadfull hole of Tartare steepe
> Through which the damned ghosts doen often
>   creepe
> Backe to the world, bad livers to torment.
>
> (II, xii, 6)

The 'Rocke' faces it,

> On whose sharpe cliftes the ribs of vessels broke:
> And shivered ships, which had beene wrecked late
> Yet stuck with carkases exanimate.   (II, xii, 7)

No 'fish nor fowl' approach, except for savage seabirds, who watch for wrecked victims:

> ...yelling Meawes, with Seagulles...
> And Cormoyraunts, with birds of ravenous race.
>
> (II, xii, 8)

These have the office of Shakespeare's fishes, by which the drowned men are 'gnaw'd upon'. Possible but not certain echoes from this

voyage of Guyon's occur in the dream: all that can be said perhaps is that in such a context 'dreadful noise', 'fearful', 'waters', 'of the Main', 'billows', 'ugly', 'sights' are common to Shakespeare's vocabulary and Spenser's, though for some of them there are closer parallels in other probable sources.[1] Nevertheless it is worth comparing with Shakespeare's 'full of fearful dreams, of ugly sights', 'billows of the main', 'dreadful noise of waters', a number of phrases in Guyon's voyage: when there are closer parallels with Shakespeare elsewhere, these may still have linked Guyon's voyage and its wrecks and gnawed corpses with the other contexts in his imagination. In that Canto Spenser has 'dreadfull noise' (of sea-monsters: stanza 25); 'dreadfull to sight' (stanza 4); 'from midst of all the Maine/The surging waters...rise (stanza 21); 'the billowes rore' (stanza 22); 'The salt brine out of the billowes sprong' (stanza 10); the 'fearefull face' (of the 'sea-satyre'; stanza 24); and 'Most ugly shapes' (stanza 23).

The vision of sunken wrecks and treasure may not depend exclusively upon so literary a source; it may owe something, as Dover Wilson suggested, to the wrecks of the Spanish Armada.[2] Multiple inspiration is characteristic of Clarence's dream. When the royal women lament, or Anne is courted, a focal source is discernible – in *Troades*, or in the Lycus episode of *Hercules Furens* – to which the other sources appear to have accrued.[3] But in Clarence's dream, the investigator's impression is of a molten confluence of influences fusing together at a high temperature and pressure of creative imagination, to yield the most eloquent poetry in the play. If one inspiration more than another contributed to that result, no doubt it came from Spenser.

[1] Cp. above, Golding, IV, 604f, XI, 644; *Octavia*, 712f; *Spanish Tragedy*, I, i, 55f; *The Faerie Queene*, II, vii, 26, III, iv, 43, viii, 37, quoted above, pp. 145–7, 149.

[2] *Richard III*, p. 185 (n. on ll. 24–33).

[3] See my article, cited above, p. 145 n. 1.

© HAROLD F. BROOKS 1979

DEEP PLOTS AND INDISCRETIONS IN 'THE MURDER OF GONZAGO'

M. R. WOODHEAD

I

The question of whether or not Claudius should see the dumb-show preceding 'The Murder of Gonzago' is one of the hoariest in *Hamlet* criticism; but it remains an essential one, because on that scene, a turning-point in the play, hangs much of the relationship between Hamlet and Claudius. There appears, as things stand, to be an inconsistency, a dramatic inelegance even, which some are tempted to explain in terms of the complexity of the texts and the possibility that this very long play contains alternative versions springing from differing conditions of performance; yet to omit the dumb-show altogether in production, as is occasionally done, might put us in danger of misinterpreting that vital scene, and that relationship. In what is still the fullest account, John Dover Wilson concludes that the dumb-show is necessary to the audience but not to the characters in the play.[1] Indeed, he argues, Hamlet is seriously upset at the likelihood that this addition to the programme (unexpected, in Dover Wilson's opinion) will spoil everything; but since all goes smoothly after all, *ergo* the King cannot have seen it. This drives producers to find something else for him to do: to have him drinking jocund healths, perhaps, or dallying with the Queen.

Alternatively the scene may be smoothed out in performance by adherence to the 'second tooth' theory, which claims that one representation of his crime is tolerable for Claudius but that he cracks at the second. 'The real weakness' of this, Dover Wilson tells us, 'is that there is not a word in the text that can be quoted in support of it'; and 'an argument entirely lacking in textual support...must assuredly be considered very hazardous'.[2] Yet unfortunately there is not a word in the text to suggest that the King is too preoccupied to see the dumb-show: Dover Wilson himself, on the analogy no doubt of the 'lost stage direction' in the 'Nunnery' scene, has to add to his text a direction for the King and Queen to 'continue in talk with Polonius throughout'.[3]

There has been much to do on both sides, before Dover Wilson and after. The two facets of the problem – did the King see the dumb-show, and how does he react to the poisoning in the play proper? – cannot be considered in isolation: the former is dependent on the latter, and some critics who want Claudius to behave in a certain way find themselves tailoring the dumb-show to fit. My own approach starts from what I hope is a common-sense view of the first question and attempts to reconsider the case as it stands, without resorting to tooth-drawing, missing stage directions or more complex theatrical, textual or symbolic interpretations.

Halliwell-Phillips, in his edition of 1865, allows himself a plaintive but fateful query:

[1] *What Happens in Hamlet* (2nd edn, 1937); referred to hereafter as *WHH*.
[2] *WHH*, pp. 151–2.
[3] *Hamlet*, New Cambridge Shakespeare (2nd edn, 1936; hereafter *NCS*), p. 70.

151

Is it allowable to direct that the King and Queen should be whispering confidentially to each other during the dumb-show, and so escape a sight of it?[1]

It is a disarming suggestion, certainly, and Dover Wilson gives it powerful support. C. J. Sisson too finds it more than 'allowable': for him it is 'a question of missing stage-directions...above all, a "producer's problem" ': in short, 'the audience must see it and the King must not'.[2] More recently, Richard Flatter suggested that the crucial moment occurs only when the unusual method of the poisoning proves to the King that this is not just any old murder.[3] Once convinced, he jumps up instantly ('violently and impulsively', adds Mr Flatter, offended by Dover Wilson's suggestion that he 'totters'). Yet another stage direction is now required, so that Hamlet, 'thinking he is threatened, draws his sword', thus proving to the Court at large that he is a 'homicidal maniac'. Because of the suddenness and violence of the King's reaction, the previous poisoned ear must have been carefully hidden. Mr Flatter explains that the dumb-show must have been performed, at the Globe, 'on the middle balcony to the accompaniment of continuous music.... Claudius and the others, seated beneath the balcony, are prevented from seeing the proceedings above their heads; they merely listen to the music.'[4] (Presumably they do see Hamlet and Ophelia, 'placed on the apron stage', gaping up into space, commenting and pointing.) It is a lovely idea, reminiscent of the lady in Apuleius who cuckolded her husband on top of a wine-barrel inside which he was groping around trying to find a leak. Less risible, perhaps, is S. R. Watson's claim[5] that if the Danish Court looked anything like that at Whitehall, where *Twelfth Night* had lately been duly played according to Leslie Hotson's theories, with the King and Queen on one side and the remainder of the Court, 'we may assume', on the two others, then 'there could be no question whether or not the king sees and understands the dumb-show'. Though the subsequent comparison of Hamlet and the recorders with Feste's epilogue will not impress, Miss Watson does appear to be straining, through the medium of Professor Hotson, after J. M. Nosworthy's eminent reasonableness fifteen years earlier: the audience 'will naturally assume that Claudius sees what they see'.[6]

In addition to hypotheses of stagecraft, with their Missing Stage Directions, there is an occasional symbolic approach, where what at first looks like clumsiness is justified by arguments about themes and images in the play as a whole. So for Norman Holland the King's failure to react to the mime, which he did see, is crucial. The play is *all about ears*, for the ear 'links the complex of images and ideas associated with the body, disease and poison to the play's frequent references to language'. Claudius cannot react to the mere *sight* of the poisoning: 'if he did, it would destroy Shakespeare's careful distinction between words and actions'.[7] This is a sound point, to which we shall return; but does it account for the dumb-show to say that it is there solely in order that the King shall symbolically *not* react to it until Hamlet, tit-for-tat, pours verbal poison into his uncle's ears through his 'dozen or sixteen lines'? Do people behave like that?

In going to cuffs in the question myself, I must make clear at once that I intend in what follows to suggest that the King did see the

---

[1] Quoted in the New Variorum edn (Philadelphia, 1877), i, 242–3, and in *NCS*, p. 201.

[2] 'The Mouse-Trap Again', *RES*, XVI (1940), 129–136, pp. 131, 134.

[3] 'The Climax of the Play Scene in *Hamlet*', *SJ*, LXXVII–VIII (1952), 26–42, p. 29.

[4] *Ibid.*, p. 36n. See the same author's *Hamlet's Father* (1949), pp. 47–56.

[5] Sara R. Watson, 'The "Mousetrap" Play in *Hamlet*', *N & Q*, CC, n.s. II (1955), 477–8.

[6] J. M. Nosworthy, 'A Reading of the Play-Scene in *Hamlet*', *English Studies*, XXII (1940), 161–70, p. 163.

[7] N. N. Holland, 'The Dumb-show Revisited', *N & Q*, CCIII, n.s. V (1958), 191. See below, p. 155.

dumb-show, and consequently to account more clearly for his conduct upon the second representation of the murder. Dover Wilson insists that 'we must show either that the King was not watching the dumb-show...or that he was not unmoved as he watched it'.[1] I propose that we need not demonstrate either: and that though criticism rightly shies away from easy answers, it is possible that we have not perhaps been asking all the right questions.

II

In all three texts of the play (though not, for what it is worth, in *Der bestrafte, Brudermord*, which limits itself to mime) we have both the explanatory dumb-show and the interrupted play itself. Claudius, it would appear, sits through the former unmoved but at the climax of the play itself more than blenches, his 'occulted guilt' having been clearly demonstrated to Hamlet and Horatio. If Claudius did see the dumb-show, why (it is asked) did he not either break down at that first representation of his crime, or take steps to spare himself the embarrassment and danger of the sequel? Without textual evidence to show otherwise, it is natural to assume, as Professor Nosworthy does, that the entire stage audience saw both performances. S. L. Bethell is equally reasonable:

If Shakespeare had intended Claudius not to see the dumb-show, he would have inserted something quite definite into the dialogue to inform the audience of the position. The Elizabethan drama relies fundamentally on words, not 'business', and any special business is clearly indicated in the text.[2]

In other words, we should expect, if not a stage-direction, at least a 'come hither, good Polonius' in the text itself. But the absence of such evidence does not in itself prove that the King saw both performances. In order to begin to sort out the problem we must enquire whether both are indeed necessary to the play of *Hamlet*, or whether we have a flexible text which on tour, at Court, or in other special circumstances could be modified to eliminate four speaking parts in exchange for a brief mime – as happens in *Der bestrafte Brudermord*.[3] If the latter can be shown to be the likeliest solution, the matter may be left to the producer's blue pencil.

That the controversy is still current would seem to militate against this proposition; and the three texts, giving us both performances, are no help in this respect. The first Quarto, no doubt reporting a performance or performances, includes not only the dumb-show but a version of Hamlet's comments on it, though it lacks Ophelia's helpful direct reference, 'belike this show imports the argument of the play' (III, ii, 135).[4] The interruptions to both dumb-show and play make it hard to believe that any authorised version could ever have omitted one or the other; and certainly the dumb-show, in giving both the murder and the seduction consequent upon it, is useful in informing the audience that the play will be more than 'something like' Claudius's crime. As Professor Nigel Alexander points out,[5] the play scene in full is essential to the vision of the past – the killing of King Hamlet – and the future, in view of that significant alteration (or slip), 'nephew to the King' (l. 238). Can we, then account for Claudius's behaviour on the assumption that the scene is as Shakespeare wrote it, or must we run to the cover of a missing stage-direction or one of Dover Wilson's winks to the audience?[6]

[1] *WHH*, pp. 150–1.
[2] S. L. Bethell, *Shakespeare and the Popular Dramatic Tradition* (1944), p. 154. Cf. H. Granville-Barker, *Prefaces to Shakespeare*, 3rd series (1937); complete edn (1972), p. 87.
[3] See for example M. H. Dodds, 'Hamlet: the Dumb-Show', *N & Q*, CLXIX (1935), 334–5.
[4] Quotations and line-references are from the edition of Peter Alexander (1951).
[5] *Poison, Play and Duel: a Study in Hamlet* (1971), pp. 91–118.
[6] *The Fortunes of Falstaff* (1943), p. 51. Cf. the 'significant glances' in his note on v, ii, 257; *NCS*, p. 253.

'*The trumpet sounds. Hautboys play*' (l. 130):[1] the entire Court, surely, is brought to attention, and Hamlet's scandalous behaviour to Ophelia, which has no doubt caused some shocked whispers, is put aside. There is no sign that he himself is surprised or discomfited by the dumb-show which follows: his comment on it, 'Marry, this is miching mallecho: it means mischief' (l. 134) hardly serves to inform us of a piece of treachery by the players likely to result in the premature exposure of the whole point of the play. (What does it matter when Claudius is exposed, so long as exposed he is?) All Hamlet is saying is that the situation is one which will lead to danger, for the characters in the play and for one particular member of the audience. Nor does Ophelia appear alarmed by the comment; and though 'we shall know all by this fellow' (l. 136) certainly again has a relevance for Hamlet that it lacks for the rest of the Court, it is a reply to her, not a gasp of horror, since his next words, 'the players cannot keep counsel; they'll tell all', are a comment (ironically, from Hamlet) on the habit of characters in plays to expound to the audience in prologue or soliloquy. An actor is nothing unless he *tells* that audience something: it is in the nature of a player to unpack his heart with words. Indeed, Hamlet's comment on the Prologue (l. 147) suggests that he wants *more* explanation, not that he is worried about premature exposure. But he reverts to bawdy by-play: the text so far does not indicate that anything has gone wrong.

We know of no other Elizabethan play which makes use of this kind of dumb-show, reduplicating the substance of what is to follow in an expository, not a symbolic or esoteric way;[2] but though this has caused some concern, it is misleading to build a case against the dumb-show for that reason. Nor is it necessary to suppose a distaste for such spectacles in Hamlet. When he attacks 'inexplicable dumb shows, and noise' (l. 12) he means strutting and bellowing: sawing the air with the hands *and* mouthing speeches. When the word is not suited to the action and the action to the word both will become 'inexplicable'.[3] The sentence is syntactically ambiguous: it may be that his elitist taste in theatre (for the Priam play 'pleas'd not the million') leads Hamlet to denigrate the taste of the groundlings, who are capable of, that is able to take in, only such rant. But this show, wordless and intended to be so, is far from inexplicable. It is the gesturing of Lucianus in the play proper that calls forth adverse criticism: 'Begin, murderer; pox, leave thy damnable faces and begin' (l. 247). All in all, the evidence that Hamlet dislikes dumb-shows in general or this one in particular is extremely sketchy.

Does 'The Murder of Gonzago' itself offer any evidence for or against Claudius's having seen the mime that preceded it? When it is well under way Hamlet breaks in to ask the Queen, 'Madam, how like you this play?' (l. 224) and the King takes the opportunity afforded by the break to ask 'Have you heard the argument? is there no offence in't?' – the question, no doubt, of a man who is getting rather nervous. This line is the keystone of the argument for those who claim that Claudius cannot have seen the mime: for Dover Wilson, 'the repetition of the word "argument" was designed by Shakespeare to underline for us the King's ignorance of the dumb-show'.[4] But the remark can readily be interpreted in terms of the theatrical concerns which run throughout *Hamlet*, a play which was after all written at a

---

[1] Alexander's stage-direction: the trumpet is from Q2, the hautboys from F. Q1 has no music-directions.

[2] See B. R. Pearn, 'Dumb-show in Elizabethan Drama', *RES*, XI (1935), 385–405; S. L. Bethell, *Shakespeare and the Popular Dramatic Tradition* (1944), p. 158; D. Mehl, *The Elizabethan Dumbshow* (1965), esp. p. 113.

[3] Dr Johnson glosses the phrase 'shows without words to explain them' (see New Variorum edn (Philadelphia, 1877), i, 226); this fails however to account for the 'noise'.

[4] *WHH*, p. 159.

crucial time for the drama. Why should not Claudius, like his nephew, take an interest in contemporary theatre? Why should he not, like Rosencrantz and Guildenstern, be aware of the great success lately enjoyed by the children's companies? What might at first glance appear to be a good old-fashioned thriller could easily be taken by the King as 'some satire, keen and critical' (*MND*, v, i, 54), the sort of thing that had been rendering the traditional theatres unfashionable and forcing these Danish players on to the roads.[1] Though the play could be brushed off as harmless blood-and-thunder, Hamlet's reply tells us that it is indeed more than that, for he voices the standard excuse of the satirist, that even if the play is 'a knavish piece of work' it need not offend the innocent.[2] 'Your Majesty, and we that have free souls, it touches us not. Let the galled jade wince, our withers are unwrung' (l. 236). Or as Jaques put it:

> Let me see wherein
> My tongue hath wrong'd him: if it do him right,
> Then he hath wrong'd himself; if he be free,
> Why then my taxing like a wild-goose flies,
> Unclaim'd of any man. (*AYLI*, II, vii, 83–7)

It seems highly probable that Claudius did see the dumb-show, and that he had to sit through it unruffled although he could not miss its application to his own crimes: so we must next ask why he blenches at the play itself. Is it simply – to expand Holland's ears and eyes[3] – that the *pictura* will not have enough life in itself without the *poesis*? Hamlet quotes the description of Pyrrhus, who 'as a painted tyrant...did nothing' (II, ii, 475–6) and Claudius later urges on Laertes with the leading question,

> Laertes, was your father dear to you?
> Or are you like the painting of a sorrow,
> A face without a heart? (IV, vii, 107–9)

Or is it indeed something to do with a failure of nerve – the 'second tooth'? A gruesome

episode in a film can be more shocking on a second viewing, and the ghastliness of the blinding of Gloucester is largely the result of the slow and inevitable build-up to it: so perhaps Claudius cracks simply because he now knows what he will have to sit through. Miss Cicely Havely notes that 'his equanimity has never deserted him before'.[4] Of course it has not hitherto, we presume, been put to such a test, but we must remember that we are dealing here with a man of great presence of mind and strength of will. The course of the play scene, over the dialogue of 'The Murder of Gonzago', represents a conflict of wills, a 'silent battle' as Granville-Barker called it:

On the defensive is the King, whose best tactics, without doubt, are to brave the business out, calmly, smilingly, giving no slightest sign that he sees anything extraordinary in it; for the attack, Horatio, whose steady eye – he has assured us – nothing will escape, and Hamlet, a-quiver with suppressed excitement, who after a while will try – still vainly – by

---

[1] In *Hamlet* the company is forced on to the roads by unpopularity; but there is, I think, no evidence that any Elizabethan companies were unsettled to such an extent by the children's companies. Dover Wilson cites Dowden on II, ii, 245–7: 'fashionable gallants are afraid to visit the common theatres, so unfashionable have the writers for the children made them' (*NCS*, p. 178), but it seems rather that the sharpness of the satire in the private houses is alluded to: fashionable gallants who fancy themselves able to defend themselves with their swords are afraid of the children's attacks on the public stages. That the satirist's pen should be made of a goose-quill is a paradox noted by Sir Toby Belch in spurring Sir Andrew on to a particularly cutting piece of invective (*TN*, III, ii, 45). The goose was apparently pigeon-livered, and lacked gall (see E. A. Armstrong, *Shakespeare's Imagination* (revised edn, Lincoln, Nebraska, 1963), ch. VII, esp. pp. 60–1).

[2] The same view is expressed in Hamlet's 'a knavish speech sleeps in a foolish ear' (IV, ii, 22), after the sarcastic 'sponge' episode.

[3] N. N. Holland, 'The Dumb-show Revisited', *N & Q*, CCIII, n.s. V (1958), 191.

[4] 'The Play-Scene in *Hamlet*', *E in C*, XXIII (1973), 217–35, p. 223.

mocking look and word, to pierce that admirable composure.[1]

For this mood of suppressed excitement (excellently re-created in Granville-Barker's commentary) the dumb-show has been the cue.[2] Since Claudius must know the truth, the long process of 260 lines up to his cry builds up a great tension in the audience. Will he crack? How much longer can he sit it out? Granville-Barker makes it quite clear that Hamlet's words increase that tension, while long ago W. W. Lawrence wrote that Hamlet here 'reaches a pitch of almost uncontrollable nervous excitement'. And though he adds that Claudius is 'not strong enough to endure the emotional strain of the action of the poisoning', he mentions again that 'Hamlet, unable longer to contain himself, leaps up and cries out'.[3] Lawrence and Granville-Barker are saying two things at once: that Hamlet is getting wilder and wilder, and that the King cracks at the second representation. But do we need both explanations? Is it indeed such a 'silent battle'?

III

We have considered some of Hamlet's interruptions, but one requiring further comment is that which precedes Lucianus's speech:

Begin, Murderer; pox, leave thy damnable faces and begin. Come; the croaking raven doth bellow for revenge.(l. 247).

Dover Wilson adds quotation-marks to stress his point that these lines include 'a satirical condensation' of *The True Tragedy of Richard III*, probably 'familiar to Shakespeare's audience as a stock absurdity of the revenge drama' (although the *True Tragedy* is not principally revenge drama).[4] Consequently Hamlet is here 'exhorting the player, in bitter sarcasm, to bellow the critical speech of the evening in the rumbustious, ranting manner of the old chronicle plays'.[5] It would not be uncharacteristic of Hamlet to indulge in literary criticism

at this point (although the shift of tone from the previous angry orders to sarcasm might be difficult for an actor to make sense of): his behaviour in leaping into the grave, far from being a moment when he 'utterly loses mental control',[6] is a furious but dangerously sane denunciation of Laertes's histrionic rant, the reaction primarily of a literary critic. But the quotation is not parodic in intent. Like the burlesque of Kyd after the play (ll. 287–8), it is a quotation with a point to it, and a point greater than to show up the bad acting of Lucianus. The subject of the line (and of several others in its context in the *True Tragedy*) is *revenge*. Perhaps 'The Murder of Gonzago' is a revenge tragedy – though if it is, the dumb-show gives us no hint of it – but it is a little excessive for Hamlet to urge on revenge before ever there has been a murder committed. His excitement is indeed becoming 'uncontrollable'. Still the King makes no remark, and there is no sign in the text of any adverse reaction. We must now confront, therefore, the very moment which changes him, and which also affects his courtiers: the moment when, as Mr Flatter puts it,

the two, uncle and nephew, are suddenly without masks: either of them knows the other knows. All at once, within a few seconds, they have become what they remain to the end: deadly enemies.[7]

It is clear, moreover, from later developments, that the rest of the Court too is aware that something has gone seriously wrong, some-

[1] *Prefaces to Shakespeare* (1972 edn), p. 88.

[2] *Ibid.*, p. 89n.

[3] W. W. Lawrence, 'The Play Scene in *Hamlet*', *JEGP*, XVIII (1919), 1–22, p. 19.

[4] Dover Wilson quotes the phrase 'satirical condensation' (*NCS*, p. 204) from R. Simpson's original note in *The Academy*, 19 December 1874; see New Variorum, i, 257.

[5] *WHH*, p. 162.

[6] G. Wilson Knight, *The Wheel of Fire* (4th edn, 1949), p. 22.

[7] 'The Climax of the Play Scene in *Hamlet*', p. 30.

thing which virtually condemns Hamlet to 'restraint' and then attempted murder. Mr Flatter has raised a valuable point: why is it that the whole Court seems shocked? Certainly the Queen, Rosencrantz and Guildenstern, and later Laertes have some evidence for Hamlet's dangerousness, albeit not the right evidence. Something more than hints is required; while Professor Robson's contention that 'the King cannot stand any more' but that all is in fact carried off with perfect outward decorum[1] does not take account of that general commotion, or of Hamlet's own triumphant crowing. Outward calm here would be a terrible anticlimax: 'there is no sign that the King was publicly exposed, and much to indicate that he was not' is true of his actual crime, but not, surely, of his being so unnaturally distressed: and distressed he is. 'Give me some light. Away!' can hardly be convincingly spoken as a yawn.[2] How have Hamlet's 'pranks' become suddenly 'too broad to bear with' (III, iv, 2)? Surely Claudius's mask slips for the moment, and the whole Court sees – though it does not imagine why – that he is deeply upset by something that Hamlet has just done. Let us look at 'the talk of the poisoning' a little more closely.

Professor Nosworthy argues that Hamlet contrives a fourfold plot: the dumb-show, the play, the interpolated comments during the performance and the 'dozen or sixteen lines'.[3] The last, he believes, is never uttered, but his third phase has been given little attention, apart from lip-service to 'uncontrollable nervous excitement'. Lucianus's lines (it is inconceivable that such a play would not contain a murder speech, and I can see nothing particularly pointed in this one, save the actual pouring into the ear) drive Claudius, we are told, to that final breaking-point. But Shakespeare did *not* write this:

Lucianus.
Thou mixture rank, of midnight weeds collected,

With Hecat's ban thrice blasted, thrice infected,
Thy natural magic and dire property
On wholesome life usurps immediately.
                    [*Pours the poison in his ears.*][4]

. . .
Ophelia.
          The King rises.
Hamlet.
          What, frighted with false fire?
                              (III, ii, 251–4,259–60)

Yet this is what critics and producers – perhaps even audiences – seem to think they see there. Lucianus makes his speech, pours his poison, and the King jumps up panic-stricken. But the above misquotation omits the lines of Hamlet that immediately follow Lucianus's action: those tumbling, breathless, repetitive and totally irrelevant lines that break so gloriously into the ponderous couplets of the stage villain. Hamlet's excitement has completely got the better of him: the play is lost in his unmistakable crescendo of fury. The King is indeed upset by 'the talk of the poisoning': but whose talk? Not by the archaic mouthings of Lucianus.

[1] W. W. Robson, *Did the King See the Dumb-Show?*, inaugural lecture (Edinburgh, 1975), p. 19.

[2] It must be admitted that in the version of Q1 this is how the line does come out:

> . . .one wholesome life vsurps immediately. *exit.*
> *Ham.*
>   He poysons him for his estate.
> *King.*
>   Lights, I will to bed.
> *Cor.*
>   The King rises, lights hoe.

Possibly, if this text records a performing version, the King's speech should be taken as implying a quiet treatment of the crisis (cf. Robson, *loc. cit.*). But it will be noticed that Hamlet is still required to make a final interruption before the King, in whatever mood, breaks off the performance. Lucianus's *exit* is surely wrong, as Polonius's 'Give o'er the play' tells us (l. 262). Perhaps the reporters of Q1 had lost track of the purpose of the scene and supposed the performance to be over.

[3] 'A Reading of the Play-Scene in *Hamlet*', p. 165.

[4] Stage-direction from F: Q2 has no direction of any kind, and Q1 a perfunctory *exit* (see above note 2).

Hamlet has gone too far, is too overwhelmed by his own business and desires to care about the play. He leaps up from his position as chorus to Ophelia to take the whole of the action to himself and bring prematurely to its point the whole deadly purpose of the charade.

'A poisons him in the garden for his estate, his name's Gonzago, the story is extant, and written in very choice Italian, you shall see anon how the murderer gets the love of Gonzago's wife.[1]

IV

Hamlet is a long play by any standards. In a modern edition the action up to the point at which the King rises covers over 2,100 lines, slightly longer than *Macbeth* in its entirety; and the events after the play, the journey to England, and the madness and death of Ophelia, let alone the catastrophe, are still to follow. Since there is no play in any of the sources of *Hamlet* that we know of, the first audiences (of an *Ur-Hamlet* perhaps) would be thrown completely off course by this version, if they knew the story; the chances are, in any case, that they would think that they had here reached the climax of the play. Why should not Hamlet, like Hieronimo and Titus Andronicus before him, use a play, masque or spectacle to accomplish a sensational public revenge?[2] We recall Kyd's brilliant demolition of the whole business of dramatic illusion at the climax of his hero's schemes:

Haply you think, but bootless are your thoughts,
That this is fabulously counterfeit,
And that we do as all tragedians do:
To die today, for fashioning our scene,
The death of Ajax, or some Roman peer,
And in a minute starting up again,
Revive to please tomorrow's audience.
No, princes.[3]

The logical consequence of this Mousetrap ought to be Hamlet's taking over and telling Claudius to his teeth – in the presence of the

Court – 'thus didest thou'.[4] But the play scene does not work like that: the audience is being misled. And indeed Hamlet seems never to have had any such purpose: his intention was simply to prove his uncle's guilt so as to be able to kill him in 'perfect conscience' (v, ii, 67). The very putting on of the play was a snap decision – 'Do'st thou hear me, old friend; can you play "The Murder of Gonzago"?' (II, ii, 529) – and it is rationalised in the soliloquy which follows:

> I have heard
> That guilty creatures, sitting at a play,
> Have by the very cunning of the scene
> Been struck so to the soul that presently
> They have proclaim'd their malefactions.
>
> (ll. 584–8)

This sounds as if he intended to leave Claudius to heaven: to lead him, 'struck to the soul' or conscience-stricken rather than simply upset, to 'proclaim' his crimes by making a public confession; but this is wrong too, for the dark understatement 'I'll know my course' at once stresses and hides the fulfilment of the ghost's command. Hamlet has turned schemer.

Perhaps there are three Hamlets: the dreamer and philosopher, the scheming revenger, and the man of action. These roles tend to interfere with each other. As later critics have pointed out to balance the nineteenth century's moody, melancholic procrastinator, Hamlet is, on occasion, singularly active:[5] one who gets so

---

[1] On this occasion I have ventured to revert to the punctuation of Q2, since Alexander's habitually heavy pointing destroys much of the excitement in this speech.

[2] I am anticipated in this by Nosworthy, 'A Reading of the Play-Scene in *Hamlet*', p. 169.

[3] *The Spanish Tragedy*, ed. P. Edwards (1959), IV, iv, 76.

[4] Alexander's reading of IV, vii, 57, where Q2 has 'didst', F 'diddest' and Q1 'thus he diest'. Dover Wilson's 'diest', spoken in the act of cutting someone's throat, seems to overstate the obvious.

[5] See for example Hardin Craig, 'Hamlet as a Man of Action', *HLQ*, XXVII (1963–4), 229–37.

carried away during the sea-fight that he boards the pirate ship; one who will dare all in confronting the ghost though wise friends warn him not to tamper with it; an excellent duellist; the hasty and careless slaughterer of Rosencrantz and Guildenstern; precipitate in leaping into the grave, rash and bloody above all in killing Polonius. This Hamlet must be set against the cunning revenger who weighs up the chances of his victim's damnation and who for some reason has lately been 'in continual practice' at fencing even though he professes to have 'forgone all custom of exercises' (V, ii, 202; II, ii, 295). Hamlet himself speaks of rashness as against scheming when he recounts his adventures with the pirates:

> Rashly,
> And praised be rashness for it – let us know,
> Our indiscretion sometimes serves us well,
> When our deep plots do pall . . .   (V, ii, 6–9)

It is most certain that Hamlet's own 'deep plots' – the careful confirmation of the Ghost's accusations, the weighing of the evidence – are matched always by a series of indiscretions which complicate or confuse them. Carefully planned though it was, just such an indiscretion comes to the fore in the play scene. Although Hamlet is able as a result to 'take the ghost's word for a thousand pound' (III, ii, 280), the plan has gone quite awry. Hamlet's rash, unthinking interruptions have spoiled it completely. And here at last we may return to the question with which we began (and from which we have come some way): if the King was unmoved by the dumb-show, why was he upset by the poisoning in the play proper? To ponder such a problem is to beg the question. It is Hamlet's commentary, quite extraneous to the original plot, that terrifies Claudius. The King was unmoved by the dumb-show because he was unmoved by the play itself.

V

We are dealing here with a villain of some complexity: a poisoner with a deep love for the woman he has won; a murderous usurper who not only has the courage to face Laertes and his angry mob single-handed but the gall to justify himself with the divine right of kings (IV, v, 119–22). The prayer scene in particular reveals his humanity and complexity, as well as the sheer impossibility of his situation (which Shakespeare was to develop: for *Macbeth* is in an important sense a rewriting of *Hamlet* with Claudius as the hero).[1] A man of Claudius's strength of will and presence of mind is not likely to flinch at the representation of his crime, shocked as he may be in private at its discovery. Certainly the events of the play scene catch his conscience, but despite Polonius's emotion at the rehearsal, the ability of the drama radically to influence its audience remains dubious, since any offensive point may be laughed off with affected nonchalance. 'They that are most galled', says Jaques, '. . . they most must laugh' (*AYLI*, II, vii, 50).[2] Gertrude's studied indifference to the insults offered her is a more typical reaction. But it is not the play that upsets her husband: it is Hamlet's direct, unfictionalised 'tenting'.

Like the madness (also a snap decision, and one which has the unfortunate effect of focusing attention on Hamlet) the decision to put on the play was a dangerous one. Through it, Hamlet certainly satisfies himself of the King's guilt, but only at the cost of coming out virtually with a direct accusation, which the rest of the Court must hear: 'Thus didest thou'. If the King could have taken the choice of play as an unfortunate coincidence, Hamlet's crescendo of rage must make the case quite plain. Hamlet knows that Claudius is guilty: Claudius knows that he knows. As with the madness, he actually draws attention to his plot, and it is

---

[1] The point has been made by Granville-Barker, *Prefaces* (1972 edn), p. 216; cited in Nosworthy, 'A Reading of the Play-Scene in *Hamlet*', p. 164.

[2] Cf. Marston's satirical figures, notably in *Antonio's Revenge*, IV, i.

little wonder, even without the casual slaughter of Polonius, that the King plans the potentially lethal trip to England. Horatio, quietly observing from his corner, would never have allowed himself to get into such a position. Both Hamlet and Claudius have a strain of the actor about them, but Hamlet lacks, disastrously, the *sang-froid* that his uncle–father displays in his role. Clowning before the assembled Court in this scene, he should have remembered his own advice to the company's clowns (III, ii, 37) to 'speak no more than is set down for them'.

The theatrical element throughout *Hamlet* alerts the audience to the business of dramatic illusion, and could lead it therefore to expect a Kydian unmasking: but in that too it is being misled. Nowhere, not even in the prayer scene (for revenge should be public and justified to that public) has Hamlet a better chance of turning the tables and settling the score, but he simply does not think about it. The surprising turn the play scene takes deprives us of the revenge-motif we have been building up. In fact, the play scene is one of a series of ironies, the crowning one being that Hamlet never does avenge his father's death, except in the most off-hand and accidental way: he kills Claudius in direct retaliation for the mortal wound he has himself been given.

The irony of the play scene itself is complex. We are on the edge of our seats to see if Claudius will blench at the dumb-show. He does not: he is in perfect control. Perhaps then he will be able to stomach words as well as actions. But when the play is under way Hamlet's 'rashness' or indiscretion overrides the apparent failure of his plot: the King is in the end deeply upset, though not for the right reasons, and Shakespeare has stood the situation on its head once again. Perhaps we are now to get the bloody *dénouement* after all: but in yet a third, consummate *volte-face* Shakespeare whisks the opportunity away once again from his hero and from us: the King rushes out and

Hamlet is left on the bare, disordered stage to parody Hieronimo and make up little jingles. The scene has been one of exquisite tension, the two men confronting each other directly and the play in the end little more than a backdrop to the reality it apes; but the effect of that confrontation has been for Hamlet to present himself naked to his enemy, an enemy not to be frighted by false fire but ready to take any steps to guard against the real thing.

VI

The apparent awkwardness of the duplicate presentation of Claudius's crime, then, has led many scholars over the years to argue that the King cannot have seen the dumb-show. Or, secondly, they have tried to show that he was moved only by its second representation as the process of breaking his nerve was a gradual one (or because the first, upstairs, wordless or perhaps only dimly lit,[1] had not fully convinced him that he was discovered). Less frequently critics have urged a restrained treatment of both representations – which however leaves both Hamlet's triumph and the evident shock of several other persons out of account. I have here attempted yet a fourth solution: that the King did see the dumb-show but cannot have been moved to break down at that point because the subsequent play, in itself, was not to upset him publicly either. If the play works at all, it has a far greater effect on Hamlet than on his uncle, for as Jaques said (*AYLI*, II, vii, 53–7), people may 'smart' inwardly when they are attacked but do very foolishly 'not to seem senseless of the bob'. Claudius is upset not by the play but (reasonably enough) by the direct accusation which Hamlet blurts out, overcome with excitement at the progress of his plot. Rashly – and we cannot praise rashness for it – he has produced the right effect for the wrong reason: assured himself of Claudius's guilt only at the cost of making his own knowledge and

[1] See *N & Q* CLXIX (1935), 305.

consequent dangerousness quite explicit. It is unlikely (unless we resort to Greg's old theory that 'The Murder of Gonzago' did *not* closely resemble Claudius's crime, Hamlet having been misinformed in that respect by an hallucinatory ghost)[1] that the King could have brushed off the choice of play as a mere coincidence: things were bad enough already for Hamlet, without his totally unambiguous interruption. It is Hamlet, if anyone, who has been worked into a frenzy by this example of *mimesis* – and it is his own performance that brings the house down.

'The Murder of Gonzago' is not satiric drama, as it turns out, though it does not lack social comment. Yet the effectiveness of the drama in moving its spectators is not proven. The deep involvement of the players in *Hamlet* betrays a pessimistic view of the possibilities of theatre as a directly functional weapon. Hamlet's discussions and rehearsals with the actors prove to be more than fascinating but incidental documents of theatre history: they are central to the play, in that they turn the spotlight not only on to the activities of the new satiric children's theatres but also on the failure of the expected Kydian catastrophe. 'He that plays the King' is too sophisticated an actor himself, and the only way to affect him positively is to smash the dramatic illusion, tear off the mask and transfix him with a 'thus didest thou'. And indeed, to his disadvantage, that is what the hot-headed prince does. The King asked if there were any 'offence' in the play. Although we are deprived of the Kydian conclusion which we might have been expecting, but which was never planned, Hamlet has accidentally, and certainly rashly, sprung his own mousetrap not through the power of dramatic art but by leaping forward and virtually coming out with the true revenger's answer: 'Yes, by St Patrick, but there is...and much offence too.'

[1] 'Hamlet's Hallucination', *MLR* XII (1917), 393–421.

© M. R. WOODHEAD 1979

'WHAT IS'T TO LEAVE BETIMES?' PROVERBS AND LOGIC IN 'HAMLET'

JOAN LARSEN KLEIN

When he created Denmark's corrupt court, Shakespeare played fast and loose with common sixteenth-century adages which then formed the great bulk of moral philosophy. At the same time he skillfully mishandled the rules of logic then commonly used to prove the *dicta* of proverbial wisdom. Shakespeare did so, I think, in the confidence that his audience which was taught from childhood to speak in proverbs and act on precepts would recognize his distortions and judge accordingly. Erasmus's *Adagia*, of course, was the great source for Renaissance collections of proverbs. It was thus also the principal textbook of moral philosophy, which William Baldwin defined as 'the knowledge of precepts of al honest maners . . . necessary for the comely gouernaunce of mans lyfe'.[1] Furthermore, said Baldwin, 'it is the duetye of . . . Logike, to make reasons to proue and improue . . . Ethike, which is moral Philosophye' (f. 2). In *Hamlet*, Shakespeare sometimes manipulated the proverbs of moral Philosophye' (fo. 2). In *Hamlet*, Shakespeare cipate discoveries. More often, however, Shakespeare made the characters clustered about Claudius and Claudius himself define their being and their actions in terms of proverbs which are false either because they are somehow garbled or because they reflect moral values which clearly no longer obtain in Elsinore. Polonius in particular mangles proverbs which were normally used by good fathers and wise counsellors in the sixteenth century. He also contorts logic in his misguided attempts to uncover truth. Only Hamlet ques-

tions the abuse of precepts and logic. Only Hamlet tries to use proverbial wisdom to its proper end, right action, and logic to its proper end, the separation of 'trueth from euery falshod'.[2] Because Hamlet's own ends in

[1] William Baldwin, *A Treatise of Morall Philosophie Containing the Sayings of the Wise*, 'the fourth time. . . inlarged by Thomas Paulfreyman' (1584), fos. 2–2ᵛ. Baldwin said 'All that haue written of Morall Philosophie, haue for the most part taught it, either by precepts, counsailes and lawes, or els by prouerbs, & semblables' (fos. 3–3ᵛ). On this point see also William Kempe, *The Education of Children* (1588), sig. F2: 'all knowledge is taught generally both by precepts of arte, and also by practise of the same precepts'. Erasmus, of course, insisted on the didactic value of his adages. See 'Prolegomena', 'vi. ad quot res utilis paroemiarum cognitio', in *Collectanea Adagiorum Veterum, Opera Omnia*, vol. ii, ed. J. Clericus (Leiden, 1703: facsimile rpt. Hildesheim, 1961), pp. 6–7. It is difficult, if not impossible, to distinguish among common and learned proverbs, precepts, laws, similitudes, and other small forms. See B. J. Whiting, *Proverbs, Sentences, and Proverbial Phrases from English Writings Mainly Before 1500* (Cambridge, Mass., 1968), pp. xii–xvii. All quotations from Shakespeare unless otherwise indicated are from *The Complete Works*, gen. ed. Alfred Harbage; *Hamlet*, ed. Willard Farnham (Baltimore: Penguin Books, 1969). There are more explicit proverbs in *Hamlet* than in any other play Shakespeare wrote. See Charles G. Smith, *Shakespeare's Proverb Lore* (Cambridge, Mass., 1963), pp. 143–4, and M. P. Tilley, *A Dictionary of the Proverbs in England in the Sixteenth and Seventeenth Centuries* (Ann Arbor, Mich., 1950), p. 807. Neither Tilley nor Smith, however, consider incomplete, disguised, or otherwise buried proverbs.

[2] Thomas Wilson, *The Rule of Reason Conteinying the Arte of Logique* (1553), ed. Richard S. Sprague (Northridge, Cal., 1972), pp. 10–11. See also Baldwin, *A Treatise of Morall Philosophie*, fo. 2.

the play are beyond the reaches of reason, however, he is finally forced to abandon proverbial human wisdom as a guide to action and the rule of his own reason as the way to truth.

As I said before, Shakespeare sometimes uses proverbs so that his audience can anticipate discoveries or events. He uses the old proverb about murder – 'Mordre wol out' – for instance, in such a way as to enable his audience to anticipate, perhaps later to confirm, the ghost's revelation. When Hamlet tells himself, before he sees the ghost, that 'Foul deeds will rise,/Though all the earth o'erwhelm them, to men's eyes' (I, ii, 257–8), Shakespeare plays upon the expectations of an audience conditioned to hear that it is murder that will out. Shakespeare drives the possibility of murder home to his audience long before Hamlet is willing to believe it when he plays Hamlet's half-committed 'That one may smile, and smile, and be a villain' (I, v, 109) against the communal memory of more familiar versions of this proverb – such as the proverb he used to characterize the future Richard III: 'Why, I can smile, and murder whiles I smile' (*3 Hen. VI*, III, ii, 182). Shakespeare confirms his audience in the truth that cannot be hid when Hamlet, finally ready to test the King, restates the proverb in language which elaborates but does not change the proverb's ordinary meaning: 'For murder, though it have no tongue, will speak/With most miraculous organ' (II, ii, 579–80).[1]

Shakespeare transforms Polonius into a parody of concerned fatherhood when Polonius abuses the proverbial material which made up the advice Renaissance fathers traditionally gave their sons. Polonius begins his advice to Laertes, for instance, by omitting any reference to man's first duty to God – and the consequences of neglecting it – even though Renaissance admonitions to parting sons always began with such a reference. Polonius does not tell Laertes, in Florio's words, to

'Loue onely...[God] and faile not,/Else what you doe preuailes not.'[2] Polonius concludes his list of time-worn precepts – in which he has idiosyncratically enlarged only upon the subject of clothes – by truncating common proverbs and perverting logic with such determination that only a cruel and dangerous verbal facade is left:

> This above all, to thine own self be true,
> And it must follow as the night the day
> Thou canst not then be false to any man.
>
> (I, iii, 78–80)

Polonius fails to preface this last 'precept' – which he seems to have invented – with the ubiquitous sixteenth-century adage: 'Nosce teipsum.'[3] Then, as Polonius directs Laertes to be true to himself 'above all', he perverts the second duty of man: 'Christ commandeth men to doe,/Euen as they would be done vnto'

[1] See Whiting, *Proverbs, Sentences and Proverbial Phrases*, M806; Tilley, *Dictionary of Proverbs*, M1315. See *MV*, II, ii, 72–4 for Shakespeare's use of this proverb in a humorous context: 'Truth will come to light; murder cannot be hid long – a man's son may, but in the end truth will out.' For smile, see Whiting, S404; Tilley, F16.

[2] John Florio, *Second Frutes* (1591; facsimile rpt. Gainesville, Fla., 1953), p. 93. Florio continues: 'The end cannot but sort to good effect, where the help of God is called vpon in the beginning.' For earlier instances of the tradition (perhaps genre) of advice to parting sons, see Rudolphe E. Habenicht, 'Introduction' to *John Heywood's A Dialogue of Proverbs*, 1546 (Berkeley, 1963), pp. 3–8. See also Doris V. Falk, 'Proverbs and the Polonius Destiny', *SQ*, XVIII, 1 (Winter, 1967), 24–30. For Christ's two commandments, see Matt., XXII, 36–40 and The Catechism in *Liturgical Services of the Reign of Queen Elizabeth*, ed. W. K. Clay, The Parker Society (Cambridge, 1847), p. 213: 'My duty towards God is, to believe in him, to fear him, and to love him....To put my whole trust in him....My duty towards my neighbour is, to love him as myself. And to do to all men as I would they should do unto me.'

[3] Maynard Mack, Jr in *Killing the King* (New Haven, 1973), p. 95, suggests that Polonius passes over crucial problems 'such as what the self is to which one must be true'. See Tilley, *Dictionary of Proverbs*, K175.

(Florio, p. 103). Here Polonius seems to be directing Laertes to base his actions on egocentric motives. To put it another way, Polonius seems to be directing Laertes to neglect the two commandments of Christ upon which the bulk of Renaissance moral philosophy was based. Polonius's false precept abuses logic, too, because it is what sixteenth-century logicians called a 'repugnant' proposition – that is, a syllogism in which the conclusion does not follow from properly expressed major and minor propositions.[1] For Polonius's major proposition as well as his conclusion are both conclusions derived from other unstated, dubious major propositions. (All men are true to themselves. No man is false to another man.) Finally, not only is Polonius's syllogism faulty and his analogy false, but his analogy is also part of a traditional 'similitude' which, in *The Ship of Fools* and elsewhere, is far from optimistic: 'After the day cometh the nyght/So after pleasour oft comys payne.'[2]

When Polonius attempts to counsel Claudius, his misuse of proverbs and his corruption of logic egregiously reveal his own inadequacy as a counsellor. Polonius blindly refuses, for instance, to 'waste' time on important Renaissance topics which are particularly relevant to the corrupt court. He will not expostulate 'What majesty should be, what duty is' (II, ii, 87). When Polonius does counsel the King, his propositions obviously parody syllogistic logic itself. He says of Hamlet, for instance: 'That he is mad, 'tis true: 'tis true 'tis pity,/And pity 'tis 'tis true' (II, ii, 97–8). Far from proving Hamlet mad, however, his circular reasoning loses even its false major proposition. But the logical conclusion which Polonius does not reach reveals that lack of pity for Hamlet which governs the actions of both Claudius and his minister. Thus, although Polonius, like Hamlet, searches for truth, it is in character for Polonius to say that he will look for truth in a center whose sphere is never defined (II, ii, 158–9) and find it out by

indirections (II, i, 66). That indirections find out only more indirections, however, was indicated by Shakespeare when he put the same proverb in the mouth of double-dealing Cardinal Pandulf (*King John*, III, i, 275–7), by York in *Richard II* when he rephrased the Biblical proverb, 'To find out right with wrong – it may not be' (II, iii, 145), and by another common proverb which asserts that 'Ther is but one way to goodnes, but the waies to euill are innumerable' (*A Treatise of Morall Philosophie*, fo. 120ᵛ). Polonius is not decapitated as he said he ought to be if he could not discover the 'truth' about Hamlet (II, ii, 156). But Polonius dies, ironically, only because he put himself in hiding. As the proverb says, it is the nature of truth to be open and plain.

Claudius comes on stage stuffed with proverbs which are twisted in ways which call attention to his duplicity. He says that it would have befitted the court to mourn the death of his brother longer:

> Yet so far hath discretion fought with nature
> That we with wisest sorrow think on him
> Together with remembrance of ourselves.
>
> (I, ii, 5–7)

Discretion proverbially fights with valor, however, as Falstaff ignobly said, not with nature (*1 Hen. IV*, v, iv, 118–19). Common proverbs not only emphasized the difficulty of

[1] Thomas Wilson identifies the main kinds of argument, *The Rule of Reason*, pp. 56–88: perfect, incomplete, and false syllogisms; induction; example. Thomas Blundeville in *The Art of Logike* (1599), sig. Q2, follows Wilson's identifications and goes on to emphasize that 'the Syllogisme is the chiefest, whereunto all others are referred as thinges vnperfect'. On false syllogisms, see Wilson, 'The repugnauncie of Proposicions', pp. 49–51, and Lewis Evans, *The Abridgement of Logique* (London? 1570?), sig. [Bviᵛ]. Wilson says that in order to construct a perfect syllogism, 'the first proposition [must] be vniuersal', p. 60.

[2] Alexander Barclay, trans., *The Ship of Fools*, ed. T. H. Jamieson (Edinburgh, 1874; rpt. New York, 1966), II, 319.

conquering nature, moreover, but also emphasized, as Lyly did, 'that if wee followe and obey Nature, we shall neuer erre'.[1] Thus Claudius is made to suggest that he has conquered what little natural good he possessed. That good nature which is demonstrably lacking in Claudius, furthermore, is proverbially content with little – as Boethius explained at length.[2] More closely related to Claudius's nature is the proverb about wise sorrow which is lessened with meat. For he has consoled his 'wisest sorrow' over a dead brother with that brother's kingdom and queen. Indeed, Shakespeare makes Claudius suggest that he always remembers his own interests first. Common proverbs, however, say that selfishness usually leads to failure: 'selfe do, selfe haue': 'Selfe wyl moost comonly dothe mor harme then good.'[3] Claudius approaches the conclusion of the first part of this speech – which reveals so clearly that self he needs to hide in order to survive – by alluding to a proverb translated early in the sixteenth century from Erasmus in the *Dicta Sapientum*: 'The wepyng of an heire is dissembled laughyng, yea he reioyceth though he wepe' (Tilley, E248). Claudius has married 'Th' imperial jointress', he says:

> as 'twere with a defeated joy,
> With an auspicious and a dropping eye,
> With mirth in funeral and with dirge in marriage.
>
> (I, ii, 10–12)

Claudius concludes this 'sentence' by misrepresenting justice itself, whose 'equal scale' was supposed to weigh right and wrong, not 'delight and dole' (I, ii, 13).

Rosencrantz and Guildenstern are also made to point to Claudius's perversions of justice through the misapplication of religious and political aphorisms. When Rosencrantz and Guildenstern are directed to become Hamlet's jailors, they tell Claudius:

> Most holy and religious fear it is
> To keep those many many bodies safe
> That live and feed upon your majesty.
>
> (III, iii, 8–10)

Their concern for well-fed bodily safety rather than spiritual salvation, however, is neither holy nor religious. Indeed, as Polonius and Claudius did earlier, so here too Rosencrantz states the basic egocentricity which impels him and Guildenstern to depend (in its Latin sense) upon Claudius, and directs Claudius to think only of himself:

> The single and peculiar life is bound
> With all the strength and armor of the mind
> To keep itself from noyance, but much more
> That spirit upon whose weal depends and rests
> The lives of many.   (III, iii, 11–15)

The bodies, furthermore, which feed on Claudius are kept safe by him only to preserve himself from a danger which he, too, regards as a physical 'Hazard' (III, iii, 6) and which he intends through Rosencrantz and Guildenstern to fetter (III, iii, 25). However much Rosencrantz and Guildenstern may think they flatter the king, therefore, their lines seem to be designed ironically by Shakespeare to remind his audience of the Renaissance view of tyranny – not the rule of a good king. As Erasmus said in *The Education of a Christian Prince*: tyrants 'look out for their people only in so far as it redounds to their personal advantage, hold their subjects in the same status as the average man considers his horse or ass. For these men take care of their animals, but all the care they give them is judged from

---

[1] Tilley, *Dictionary of Proverbs*, N41. See also Smith, *Shakespeare's Proverb Lore*, 213. Sidney in *An Apology for Poetry*, ed. Geoffrey Shepherd (1965), p. 100, says the moral philosopher directs man to ' "follow Nature...and thou shalt not err." '

[2] Chaucer, *Boece*, Book II, Prosa 5 in *The Works*, ed. F. N. Robinson (Boston, 1957), p. 335: 'For with ful fewe thynges and with ful litel thynges nature halt hir apayed.' See Tilley, *Dictionary of Proverbs*, N45.

[3] Heywood, *A Dialogue of Proverbs*, p. 110: 'Boldly and blyndly I ventred on this...I dyd it my selfe: and selfe do, selfe haue,/But a daie after the fayre, comth this remors.' See Whiting, *Proverbs, Sentences and Proverbial Phrases*, S143, S144; Tilley, *Dictionary of Proverbs*, S217.

the advantage to themselves, not to the animals.'[1] When Rosencrantz describes how 'The cess of majesty/Dies not alone, but like a gulf doth draw/What's near it with it' (III, iii, 15–17), Shakespeare was reminding his audience of common allusions to Scylla and Charybdis as well as to the ship of state driven by vice: 'Like as a crazed shippe by drinkinge in of water, not onely drowneth it selfe, but all other that are in hir; so a ruler by using viciousness destroyeth not himselfe alone, but all other beesides that are vnder his gouernance' (*A Treatise of Morall Philosophie*, fo. 186ᵛ).[2] In their clumsy attempt to flatter Claudius, then, Rosencrantz and Guildenstern have successfully painted the tyrant's picture and made their 'boist'rous ruin' a matter of time 'when' (III, iii, 22, 20). Rosencrantz's and Guildenstern's lines, therefore, have nothing to do with that hallowed and gracious time Marcellus evoked at the beginning of the play. Here is nothing but the frightened (and commonplace) perception of the chaos a wickedly selfish king causes inevitably.

In this play, only Hamlet questions the sententious material which other characters consistently misuse in the attempt to maintain their own false appearances. After 'The Mousetrap', for instance, as Rosencrantz and Guildenstern continue doggedly and unnecessarily to pry into the 'cause' of Hamlet's distemper, Hamlet responds with a proverb which he cannot bring himself to finish perhaps because the ambition it suggests – a 'cause' first proposed to Hamlet by Rosencrantz and Guildenstern themselves (II, ii, 248–62) – seems to him now, as before, most pitiful. But he defines the proverb by kind, as other characters do not, and he deliberately identifies its mustiness with Denmark's pervasive rot: ' "while the grass grows" – the proverb is something musty' (III, ii, 329–30). Indeed, as Hamlet has become aware of the true nature of his false friends, he has made increasingly ironic use of customary forms of address based

on adages which defined true friendship. Before he knows they have come to Elsinore to betray his friendship, Hamlet welcomes Rosencrantz and Guildenstern unaffectedly, without the implicit warning that the explicit awareness of forms suggests: 'My excellent good friends!... Good lads, how do ye both?' (II, ii, 222–3). When Hamlet only partly suspects that Rosencrantz and Guildenstern are false, he cautions them through a metaphor which recalls the 'broad waye that leadeth to destruction' (Matt., VII, 13):[3] 'But in the beaten way of friendship, what make you at Elsinore?' (II, ii, 266–7). When Hamlet is sure that Rosencrantz and Guildenstern are false, he tells them outright that the courtesies of friendship (where friendship is lacking) are 'fashion and ceremony', matters of garb and fair outward shows (II, ii, 362–6). Indeed, when

[1] Trans. Lester K. Born (New York, 1936), p. 161. See also Guevara, *The Diall of Princes*, trans. Thomas North (1557), Bk. I, ch. 20, fo. 26, and his contrary statement about the good king, bk. I, ch. 36, fo. 50ᵛ, who will 'vse his subiectes as hys children...for generallye the good father can not suffer hys chyldren to be in daunger.' In *The Governor*, ed. S. E. Lehmberg, Everyman's Library (1962), bk. II, ch. I, p. 97, Elyot not only translated Erasmus's statement about the tyrant, but added also that governors should consider 'that neither noble progeny, succession, nor election be of such force, that by them any estate or dignity may be so established that God being stirred to vengeance shall not shortly resume it, and perchance translate it where it shall like him' (bk. II, ch. I, p. 95). See also *A Treatise of Morall Philosophie*, bk. III, ch. 4, fo. 63.

[2] See, for instance, Geffrey Whitney, *A Choice of Emblemes* (Leyden, 1586), sig. B2, *Res humanae in summo declinant*: 'When Seas do rage, [the ship] is swallowed in the waue....Which warneth all, on Fortunes wheele that clime/To beare in minde how they haue but a time.' See also sig. F2, *Mens immota manet*: we should 'shape our course, so right while wee bee heare:/That Scylla, and Charybdis, wee maie misse,/And winne at lengthe, the porte of endlesse blisse.'

[3] All biblical references are to *The Geneva Bible*, intro. Lloyd Berry (1560, facsimile rpt. Madison, Wisconsin, 1969).

Hamlet holds the mirror up to Claudius and Gertrude in 'The Mousetrap', he does not neglect a common proverb about false friendship which applies particularly well to Rosencrantz and Guildenstern ,who are also watching this play: 'For who not needs shall never lack a friend,/And who in want a hollow friend doth try,/Directly seasons him his enemy' (III, ii, 199–201. See Whiting, F635, F659, F667, F672, F673).

When Hamlet addresses Horatio, however, his courtesy is unambiguous and he uses proverbial references with all the force of their positive moral and historical import. In this play, Horatio embodies the common Renaissance adage: 'Amicus alter ipse.' Hamlet says this to Horatio at their first encounter: 'Horatio – or I do forget myself' (I, ii, 161), and they exchange the name 'good friend' (I, ii, 163). At the close of his letter to Horatio, Hamlet emphasizes the lasting relationship which this adage implies: ' "He that thou knowest thine, Hamlet" ' (IV, vi, 29). Hamlet enlarges upon the meaning of this adage when he summons up its familiar exemplars. He calls Horatio 'Damon dear' (III, ii, 271) after 'The Mousetrap', and thus suggests the potentially sacrificial nature of their friendship as well as his own likeness, at this point, to the condemned Pithias. In the graveyard, Hamlet implies that Horatio is Hephaestion to his Alexander (v, i, 186–204). That Hamlet is right about Horatio is shown by Shakespeare at the end of the play when Horatio, 'more an antique Roman than a Dane' (v, ii, 330), attempts to join Hamlet in death.[1]

Although Horatio is Hamlet's 'alter ipse' in the play, Horatio is not Hamlet's only friend. Hamlet calls Marcellus, Bernardo, and Horatio his friends at the beginning of the play: 'good friends,/As you are friends, scholars, and soldiers' (I, v, 140–1). They prove their friendship by keeping their oath not to reveal 'aught' of Hamlet (I, v, 179) – for Claudius never suspects a ghost. Hamlet also calls the players his 'friends' – five times in the space of a few lines – and, identifying himself with them, thinks he could get a 'fellowship in a cry of players' (II, ii, 411–21; 521–30; III, ii, 267–8). Unlike Rosencrantz and Guildenstern and like Horatio, these actors prove the old adage that says true friends help at need. The players help Hamlet 'for a need' as he asks them to (II, ii, 525–6), and they do so, apparently, without seeking a reward.[2]

Ironically, Hamlet consistently and accurately uses familiar proverbs about custom (established by custom) to condemn the 'uses' of his new world (I, ii, 134). He does so because it is custom that proverbially makes all actions, especially wicked ones, a property of easiness: 'use of evill maketh us thinke it no abuse.'[3] In

[1] Tilley, *Dictionary of Proverbs*, F696. Taverner, in *Proverbs or Adages*, intro. DeWitt T. Starnes (London: William How, 1569, facsimile rpt. Gainesville, Fla., 1956), fos. 66–66ᵛ, translates Erasmus's adage: 'Frendship (saieth Pithagoras) is equalitie, and all one minde or will, and my frende is as who should say an other I.' See *A Treatise of Morall Philosophie*, fo. 182ᵛ, and the chapter, 'Of friends, friendship, and amitie,' fo. 80. This adage is the subject of Shakespeare's sonnet 39 and is alluded to in 31 and 36. See the last song in Richard Edwards's *Damon and Pithias* (1571; rpt. The Malone Society, Oxford, 1957), sig. h [4], ll. 2240–8. Tilley, *Elizabethan Proverb Lore* (New York, 1926), p. 164, no. 270: 'Alexander esteemed Hephaestion a second Alexander, according to the proverb Amicus alter ipse, that is, two friends are one soul and one body.' See James I. Wimsatt, 'The Player King on Friendship', *MLR*, LXV (1970), 1–6, for the classical bases of the relationships between Hamlet and Horatio, Rosencrantz, and Guildenstern.

[2] See Whiting, *Proverbs, Sentences and Proverbial Phrases*, F634, for the ubiquity of 'A friend in need'; Tilley, *Dictionary of Proverbs*, F693–4; Smith, *Shakespeare's Proverb Lore*, 2. Taverner suggests that the phraseology Shakespeare uses (a 'need') is specifically English: 'A frende certaine is espied in a thing incertaine, that is to say, in aduersitie, where a mans matters are inconstant, doubtfull, and full of daunger. And therefore yf thou will do wel, do as the english prouerbe biddeth the. Proue thy friend, ere thou haue nede' (fos. 64–64ᵛ).

[3] Pettie, *A Petite Pallace of Pettie His Pleasure*, ed. Herbert Hartman (Oxford, 1938), p. 124. Pettie

the closet scene, for instance, Hamlet rages bitterly against 'That monster custom' (III, iv, 162). He would 'wring' Gertrude's heart 'If damnèd custom have not brazed it so/That it is proof and bulwark against sense' (III, iv, 38–9). Hamlet takes the consequences of pursuing wicked customs to their furthest conclusions: custom is a devil 'who all sense doth eat' (III, iv, 162), who armors the heart against the witness of the senses, who causes the senses themselves to become apoplexed and disjunctive (III, iv, 79–80). After Hamlet has defined custom and sense as opposites, he goes on to identify the senses with nature itself. In so doing, he adopts the oldest of the adages about custom: 'use almost can change the stamp of nature' (III, iv, 169). When Hamlet interpolates 'almost' into Erasmus's (and behind Erasmus, Plato's) more common 'Usus est altera natura', however, he reveals his hope that Gertrude will assume the 'use of actions fair and good' (III, iv, 164). Like all Christian moralists, therefore, Hamlet concludes that Gertrude can both confess her sins and leave them. In Barclay's words:

In olde sores is grettest ieopardye
Whan costome and vse is tourned to nature
It is right harde to leue: I the ensure
Therefore if that thou lewdly fall in syn
By thy frayle flesshe, and the fals fendes trayne
Take nat the vse, contynue nat therin
But by confessyon shortly ryse agayne.

(*The Ship of Fools*, 1, 164)

On the other hand, just as repeated actions take on the authority of custom, so repeated words, first a fashion following the 'tune of the time' (v, ii, 181–2), become proverbial after long use.[1] Hamlet makes it clear, however, when he metaphorically links the habit, frock, or livery of custom with Osric's unsettled hat, that fashion and custom, equally suspect, differ only in duration. It is by testing that they are both proved, and proving is the work of time, experience, and logic. But Hamlet has no time

– though critics have called him dilatory – and he has returned from Wittenberg a scholar. It is thus in character that Hamlet should consistently use the ways of logic to get at truth.

Hamlet, the scholar, says he will remember the ghost by erasing from the table of his memory 'All saws of books, all forms' (I, v, 100) but, as we have seen, he does not. He also keeps to the rules of logic. Just as Hamlet remembers and questions proverbial wisdom, so too, he remembers and questions traditional ways of arguing: by syllogism, induction, and example (*The Rule of Reason*, pp. 56–88). In fact, Hamlet is conscious of false reasoning throughout the play. He answers Claudius's false assertion that he is Hamlet's 'loving father', for instance, with a false syllogism – the reduction to absurdity: 'My mother – father and mother is man and wife, man and wife is one flesh, and so, my mother' (IV, iii, 49–51). Hamlet's absurdity is 'false' for another reason, too, for its corrupt reasoning accurately reflects Claudius's corruption of marriage.[2]

Although Hamlet constantly plays with the false logic a false court encourages, however,

continues: 'sinnes oft assayed are thought to bee no sinne.' See also Whiting, *Proverbs, Sentences and Proverbial Phrases*, C645–53; Tilley, *Dictionary of Proverbs*, C933–4; Smith, *Shakespeare's Proverb Lore*, 49; Baldwin, *A Treatise of Morall Philosophie*, fo. 175. Horatio, of course, identifies the gravedigger's lack of feeling with 'custom' (v, i, 64). Ironically, Shakespeare makes Claudius's messenger suggest that custom and antiquity ratify language as well as prop up Claudius's reign (IV, v, 103–6).

[1] The relationship between customs in manners and customs in language was described at length by Richard Mulcaster in *The First Part of the Elementarie* (1582), sig. Lii–L[iv].

[2] On one flesh, see *Liturgical Services of the Reign of Queen Elizabeth*, p. 223: 'So men are bound to love their own wives as their own bodies. He that loveth his own wife, loveth himself: for never did any man hate his own flesh, but nourisheth and cherisheth it.' See also Genesis, II, 23–4. Claudius abandons Gertrude when he lies about her collapse (v, ii, 297).

he uses logic seriously to prove the primary question of moral philosophy: what is man? In asking this question, Hamlet sets himself apart from most other characters in the play, whose questions mainly concern Hamlet's 'madness'. (Besides, these other characters are in no position to ask final questions – as Claudius begins to realize when he tries to pray.) Moreover, Hamlet's growth throughout the play can be charted partly in terms of the different ways in which he answers that question about man which no one else thinks of asking. Early in the play, for instance, Hamlet defines man and thus right action in terms of his dead father. Later, when he realizes how radically and perhaps permanently his world has changed for the worse, the example of his father is no longer practicable. Instead, Hamlet suggests that now only he, alienated and indifferently honest, can serve to measure right action. When Shakespeare provides Hamlet very late in the play with new examples of heroic activity, Laertes and Fortinbras, they prove to Shakespeare's audience and to Hamlet the futility of acting on the basis of human examples. It is further ironic that Hamlet's last attempt to use traditional reasoning in order to validate the example set by Fortinbras ends in the collapse of logic itself. Because neither experience, example, nor logic provide Hamlet with satisfactory answers about man's being and end, therefore, Hamlet comes at last to prove the limits, perhaps even the irrelevance, of experience and reason both.

Before he sees the ghost, Hamlet says of his father: "A was a man, take him for all in all,/I shall not look upon his like again' (I, ii, 187–8). Hamlet further characterizes the king whom Horatio remembers as 'goodly' (I, ii, 186) in terms of examples set by classical gods and heroes: Hyperion, Jove, Mercury, and Hercules. Hamlet will not see the like of his father again, however, and in this fearfully Christian play, the classical gods are also dead. Thus, when Hamlet defines this piece of work, man,

for the edification of his false friends, I think we are meant to see only bitter irony in his definition – given the lies that precede his extraordinary hyperbole and the context of its presentation. Hamlet knows very well why he has lost all mirth and forgone all customary exercise; Denmark is now as sterile as it is pestilent. Nowhere in Denmark, furthermore, certainly not in the person of its king or his servants, has Shakespeare shown us a man who embodies *in esse* what the philosopher Pico in his analogue to Hamlet's lines said existed only *in potentia* and what the gloss to the primary analogue in the eighth Psalm said was true of man only at his first creation:[1] 'What a piece of work is a man, how noble in reason, how infinite in faculties...in action how like an angel, in apprehension how like a god' (II, ii, 300–3). As Hamlet tells us repeatedly, only his father was god-like; only his father at this moment in the play (despite those purgatorial fires) can be thought of as a 'radiant angel' (I, v, 55). Indeed, only the spirit of Hamlet Sr is now that ghostly fifth element of which heavenly bodies are composed, a 'quintessence of dust' (II, ii, 304–5). Thus Hamlet implies what both analogues to these lines stated: that most men are enslaved by their appetites, bestially sleeping and feeding, condemned to dusty death. After defining man as he once might have existed ideally, Hamlet proceeds with terrible irony to ask Rosencrantz and Guildenstern a question about the present

---

[1] Pico della Mirandola, *On the Dignity of Man*, trans. Charles G. Wallis, intro. Paul J. W. Miller (Indianapolis, Ind., 1965), pp. 5–6. Psalmes, VIII: 'When I beholde thine heauens, *euen* the workes of thy fingers, the moone and the starres which thou hast ordeined, What is ᵇman, *say I*, that thou art mindful of him? and the sonne of man; that thou visitest him? For thou hast made him a litle lower then ᶜGod, and crowned him with glorie and worship. ᵇIt had bene sufficient for him to haue set forthe his glorie by the heauens, though he had not come so low as to man, which is but dust. ᶜTouching his first creation' (fo. 236).

moment: 'And yet to me what is this quintessence of dust?' This question, which follows Wilson's sixth division of the question,[1] goes unanswered. But it seeks, among other things, to define the relationship now obtaining between Hamlet and his father's attending spirit. Soon after, in this same scene, Hamlet asks by implication a similar question about the relationship between himself and his still living mother: 'What's Hecuba to him, or he to Hecuba,/That he should weep for her?' (II, ii, 543–4).

When Hamlet next appears on stage, he is considering yet another variant of the central question of moral philosophy: 'To be, or not to be' (III, i, 56) – although he puts Wilson's important first division of the question into the subjunctive.[2] As Hamlet takes up Wilson's second division, 'what it is', in a 'speache, whiche sheweth the very nature of the thing' (*The Rule of Reason*, on definition, p. 37), he contradicts everything he said earlier to Rosencrantz and Guildenstern about man's divine parts and mortal end. Here we are told that to be a man is to suffer outrageous troubles, not to be one is to hasten to unknown and dreadful ills. We are told that to come into being is to inherit heartbreak and shock; that to live is to endure, beaten and weary; that it is the disposition of all men of patient merit to go heavily. But Hamlet does not refer specifically to his own terrible dilemma in these lines. Instead, he uses the collective 'we' throughout, and thus makes his speech apply generally to all suffering, good men. As he meditates on the whole state of man, Hamlet reworks the proverbial bases of his statements within the framework of logical argumentation.[3] With all its power, therefore, this speech must be nonetheless understood in part as a controlled meditation upon a popular *sententia* – which the sight of Ophelia stops abruptly.

When Hamlet encounters Ophelia, his question about man's being and end changes as radically as does his diction. Indeed, Hamlet's

new questions and their half-answers seem to repudiate the philosophical framework, if not wholly the proverbial substance, of his previous 'question'. Hamlet now does not ask a traditional philosophical question about man-in-general. His questions to Ophelia are bitter, direct, and personal. They concern his relationship to Ophelia and Ophelia's relationship to the corrupt court. Is she honest? Fair? Why would she breed sinners? Where's her father? (III, i, 103, 105, 121–2, 130) Pico's old view of man – located somewhere between the beasts and the angels – is contracted in a harsh, personal, informal question which Hamlet directs to himself: 'What should such fellows as I do crawling between earth and heaven?' (III, i, 127–8). This new question, among its other implications, suggests that Hamlet has

[1] Hamlet divides his question throughout the play in ways that resemble Wilson's eight divisions: whether a thing 'be, or no', 'what it is', 'what the partes are', 'what the causes are', 'what are the effectes', 'what are like', 'what contrarie,' 'what example there is…to proue it' (p. 45). For a discussion of Wilson's eight divisions of the question, see Wilbur S. Howell, *Logic and Rhetoric in England, 1500–1700* (Princeton, 1956), pp. 21–3.

[2] Hamlet's development of what Wilson would have called a 'double question' (p. 12) has a long philosophical history. T. W. Baldwin in *William Shakespere's Small Latine & Lesse Greeke* (Urbana, Illinois, 1944), II, 603–8, traced it back to Cicero's first question in the *Tusculan Disputations*. William Baldwin, among others, debated Cicero's question 'Of death not to be feared' in a Christian context and with the tendency towards generalization which characterizes Hamlet's lines (*A Treatise of Morall Philosophie*, fo. 99ᵛ).

[3] Hamlet radically reshapes proverbs here. On 'sea of troubles', see Whitney, sig. S: *Constantia comes victoriæ*; Whiting, *Proverbs, Sentences and Proverbial Phrases*, S107, S111, S114; Tilley, *Dictionary of Proverbs*, S173; *Second Frutes*, p. 17. On flesh: Whiting, *Proverbs, Sentences and Proverbial Phrases*, F272. On the rub: Tilley, *Dictionary of Proverbs*, B569, R196; *Rich. II*, III, iv, 4–5. The editors of *SQ*, XXIII (Winter, 1972), 106, reproduced Whitney's emblem of a man swimming in the sea of life with 'fardle on his backe'. On conscience, see Tilley, *Dictionary of Proverbs*, C601, C606.

moved away from his recent generalized vision of man as a suffering being. Here he seems to have come to a new, desperate realization that he, 'indifferent honest' (III, i, 122), 'crawling between earth and heaven' is alone responsible for what he should 'do', and that a dreadful part of what he does is a lie. Moral philosophy and logic have not aided Hamlet in his newest acquisition of 'knowledge'. Nor have they played a part in his terrifying indictment of her whom he once loved.

In 'The Mousetrap', Hamlet returns for the last time to consider that better world which existed before the death of Hamlet Sr, and to consider, as well, the examples set by his then living father and still faithful mother. But he does so, ironically, only so that the image of a true marriage and of the murder of a true king will force both Gertrude and Claudius into admissions of guilt. In this context Hamlet introduces another philosophical double question related to his central question about man: 'For 'tis a question left us yet to prove,/ Whether love lead fortune, or else fortune love' (III, ii, 194–5). But Hamlet knows well that this question was proven by means other than logic before his return from Wittenberg:

...my uncle is King of Denmark, and those that would make mows at him while my father lived give twenty, forty, fifty, a hundred ducats apiece for his picture in little. 'Sblood, there is something in this more than natural, if philosophy could find it out.

(II, ii, 355–60)

Philosophy cannot find it out, however, which makes its rhetoric in 'The Mousetrap' as empty as the characters are feigned.

When Hamlet comes again to ask the question which is central to his concerns and peripheral to those of nearly everyone else, he puts it in a new context, one which tends to destroy the value of human example, proverbial human wisdom, traditional logic, and, therefore, unaided human reason. Immediately after Hamlet has been taken prisoner, he is pre-sented with another example of the warrior prince – Fortinbras. But Fortinbras is an anti-hero. He is almost a parody of conquerors like Alexander and Caesar. For Fortinbras goes to win a little 'patch of ground' not worth the farming (IV, iv, 18), which he will turn into a grave 'not tomb enough and continent/To hide the slain' (IV, iv, 64–5). Hamlet knows, however, that Fortinbras is pursuing a 'fantasy and trick of fame' (IV, iv, 61); that he is a child soldier, making 'mouths at the invisible event' (IV, iv, 50); that, like a reckless libertine, he is 'puffed' with 'divine ambition' (I, iii, 49; IV, iv, 49) – although Fortinbras's ways are not god-like. In fact, Hamlet knows that Fortinbras's big war is only a question of straw – about to be debated in deadly earnest, however, by more than 'Two thousand souls and twenty thousand ducats' (IV, iv, 25).

Hamlet clearly sees the futility and waste of this straw quarrel. He contradicts everything he has learned from precepts and logic, therefore, when he lets himself believe that Fortinbras will find honor in this battle. Hamlet even more dangerously contradicts the reasonable conclusions he drew himself from questions put to Fortinbras's captain when he says that the occasion provided by this new example of self-aggrandizement not only informs against him but also exhorts him to action he is, at the moment, powerless to carry out. It is, then, in a context of spurious heroism and futile debate that Hamlet once more puts his traditional question:

> What is a man,
> If his chief good and market of his time
> Be but to sleep and feed? A beast, no more.
> Sure he that made us with such large discourse,
> Looking before and after, gave us not
> That capability and godlike reason
> To fust in us unused. (IV, iv, 33–9)

As Hamlet continues to answer the question, he suggests that it is he who lets all sleep in bestial oblivion, in contrast to Fortinbras, 'a delicate and tender prince' (IV, iv, 48), the capable man, godlike in reason (though we do not see Fortinbras reason). Earlier in the play, however, Horatio told us that Fortinbras ruthlessly 'Sharked up a list of lawless resolutes/ For food and diet to some enterprise/That hath a stomach in 't' (I, i, 97–100). And Hamlet tells us here that the food and diet of Fortinbras's newest enterprise are twenty thousand men, ready for slaughter like beasts, going to their graves like beds. Shakespeare makes it clear, therefore, that Hamlet's commonplace view of man become beast in no way characterizes himself, as he claims. Bestiality has rather been enforced upon 'this army of such mass and charge' (IV, iv, 47) by that prince who commands it. All these anonymous, sold men are made to resemble Rosencrantz and Guildenstern, who themselves sold the market of their time to Claudius to become members of the many bodies feeding upon the king (III, iii, 9–10). So it is Fortinbras, another predator, whom Shakespeare identifies with Claudius. Thus, although Hamlet comes to the opposite conclusion, this scene seems to be designed to prove the close kinship between the present and future kings of Denmark as well as the deadly consequences visited upon those they rule.

In his last soliloquy Hamlet no longer seems to possess anything like right reason. He does not even seem capable of logical discourse. His own reason, which ought to arbitrate right action, instead, he thinks, hinders him from action: is it 'some craven scruple/Of thinking too precisely on th' event' (IV, iv, 40–1)? Aristotle, however, upon whose logic the Renaissance based its divisions, said that questions were supposed to be divided into four parts precisely. Nor would any logician suggest that quartered thought 'hath but one part wisdom/And ever three parts coward' (IV, iv, 42–3) – for logic works towards truth, not with motives. Thus Hamlet abandons reason and in its place sets up 'Examples gross as earth' to urge him to action (IV, iv, 46). He

does so even though he says in this same soliloquy that reason should not be sold, bestially, to that earth which he had earlier thought 'rank and gross in nature' (I, ii, 136). Hamlet mistakes divinity, too, first when he ascribes it to ambition, and second when he associates it with that outrageous fortune which he (and Shakespeare) identified with Rosencrantz, Guildenstern, and their master (II, ii, 226–33; III, i, 58). Hamlet's description of Fortinbras, 'with divine ambition puffed... Exposing what is mortal and unsure/To all that fortune, death, and danger dare,/Even for an eggshell' (IV, iv, 49–53), recalls his exposition of the dangers of fortune and dying in III, i, 56–88, and his concluding line is proverbial. Indeed, Hamlet's lines here seem to echo More's 'To them that trust in fortune.' But the example that Hamlet says he admires in his unreasoned, illogical soliloquy, More condemns:

> Before her [Fortune] standeth Daunger and Envy,
> Flattery, Dysceyt, Mischiefe and Tiranny.
> About her commeth all the world to begge.
> He asketh lande, and he to pas would bryng,
> This toye and that, and all not worth an egge.[1]

'Rightly to be great/Is not to stir without great argument' (IV, iv, 53–4). Although Hamlet does not prove this proposition, Shakespeare has made his audience understand that honor can not be found in useless, bloody quarrels. The imminent and unnecessary death of twenty thousand men does not shame Hamlet's inforced inaction. Hamlet's thoughts, furthermore, are never as bloody as those of Fortinbras must be. But Hamlet's thoughts are not, on that account, 'nothing worth' (IV, iv, 66). Instead, they are lost in a wood of Errour out of which, Hamlet will soon come to believe, they can be led only by him 'that made us' (IV, iv, 36). That next step is taken after Hamlet's deep plots have palled, and he allows

[1] *The English Works of Sir Thomas More*, ed. W. E. Campbell (1931), *Early Poems*, I, 340.

a divinity, not his own troubled reason, to shape his end.

Hamlet suggested to Horatio early in the play that man's reason is limited: 'There are more things in heaven and earth, Horatio,/Than are dreamt of in your philosophy' (I, v, 166–7). It was Horatio, however, who said that the sea of troubles which the ghost drew Hamlet to look on could deprive Hamlet of his 'sovereignty of reason' (I, iv, 73). That reason and its rules are fallible by nature, moreover, especially in the face of infinite wisdom, was a Christian commonplace in the sixteenth century. It was stated by Pico in the same oration that celebrated the dignity of man (pp. 11–12). It was repeated in commonplace books, catechisms, and the liturgy: 'The beginning of the fall of man was trust in himself. The beginning of the restoring of man was distrust in himself, and trust in God' (Godly Prayers, *Liturgical Services of the Reign of Queen Elizabeth*, p. 254).[1] Because man's reason is not only limited to matters on earth, but also faulty by nature, Hamlet's first reaction to the ghost's words was badly mistaken. Hamlet was not 'born to set it right' (I, v, 189). Not until his transforming sea voyage, however – as I think Maynard Mack was suggesting twenty years ago – does Hamlet reach the intuitive faith which allows him to will action in accord with providence,[2] rather than the dictates of reason. Only in this way can Hamlet reconcile human revenge with divine justice. But he pays a terrible price for his achievement, for he abandons those proverbial humanistic rags of thought understood so much worse and relied upon so much more heavily by everyone else in the play together with the rules of reason that prove them. Shakespeare expresses Hamlet's achievement in explicitly biblical proverbs and in sparse, monosyllabic diction. Hamlet's new language exemplifies what wisdom literature said about the way truth is expressed: 'Trouthes tale is simple, he that meaneth good faith, goeth not about to glose his

communication with painted wordes' (Taverner, fo. 14ᵛ). Hamlet's anger at Laertes's rant over the body of Ophelia takes the form of bitter parody. Underlying it is none of the meaning which could always be found before in Hamlet's wild and whirling words. Hamlet's ironic parody of and commentary on Osric's parade of words denies substance to them and, indeed, to Osric himself.

Shakespeare goes equally far, especially in the graveyard, to suggest the limitations of logic. Hamlet exercises his reason here (using the 'heaping argument')[3] in order to reduce one of the greatest examples of human heroism to absurdity: 'Alexander died, Alexander was buried, Alexander returneth to dust; the dust is earth; of earth we make loam; and why of that loam whereto he was converted might they not stop a beer barrel?' (v, i, 196–9). Shakespeare reinforces Hamlet's new understanding of the inability of reason to question that providence which is beyond human reason when he makes the primary exponent of the rules of reason in the graveyard not Hamlet, but rather the foolish and forgetful gravedigger. It is the gravedigger who argues the case for Ophelia's burial in sanctified ground with the

---

[1] Bèze in *A Booke of Christian Questions and Answers*, trans. Arthur Golding (1572), sig. G[7ᵛ]–G[8], posed the question: 'Is not reason, reason then? An. Yes vndoubtedly, and it allwayes becommeth better sighted by serching, but yet it is alwaies faulty till it be regenerated.' See also *A Treatise of Morall Philosophie*, 'Of Faith and Truth', fo. 145ᵛ.

[2] 'The World of Hamlet', *The Yale Review*, XLI (1952), rpt. in *Twentieth Century Interpretations of Hamlet*, ed. David Bevington (Englewood Cliffs, N.J., 1968), p. 62. On this point I also generally follow Fredson Bowers, 'Hamlet as Minister and Scourge', *PMLA*, LXX (1955), rpt. in *Twentieth Century Interpretations of Hamlet*, p. 91; Eleanor Prosser, *Hamlet and Revenge* (Stanford, Cal., 1967), p. 229; Bertram Joseph, 'The Theme' in *Twentieth Century Interpretations of Hamlet*, pp. 96–103; Geoffrey Bullough, 'Introduction' to *Narrative and Dramatic Sources of Shakespeare* (1973), VII, 58–9.

[3] Lewis Evans, *The Abridgement of Logique*, sig. Ciiᵛ. See also Wilson, *The Rule of Reason*, pp. 75–6.

Ciceronian logic of the philosophers and the terminology of Elizabethan lawyers.[1] But Hamlet questions the limits of law, too, when he asks where, after death, are a lawyer's 'quiddities', 'his quillities, his cases, his tenures, and his tricks' (v, i, 92–3). The anonymous 'other' clown, furthermore, makes it clear that Ophelia was given her 'maimèd rites' not for reasons of logic or law, but because of her position at court: 'Will you ha' the truth on't? If this had not been a gentlewoman, she should have been buried out o' Christian burial' (v, i, 21–3). It is nevertheless in the graveyard that Hamlet asks the last question about man that human reason and experience can propose: 'Did these bones cost no more the breeding but to play at loggets with 'em?' (v, i, 85–6). The only answer Hamlet makes (which is none at all in terms of final causes) is to identify himself with all mankind. His bones 'ache to think on't' (v, i, 86). The limits of reason, therefore, are finally defined tangibly and spatially by bones in a grave and temporally by historical time from Adam's 'till doomsday' (v, i, 56). This is all of human being that living human reason imperfectly can know, and it is not enough.

After Hamlet leaves the graveyard, he no longer poses questions about man. Instead he defines man with a new simplicity which suggests both temporal and eternal perspectives: 'a man's life's no more than to say "one" ' (v, ii, 74). When Hamlet speaks to Horatio about how he truly feels, he uses a plain statement which associates him with the good soldier, Francisco, who was also 'sick at heart' (I, i, 9): 'thou wouldst not think how ill all's here about my heart' (v, ii, 201–2). But Hamlet no longer trusts the auguries of his heart, however much he feels them. Nor will he, as Horatio urges, trust the dislikings of his mind. Hamlet no longer anatomizes, no longer speaks in the 'old ends' of proverbs – that large, vivid, motley, by definition and by organization fragmentary collection of human wisdom.

Hamlet's diction is explicitly theological and his proverbial fragment is biblical: 'There is special providence in the fall of a sparrow' (v, ii, 208–9).[2] Here Hamlet contradicts the different and dangerous assertion of providence made by Claudius, who would have restrained through his own temporal 'providence' 'This mad young man', and who would murder Hamlet to gain 'An hour of quiet' (IV, i, 17–19; v, i, 285). Then Hamlet declares his faith in terms that seem at last to answer conclusively and affirmatively the question 'To be or not to be.' At the same time that Hamlet affirms being, however, he denies to man the capacity to know truly anything here on earth:

If it be now, 'tis not to come; if it be not to come, it will be now; if it be not now, yet it will come. The readiness is all. Since no man of aught he leaves knows, what is't to leave betimes? Let be. (v, ii, 209–12)

At the play's end, therefore, Hamlet has forgone the scholarly and philosophical uses of reason. He has willed himself instead to accept on faith the belief that providence will guide him to that final vengeance which is the Lord's. It was the 'dread of something after death' which puzzled the will (III, i, 78–80). It was her reason which pandered Gertrude's will (III, iv, 89). Only with the surrender of the will to that providence about which man cannot reason is action for Hamlet (if not for Shakespeare) consonant with divine justice. When Hamlet affirms being, however, he never tells us precisely what 'it' refers to,

[1] For Delver's knowledge of Ciceronian logic, see T. W. Baldwin, *Small Latine & Lesse Greeke*, II, 120–2. For Delver's knowledge of the Hales case, see, among others, Kittredge's summary in his 'Notes' to *Hamlet*, v, i, in *Sixteen Plays of Shakespeare* (Boston, 1946), pp. 1,093–4.

[2] The Epistle to Elizabeth which prefaces the Geneva Bible makes it clear that besides faith, only 'the worde of God...is sharper then any two edged sworde to examine the very thoghtes and to iudge the affections of the heart, and to discouer whatsoeuer lyeth hid vnder hypocrisie and wolde be secret from the face of God and his Churche' (sig. ✱✱ii^v).

although he repeats that ambiguous pronoun emphatically seven times before the duel and once as he lies dying. We can only be sure that 'it' refers to more than Hamlet's own death. As the reference to the sparrow's fall suggests, presumably 'it' refers to all God's working on earth, His 'Looking before and after'. If this is so, the whole range of meaning included within 'it' cannot be described by philosophy or even by scripture, which shows us divine truth 'though a glasse darkely'. Hamlet can only suggest the fullness of his new knowledge – which is based on the familiar paradox that human knowledge is necessarily incomplete – through significantly truncated syntax and simple diction: 'O, I could tell you – /But let it be' (v, ii, 326–7). What remains to be for Hamlet may be everything: the everlasting peace and inexpressible truth he looks to when he says 'the rest is silence' (v, ii, 347). What remains for those few left alive at the play's end – indeed for all of us who are Shakespeare's audience – may be that other unanswered question embedded in Hamlet's final affirmation: 'what is't to leave betimes?' (v, ii, 212).

'THE TEMPEST': LANGUAGE AND SOCIETY

STANTON B. GARNER, JR

'Where the devil/should he learn our language?'
(II, ii, 66–7)[1] wonders Stephano when he finds
the terrified Caliban, echoing Ferdinand's first
reply to Miranda:

> My language? heavens!   (I, ii, 429)

Insignificant as this appears at first, it is new;
never before in Shakespeare's plays have
characters called such attention to the fact that
they might *not* speak the same language. Both
Mortimer in I *Henry IV* and Henry V marry
women of different tongues, but these ladies
actually sing or speak on stage in their native
languages, and the underscored confusion
provides humor and charm. Elsewhere, dramatic license circumvents the difficulty, as
Sicilians and Bohemians, Danes and Nor-
wegians, Romans and Egyptians all converse,
with our assent, in standard Elizabethan
English. *The Tempest*, though, is different, and
these two remarks are only one way in which
Shakespeare calls attention to characters speaking. The question of language lies at the
thematic center of *The Tempest* – a play where
drops of water 'swear', thunder 'pronounces',
and billows 'speak'; a play where the controlling
pulse derives ultimately from a magician's
arcane book. Shakespeare, in his final romance,
returns with uncompromising directness to a
problem which concerned him in earlier plays:
the inescapable inadequacies of language as a
medium for expression and communication.[2]
Like its characters, *The Tempest* demonstrates a
heightened sensitivity to words, exploring

these inadequacies and searching for a way to
make language an acceptable basis for social
order.

That language should betray its limitations
so clearly throughout *The Tempest* is not
surprising in light of the island experience. For
one thing, the boundaries of speech are continually blurred by the island's inescapable
non-verbal element. Language occupies only
a middle ground in the range of sounds in this
remote world. Above it hovers the enchantment
of music, for which Ariel serves as symbolic
manifestation. Below it spreads the haunting
and disturbing sub-stratum of the inarticulate –
the 'hisses', 'groans', 'howls', and 'roars' of
Caliban's world. It is in part due to the illusory
and strange existence of these other realms of
sound that the island presents such an enchanting and disquieting milieu for the
characters who land there and that ordinary
means of communication become less secure.
Fooling, distorting, and controlling, the sounds
of the island draw the wanderers into states of
bewilderment and amazement. Certainty moves
into uncertainty as reality on the island becomes
dreamlike illusion. To Gonzalo's 'Whether

---

[1] Quotations are from *The Riverside Shakespeare*,
ed. G. Blakemore Evans (Boston, 1974).

[2] Among others, *The Tempest* recalls *King Lear*, a
play complexly concerned with the failures of language.
See Sheldon P. Zitner, '*King Lear* and Its Language',
in *Some Facets of 'King Lear': Essays in Prismatic
Criticism* (Toronto, 1974), pp. 3–22. See also Anne
Barton (Righter), 'Shakespeare and the Limits of
Language', *Shakespeare Survey 24* (Cambridge, 1971)
pp. 19–30.

this be,/Or be not, I'll not swear', Prospero replies:

> You do yet taste
> Some subtleties o' th' isle, that will [not] let you
> Believe things certain.   (v, i, 122–5)

The relationship between words and the reality they symbolize has shifted; verbal certitude, stressed throughout this play in the pacts between Prospero and Ariel, Caliban and Stephano, and Ferdinand and Miranda, is directly challenged by the island's illusory presence.

Movement away from certainty poses another threat to the reliability of language and the security of words, because this environment also represents a new world of experience, emotion, and possibility. Inner dreams now appear capable of realization as the island's seductive strangeness encourages characters to retreat into and act out their individual fantasies. Antonio's articulation of Sebastian's dream –

> My strong imagination sees a crown
> Dropping upon thy head –   (II, i, 208–9)

is scarcely less possible than Stephano's: 'the King and all our company else being drown'd, we will inherit here.' (II, ii, 174–5). Characters, from Caliban to Ferdinand, fall victim to the play's peculiar centrifugal force and walk singly in extreme visions of ambition, guilt, and love – amplifying the 'compartmentalization' that Anne Righter has found so prevalent in *The Tempest*.[1] The separate wanderings underscore a more fundamental psychological isolation and render visual the distance that words must bridge in order to communicate. With heightened emotions to express and isolated characters to bring together, language is brought to the test as an acceptable medium for communication, a test it largely fails in the early acts of *The Tempest*. Words, forced to the surface and away from ordinary situations and meanings, themselves become strange, and their limitations highlighted. In the play's distorting light we see realized the inherent dangers that words and their misuse can represent to society, as language gradually reveals itself to be a wedge of divisiveness and a tool for manipulation.

The difficulty attending communication between characters in *The Tempest* has been increasingly recognized by critics in recent years. Much of this attention has focused on the early dialogue between Prospero and Miranda, probably the closest relationship the early acts provide, and on Prospero's continual interruptions throughout his narrative to question his daughter's attention. With other characters, most noticeably the mirroring groups of courtiers and clowns, this inability to communicate accurately and effectively is extended, and language actually intrudes divisively to deepen character isolation.

Such intrusion is most marked within the Court Party, especially as its members regroup and try to come to terms with their situation and their loss. Language, in this 'strange' setting, tends to frustrate understanding; words, reliable enough in old situations, become ineffective in the new. Gonzalo, whose words Antonio labels 'deep chat' (II, i, 266), continues to speak with the verbosity that marked him in the first scene. Although we must recognize the venom that characteristically infuses Antonio's language, this judgement conforms to our previous exposure to Gonzalo aboard ship, where he spoke far more than any other courtier and showed perhaps too much fondness for his prophecies about the Boatswain's 'gallows' complexion (I, i, 28–33, 46–8, 58–60). Gonzalo's words are a measure of his optimism and well-meaning, but they also indicate a naïveté which prevents him from accurately judging their effect. Alonso is inconsolable in his grief, and Gonzalo's words of comfort only

[1] Anne Righter, ed., *The Tempest*, New Penguin Shakespeare (Middlesex, 1968), p. 30. I am indebted to Professor Righter's introduction for some enlightening perspectives on the play and its language.

confirm his sense of individual loss. In spite of his intentions, these words have an almost reverse effect, and they rebound back on him when his ill-judged reference to Claribel's marriage, the occasion for the unfortunate voyage, receives the sharp rebuke: 'You cram these words into mine ears against/The stomach of my sense' (II, i, 107–8). The medium intrudes with an almost physical bluntness. With word so poorly suited to situation, communication fails; as Alonso flatly states, 'thou dost talk nothing to me' (II, i, 171). Sebastian's words to the King, too, different though they are, not surprisingly widen the emotional distance, as their naked reproachfulness further drives Alonso into himself. Gonzalo's reprimand rings true: 'The truth you speak doth lack some gentleness,/ And time to speak it in' (II, i, 138–9). Both uses of language violate the moment, and their verbal inappropriateness serves only to generate antagonism.

This fundamental division is intensified by the use both Antonio and Sebastian make of words as vehicles for humiliation, what Coleridge called 'the tendency in bad men to indulge in scorn and contemptuous expression' with the end of 'making the good ridiculous'.[1] Shakespeare from the start carefully underscores the verbal nature of their derisiveness:

Gonzalo.
    When every grief is entertain'd that's offer'd,
    Comes to th' entertainer –
Sebastian. A dollar.
Gonzalo. Dolor comes to him indeed, you have spoken truer than you purpos'd.
Sebastian. You have taken it wiselier than I meant you should.
Gonzalo. Therefore, my lord –
Antonio. Fie, what a spendthrift is he of his tongue!

Language becomes, in their hands, a tool for calculated superiority over their victims, in this scene Gonzalo and Adrian. Language's ambiguities and richness, no longer a source of subtlety and complexity, serve as the basis for pointless distinctions and derisive jokes. Gonzalo's Commonwealth speech is viciously attacked by Antonio and Sebastian, whose words become destructive in the sophistical logical points they draw:

Sebastian.
                Yet he would be king on't.
Antonio. The latter end of his commonwealth forgets the beginning.

(II, i, 157–9)

Whether or not Shakespeare intended Gonzalo's speech as a satire of primitivistic utopias is problematic; what is clear in these lines is how ridiculous language can make it appear. By attacking and manipulating words to their advantage, Antonio and Sebastian effectively circumvent his meaning. Consummate sophists, they play with non-referential language, severing words from a concern for truth. The two substitute verbal for imaginative power and make language an instrument of their superiority.

Barbed words virtually obscure communication as the scene continues; divorced from any attempt at understanding, language isolates and victimizes. Critics have long puzzled over what Frank Kermode calls 'the apparent irrelevance'[2] of lines 77–102, the extended verbal play on 'widow Dido'. These lines occupy a central position in a scene portraying the different divisive misuses of words. The 'dreary puns'[3] and irrelevancies of this passage, also characterizing much of the humor of Stephano and Trinculo, are intentional and controlled; their very triviality is the essence of the 'destructive intelligence'[4] operating through words. Rarely in Shakespeare has the pun tasted so flat; he seems, indeed, suddenly

[1] *Coleridge's Writings on Shakespeare*, ed. Terence Hawkes (New York, 1959), p. 206.
[2] Frank Kermode, ed., *The Tempest*, New Arden Shakespeare (1954), p. 47.
[3] Lytton Strachey, 'Shakespeare's Final Period', in *Books and Characters* (New York, 1922), p. 68.
[4] Derek Traversi, *Shakespeare: The Last Phase* (1954), p. 213.

to have grown disenchanted with his fatal Cleopatra. Singularly lacking humor,[1] puns, throughout the play, are usually used at some-one else's expense. Verbal distinction now serves to confuse, not clarify, understanding. The moral chaos implicit in this misuse of words is emphasized by the recurrent theme of equivocation in *The Tempest*:

Antonio. He misses not much.
Sebastian. No; he doth but mistake the truth totally.

(II, i, 57–8)

Extended in this direction, such speech results in a complete breakdown of communication, a condition of moral and social anarchy actually realized two acts later when Ariel's disembodied 'thou liest' – sounds which are literally separated from person, situation, and meaning – plunges Caliban, Stephano, and Trinculo into the confusion of fractured communication.

Words divide in *The Tempest*, but as tools for manipulation and seduction they are brought to even more insidious use and involve equally serious social implications. The play is ripe with personal and political conspiracy, from the start self-consciously verbal. As the main conspiracies of Antonio and Caliban unfold, so carefully paralleling each other, our attention is specifically drawn to the verbal mechanism through which they take form and to the manipulative power of words, shifting and remolding reality, to work on the human imagination.

Throughout Antonio's seduction of Sebastian, we are continually made aware of the spoken medium through which the two men communicate. The opening lines of the dialogue reveal their almost obsessive awareness of their words:

> *Antonio.*
>
> What might,
> Worthy Sebastian, O, what might –? No more –
> And yet methinks I see it in thy face,
> What thou shouldst be. Th' occasion speaks thee, and
> My strong imagination sees a crown

> Dropping upon thy head.
> *Sebastian.*
>
> What? art thou waking?
> *Antonio.*
>
> Do you not hear me speak?
> *Sebastian.*
>
> I do, and surely
> It is a sleepy language, and thou speak'st
> Out of thy sleep. What is it thou didst say?
> This is a strange repose, to be asleep
> With eyes wide open – standing, speaking, moving –
> And yet so fast asleep.
> *Antonio.*
>
> Noble Sebastian,
> Thou let'st thy fortune sleep – die, rather; wink'st
> Whiles thou art waking.
> *Sebastian.*
>
> Thou dost snore distinctly,
> There's meaning in thy snores. (II, i, 204–18)

The island is at work; this land of dreams nurtures the seeds of ambition with the insistence of Inverness Castle, the scene of an exchange remarkably similar to this one. But these and subsequent lines also demonstrate the caution taken by the two men as they move toward a common understanding, toward joining 'speaking' with 'meaning'. Communication does not come readily, nor is Sebastian easily seduced. He seems to resist the suggestion, particularly later when he lists possible obstacles, and even betrays a considerable degree of surprise at mention of the plot: 'What stuff is this? How say you?' (II, i, 254). It becomes increasingly evident that, in spite of Sebastian's eagerness to reach the deeper 'meaning' in Antonio's words, Alonso's death has not been fully considered or articulated, but rests in the dormant stage of inclination.

It is the nature of Antonio's seduction to provide the needed articulation, exploiting

[1] Righter, referring to Stephano and Trinculo, comments that 'It is difficult to find the ghost of a laugh in those weary explorations of the possible double meanings inherent in "standard", "go", and "line".' Righter, ed., *The Tempest*, p. 18.

language to nurse that inclination into something detailed, substantial, and possible. As he moves from prose into verse, he shows himself to be a master rhetorician, blending logical deliberateness with imagistic power. He structures an argument which deals with Sebastian's doubts almost syllogistically (proposition: 'Say this were death/That now hath seiz'd them' [II, i, 260–1]), and, like Milton's Satan, he presents his own experience for Sebastian to take as 'precedent' (II, i, 286).[1] But the true effectiveness of Antonio's seduction, like Iago's, lies in his use of words to conjure up images, a poetic use of language to make the abstract tangibly and visibly concrete. He describes the distance between Naples and Tunis, the home of Claribel, Alonso's heir as,

> A space whose ev'ry cubit
> Seems to cry out, 'How shall that Claribel
> Measure us back to Naples? Keep in Tunis,
> And let Sebastian wake.'   (II, i, 257–60)

And conscience is carefully imaged as an easily manageable blister (II, i, 276–7). Through this deliberate manipulation of logic and image, Antonio succeeds in sketching out the details of the plot into a coherent visual picture, one which he sets in front of Sebastian as an almost realized act:

> Here lies your brother,
> No better than the earth he lies upon,
> If he were that which now he's like – that's dead,
> Whom I with this obedient steel, three inches of
>   it,
> Can lay to bed for ever.   (II, i, 280–4)

The 'sleep' of Antonio's initial suggestion has been subtly reworked into the sleep of death, a natural metaphor for the sleeping Alonso. The hypothetical 'were' operates in a state of tension with the present tense and, reinforced by the recurrent 'now', creates a verbal tableau where future blends with present, the impossible becomes possible, and illusion is given reality's trappings. Coleridge writes that 'By

this kind of sophistry the imagination and fancy are first bribed to contemplate the suggested act and at length to become acquainted with it.'[2] By the scene's end, Sebastian is seduced – an easy step, for all he must do is assent to the imaginative picture which Antonio's words have drawn.

At the same time, though, we must recognize that the two men never attain genuine communication, a true sharing of motive and understanding. They establish a partnership, but unlike the communion of Ferdinand and Miranda later in the play, it is almost entirely verbal, characterized elsewhere by frequent verbal games and 'asides'. Bearing sinister resemblance to Prospero, Antonio uses language as a means of control. Sebastian, close as he may feel to him, has undergone a deliberate and careful manipulation designed to play on his suggestibility; he is more victim than compatriot and, like the other courtiers in Antonio's description of humanity, takes 'suggestion as a cat laps milk' (II, i, 288).[3]

Throughout this scene and, indeed, throughout the play, Antonio himself remains an enigma. Never do we discover the motives behind his seduction: Sebastian's mercenary concession at the end of the dialogue that 'One stroke/Shall free thee from the tribute which thou payest' (II, i, 292–3) seems almost an afterthought. Shakespeare's other major villains – Edmund, Claudius, Richard III, and even Sebastian – all have moments when the mask of language slips to reveal an inner core of motives, fears, and perhaps a flash of humanity. Antonio, though, joins Iago alone in his apparent self-sufficiency and in his use of language as an impenetrable barrier to the workings of his personality. His language

[1] Kermode's text. Evans (II, i, 291) preserves the First Folio 'president'.
[2] *Coleridge's Writings on Shakespeare*, pp. 206–7.
[3] For a close reading of this scene and some interesting comments on Antonio, see Traversi, *Shakespeare: The Last Phase*, pp. 213–22.

exists independent of those feelings that give it form and meaning; instead of revealing character, his words obscure it. Animated by the vague impulse toward regicide and fratricide which represents much of the anarchic threat within the play, his words become tools with frightening potential for evil.

The opposite holds true for the other seducer, Caliban, whose words serve continually to express the motives of a recognizably bestial nature. From the start his presence has pointed to a different limitation inherent in words and posed a direct challenge to Prospero's view of language as a civilizing agent. In Miranda's claim to have given him the ennobling power of expression –

> When thou didst not, savage,
> Know thine own meaning, but wouldst gabble like
> A thing most brutish, I endow'd thy purposes
> With words that made them known –
>
> (I, ii, 355–8)

even Caliban sees the irony:

> You taught me language, and my profit on't
> Is, I know how to curse. The red-plague rid you
> For learning me your language! (I, ii, 363–5)

The 'purposes' of a savage, whom Prospero learns to recognize as 'A devil, a born devil, on whose nature/Nurture can never stick' (IV, i, 188–9), can issue verbally into nothing but curses; vicious expression is, for Caliban, compulsive: 'His spirits hear me,/And yet I needs must curse' (II, ii, 3–4). For Caliban, language can act only as his nature asserts. In his seduction of Stephano, therefore, his resentment toward Prospero makes itself felt in the expressive violence of his imagery: 'I'll yield him thee asleep,/Where thou mayst knock a nail into his head' (III, ii, 60–1). Unlike Antonio, Caliban conceives his plot out of discernible motives and sets it naturally into words which reflect them.

But in so doing, he becomes manipulator. Language, which Prospero conceived of as a civilizing force, not only fails with Caliban but, by acting as such a perfect medium which allows his bestial nature to express itself in verbal terms beyond his usual 'gabble', it also represents, in Derek Traversi's words, 'the cause of a dangerous extension of the capacity for ill'.[1] Although lacking Antonio's verbal sophistication, he is able to put his emotions into a seductive and suggestive medium and communicate them to others. In the haze of liquor, which Stephano holds out to Caliban as 'that which will give language to you' (II, ii, 83) and which serves only to loosen his tongue and make him bolder in suggestion, we see a plot take verbal form in much the same way as its earlier counterpart. 'Occasion speaks' to Stephano with a similar subtle effectiveness. Caliban, whose lines are generally acknowledged to be among the play's finest, draws an intensely visual picture of the lush island governed from an Olympian center by the drunken butler: 'I'll show thee every fertile inch o' th' island;/And I will kiss thy foot. I prithee be my god' (II, ii, 148–9). To obtain Miranda and total rule, all Stephano must do, like Sebastian, is assent to the verbal image. This conspiracy never achieves the threat of the plot between Antonio and Sebastian, Ariel and drink ensuring a comic atmosphere where action is frustrated and consequence denied. But throughout this scene, the manipulative use of language to give form and purpose to anarchic impulses remains, and the sinister power which words exert over the human imagination is implicit in Sebastian's Macbeth-like declaration: 'Give me thy hand. I do begin to have bloody/thoughts' (IV, i, 220–1).

Language, then, by acting as such an irresistible instrument of seduction in the early acts of *The Tempest*, reinforces the illusion that tends to surround characters in isolation;

[1] Traversi, *Shakespeare: The Last Phase*, p. 232.

by acting divisively, it widens those fundamental distances. Speech, which Tasso placed
above reason as 'what primarily distinguishes
man from the animals',[1] gradually undermines
the social imperative from which it evolved:
the need to communicate. Even Prospero, the
verbal magician at the play's center, cannot
escape the fact that the medium which he
exercises with such total authority over the
elements remains remarkably ineffective in
reaching the souls of others: his almost
spiritual understanding with Ariel is countered
by Caliban's sullen resistance, and the force
with which his words pierce to the inner fiber
of the guilt-torn Alonso is balanced by the
active defiance of Antonio and Sebastian.
These marked failures represent failures of
language and would seem to bear somber
implications for poet and dramatist. And when
we consider, at the same time, the shifting
suggestiveness of Antonio's words and the
vehement execrations of Caliban's, we might
be tempted to imagine a Shakespeare disillusioned with the very medium of his art.
But this play, in spite of its compactness and
general verbal asceticism, reflects no weakening
of poetic force; one could argue, along with
Henry James, that Shakespeare's verse has
never served as a more expressive medium.[2]
Prospero's island, an illusory land of fantasy
and disequilibrium, has brought language into
a state of crisis and threatens to throw verbal
interaction into chaos.[3] But Shakespeare
realizes that without language and communication, poetic, moral, and social structure
descends into the inarticulate 'howls' and
'hisses' of the island's sub-stratum, just as the
harmony of Prospero's carefully planned
marriage masque crashes into 'strange, hollow,
and confused noise' (stage direction after IV, i,
138). Man must live with language, imperfect
as it is; chaos and mute silence seem to be, for
Shakespeare, unacceptable alternatives. The
characters in The Tempest must, in a sense,
rescue language from the island's confusion,
rediscover some basis for verbal communication and, in so doing, make such a limited
medium serve as the foundation for the new
order, embodied in Ferdinand and Miranda,
which will begin when they leave the island and
set sail for Naples.

For the two lovers, though, the road to this
discovery is littered with obstacles; they, too,
participate initially in the island's verbal
confusion. Actually, their conversation is over
before they ever begin to speak, their glances
saying all: 'At the first sight/They have
chang'd eyes' (I, ii, 441–2). In sharp contrast
to the verbal rapport of Sebastian and Antonio,
the bond of Ferdinand and Miranda is the first
instance of a genuinely non-verbal understanding in The Tempest, a play which itself
relies upon an unprecedented amount of music
and spectacle. But their inner speech cannot at
this stage be translated into words, and the
verbal attempts only confuse and distort their
simple, spiritual understanding. Ferdinand, concerned in part with how he *should* speak, begins
by casting his sudden love into hyperbole
and even proposes suiting his behavior to his
rhetoric:

> Most sure, the goddess
> On whom these airs attend! Vouchsafe my pray'r
> May know if you remain upon this island,
> And that you will some good instruction give
> How I may bear me here.   (I, ii, 422–6)

Between formal concerns for proper behavior

[1] Torquato Tasso, *Discourses on the Heroic Poem*,
trans. Mariella Cavalchini and Irene Samuel (Oxford,
1973), p. 139.

[2] Henry James, 'Introduction to *The Tempest*'
(1907), rpt. in *The Appreciation of Shakespeare*, ed.
Bernard M. Wagner (Washington, 1949), pp. 477–8.
James writes: 'The face that beyond any other, however, I seem to see *The Tempest* turn to us is the side
on which it so superlatively speaks of that endowment
for Expression.... The resources of such a style, the
provision of images, emblems, and energies of every
sort, laid up in advance, affects us as the storehouse of
a king before a famine or a siege....'

[3] It literally does, as the subplot clowns are drawn
into a bog and the courtiers into powerless silence.

and the inflating language of romantic adoration, his words, despite their underlying sincerity, escalate far beyond the simplicity of those original, all-speaking glances. Righter calls their initial conversation 'perplexed in the extreme'.[1] Language operates in conflict with the non-verbal and indeed seems to hinder more than help, especially with the intrusion of Prospero, whose words throw Miranda into a state of confusion, as reality actually clashes with the appearance of words: 'My father's of a better nature, sir,/Than he appears by speech' (I, ii, 497–8).

One of the significances of the log-bearing scene is the way in which Ferdinand and Miranda together manage to overcome the obstacle posed by language. Ferdinand returns to the hyperbolic rhetoric of their earlier meeting, but at the same time seems suspicious of his words, contrasting what he feels to be true love with the verbal illusion of his previous liaisons:

> Full many a lady
> I have ey'd with best regard, and many a time
> Th' harmony of their tongues hath into bondage
> Brought my too diligent ear. (III, i, 39–42)

We can sense a strong tension between language and the emotional demands of the moment, a tension which Miranda tries impulsively to overcome: 'But I prattle/Something too wildly' (III, i, 57–8). The solution, which they both discover, lies in reducing the words they use to the simplicity and honesty of the love they feel. They abandon romantic hyperbole and formality, as their love forces them into a more direct and expressive diction, one capable of articulating and verifying the commitment each wants to make. Ferdinand is the first to speak in firm, declarative words:

> Hear my soul speak:
> The very instant that I saw you, did
> My heart fly to your service, there resides,
> To make me slave to it, and for your sake
> Am I this patient log-man.

Miranda.	Do you love me?
Ferdinand.	

> O heaven, O earth, bear witness to this sound,
> And crown what I profess with kind event
> If I speak true! if hollowly, invert
> What best is boded me to mischief! I,
> Beyond all limit of what else i' th' world,
> Do love, prize, honor you. (III, i, 63–73)

Miranda, too, adopts the language of the soul, which has now become charged with expressive power:

> But this is trifling,
> And all the more it seeks to hide itself,
> The bigger bulk it shows. Hence, bashful cunning,
> And prompt me, plain and holy innocence!
> I am your wife, if you will marry me;
> If not, I'll die your maid. (III, i, 79–84)

Language has become, in this scene, no longer divisive or manipulative, but a source of binding and power. Solidly founded on their inner communion, it escapes the illusory non-reference that has so noticeably distinguished it elsewhere; words find their link with person, situation, and meaning. 'Soul' and 'heart' resonate through this passage as the only true source of genuinely expressive language.[2] And as the two finally speak what they mean, language is redeemed as an agent of social cohesion. By placing their most inexpressible feelings in words, they have confirmed and strengthened their mutual commitment; articulated in the language of direct pledge, their bond is complete. In one of The Tempest's many paradoxes, only by understanding and

---

[1] Righter, ed., The Tempest, p. 33.

[2] Their discovery is one which Shakespeare has reaffirmed before as a way of redeeming language, from Berowne: 'Honest plain words best pierce the ear of grief' (LL Lost, v, ii, 753) through Troilus: 'Words, words, mere words, no matter from the heart' (Tr. & Cress., v, iii, 108) and Edgar: 'Speak what we feel, not what we ought to say' (Lear, v, iii, 325). Miranda's 'plain and holy innocence' reminds us, too, of Juliet's ingenuous, yet liberating directness during the balcony scene (Rom. & Jul., II, ii, 85–106).

using language are the two lovers liberated from it. When they are revealed at chess to the Court Party in the final scene, their conversation shows the extent to which they have moved beyond the divisive potential of words and the ease with which they now operate through them in ordinary speech:

> *Miranda.*
> > Sweet lord, you play me false.
> *Ferdinand.* No, my dearest love,
> > I would not for the world.
> *Miranda.*
> > Yes, for a score of kingdoms you
> > should wrangle,
> And I would call it fair play. (v, i, 172–5)

Ferdinand and Miranda begin the descent from the island's illusion and verbal disequilibrium, a movement which characterizes the end of *The Tempest*. Words have become an acceptable medium for their relationship and, by extension, for the social order which they now represent. Shakespeare, in the final moments of the play, invites all the characters to join this newly-formed order. Prospero, who has controlled and participated in the elaborate illusion, abjures his verbal control over the courtiers and renounces his magic.[1] They enter, submerged in the charmed 'speechlessness' to which they have been reduced. Gradually, the island's effects begin to wear off, the 'ignorant fumes' that have covered their 'clearer reason' lift (v, i, 67–8), and the world of fantasy and illusion now seems itself the dream. But the presence of verbal confusion, with its own dream-like seductions and obstructions, is harder to dispel. Their experiences have served to undermine their assumptions about the relationship between language and reality; Gonzalo's 'Whether this be/Or be not, I'll not swear' (v, i, 122–3) recalls his earlier uncertainty about the fantastic claims which 'Each putter-out of five for one will bring us/Good warrant of' (III, iii, 48–9). Truth emerges from illusion,

though, and little by little they regain control over their senses and their speech. But for Alonso and Gonzalo, at least, the experience of language plunged into confusion and speechlessness remains in their memories; they speak haltingly and tentatively, questioning for certainty, unwilling to commit themselves to words that might misrepresent what they perceive.

This awareness of language's inadequacies makes itself felt most strongly in the quality of silence which frames the final scene. We are impressed not so much by what is said, but by how much is left unsaid where we might expect explanation. The matter of Alonso's past treachery, bearing heavily on his mind, is cut off at first mention. Similarly, Prospero breaks with other Shakespearian last scenes by choosing not to reveal publicly the crimes of the villains: 'At this time/I will tell no tales' (v, i, 128–9). The sheer fact of recognition, independent of words, constitutes all the exposure the moment needs. In both cases, the dissonance of such revelations would needlessly complicate the pervading tone of reconciliation. Sebastian's sneering aside – 'The devil speaks in him' (v, i, 129) – betrays the extent to which, by remaining outside the circle of reconciliation, he does not share this new awareness of language – an awareness which will accompany the characters back to Naples and which represents, in many ways, *The Tempest*'s achievement. If the members of society, like the returning characters, cannot all attain the perfect communion of Ferdinand and Miranda, they can remain sensitive to their language, its limits, and its potential for misuse.

The joy and wonder of the final scene, however, like the love of Ferdinand and

---

[1] He does this as a result of what might ultimately be the most important piece of language in *The Tempest*: Ariel's intercession on behalf of the distracted courtiers, which sways his inclinations to the side of mercy (v, i, 7–20).

Miranda, asks for expression. Gonzalo, who in earlier scenes applied word to situation with less than consistent appropriateness, remains uncharacteristically quiet during much of the reconciliation and chooses to speak only after wordless participation. His language, though, is different:

> I have inly wept,
> Or should have spoke ere this. Look down, you gods,
> And on this couple drop a blessed crown!
> For it is you that have chalk'd forth the way
> Which brought us hither.
> *Alonso.*   I say amen, Gonzalo!
> *Gonzalo.*
>   Was Milan thrust from Milan, that his issue
> Should become kings of Naples? O, rejoice
> Beyond a common joy, and set it down
> With gold on lasting pillars: in one voyage
> Did Claribel her husband find at Tunis,
> And Ferdinand, her brother, found a wife
> Where he himself was lost; Prospero, his dukedom
> In a poor isle; and all of us, ourselves,
> When no man was his own.   (v, i, 200–13)

Although his speech is filled with his undying optimism, it indicates at the same time a new and more sophisticated use of words. The logic of his words, apparently colliding with itself, gives Gonzalo an expressive power he lacked earlier. By elevating language, linear and logical, to paradox, he becomes spokesman for the moment and comes closer than any other character to expressing the emotions 'beyond a common joy' that undeniably permeate this scene. Gonzalo's words, which Alonso agrees with for the first time in the play, implicitly acknowledge the presence of an inexpressible realm, but also indicate his resolve to make language approximate that realm.

Still, the notes of the final chord do not all sound in harmony. Caliban enters to remind us of the presence of unalterable natures for whom language can never be redeemed. Then

there is the exposed Antonio, whose silence during the entire scene is the most disturbing bit of language in the play. It communicates the inscrutability which has characterized him throughout. Words have served all along as the sole basis of his interaction with others; their loss leaves him nothing. Stripped of the tools of its control, the 'destructive intelligence' turns inward on itself and retreats into silence.[1] It is fitting that, as others make a similar inward journey and uncover the roots of human communication, Antonio's words should be rendered impotent. His loss, after all, is society's gain.

Prospero ends the play by promising to reveal all at a later time. Language, now free of the island's distortions, moves back into the ordinary: Prospero's account will furnish 'a chronicle of day by day' (v, i, 163). Civilization depends on language and the certainties of words; society relies on communication. Shakespeare seems unable to conceive of a world like Montaigne's primitive paradise where 'The very words that import lying, falshood, treason, dissimulation, covetousnes, envie, detraction, and pardon, were never heard of...'[2] Evil necessitates such words, and *The Tempest* does not falsify the world to which it returns. The balance is delicate and faithful: Prospero, Alonso, Ferdinand, and Miranda will always have to cope with the potential for verbal confusion. But an understanding of the nature of words, the island's gift, provides a corrective – recognized, the anarchic misuse of words which Antonio and Caliban represent can be controlled. Their corruptive presence does not diminish the need

[1] His presence poses a challenge similar to the last words spoken by an unmasked Iago: 'Demand me nothing; what you know, you know:/From this time forth I never will speak word' (*Oth.*, v, ii, 303–4). Nowhere does Antonio resemble Iago more than in the silence of his complete self-containment.

[2] 'Of the Caniballes', *The Essayes of Lord Michaell de Montaigne*, trans. John Florio (1603), p. 102.

to make language, imperfect as it is, an acceptable basis for communication. *The Tempest* affirms that language can be redeemed by an awareness of its inadequacies and that, in its purest moments, founded on soul-spoken simplicity and feeling, it can genuinely bind and communicate.

PICTORIAL EVIDENCE FOR A POSSIBLE
REPLICA OF THE LONDON FORTUNE
THEATRE IN GDANSK

JERZY LIMON

It is widely known amongst scholars of the Elizabethan and Jacobean theatre that the contemporary English 'Continental' companies were extremely active and popular in the Protestant and Catholic countries of Western and Central Europe for many decades. However, the news that at the beginning of the seventeenth century a permanent public theatre was built in the city of Gdansk[1] on the Baltic coast, and that this theatre was modelled on London's Fortune, will be received with a large dose of understandable scepticism. The Fortune, of course, has been one of the 'favourite' theatres of reconstructors, but in spite of the fact that it is actually the only London theatre about which a vast amount of valid written evidence is preserved, with the builder's contract being most important, its numerous modern reconstructions have mostly been of a highly conjectural nature. This discrepancy arises from the lack of pictorial evidence for the reconstructors; the only substitute being to take some details from other sources, like De Witt's drawing of the Swan or Hollar's 'Long View of London', and fuse them together with the features of the Fortune as described in the contract. This situation gave rise to a series of eclectic designs composed of elements taken from various sources.

The aim of this article is to suggest indirect pictorial evidence for the Fortune, a seventeenth-century engraving showing a public theatre in Gdansk (plates IIA and B), which – in the opinion of the writer – may be

used, with some restrictions, as a valid source for any future reconstructions of the Fortune.

Although the similarity of the Gdansk theatre to the Fortune is striking, it remained unnoticed until recent years.[2] This may have been due to the generally accepted opinion that the architecture of Elizabethan and Jacobean theatres was unique and restricted to England only. Thus, our second task will be to establish how this English theatrical form made its way as far east as Gdansk, and was the cultural background of such an unprecedented and peculiar 'import' of an architectural concept.[3]

[1] The Polish form 'Gdansk' is used here instead of the German 'Danzig'. Although the details of the etymology of these words lie beyond the scope of the present inquiry, it is worth noting that 'Gdansk' is not a new name created to replace the other, and it has been used simultaneously with the Latin form 'Gedanum' for centuries. During the Elizabethan and Jacobean periods in England the most common name used in reference to this city was 'Dansk' (often confused with Denmark), which obviously derives from the Polish form 'Gdansk'.

[2] See my article 'Przypuszczalne związki teatru w gdańskiej "Szkole Fechtunku" z teatrem "Fortune" w Londynie', *Pamiętnik Teatralny*, 1 (Warsaw, 1977), pp. 29–38.

[3] A theatre at Nuremburg erected in 1628 seems to belong to the same 'school' and is – in its general appearance – similar to the Gdansk playhouse. Since the Fortune burned down in 1621, it seems that it could actually have been modelled on the Gdansk theatre. An engraving dated 1651 showing the interior of the Nuremberg playhouse is reproduced by Gustav Könnecke in *Bilderatlas zur Geschichte der*

Let us begin with the engraving proper, which is attributed to a Dutch artist, Peter Willer; he included it in his cycle of illustrations made for the first written history of Gdansk by Reinhold Curicke. This was written in 1645, but – due to a conflict with censors – was not printed until 1687.[1] Since Willer was active in Gdansk from 1664 (previously he had been employed by the King of Poland, Vladislaus IV, in Warsaw), the engraving must have been made between 1664 and 1687. It shows the south-western corner of the Main City, which was the centre of old Gdansk, with the object of our interest in the foreground. Behind the theatre some municipal buildings are shown (hence the engraving is entitled 'der Stadthoff'); these were erected by Jerzy Strakowski in the 1620s. The towers which were built in the second half of the fourteenth century are the remains of a medieval defence system. All of these, with the exception of the theatre, have survived to our times. Unfortunately, Willer's engraving remains the only pictorial evidence for the Gdansk theatre; this is readily accounted for by the fact that the building adjoined a huge military defence system that encircled the city, and on numerous views and panoramas it is simply concealed by one of the bastions.[2]

The theatre itself is apparently a wooden structure erected on more solid foundations, presumably made of stone, which – as in the Fortune contract – seem 'to be wroughte one foot of assize att the leiste aboue the grounde'. The frame consisting of four sides encloses an inner yard and is covered with a single-sloped roof, which leads us to suspect that the galleries were not very deep. It seems probable that the roof was tiled, especially in view of the fact that tiles are clearly marked on the right wing. A large double-hung gate, reinforced with iron hinges and opening outwards, forms the main entrance. No direct evidence can be provided for the actual location of the stage. At least two possibilities may be taken into consideration. First, that it was situated opposite the

main entrance. Second, that it adjoined the facade of the right-hand side of the frame. The latter possibility may be additionally supported by the fact that the buildings outside the theatre adjacent to this side could have been a part of the tiring-house which was also equipped with a separate entrance for the players. A similar arrangement in London is shown, for instance, on Norden's map of 1593 where two buildings adjoining the Beare house seem to be a part of the theatre.

The front facade of the Gdansk theatre, made of vertical wooden boards, is supported by a system of seven buttresses but we have no evidence whether these had been erected according to the builder's plan or, which seems more probable, were added afterwards when there was a danger that the building might collapse. The number of buttresses on each side of the main entrance is not equal, for we have four on the left-hand side and three on the right, where the corner buttress is for some reason missing. This could have been either the artist's omission or caused by the fact that this part of the facade was sufficiently supported by the adjoining building.

The staircases are not visible, which leads us to suspect that they were incorporated into the frame. In the Fortune contract it is stated that the 'steares' are to be constructed in the same way as the ones in the Globe, which, in fact, does not solve the problem since we do not have firm evidence about whether in the latter case the staircases were attached to the

deutschen Nationallitteratur (Marburg, 1895). Some information about this theatre is also provided by F. E. Hysel in *Das Theater in Nürnberg von 1612 bis 1863 nebst einem Anhange über das Theater in Fürth* (Nuremberg, 1863).

[1] *Der Stadt Danzig Historische Beschreibung* (Danzig and Amsterdam, 1687).

[2] Early seventeenth-century panoramas of Gdansk were made by I. Dickmann (1617) and his copyists: Peter van der Keere (1618), Claes Jansz Visscher (1620) and M. Meriam (1640). An English copy of Dickmann's panorama was published by J. Fielding in the 1780s (entitled *Danzick in Polish Prussia*).

frame or incorporated into it. Since on Hollar's 'Long View of London' the Second Globe is equipped with external stairs, most reconstructors have insisted that it must have been the same in the Globe of 1599. The lack of windows in the Gdansk theatre is not surprising in view of the fact that the only ones referred to in the Fortune contract are 'windows and lightes glazed to the saide Tyreinge howse', so presumably they would not have been visible even if the engraving had shown the Fortune. There is also no hut, but again we do not have any evidence for one in the Fortune.

Although the whole frame has a somewhat trapezoid shape it is not unlikely that it might have been in fact square, if we take into consideration some inaccuracies in perspective and the presumed attempt of the artist to show as much of the interior as possible. Thus, he managed to show the top gallery for spectators in the two sides of the frame, one opposite the main entrance (which is backed by a pitched roof of a building behind the theatre), and the other adjoining it on the left-hand side. The shape of these galleries recalls both the pictorial evidence we possess of London theatres and their reconstructions as well. It is worth noting that in the lower part the galleries are equipped with solid protections instead of railings and are surmounted by lambrequin ornamentation.

The roof above the front facade bears a diagonal Latin inscription AVDII VVE, an abbreviation which most probably stands for ADVII verbum VERitatis, meaning 'I listened to the word of truth', which obviously suggests the theatrical function of the building. The strange-looking projecting element on the right-hand side is a chimney constructed in 1646 when heating was installed in a special compartment of the gallery for the Queen, Maria Ludvica Gonzaga, wife of Vladislaus IV, when in February an Italian opera was staged there in her honour as a part of celebrations to welcome her to Gdansk. It seems likely that this compartment was arranged below the chimney, which gives additional support to the idea that the stage was on the right-hand side rather than opposite the main entrance. One of the courtiers accompanying the Queen, J. Le Laboureur, wrote a brief but nevertheless interesting description of the theatre,[1] in which he noted that it was a wooden structure, with several galleries for spectators ('avec plusieurs galleries') some of whom stood in the yard, around the stage, which was a common custom in London theatres. He also provides us with a striking piece of information, estimating the number of spectators as 3,000, which is exactly the same as that recorded by De Witt in 1596 and confirmed by the Spanish ambassador who visited the Second Globe in 1624.

Unfortunately, we do not possess the precise measurements of the Gdansk theatre and we can only deduce them from the height of the people standing near – a calculation which, of course, cannot be accurate. But given the number of spectators, we can come to the general conclusion that – even if the capacity of the theatre is exaggerated (as it just as well could be in the case of the Swan and the Second Globe) the Gdansk theatre was similar in size to a 'typical' London playhouse. Although the number of galleries is not mentioned, the quoted 'plusieurs' means more than two, and taking into account the height of the human figure standing just by the front facade of the theatre, and the size of the entrance gate, we may state in all probability that the frame consisted of three galleries.

As far as the physical conditions of the stage are concerned, we have to take into consideration the fact that no pictorial evidence is available, and thus we have to rely exclusively on written sources, amongst which the most important are stage-directions included in plays performed in Gdansk, especially in those written by native authors for that particular

[1] *Relation du voyage de la Royne de Pologne* (Paris, 1647), p. 157.

stage. It should be remembered that in the first half of the seventeenth century, Gdansk was not only the largest and wealthiest city in this part of the Continent (with over seventy thousand inhabitants), but was also an important cultural centre, with literary and theatrical circles founded by scholars and students of the Academic Gymnasium, poets and playwrights. Due to the fact that Gdansk was a multi-national city, literature was written in a number of languages, above all in Latin, German and Polish. Unfortunately, most of the plays staged at the Gdansk theatre are known only by their titles or by the names of their authors; only a few dramas written to be staged in that theatre have been preserved, either in print or manu-script, and are available at the library of the Polish Academy of Science in Gdansk.

But in spite of this unfortunate scarcity of material, some useful information may be gathered from an analysis of stage-directions in the extant plays. For instance, in an anonymous Polish play *Tragedia o bogaczu y Łazarzu...* (A Tragedy of a Rich Man and Lazarus...) written in 1643,[1] we have a number of interesting facts provided by the text. Actors made their entrances and exits through the door (doors?), which are several times mentioned. Simple stage properties were used, such as a bed, a table, chairs; music was played and a trumpet blown. Some sort of machinery must have been used, since we encounter entries like 'Neptune comes on a dolphin swimming over the sea' (F. 12), 'Angels take Lazarus's soul to the bosom of Abraham' (F. 28), 'A Virgin will come on a ship sailing over the sea' (F. 19), and there must have been at least one trap, in this case leading to the 'abyss' (F. 31). The stage may also have been equipped with a place for concealment since in one of the entries the actors are directed to 'hide and whistle' (F. 25). Although some of these may be interpreted as literary directions it is worth noting that the technical device of arranging 'a sea' on stage had been known in Poland before the play was

written. It is, for instance, described in a treatise by Casimir Sarbiewski *De perfecta poesi*, (On Sublime Poetry), written *c.* 1626. (Sarbiewski was a notable seventeenth-century Polish poet and scholar; some of his poems appeared in an English edition under the title *The Odes of Casimir*, translated by G. H., London, 1646). Sarbiewski gives the following technical instruction: 'Because the action of a tragedy or a comedy sometimes takes place on the sea, the boards of the theatrical platform must be arranged in such a way that they can be lifted slightly from one side and thus we achieve the illusion of waves after having covered the lower part with pleated cloth of interwoven silver and blue silk. The boards should be set in motion to give the impression that the sea twinkles with a bright glitter.'[2]

On the other hand, the numerous German prose versions of English plays, even if performed in Gdansk by the English wandering companies, cannot be taken into consideration in our analysis of stage conditions in the Gdansk theatre, simply because these plays were not written for that particular stage. Even the two manuscripts that have been miracu-lously preserved in the library of the Polish Academy of Science in Gdansk, and which presumably come directly from one of the English companies, cannot for the above-mentioned reason serve as valid evidence.[3]

[1] In the collection of the library of the Polish Academy of Science in Gdansk: MS 2429.

[2] Quoted after B. Król-Kaczorowska, *Teatr dawnej Polski, Budynki Dekoracje Kostiumy* (Warsaw, 1971), pp. 100–1.

[3] The first play, *Tiberius und Anabella*, is a German version of John Marston's *Parasitaster, or the Fawne*, and was, for instance, in the repertory of John Green's company, which frequently visited Gdansk. The second, *Der Stumme Ritter*, is Lewis Machin's *The Dumb Knight*, and was in the repertory of John Spencer's company, which also performed there often. Both of these were printed for the first time by J. Bolte in *Danziger Theater im 16. und 17. Jahrhundert* (Hamburg and Leipzig, 1895), pp. 169–267. It may also be noted here that in the Gdansk library there is a

Summing up, we may conclude that the stage of the Gdansk theatre was presumably a removable raised platform, erected *ad hoc* before the performance just like, for instance, that in the Hope theatre. It was probably arranged in the same way as in London theatres, i.e. projecting into the yard and at the back adjoining the tiring-house facade. It must have been reasonably large and equipped with at least one trap, a place for concealment, and some sort of machinery. It should be noted here that the building also functioned as a fencing school and in documents is referred to as 'Fechtschulen'. In a relatively puritan city like Gdansk, there had to be not only a moral pretext for erecting a permanent theatre, but also an economic one: officially theatrical performances could take place during the Dominic fair in August, and sometimes in July, but plays and operas were staged occasionally during the whole year. For instance, performances of various plays were recorded in February 1629, June 1631, September 1636, February 1646, January 1648 etc.[1] Besides fencing exercises and tournaments, animal baiting took place there, which is another feature in common with some London play-houses.[2]

In spite of the fact that the stage of the Gdansk theatre may have differed in detail from that of the Fortune, the general resemblance it bears to the Fortune is remarkable. The fact that two theatres, obviously belonging to the same architectural type and similar in a number of details, were built almost simultaneously in two cities so far apart cannot be a matter of mere coincidence. The Gdansk theatre is first mentioned in documents on 30 May 1600 – i.e. several months after the Fortune contract had been signed – when one Conrad Heidemann made application to the City Council for permission to build a 'Fencing School' in which other performances would also take place ('allerley Schawspill').[3] However, this astonishing coincidence of dates cannot lead us to suspect that it is Conrad Heidemann who was responsible for such a rapid import of a theatrical concept, for we have no proof that his project of 1600 was the same as was realized later on, since he was not given a permit in that year and is not mentioned in any theatrical documents again. The first evidence of theatrical performances in the Fencing School comes from 1612, which means that the theatre must have been built some time between 1600 and 1612.[4]

The question remains, how did this indisputably English theatrical form make its way to Gdansk? No doubt a number of Gdansk citizens, merchants, travellers and students, visited London, and obviously the London theatres were known at least to some people in addition to the members of the large English colony in Gdansk (which in the seventeenth century was actually the largest English colony on the Continent, reaching almost one thousand people). Some written evidence can be provided. For instance, the anonymous author of *Descriptio Urbis Londini in Anglia*, written in Gdansk before 1615,

collection, unique in Poland, of Elizabethan and Jacobean plays, all of which are original London sixteenth-and seventeenth-century editions. This may serve as strong evidence of the exceptional popularity of English drama in Gdansk.

[1] Bolte, *Danziger Theater*, pp. 41–78.

[2] Written evidence may be provided for this. See *ibid.*, p. 42.

[3] *Ibid.*, p. 42.

[4] In an application to the City Council in Gdansk of 20 July 1615, a company of Brandenburg players asked for leave to play in the 'Fechtschullen', where their 'Antecessor vor dreyen Jahren' had also given performances. This 'vor dreyen Jahren' means, of course, in 1612. Numerous applications of various English companies are in the collection of the State Archives in Gdansk (Wojewódzkie Archiwum Państwowe w Gdańsku), catalogue number: 300, 36/67. These were reproduced by Bolte (1895). It is worth noting that although Bolte managed to gather a surprising number of documents referring to the Gdansk theatre, he was unable to find any pictorial evidence of it.

mentions 'comaediarum theatra' as places of interest he recommends seeing in London.[1] The idea that the missing Fortune plan was brought to Gdansk seems to be too implausible to be taken seriously, although – on the other hand – the truth may be as simple as this. The most convincing explanation in this case is that the notion of erecting an English-type theatre in Gdansk had been suggested to its founders by the actors of the English Continental companies, especially those who had either performed in the Fortune itself or had close relations with the theatrical life of London and who may be traced in Gdansk from 1600 to 1612.

Even in the partially preserved documents referring to theatrical matters in Gdansk, we may observe that the visits of the English companies were surprisingly frequent; this is the case in particular in two periods: between 1600 and 1619, and 1636 and 1650. The English are first mentioned in 1587, when five actors performed an unidentified play during the Dominic fair. It seems quite probable that it was the same troupe that had visited Dresden and Elsinor a couple of months before.[2] Their names are given in the German list: Thomas Stephens, George Bryan, Thomas King, Robert Percy and Thomas Pope (the Danish list adds William Kempe and Daniel Jones), all of whom were at that time members of Leicester's company. Three of them, i.e. Pope, Bryan and Kempe reappear amongst Strange's men and thereafter in the Lord Chamberlain's company.[3] The first visit of the English actors to Gdansk may have been treated as a sort of 'reconnaissance' of this part of the Continent and we can speak of regular performances given by them after 1600. The three companies that we encounter in Gdansk documents before 1612 are those of Robert Browne, John Green and John Spencer.

Undoubtedly, the most interesting of the three actors mentioned is Robert Browne, an indefatigable organizer of Continental com-panies between 1590 and 1620. It is certain that he knew the owners of the Fortune, both Edward Alleyn and Philip Henslowe. He first appears as a player, with Alleyn, in Worcester's company which they eventually left together with Richard Jones in 1587 when they joined the Lord Admiral's men. And there is no question about his acquaintance with Henslowe, at least after 1593, when Henslowe in a letter informed Alleyn about the death from plague of Browne's family.[4] One cannot avoid the impression that the activity of the English players on the Continent, especially at the turn of the century, centred on Robert Browne, who paid several long visits there and took with him a number of actors, some of whom split off

[1] An unpublished Latin manuscript is extant in the collection of the library of the Polish Academy of Science in Gdansk: MS 1654, pp. 1–36. A number of interesting 'Anglicana' are also kept there, for instance, letters written by Henry VIII to among others, the scholar Melanchton, or a Latin description of the visit paid by Frederick V, the Palatine of Rhein, to London in 1612/1613.

[2] Bolte, *Danziger Theater*, pp. 22, 25; see also S. Herz, *Englische Schauspieler und englisches Schauspiel* (Hamburg and Leipzig, 1903), p. 3.

[3] It is not unlikely that they are responsible for providing Shakespeare – who soon after their return to England became their companion – with various pieces of information about Poland, which – in turn – he inserted into *Hamlet*. For instance, in IV, iv, Hamlet asks the Captain: 'Goes it against the main of Poland, Or for some frontier?' and receives an answer:

> Truly to speak, and with no addition,
> We go to gain a little patch of ground
> That hath in it no profit but the name.
> To pay five ducats, five, I would not farm it;
> Nor will it yield to Norway or the Pole
> A ranker rate, should it be sold in fee.

This seems to recall the constant minor conflicts between Denmark and Poland in the second half of the sixteenth century, especially in the Gdansk region. There is no doubt that the English actors visiting Gdansk and Elsinor in 1587 must have heard various 'histories' about recent happenings, skirmishes and brushes with the enemy about 'little patches of ground' the only result of which was unprofitable bloodshed.

[4] See Walter W. Greg (ed.), *Henslowe Papers* (1907), p. 37.

into independent associations. Unfortunately the frequent failure of the archives to record individual names makes it extremely difficult to trace the precise tours of these groups and in many cases we have to base our discussion on conjectures or our sense of probability. The three major attempts to bring the scraps of evidence into order, undertaken first by A. Cohn, then S. Herz and E. K. Chambers[1] are not free from omissions and mistakes. Since our present task is not to examine in detail the complex problem of the English Continental companies in general, but to concentrate on those which visited Gdansk between 1600 and 1612, some compression of the material will be necessary. In what follows I propose to describe in chronological order the visits paid to Gdansk by English actors within that period.

1601

An English company of players performed in Gdansk during the Dominic fair. The evidence is provided by an application for leave to play from a rival company from Bergen submitted to the City Council on 23 August, in which 'Engelschenn' who had performed before are several times mentioned.[2] Although Herz classified this group as unidentified,[3] it is not impossible that it was Robert Browne's, since at that time his company was the only one not attached to any court. Before his visit to Gdansk he is last mentioned in Strasbourg in June and he reappears in Munich in October. This gap of several months could have been filled by the trip to Gdansk and back to Germany.

1605

Another group of English actors came to Gdansk during the Dominic fair, this time under the title 'Brandenburg Comedianten und Musicanten'. It has been agreed amongst scholars that the company attached to the

court of Margrave Christian Wilhelm Brandenburg in Halle since 1603 was that of Richard Machin, George Webster and Ralph Reeve, former companions of Browne.[5] After having performed in Gdansk they went to Elbląg (Elbing) where they are mentioned in the archives on 14 August when the Town Council complained about 'disgraceful things' in their comedy staged a day before ('weil sei gestern in der Comödie schandbare Sachen furgebracht').[6] From Elbląg (which is about thirty miles from Gdansk) they went further east, for we meet them in Königsberg (Now Kaliningrad, USSR) on 3 October when they received 75 Marks from the Duchess, Maria Eleonora.[7]

1607

During the Dominic fair John Green appeared with his men all of whom had been members of Browne's company. Browne was first

---

[1] See Albert Cohn, *Shakespeare in Germany in the sixteenth and seventeenth Centuries: an Account of English Actors in Germany and the Netherlands and of the Plays Performed by Them During the Same Period* (London and Berlin, 1865); E. K. Chambers, *The Elizabethan Stage* (Oxford, 1923), II, 261–94; Herz, *Englische Schauspieler*; the theatrical life in Gdansk was also analysed by G. Gross in her doctoral thesis *Das Danziger Theater in der ersten Hälfte des 17. Jahrhunderts* (Leipzig, 1939) and briefly by W. Krause in the introduction to his *Das Danziger Theater und sein Erbauer Carl Samuel Held* (Danzig, 1936). Krause was the first one to identify the Fencing School in Willer's engraving as the actual theatre. He also noticed its general similarity to the contemporary London theatres, but to the Globe rather than the Fortune, which in fact he did not even mention.

[2] Bolte, *Danziger Theater*, p. 31.

[3] Herz, *Englische Schauspieler*, p. 63.

[4] Chambers, *The Elizabethan Stage*, pp. 278–9.

[5] Bolte, *Danziger Theater*, pp. 33–4; Herz, *Englische Schauspieler*, pp. 38–9.

[6] Bolte, *Danziger Theater*, p. 34; Cohn, *Shakespeare in Germany*, p. lxxx; see also E. A. Hagen, *Geschichte des Theaters in Preussen...*, (Königsberg, 1854), p. 53.

[7] Bolte, *Danziger Theater*, p. 34; Hagen, *Geschichte des Theaters in Preussen*, pp. 47, 53.

accompanied by Green at Strasbourg in 1606. At that time among members of his company we find Richard Jones and Robert Ledbetter, late of the Lord Admiral's men. Richard Jones, whom Browne had known at least since 1589, was a well known player in the Lord Admiral's company until February 1602,[1] and is the first actor on the Continent (and in Gdansk) who is definitely known to have performed in the Fortune. By spring 1607 Green had succeeded Browne in the leadership of the company, which held together for a while longer. Browne's name disappears from Continental records for a decade. All we know about him is that he was a member of the Queen's Revels syndicate in London in 1610 and he wrote a letter to Alleyn from Clerkenwell on 11 April 1612.[2] Before coming to Gdansk, Green's company visited Elbląg where they had applied for leave to play on 16 July 1607, which was granted provided that the performance would take place in a private house.[3] In winter of the same year their repertory included: *The Prodigal Son, A Proud Woman of Antwerp, Dr Faustus, The Duke of Florence and a Nobleman's Daughter, Nobody and Somebody, Fortunatus, The Jew, King Louis and King Frederick of Hungary, The King of Cyprus and the Duke of Venice* and *Dives and Lazarus*.[4]

Green's further activity in the Gdansk region is worth particular attention. Although after 1608 all trace of him is lost for several years, he reappears with eighteen men in July/August 1615 and again in July/August 1616, when they performed in the Fencing School.[5] It seems that due to the popularity of the English players the summer 'theatrical season' was extended to two months. From Gdansk they went to Warsaw to the court of Sigismund III, where they stayed from October 1616 to February 1617. It seems that their performances were very well received for they were given a letter of recommendation sent by the closest relative of the Polish Queen, the Archduke Charles, to Cardinal Dietrichstein, in which he wrote: 'they have come to us with royal recommendations and good testimonials from Poland, where they have some months exhibited such comedies at their Royal Highnesses, and have respectfully announced themselves'.[6]

Some members of Green's company can be identified. In the Gdansk application of 29 July 1616, Robert Reinolds is mentioned, who made a reputation as a clown under the name of 'Pickleherring'.[7] Another actor is Richard Jones again, who seems to have left Green around 1610 and now returned. In an undated letter to Edward Alleyn (preserved at Dulwich) he wrote :'I am to go over beyond the seas with Mr Browne and the company, but not by his means, for he is put to half a shaer, and to stay hear, for they ar all against his goinge.'[1] The opinion of Chambers that the letter was written in or near 1615, and that Jones was one of the actors who started in advance of Browne under John Green, seems very convincing, especially in view of the fact that three years later Browne

---

[1] Walter W. Greg (ed.), *Henslowe's Diary*, (1904), p. 164.

[2] *Henslowe Papers*, p. 63.

[3] Cohn, *Shakespeare in Germany*, p. lxxxii; Bolte, *Danziger Theater*, p. 35; Hagen, *Geschichte des Theaters in Preussen*, p. 53.

[4] Chambers, *The Elizabethan Stage*, pp. 281–2; Bolte, *Danziger Theater*, pp. 35–6.

[5] Their applications for leave to play and for the extension of the given period for performances are reproduced by Bolte, *Danziger Theater*, pp. 45–53.

[6] Quoted after Cohn, *Shakespeare in Germany*, p. xciii.

[7] Published by Bolte, *Danziger Theater*, pp. 48–9. It should be added that Reinolds paid frequent visits to Gdansk as a member of various companies active there in later periods and his name appears last in 1640. These groups of actors were mentioned by Peter Mundy in his diary written in Gdansk in 1642: 'Some summers come here our English comedians or players which represent in Netherlandish Dutch, having been at Königsberg before the prince Elector of Brandenburg, also at Warsaw before the King of Poland.' See *The Travels...in Europe and Asia* (Hakluyt Society), VI, 181.

[8] *Henslowe Papers*, p. 33.

came out with a new company on his last visit to the Continent and presumably joined forces with Green.[1] That Jones was still travelling by 1620 is shown by a letter written by his wife from Gdansk on 1 April 1620 (at a time when there is otherwise no record of English players), to Edward Alleyn, in which she complained that she is 'looking Evry daye to Gooe' after her husband, who apparently 'js with the prince'.[2] The mentioned 'prince' was most probably Philip Julius, Duke of Wolgast in Pomerania, at whose court Jones's presence is shown by his petitions of 1623 and 1624.[3]

1611

On 15 July the first visit of John Spencer's company is recorded in Gdansk.[4] Spencer had been associated with the Elector of Brandenburg's court in Berlin since around 1605 and from there undertook extensive travels in various countries. He made his reputation as a clown under the name of 'Hans Stockfish' and was active as leader of his company until 1623 and within that time paid several visits to Gdansk. Nothing is known about his London career, if he had one, or about the members of his company. An unrelated piece of information from Cologne tells us that a strange thing happened to the company there in February 1615, when all the players were converted to Catholicism by a Franciscan friar. There is also some indirect evidence that the company might have visited Gdansk in 1609, since in July of that year Spencer's name appears in Königsberg and it is certain that he had to go through Gdansk on his way there and back.

At present it is not possible to identify the English company which visited Gdansk in 1612 and was the first one (at least according to the records) to perform in the Fencing School. The only information about these actors comes from an application of a rival company of Brandenburg players and has already been discussed above. But the most important fact is that by 1612 a public theatre had been opened in Gdansk. Among the actors hitherto dealt with, several were recorded as being active in London after the Fortune had been built and a few of these visited Gdansk before 1612: Robert Browne in 1601 and Richard Jones with Robert Ledbetter in 1607. Of course, it may be argued that practically all the players of the Continental companies had seen at least some of the London theatres, including the Fortune, but since there is direct evidence for the three mentioned, it may be suggested that it could have been any of them who was responsible for providing somebody in Gdansk with detailed information about the architecture of the Fortune.

It should be noted that these actors were members of the Lord Admiral's company and the Fortune was 'their' theatre. That Poland was not completely unknown to this company may be evidenced by two plays that we know of from their repertory thematically connected with that country. The first one, *Voyvode*, (for which Henslowe paid £1 to Chettle on 29 August 1598 and on which he spent £17.5. for properties), was probably, as Greg suggested (*Henslowe's Diary*, part II, p. 197), 'an old play belonging to Alleyn revised by Chettle on the occasion of its revival'. In the past, a 'voivode' had mainly military duties. Today, 'voivode' is a title equivalent to governor of a province

[1] Chambers, *The Elizabethan Stage*, pp. 284, 286.
[2] *Henslowe Papers*, pp. 94–5. This company visited Gdansk again in July/August 1619.
[3] See C. F. Meyer, 'Englische Komödianten am Hofe des Herzogs Philipp Julius von Pommern-Wolgast', *Jahrbuch der deutschen Shakespeare-Gesselschaft*, XXXVIII (Berlin, 1902), pp. 209–10.
[4] Their applications to the City Council of July and August 1611 are reproduced by Bolte, *Danziger Theater*, pp. 38–40. In 1613 the company's repertory included *Philole and Mariana, Celinda and Sedea, The Fall of Troy, The Fall of Constantinople* and *The Turk*; see Chambers, *The Elizabethan Stage*, p. 289; Cohn, *Shakespeare in Germany*, p. lxxxvii and Bolte, *Danziger Theater*, pp. 37–8.

in Poland, hence the country is divided into 'voivodeships'. It seems likely that the play was written after Olbracht Łaski's visit to England in 1583. Łaski was a voivode at Sieradz and was known in England as 'Alasco', and his visit aroused a good deal of interest all over England (it was described, for instance, by Holinshed and Camden;[1] there is also a vast amount of official correspondence in this matter). The second play, *Strange News out of Poland*, was bought by Henslowe on behalf of the Admiral's men from Haughton and one 'mr Pett' for £6 on 17 May 1600 and £3 were paid for properties on 25 May. Unfortunately, nothing is known of this piece, although the very title proves that Poland lay within the range of interest of the Elizabethans.

It is also known that trade between England and Gdansk was very lively at this time and that there were significant political connections as is evidenced by a great deal of official correspondence between Elizabeth I, James I, Charles I and the City Council in Gdansk, where it is preserved in the municipal archives (Wojewódzkie Archiwum Państwowe, catalogue number: 300, 53/748–49–50; some letters are also preserved in the British Library). It is not without relevance that there are also two letters of the Earl of Nottingham, i.e. the Lord Admiral, both written to Gdansk in 1606.[2] And there were large English colonies residing in Gdansk and Elbląg (which was the centre of the Eastland Company). But these circumstances alone do not entirely explain why the English theatrical groups made their way as far as Gdansk or – as Chambers put it – 'out-of-the-way corners of Northern Europe'. There must have been some further motive, not necessarily an economic one, and the existence of a public theatre there, modelled on the newest achievements of theatrical architecture in London and providing the actors with the best acting conditions they could have imagined, may have provided the temptation and encouragement that brought them there. At

any rate, the visits of the English actors to Gdansk became more frequent during and after the first decade of the seventeenth century.

The Fencing School in Gdansk functioned as the city's only theatre for two hundred years. Being a wooden structure it underwent numerous repairs, renovations and reconstructions. It was repaired in 1635 and a sort of 'Lord's room' for the rich citizens was installed within the frame. In 1646 heating was installed in one of the compartments of the gallery, as mentioned above. In 1695 three rows of benches were dismantled in order to accommodate a 'choir' for an orchestra. The building was repaired again in 1714, and in 1730 a roof was constructed over the whole, after which the entire theatre was heated. The theatre's condition was appalling by the end of the eighteenth century and Joanna Schopenhauer, the philosopher's mother, complained in her memoirs that it looked like a shed rather than a theatre ('baufälligen bretternen Bude, die eher einer Schenne als einem Theater gliche'). It was repaired again in 1795, but this did not help much. It was last mentioned in 1809 and the playhouse was presumably dismantled afterwards (since a new theatre had been built) and on its site a synagogue was soon erected, but this did not survive the Nazi occupation.[3]

The Gdansk public theatre, erected within the first decade of the seventeenth century,

---

[1] See R. Holinshed, *Chronicles of England, Scotland and Ireland*, v (1808), 505–7; W. Camden, *Annales rerum Anglicarum et Hibernicarum regnante Elizabeth*, (Amstelodami, 1677), p. 389.

[2] One of Nottingham's letters is addressed to Dr Bruce, 'His Majesty's Agent in Poland'. Bruce was probably the author of an extremely interesting manuscript, preserved at the British Museum, *Relation of the State of Polonia and the United Provinces of that Crown Anno 1598*, which was first published by T. H. Talbot in *Elementa ad fontium editiones*, vol. XIII, (Rome, 1965). For trade relations between England and Gdansk see H. Zins, *England and the Baltic in the Elizabethan Era*, (Manchester, 1972).

[3] Documentary evidence is provided by Krause, *Das Danziger Theater*, pp. 11–13.

seems to be a unique example of an English theatrical model implanted in a foreign country. It has a number of general features in common with the London playhouses. We may say that the origin of its architecture is probably to be sought in London's Fortune. Both of these theatres were square wooden structures, containing three galleries built round an open inner yard (which accommodated both the stage and some of the spectators), and their capacity (i.e. the actual size) was, if not the same, not very different. They were built almost simultaneously, shared some of the same actors (who seem to have been responsible for bringing the idea and architectural details to Gdansk) and a number of the same plays were staged in both of these theatres. The congruity of the Gdansk theatre, as shown on Willer's engraving with the features of the Fortune as described in the contract, enables us to incorporate this engraving into the meagre file of indirect pictorial evidence for Elizabethan and Jacobean theatre architecture. It may also serve as a valid source for any future reconstructions of the Fortune.

A YEAR OF COMEDIES: STRATFORD 1978

ROGER WARREN

Apart from Peter Brook's production of *Antony and Cleopatra* (opening too late for review), the 1978 season at Stratford-upon-Avon consisted entirely of comedies, ranging over the entire spectrum: *A Midsummer Night's Dream* (revived from 1977, when it was enthusiastically reviewed here), *The Taming of the Shrew, The Tempest, Measure for Measure, Love's Labour's Lost*, and (at the Other Place, the RSC's Stratford studio) *The Merchant of Venice*. It presented an interesting mixture of old and new in that two RSC directors of long standing, Clifford Williams and John Barton, had directed *The Tempest* and *Love's Labour's Lost* before at Stratford, during the Peter Hall regime, whereas Michael Bogdanov and Barry Kyle were in sole charge of plays in the main house for the first time.

I

The opening of Michael Bogdanov's *Taming of the Shrew* exploited the current fashion for blurring the distinctions between theatrical 'realism' and 'artifice', presumably to emphasise enduring 'relevance'. After being unexpectedly faced with old-fashioned painted scenery, the audience was suddenly startled by a deceptively genuine squabble between an usherette and a drunk member of the audience without a ticket. 'No bloody woman is going to tell me what to do!' he cried, thus making the play's relevance plain. Leaping on to the stage, he tore apart all the illusory scenery, revealing a respectably contemporary series of rusty metal

frames, staircases, and cat-walks. He collapsed; the lights dimmed to a spot on him, and rose to reveal the Lord and his huntsmen in sinister outline, smoothly complacent in modern red hunting outfits. 'O monstrous beast, how like a swine he lies' became the smugly superior comment of material well-being upon the down-at-heel. This contrast was subsequently picked up in the play itself: the Lord became Baptista, a wealthy tycoon surrounded by servants in impeccably cut morning suits, and Petruchio adopted his earlier drunk persona in the wedding scene, to achieve maximum contrast with the society outfits of the others, and to underline his emphatic 'To *me* she's married, not unto my clothes.'

The problem with most such ingenious adaptations is that they are hard to sustain; they may confuse as much as they illuminate. Apart from merely suggesting that the male/female struggle for domination is still a live issue, there was no natural transition from Sly to Petruchio: Sly just slipped off, and reappeared, riding a motor-bike, as Petruchio. The connection between hunting and Petruchio's taming methods was stressed by the doubling and by horn calls at the end (a 'death'?); but the connection wasn't really very illuminating, since in the Induction it is the Lord/Baptista who is the hunter, not Sly/Petruchio. The contrast between smoothness and scruffiness became muddled when the servants at Petruchio's country house, led by a Curtis presented (but not re-named) as a briskly efficient air hostess, were dressed in the same smart morning suits as Baptista's servants, were indeed the same servants. I could not see the point of this discrepancy between master and men, aggravated by retaining the lines about their pumps, hats, and daggers, though virtually all of Sly's lines, for instance, had been freely changed to modern colloquialisms. Again, when the establishment at the wedding responded with relieved, superior laughter to Baptista's anti-climactic dismissal, 'let them go, a couple of quiet ones', were we meant to feel that the unaffected violence of Kate and Petruchio was inevitably preferable, or merely a contrast?

At any rate, the production made no attempt to soften the brutality of Petruchio's methods: the first scene with Kate was a violent physical struggle, not a wit-combat. And the creation of a world dominated by a combination of male chauvinism and material greed certainly paid off in the final scene, where the dinner-jacketed speculators sat round a circular green-baize-covered gambling table, with after-dinner brandy and cigars, to indulge in a little speculation on their latest assets – wives. This self-satisfied group, with their 'hear-hears', nods, and applause, were the perfect audience for Kate's assertion of male domination; and this setting made it much easier than usual for Kate to deliver a speech which has of recent years seemed to become impossibly difficult to bring off.

That context was just as well, for otherwise Paola Dionisotti's Kate did not achieve much more than a deep-throated rage or indignation. There was certainly no hint of possible relationship, much less affection, between her and Petruchio (who, perhaps accidentally but in any case significantly, omitted 'and love' from the line 'Marry, peace it bodes, and love, and quiet life'). Nor was there much laughter: what Petruchio calls Grumio's 'conceits' were in fact forcefully delivered complaints, David Suchet making his presence felt with every line; and Jonathan Pryce had all the necessary

distinction of presence and voice for so dominating a Petruchio while avoiding rant or monotony.

Indeed, the entire production was unusual in avoiding both tedium and, even more surprisingly, slapstick business. The sub-plot, especially, gained from the absence of the second: it was unfussily laid out and clearly delivered. What jokes there were were related to character, as when Paul Brooke's Baptista, briskly calculating the rival dowry offers on an adding machine, had to pause to look up the value of Gremio's farm stock, country market prices of course being outside an urban financial speculator's orbit.

II

Clifford Williams's previous RSC production of *The Tempest*, in 1963, was very imaginative and original: a translucent perspex wall had enclosed the stage, on which a blood-red sun was eclipsed and constantly changing shapes and colours projected; a sternly authoritarian Prospero had risen up out of the floor to oversee the shipwreck victims, drawn on to the forestage by a conveyor belt; Ariel's attendant spirits were fantastically masked, a mixture of science fiction and primitive carvings; the goddesses emerged from huge stooks of flax. All this had been uncompromisingly modern. In 1978, some modern touches remained: the blood-red sun on a front screen, behind which the shipwreck victims, absolutely stock-still, were dimly perceived; the cell was a severe, unadorned shield from the elements; Ralph Koltai's suspended silver disc which replaced the red sun in certain scenes, his gleaming tin-foil floor, and the abstract globe which served (apparently most uncomfortably) as a seat recalled the science fiction *Ring* he designed for the English National Opera. But the modern images were combined with Renaissance ones, most strikingly when Ariel descended as a harpy enclosed within a circle, arms and legs outstretched, after Leonardo's famous illustration of Vitruvius's 'Proportions of the Human Figure'; but the historical link did not inhibit him from vividly ferocious cawing as he came.

The 1978 Ariel and Caliban were developments of the earlier interpretations. Ariel (Ian Charleson) was a grave, still spirit, moving and speaking deliberately, his voice amplified at the very start and in the songs, furious with Prospero at 'Is there more toil?'. Caliban (David Suchet) was a naked, dark-skinned primitive, with a bald head and bloodshot eyes; his words were very deliberately enunciated, almost like a lesson painfully learnt; and his exploitation was strongly emphasised: 'he shall not suffer indignity', said Stephano, pinning him down by the back of the neck. What Mr Williams's 1963 programme note called Caliban's 'shamefully ironic…grovelling humility before the fine lords' and their servants came over particularly strongly since Mr Suchet's Caliban was the outstanding performance, which, like his Grumio, made sure that every single line told with unyielding power.

In 1963, uncompromising designs had reflected an uncompromising interpretation:

if there is any reconciliation at the end, there is infinitely more irresolution….A man spends his life trying to perfect his responses to the world, to control himself and nature: he still ends up senile….There is no grand order, and Prospero returns to Milan not bathed in tranquillity, but a wreck, 'where every third thought shall be my grave'.

Tom Fleming had duly presented a sour, censorious, sternly furrowed Prospero, limited but memorable. In 1978, this view was much modified, partly perhaps to suit the personality of Michael Hordern.

Instead of a voluminous robe, the 'magic garment' was an academic gown; this Prospero was schoolmasterly in manner, impatiently tapping his foot as he made Ariel repeat the origin of Sycorax. He also found much humour

in lines like the over-explanatory 'It eats, and sleeps, and hath such senses/As we have, such', or 'sit then and *talk* with her' after his stern warnings to Ferdinand about sexual abstinence. Mr Hordern's easy relaxation and extensive experience enabled him to sustain the enormous second scene: his confident delivery moved from mock indignation ('An advocate for an impostor') via anger ('Hush!') to ironic humour ('Thou think'st there is no more such shapes as he,/Having seen but him and Caliban!') in one short speech. He moved easily in and out of the great speeches without needing to 'prepare' for them: they simply arose, as they should, out of character and situation, and Mr Williams seconded this by leaving the lighting quite unchanged for 'Ye elves of hills'. Perhaps the ultimate effect was a little *too* easy: the decision to forgive seemed to be reached without all that much strain, and this despite admirable pointing of the relationship between Prospero and Ariel, including a great effort of personal strain to summon Ariel in the first place, and a shuddering gasp as he released him (relief? a sense of loss?).

This slight uncertainty at the climax derived, I think, from Mr Williams's less uncompromising approach this time. But there were great gains: Mr Williams is a master of clear exposition, using variations of movement and positioning to chart the development of that long second scene: Prospero's narration, the summoning of Ariel and Caliban, Ariel leading Ferdinand with his singing, Miranda's amusement at Ferdinand's exaggerated courtesy when he thinks her some exotic deity, all these were a constant pleasure to watch. And he always draws excellent performances from his actors: here, in addition to Mr Hordern, Mr Suchet and Mr Charleson, from Sheridan Fitzgerald, a fresh, delightful Miranda, from Richard Griffiths's white pierrot Trinculo and Paul Moriarty's bullying, unforced Stephano, both milking their lines for all possible laughs chiefly by addressing them straight to the audience; and from Paul Brooke, whose Antonio moved from complacency to conspiracy with casual ease.

If the production as a whole, with its mixture of contemporary and Renaissance images, presented the narrative clearly and satisfyingly without any particular revelation, that may reflect Mr Williams's view as expressed in the 1963 programme:

Shakespeare includes all the themes from his earlier work – kingship, inheritance, treachery, conscience, identity, love, music, God: he draws them together as if to find the key to it all, but there is no such key.

III

Christopher Morley's designs for John Barton's *Merchant of Venice* at the Other Place were late nineteenth-century, rather Chekovian in feel, especially the *Three Sisters*-like severe black mourning dresses for Portia and Nerissa, with buttoned-up necks and mutton-chop sleeves. Shylock was shabby, almost miserly, carefully preserving the stubs of the home-rolled cigarettes which constantly drooped from the side of his mouth. He contrasted sharply with Tubal, who dressed impeccably and smoked cigars, like the smart Venetians-about-town. At home, Shylock worked at a Dickensian stand-up desk, with a large pair of scales, which he subsequently brought into court. Launcelot Gobbo was a music-hall comedian, armed with concertina and klaxon horn to accompany the voices of Conscience and Fiend; these sorted oddly with a lute, on which he accompanied speeches later on: the effect was muddled, the character as ineffective as ever.

The change of period did not seem to have any such interpretive purpose as the revelation of a superficial society in Mr Barton's British Raj *Much Ado*, beyond establishing a world which simply took it for granted that the Jews should be set apart, and even, as Antonio's off-hand reply to Shylock put it, spat on. But the Jew-baiting was not over-emphasised; neither the production nor the adequate but undistinguished supporting playing distorted (or clarified) the studied ambiguity of Shakespeare's presentation of the Christians.

The real strength of the production lay in Mr Barton's masterly exploitation of the intimacy of the Other Place to present the play in the round, and thereby to concentrate maximum attention on crucial events taking place dead centre, especially Bassanio's choice, the trial, and the finale. The caskets were placed centre, simply set out on a small cane table, emphasised by a spotlight pointing down on them; Bassanio nervously circled them while Portia herself sang 'Tell me where is fancy bred', built up into a powerful, evocative ensemble when the others, grouped at the edges of the circle, joined in with 'Ding dong bell'. There was no crude suggestion that Portia gave the game away by stressing the 'ed' rhymes to hint at 'lead', but there was the oblique hint at the emptiness of outward show, seized on by Bassanio at '*So* may the outward shows be least themselves': the formality, the music, the circling movement built up to a tremendous climax: 'here choose I' was electric. The caskets were then removed and the stage cleared for Portia's and Bassanio's elaborate vows, the crucial ring held up in the hot-spot at the centre; it was similarly held up there when Portia claimed it at the end of the trial scene, the cross-reference helping to begin the transfer back to Belmont.

The trial was laid out with similar formality, heavy dark chairs and judgement table replacing the cane furniture: Shylock and Antonio sat facing one another, the Duke facing a black-draped chair to which Antonio was subsequently strapped. This created a central debating-area which became a combat-area; and by grouping everyone else around the edges, Mr Barton stressed that this is essentially a duel between Shylock and Portia, not primarily about abstract issues like

Justice and Mercy, but arising out of a particular situation. Portia started 'the quality of mercy' seated at the edge; then, warming to her task, she moved to the centre to dispute with Shylock: he brought the debate back to judicial relevance with an insistent 'I crave the law'. Thereafter Marjorie Bland and Mr Barton emphasised the vital point that Portia, having given Shylock every chance to show a mercy outside the rigid terms of 'the law', then insists equally rigidly on the enforcement of that law, including its penalties. But when Shylock, after grovelling before the Duke and shaking Antonio's hands in abject gratitude for his mercy, fumbled for his cigarette tin, dropped it, and spilled the contents, it was Portia who picked it up for him: 'give me leave to go from hence' was spoken directly to her. And his response to Gratiano's ferocious gibe about the gallows not the font was to break into the laughter with which he had shared jokes with the Christians earlier.

Patrick Stewart's Shylock was a virtuoso performance encompassing all the variety of the part, now quietly colloquial, now impassioned. Genial in public (even mocking Bassanio's 'be *assured* you may' by the way he pronounced the word), he was sober in private, even giving Jessica a quite gratuitous slap in the face before leaving for supper. He caught all the changes of mood in the Tubal scene, the quiet passion of 'no sighs but o' *my breathing*; no tears but o' *my shedding*', switching from the ecstatic 'Good news!' of Antonio's fate to despair both over Jessica's profligacy and Tubal's expenses, which he scrupulously paid out there and then with soiled notes from a pocket book in which he had calculated the 'rate' of Bassanio's loan. After a pause to light the inevitable drooping cigarette, he was struck with the idea of paying Tubal (more notes) to 'fee me an officer', answering Tubal's surprise that he should actually pursue the bond with a sharp, quiet, edged 'were he out of Venice, I can make what

merchandise I will', a commercial motive duly appreciated by Tubal.

Mr Barton balanced the complex variety of this Shylock by encouraging Marjorie Bland to bring out the variety of Portia too, pinpointing her anxieties and ecstasies in the casket scenes: 'I would/ not/ lose/ you' was intensely emphatic. I particularly admired her refusal to soften Portia's unsentimental hardness and sententiousness: 'To offend and judge are distinct offices' was a tart rebuke to a brisk Prussian officer of an Arragon, complete with iron cross, who, after pawing her with barely restrained desire, had complained with furious wounded pride and no trace of humour, 'Did I deserve no more than a fool's head?'

John Nettles's Bassanio was almost as striking, developing from nervy eloquence to a thoughtful power in response to Portia. The final sense of harmony, of the music of the spheres even, was secured partly by music and formality, the cast sitting in a circle for *al fresco* drinks, a ring of harmony broken by argument and re-formed again as Antonio restored the ring to Bassanio (again catching it in that central spot), but still more by the strength of feeling in this Portia and Bassanio.

The Merchant is much less fashionable than it was, especially in academic estimation. While this production absolutely justified earlier esteem for it, making you marvel afresh at Shakespeare's subtleties and complexities in the Shylock/Portia scenes, it also reinforced another older view that those powerful peaks make the scenes in which neither appears seem somewhat wan.

IV

Whereas Mr Barton played each scene in *The Merchant* for what it was worth, without concealing the unevenness of the play, Barry Kyle achieved the astonishing feat of unifying the much more uneven *Measure for Measure*, something I have neither seen happen before nor thought was possible. Mr Kyle did not achieve this by sensational means, nor by following the drastic expedients of others (huge cuts, changes like Isabella refusing to marry the Duke, or sheer extraneous fantasies like playing the Duke as a pantomime demon king), but by a very wary, careful, sensitive exploration of what the text actually says, combined with bold, imaginative interpretation.

The design scheme set out the play's concerns clearly but without forcing: the 'precise' Angelo was properly dressed in Puritan homespun grey, and once in power he replaced the red robes of the Duke's counsellors with black ones; the Provost and his officers wore tall black Puritan hats; Lucio by contrast was a laughing cavalier in red leather; between the two extremes, the Duke was a sober Jacobean gentleman. At the start, he gave Angelo a white robe of office edged with red flames, a symbol of his prerogative of 'mortality and mercy'. Angelo promptly made all his victims wear this device, Claudio on his Inquisition-style pointed cap as he was paraded through the streets, the bawds on the smocks which they were compelled to wear after being dragged into prison and their clothes (even wigs) torn off and piled in a huge heap centre-stage. For the trial of Pompey, Angelo sat on a specially elevated black seat high above the others, the symbolic 'deputed sword' of justice across his knees, absolute image of 'proud man, /Dress'd in a little brief authority'.

Christopher Morley's distinguished set in-geniously provided both palace and prison. A three-sided black box contained a series of doors for the palace which became stable-like cells for the prisoners, from the upper half of which they could watch the action. This sharply defined, without restricting, the acting area, and, like the costumes, emphasised the issues: the box's moveable walls swung in to enclose Angelo at his black-draped table for the first scene with Isabella, and an overhead spotlight picked out his first sign of weakening:

'She speaks, and 'tis/Such sense that my *sense* breeds with it.' After she had gone, he tried to work at his papers to keep his mind off her, and tried again after the soliloquy. He seemed trapped, cornered, by his physical situation which reflected his internal tension, caught between the demands of his office and those of his desires; a nervous glance towards those walls at 'O cunning enemy' suggested that he imagined the enemy all around him. Thus set up, Jonathan Pryce took command of the stage, powerfully expressing the turmoil and con-fusion of Angelo, especially his self-loathing even while giving his 'sensual race the rein', spitting the lines against the enclosing walls, not towards Isabella, and even showing a kind of concern for her: 'I talk not of your soul' was not a gibe, but a genuine wish not to endanger it. It was quite consistent for this Angelo to play the final scene in a daze, over-come by what he had done.

Elsewhere, too, the director sought con-sistency of character where others have failed to find it: John Nettles's excellent Lucio delivered his apparently out-of-character speech about 'full tilth and husbandry' as if he thought this was language which a novice might under-stand better. But the real achievement in this respect was to make coherent sense of the Duke. In Michael Pennington's gentle, thought-ful performance, the Duke seemed genuinely to be seeking practical solutions to the prob-lems of his office, not playing God. He obviously cared for his subjects, and his urgent attempts to reconcile Claudio with death gave the impression that the Duke felt that people had to be made to *experience* the gravity of breaking the law (whose 'bits and curbs' are, after all, '*needful*') so that his ultimate mercy might be appreciated at its true worth; and this obviously prepared us to accept his apparently gratuitously cruel treat-ment of Isabella later.

A similar sense of the need for practical solutions emerged in the excellent treatment of

Escalus's examination of Pompey, where Raymond Westwell's Escalus showed beautiful comic timing and also a ripe humanity as he gently sought to replace Elbow with a more competent constable without offending him: 'to your worship's *house*?' replied Elbow, overwhelmed at the honour. There was a very strong sense that, as Anne Barton put it in the programme, 'justice is best served by the unassuming, empirical evaluations of old Escalus', who significantly leant Angelo's symbolic sword of justice casually against the table, and who, while 'it grieves me for the death of Claudio', had to admit that there was yet 'no remedy', banging the table in frustration as, like the Duke, he stressed that the severity of the law is 'needful'.

From the point of his intervention ('a remedy presents itself' was enthusiastic), this Duke vigorously applied himself to working out the kind of pragmatic course needed: Michael Pennington's ability to deliver formal couplets formally and yet make them seem like developing thought-processes ('*Craft* against vice I must apply') meant that he involved us in his plans. His vigour re-appeared at the moated grange: amongst a pile of straw, under a large straw sun, Mariana lay drinking her sorrows away, listening to half-naked rural urchins singing 'Take O take those lips away'. She indicated the half-consumed bottle at 'I have sat here all day', and the Duke later poured himself a drink. This general lightening of the tone got the maximum humanity, and a hint of a warmly relaxing countryside outside the harsh city, from what can seem a perfunctory scene, as well as underlining the play's shift from intensity to intrigue.

There were important results: the Duke's humanity was established; Isabella, mapping out Angelo's garden and vineyard cheerfully and practically with pieces of straw, seemed willing to enter the intrigue as a secular operator, a noticeable development from her reverent, dedicated kissing of the nun's robes presented to her at her first arrival at the convent, and developed further when she tore off the veil in despair at Claudio's supposed death; most important for the general progress of the play, she and the Duke seemed to be drawn into a natural relationship through their shared activity.

The play's development was further assisted by making Angelo's distracted soliloquy in IV, iv a kind of fevered climax to the prison sequences, watched over as if in a nightmare by the prisoners who were his victims. Then this entire world was disposed of as the front section of the floor rose up to become a fourth wall to block it from sight; and, on a pure white carpet at the very front of the stage, the resolution seemed able to merge the symbolic and realistic aspects into single, highly-charged moments. Claudio, his face bandaged and in a shroud-like prison smock, returned pale and shaken from his ordeal, naturally, but with the additional suggestion that he had come from the grave: Isabella even touched him to make sure he wasn't an apparition. The tension was enormous, the sequence intensely moving, with magical echoes and yet the work of man. It was natural that Isabella should respond to her friar/Duke/preserver and that he should propose to her. After his unmasking, the Duke wore his friar's robe half-on, half-revealing his secular clothes, to sustain his ambiguous role; yet nothing seemed forced, largely because, although pushed to desperate (and sometimes harsh) measures in achieving a pragmatic solution, the Duke seemed an essentially *kind* man, tenderly uniting Juliet and Claudio, and gently urging the others to faith and happiness. In its sense of hard-won harmony, and its secure combining of realism and symbol, the play strongly resembled the 'lawful magic' of the late romances rather than, as it often seems, merely aspiring towards them: an exceptional achievement.

V

In his 1965 production of *Love's Labour's Lost*, John Barton sought to 'explore the relationships of the characters beneath the highly-jewelled surface': the 1978 version took this process further, and paid even less attention to surface glitter. True, Ralph Koltai's set was exquisitely beautiful and appropriate, enormous boughs of cascading autumnal leaves entirely enclosing a raked wooden forestage, behind which seats and a leaf-strewn floor suggested distant parkland. But there was no external glamour about the two courts, which seemed humbler, less formal, than usual: the lords took their oaths with little ceremony on a rustic seat; Rosaline cleaned the Princess's travelling boots and the travel-stained hem of her skirt in their first scene, and swept up autumn leaves with a broom in the last; the King and the Princess, especially, were very unelaborate, untidy even, in appearance, ordinary human beings rather than heads of state, especially when they first met, a rather endearingly unimpressive, bespectacled pair: a long silence indicated sudden (to them embarrassing) mutual attraction.

To cast Richard Griffiths, the company's superbly apt Bottom, Trinculo, and Pompey, as the King of Navarre was clearly a deliberate attempt to avoid the stereotype of elegant aristocracy. With his quietly conversational style, this was not a Navarre to sound the splendour of the opening speech or the lyricism of his sonnet. On the other hand, this King could switch quickly from the chop-logic about Aquitaine to a considerate 'Your *fair self* should make/A yielding '*gainst some reason* in my breast', and could attempt to soften the inhospitable blow with his 'here without you shall be so receiv'd/As you shall deem yourself lodg'd in my heart', while at the same time embarrassedly admitting the contradictory situation his oath has landed him in – 'Though so denied fair harbour in my house'. This King

and Princess seemed to be, as Mr Barton said of the Princess in his 1965 programme note, 'none too sure about how to cope with any situation'.

Michael Pennington understudied Berowne in the earlier version, and played it occasionally: a good performance in 1965 became a brilliant one in 1978. To an easy, relaxed manner for the opening he added a powerful desire for 'I forsooth in love' and an intense, almost erotic lyricism for the great defence of Love, which rightly became the climax of the first half. This scene typified the production's quality, building superbly from one humorous peak to another, without loss of humanity: the lords' poems were not guyed, but rather became the rapid, passionate release of pent-up desire, Dumaine bringing us back to earth with his resolve to send 'something else *more plain*' as well. Berowne's mockery gained particular impact from this particular interpretation of the King, Mr Griffiths physically crumpling in plump, blushing confusion.

But after this explosion of gaiety, the lords fell into the sobered realisation that they were 'all forsworn'. Mr Barton emphasised throughout the serious consequences of the oath-breaking to which the characters constantly refer, and for an important reason. As he put it in the 1965 programme,

ridiculous and impracticable, . . . it is an oath all the same, and a serious one. So when the King and the rest break it at the first sight of a woman's eyes, the girls are justified in questioning their oaths of love.

So after the second great outburst of gaiety, the Masque of Russians, the text was slightly re-arranged so that the King's earnest 'Despise me when I break this oath of mine', and the Princess's answering rage against 'perjur'd men', furiously sweeping up leaves with Rosaline's broom, became the 'fair fray' which Costard interrupted; a little later the Princess used her request to see the play ('let me o'errule you now') as an overture of conciliation.

Such relationships were sustained during

the play scene, with no sacrifice of humour or invention. The Worthies used a variety of hobby-horses, and Nathaniel's confused repetition of 'When in the world I liv'd, I was the world's commander' was caused by his gradual overbalancing under the weight of his horse and by the awkwardness of his enormously long lance: Alexander was literally 'overthrown'. But this hilarious sequence was also used in the interests of character, for the Princess and the King, working together, helped him up again and returned his lance.

The long dying fall was more effective, more astonishing than ever. As in 1965, it began with Armado's entry as Hector, accompanied by fading light and an especially haunting old Flemish melody offstage. This elegiac sequence ('The sweet war-man is dead and rotten') modulated into Marcade's entry without in any way diminishing its power or its theatrical and human magic, as the affairs of state took over and all knelt to the new Queen; Armado, still mounted on his lifts as Hector, saluted her with his rapier. Carmen du Sautoy's Princess took off her spectacles as she took on authority: 'Prepare, I say!' had an imperious command as bespectacled uncertainty gave way to new-found domination of the stage, matching the new confident fluency of her verse at this point. And because the oaths had been so stressed earlier, her stern conditions seemed a genuine necessity. As before, Mr Barton retained part of what looks like an uncancelled first draft of the final Berowne/Rosaline exchange at v, ii, 805–7,

Berowne.
　　　　And what to me, my love? and what to me?
Rosaline.
　　　　You must be purged too, your sins are rack'd;
　You are attaint with faults and perjury,

so that Rosaline could sit downstage thinking during the next exchanges, thus prompting Berowne's '*studies* my lady?'; Jane Lapotaire deflated his jaunty cocksureness easily –

though the final 'A twelvemonth?' had the wryness of a negotiated peace, Berowne the individualist to the end.

Mr Barton repeated his earlier innovation of having the final songs spoken, thereby throwing greater emphasis onto their vivid images of country life; but he extended the idea so that all the villagers echoed the 'Cuckoo' and 'Tu-whit, tu-who', and, even more important, the court, led by the King and Princess, joined in too, so that the stage became filled with harmonious echoes of country sounds – exquisitely capped by the hooting of a *real* owl above their heads, magically reinforcing Shakespeare's own final emphasis upon the ordinary realities of country life. Such an extraordinarily complex scene, which takes the breath away with its combination of gaiety and sadness, its blending of affairs of state, of the heart, of the countryside, is Mr Barton's special territory as a director. He clearly delights in probing the implications of imagery and characterisation, and is rightly unafraid of fleshing out his discoveries in terms of concrete theatrical effects and sustained, detailed characterisation which, far from over-loading the text, have the supreme advantage of increasing admiration for it, emphasising the sheer confident mastery of Shakespeare's writing in this scene.

Penelope Gilliatt wrote of Mr Barton's earlier version:

When it is done this way, the play can become a marvellous testament of a great writer finding himself; ...and the soaring generosity of the play as it climbs to its sombre ending...has the grasp of a genius who has suddenly found his life work under his hands.[1]

This magnificently realised scene fittingly concluded a season in which old and new interpretations of Shakespeare's comedies had been most profitably and satisfyingly blended.

[1] *The Observer*, 11 April 1965.

© ROGER WARREN 1979

THE YEAR'S CONTRIBUTIONS TO
SHAKESPEARIAN STUDY

1. CRITICAL STUDIES

reviewed by R. F. HILL

Several recent studies range widely over the canon analysing various aspects of Shakespeare's technique and creative process, the most original but also questionable thesis being advanced by Joan Rees.[1] She argues that the plays are not careful intellectual constructions but the result of a generative creative process in which Shakespeare's imagination responds to developments of the story line as they take place in the course of writing. Some part of the material may stimulate a burst of creative power and consequently distort the story line; again, where the story line fails to provide adequate imaginative stimulus, or where the narrative materials prove insufficient, his energy makes splendid way through new outlets. It is an attractive theory but highly speculative. It is asserted, for example, that Shakespeare realised the limitations of his material in the characters of Hero and Claudio, and that the plan of *All's Well That Ends Well* made Helena's role in the second half of the play unrewarding; the consequence was a compensatory flow of energy into the characters of Beatrice, Benedick, and Parolles. But are the situations of these characters inherently limited? The argument is available that they only appear so because Shakespeare chose to develop them in the way he has, and that the weight and interest attaching to Beatrice, Benedick, and Parolles were part of his primary conception of the plays. There are other propositions about the exigencies of Shakespeare's stories which seem not self-

evidently true, as, for example, the restrictions upon the creative process imposed by the materials of history, and the risk of anticlimax at the end of the reconciliation type story. The book appears more rewarding in its appreciation of manifestations of the 'creative surge' than in its account of them as responses to story demands – it is especially good on Shakespeare's resourcefulness in 'doing without events'. And one can certainly applaud the book's own underlying creative impulse, to assert Shakespeare's imaginative fertility in the face of modern tendencies to reduce the plays to schemes and themes.

Robert F. Willson Jr[2] analyses form and function in the opening scenes of nineteen plays. As might be predicted Shakespeare's method of launching his plays is found to vary widely so that not much can be offered by way of generalisation, except that his technique improved, moving more in the direction of foreshadowing and symbolism and away from bare exposition. One interesting aspect of this purpose is Shakespeare's presentation in some opening scenes of an action analogous to a subsequent climactic one, a particularly good example being the 'seduction of Brabantio' in *Othello*. Great originality in a field where so much work has already been done is hardly to be expected but the study further illuminates

[1] *Shakespeare and the Story: Aspects of Creation* (Athlone Press, 1978).
[2] *Shakespeare's Opening Scenes*, Salzburg Studies in English Literature (Universität Salzburg, 1977).

the imaginative unity of the plays by demonstrating how much of what is to come is foreshadowed in the opening scenes. Insistence on this feature produces some strained readings but generally the book is honest and unpretentious.

Thomas F. Van Laan[1] further explores territory which has aroused much interest in recent years, the function in Shakespeare's plays of various histrionic metaphors. Specifically he contends that 'the theatrical allusions, disguises, impersonations, and conscious or unconscious self-misrepresentation...exemplify a basic concern with role-playing that substantially affects characterization, action, structure, and theme'. Role is seen as conferring identity, and a major preoccupation of both comedies and tragedies is loss of identity with a consequent endeavour to find a new role or to assume a substitute role, the results of such processes differing radically as between comedy and tragedy. Another feature, studied closely in some of the comedies, is the discrepancy between the characters and the roles they are called upon or choose to play, and this supplies further ammunition to those disposed to attack the character of the Duke in *Measure for Measure*. Such animus against the Duke is related to a particular role, traced through a number of plays and culminating in *The Tempest*, the manipulator or 'internal dramatist'. The author believes that Shakespeare entertained an increasing suspicion of such figures, that of Duke Vincentio beginning to resemble his counterparts in the tragedies, and even Prospero is in the last analysis to be condemned as is indicated by his failure to achieve full success. This view itself indicates that there are things to question in this book, and a more general criticism would be that schematism sometimes overrides the complexities of the texts; another, that familiar things are being said in unfamiliar ways. Nonetheless, the section on *Hamlet* is good, showing what insights may follow from the

author's approach, and the book is strong in establishing continuities in Shakespeare's preoccupation with role-playing.

Ralph Berry[2] offers a collection of studies in which analysis proceeds upon two associated critical premises: that the relationship between literal and figurative language is complex and shifting, and that metaphor may be used in the sense of a controlling idea, or nexus of ideas, expressed in various configurations of the literal and metaphorical, which informs and organises the drama. As may be supposed from such a generous interpretation of metaphor the character of the studies as formal explorations varies greatly, and sometimes the reader is hard put to maintain a sense of the legitimacy of metaphor as a term for the play features described; this is especially true of the *Hamlet* essay, although what is said about the character of the Prince is illuminating. The most straightforward essays identify the 'controlling metaphor' as bastardy and legitimacy in *King John*, actor and play in *Richard III*, *tempus edax rerum* in *Troilus and Cressida*, and the Chorus in *Henry V*. The last-mentioned analysis explores the double impact of the play in terms of the Chorus version of events and the events themselves, a disparity matched by that in the play itself between the public rhetorical screen and the political realities. Berry allows that exclusive priority cannot be claimed for a single metaphoric formulation and that a play is always subject to other formulations; one welcomes such a reservation in the face of his sex–power analysis of *Coriolanus*. It is, however, hard to see how his controversial 'sonnet-world' reading of *Romeo and Juliet* possibly *could* admit any other, with its dismissal of Verona – including Romeo and Juliet – as a 'wrong-choice' society of mistaken values.

More various in its preoccupations is the

[1] *Role-playing in Shakespeare* (University of Toronto Press, 1978).
[2] *The Shakespearean Metaphor* (Macmillan Press 1978).

last book in this group, by F. W. Brownlow,[1] an intellectually alive but in some ways puzzling work. It deals with two groups of plays: the first tetralogy of history plays together with *King John* and *Richard II*; the tragicomedies, or last plays, including *Henry VIII*, *The Two Noble Kinsmen*, and *Timon of Athens*. Having reminded us that the chronology of the plays is uncertain and that the Romantic notion of organic development is dubious, the author then proceeds to discuss the plays in *sequences*, requiring us to see, among other things, developments from one play to the next. We are also told to beware of viewing the plays as autonomous creations, but rather attend to the ways in which they show 'the very age and body of the time his form and pressure'; and yet that aspect does not figure prominently in the discussion of the plays, certainly not with respect to the second sequence. An attempt is made to link the two sequences by forward and backward reference, and by using *King Lear* as a pivot. The first sequence develops towards the emergence of Shakespeare's first typically Shakespearian hero, Richard II, whose fall into pessimistic nothing prefigures *King Lear*; the second sequence moves out of the confining pessimism of *King Lear* into the wide horizons of *Pericles*, and back via *The Tempest* to a progressive eclipse of Providence in *Henry VIII*, *The Two Noble Kinsmen*, and *Timon of Athens*. However, the urge to define the particularity of individual plays pulls against a sense of the book as a unified whole. Despite the strong case made for the progression of the second sequence to a culmination in *Timon of Athens*, it is in its numerous insights, and in its analysis of individual plays, notably *The Winter's Tale* and *Henry VIII*, that the book really scores. The cargo of ideas is absorbing and challenging even if sometimes detrimental to clear exposition. The tone is supremely assured; Shakespeare can do no wrong, but his critics can. Brownlow has few qualms about author-

ship problems, and *The Two Noble Kinsmen* is said to reveal 'an artistic intelligence in complete control of its material'. The book is blemished by many typographical errors.

Most of the work noted on the non-dramatic poetry has been devoted to the Sonnets and there are just two essays to be mentioned on *Venus and Adonis*. S. Clark Hulse[2] examines its love paradoxes in the light of mythographic tradition, arguing that although there is no resolution at the discursive level of thought – the debate between Venus and Adonis is never resolved – there may be at the iconic level. Donald G. Watson,[3] rightly rejecting any simplistic moral interpretation of the poem, bases his reading on the clash of the concupiscent and irascible dispositions as embodied in Venus and Adonis. Neither position is simple or to be simply endorsed – 'The complexity of the passionate dispositions generates much of the comic irony of the poem as well as many of our difficulties in interpreting it.' The case is persuasive and accounts for much of one's complex response to the poem. (What is said about the common allegorising of the union of Venus and Mars as stated by Leone Ebreo should be compared with the view of Alur Janakiram expressed in his book discussed below.)

In 1934 L. C. Knights remarked that there was little genuine criticism in 'the terrifying number of books and essays on Shakespeare's Sonnets'. The *Casebook*[4] on the Sonnets, edited by Peter Jones, demonstrates how criticism in recent years has redressed the balance, moving away from biographical speculation to discriminating analysis of the poetry of the Sonnets. The meat of this

[1] *Two Shakespearean Sequences* (Macmillan Press, 1977).
[2] 'Shakespeare's Myth of Venus and Adonis', *Publications of the Modern Language Association*, XCIII (1978), 95–105.
[3] 'The Contrarieties of *Venus and Adonis*', *Studies in Philology*, LXXV (1978), 32–63.
[4] Macmillan Press, 1977.

collection, apart from Knights's own fine essay and an excerpt from *Seven Types of Ambiguity*, is contained in the section devoted to studies since 1952. This includes Winifred Nowottny's sensitive exploration of formal elements in the Sonnets, G. K. Hunter's important essay on their dramatic technique, and essays covering other aspects of their poetics – G. Wilson Knight on symbolism, M. M. Mahood on wordplay and on a thematic relationship between the Sonnets and the plays of Shakespeare's middle period, and Joan Grundy on the significance of the adjustments Shakespeare made to sonnet conventions. In the midst of criticism of this order the extract from Yvor Winters's depreciatory account of the Sonnets looks crude, but one supposes that its notoriety earned it a place; the same may be said of the views of John Crowe Ransom. C. F. Williamson's analysis of the contrast between the Poet's relationships with Friend and Mistress, which sees 'Man slung in the void between damnation and the Glory of God', appropriately rounds off the collection although to some the argument will look too neat. In the selection of texts and introduction biographical speculation is given short shrift and one therefore wonders why the piece by A. L. Rowse on Mr W. H. should have been included. The Graves–Riding extract deserves its place as one of the signposts in criticism of the Sonnets although the introduction might have indicated its flawed scholarship. The introduction briskly deals with basic facts and problems, and provides some discussion of critical viewpoints but does not mention structuralist analysis.

Before we deal with the major contribution to Sonnet study there are two pieces to be noted. In a brief essay which is really only illustrating the variousness and complexity of the Sonnets Paul A. Bates[1] contends that they provide a bridge from the early plays to the later. Lorena Stookey and Robert Merrill[2] play down the irony of Sonnet 94, refusing to find

hypocrisy indicated by 'show' (l. 2), and suggesting that the fearful insight of the sonnet is that the Friend is *incapable* of love rather than that he *will* not love. The argument is reasonable and a change from the burgeoning ambiguities to which we now turn.

As with the *Casebook*'s bias the concern of Stephen Booth's important edition of the Sonnets[3] is with the literary experience the poems evoke in us, but also – significant addition – with that of the Renaissance reader. Accordingly, biographical speculation, the problem of dating, Shakespeare's sexuality ('the sonnets provide no evidence on the matter') are discussed in a fairly summary fashion in an appendix, together with such matters as authenticity, the order of the Sonnets, and the text. In the notes on Sonnet 129 Booth effectively pin-points the weaknesses in the Graves-Riding views on punctuation and spelling, rightly observing that the influence of punctuation on the way a reader reads is much exaggerated. He opts for a compromise, printing in parallel the Quarto text and a modernised version which attempts to find a mid-point between the punctuation and spelling of the Quarto and modern directive punctuation and spelling, leaving the gap between the two to be dealt with discretely in the commentary. The drive of his massive commentary is two-fold; first, to provide a cultural and linguistic context for the Sonnets which will acquaint the modern reader with what meanings and associations were available to the Renaissance reader; second, to campaign for an analytic criticism that insists on plurality of meaning even where meanings detected in syntactic ambiguity, puns, overtones, and echoes run counter to the immediate sense. As

[1] 'Shakespeare's *Sonnets* and the Growth of his Dramatic Art', *Shakespeare Jahrbuch*, CXIV (1978), 70–4.
[2] 'Shakespeare's Fearful Meditation: Sonnet 94', *Modern Language Quarterly*, XXXIX (1978), 27–37.
[3] *Shakespeare's Sonnets* (Yale University Press, 1977).

to the first the reader of the Sonnets can only be grateful for the riches amassed by patient scholarship even if some readers qualify their gratitude by not putting them to the use the editor intended; for some may think that all the available meanings and associations suggested may not have been in all Renaissance minds – including Shakespeare's. This leads us to Booth's second purpose and the crux of the matter. And here one must be fair to Booth; he makes it plain more than once that in arguing for plurality of meaning the subliminal effects which complicate meaning 'cannot displace or substitute for the clear expository intentions that are ordinarily obvious in the sonnets'. However, he also insists that every meaning that the language of a sonnet is capable of suggesting is actually *in* the sonnet. Is there then nothing that Shakespeare (or any other poet) can choose *not* to say? He must use language and, inevitably, he will set down some words, or arrangements of words, (whether the process be conscious or unconscious) which suggest meanings foreign to the imaginative experience being mediated. There is another, though lesser, problem. Booth's commentary is 'explicitly designed to ensure that a reader's experience of the sonnets will as far as possible approximate that of the first readers of the 1609 Quarto'. He argues that for Shakespeare's contemporaries all the overtones, contradictions, echoes and suggestions that he teases out would have been active in their reading. But how can we know this? Our consciousness, under instruction, of such linguistic features is no guarantee that they were *in* the poem for a contemporary. Surely sensitivity in reading is much a matter of training and expectation, and what kind of consciousness a Renaissance reader brought to the act of experiencing a poem would seem, in these obscure regions at least, impossible to retrieve. Doubts like these are bound to arise for many readers where the sea of possible relevance threatens to engulf discrimination in

critical response; they cannot, however, lessen admiration for the high order of scholarship, or take from the recognition that this is an enterprise of large vision which has pondered deeply its own ways and those of others in the field.

A bridge to the comedies is provided by Alur Janakiram[1] who examines the relationship of reason and love in a number of the poems and plays. The first two chapters conscientiously sketch out representative positions of some Renaissance moral philosophers; parts of this material remain somewhat disengaged from the analyses that follow. The author is aware that much study has already been done in his field, modestly disclaiming great discoveries on his part, and it must be said that his readings of, for example, *Love's Labour's Lost*, *Much Ado About Nothing*, and *Troilus and Cressida* reach familiar ends by new routes. Nonetheless, Janakiram does make his contribution. He demonstrates that although moralists might stress a conflict between reason and love, neo-Platonic thinking, especially that of Leone Ebreo, recognised not merely discursive reason but also an 'uncommon' or intuitive reason as operative in love, thus effecting a reconciliation between reason and love. Whether or not this demonstration adequately explains, as is argued, the figure of Venus in *Venus and Adonis* is debatable, but it is suggestive in its bearing on the celebrated ambiguity of Shakespeare's depiction of love. The errata slip picks up but few of the errors in the text.

The comedies, including the problem comedies and the last plays, are studied by William O. Scott[2] from the point of view of their concern with a character's definition of self and the contingent matters of government and self-government. He explores the variety of

[1] *Reason and Love in Shakespeare* (Triveni Press, Machilipatnam, 1977).
[2] *The God of Arts. Ruling Ideas in Shakespeare's Comedies* (University of Kansas Publications, 1977).

pressures – situational, personal, public, and supernatural – which work to educe, confirm, or re-direct such self-definition. Ultimately the book has some success in showing how the comedies, under this view, have a coherence of preoccupation and development. However, the run of thought is sometimes difficult to grasp, and the author may be shooting at too many targets for the reader to follow his aim. Peter Hyland[1] offers a fresh slant on Shakespeare's use of the disguised heroine in the romantic comedies, suggesting that the device was of particular value in creating audience involvement since the secret of the disguise is shared between audience and heroine. Marianne L. Novy[2] examines the love relationships in *Much Ado About Nothing, As You Like It,* and *Twelfth Night,* showing by what processes they achieve a mutuality in love transcending the one-sideness of classical comedy and Petrarchan tradition.

Lawrence Danson's[3] book on *The Merchant of Venice* is to be welcomed for what it may do to stem the tide of irony that has been lately sweeping over the play. He notes the oddity of supposing the wholesale condemnation of the lovers in a Shakespearian comedy, and puts his foot firmly on such aberrant notions as a sexual competition between Portia and Antonio, a hand of friendship offered in Shylock's 'merry' bond, and a sly hint by Portia in Bassanio's casket scene. Danson treads a middle path between the ironist and sentimental Christian views of the play by distinguishing between the realistic and parabolic dimensions of its characters; what they 'represent' is not always matched by what they actually are. The play asks us to accept the Christian ethos and reject the Shylock ethos, while at the same time allowing sympathy for Shylock and criticism of the lovers as individuals. Moreover, Antonio and Shylock are not merely contrasted; Antonio, too, needs a lesson in charity and at the end of the trial scene he displays a charity towards Shylock

which he had earlier lacked. The book provides historical and biblical contexts to direct interpretation, and is especially helpful in its outline of the New Testament version of salvation history which sees the divine scheme for mankind only fulfilled when both Jew and Gentile shall have embraced Christ. The discussion of money-lending in the sixteenth century shows the divergence between theory and practice, a divergence not found in the Christians of Shakespeare's play; however, it does not dispel one's unease that Shylock is condemned for usury even though there was hardly any other occupation open to Jews. The 'harmonies' of the book's title are the resolutions of the dilemmas of the casket choice, the trial scene, and the ring episode, the music of the spheres in the last act lifting the meaning 'beyond the reach of discursive language'. The relating of Portia, Bassanio, and Antonio to the Graces as a 'triune dance of generosity' is a felicitous touch. It is a fair-minded and central book.

Going along with such a comforting view of *The Merchant of Venice* is that of Walter F. Eggers, Jr[4] who sees the play as qualifying commonplace equations of love and likeness, and affirming 'the possibility of love among apparently unlike people'. Less cheerful are the views expressed in four articles in *Shakespeare Jahrbuch* (1977) which are variously concerned with cultural and economic problems which they derive from the play. Anselm Schlösser[5] considers the contrast and interdependence of the worlds of Venice and

[1] 'Shakespeare's Heroines: Disguise in the Romantic Comedies', *Ariel,* IX (1978), 23–39.
[2] ' "And You Smile Not, He's Gagged": Mutuality in Shakespearean Comedy', *Philological Quarterly,* LV (1976), 178–94.
[3] *The Harmonies of 'The Merchant of Venice'* (Yale University Press, 1978).
[4] 'Love and Likeness in *The Merchant of Venice',* *Shakespeare Quarterly,* XXVIII (1977), 327–33.
[5] 'Zur Dialektik in *Der Kaufmann von Venedig',* *Shakespeare Jahrbuch,* CXIII (1977), 35–44.

Belmont; Fritz Bennewitz and Dieter Görne,[1] writing about a production of *The Merchant of Venice* at the Weimar Theatre, are similarly concerned and see the harmony of Belmont as an illusion shattered on contact with Venice. Thomas Sorge[2] sees the play as an artistic expression of the fight of Renaissance humanism in a period of accumulation of capital of which Shylock is symbol. Shylock also comes off badly in the article by Adel Karasholi;[3] the Jew was presented by Shakespeare as a usurer not as a tragic representative of a suppressed minority.

It is a relief to move on to the remainder of the comedies and less shackled criticism. Anne Paolucci[4] suggests an answer to the problem of the time scheme in *A Midsummer Night's Dream*; normal time, as pointed by references in the 'frame' scenes, is suspended in the magic wood where time cannot be measured in the usual way, and thus an apparent gap in time is bridged. Hans Jürg Kupper[5] writes on the effects aimed at by Shakespeare in alternating prose and poetry in the language of the young lovers. Margaret Boerner Beckman[6] rejects any reading of *As You Like It* which takes sides in the play's opposition of values; she argues for a reconciliation of opposites epitomised in the conflicting aspects of Rosalind's character and her androgynous status. David Willbern[7] proffers another version of the view that the romance world of *Twelfth Night* is undercut by the melancholies of Malvolio and Feste which are never resolved; the argument requires us, among other things, to be very solemn about the carnality of 'her very C's, her U's, and her T's', and to find significance in the loose end about Malvolio and the captain. William Carroll[8] examines the uses and abuses of imagination in *The Merry Wives of Windsor*, thus linking the play to the mainstream of Shakespeare's work, and indicating that the play is worthy of more serious attention than it is usually accorded. The essay is perceptive and interesting throughout, notably in the parallel drawn between Ford and Falstaff,

although perhaps trying to gather too many ideas under one umbrella.

Two essays on the problem plays are concerned with form. David M. Jago[9] finds the dramatically unsatisfying form of *Troilus and Cressida* intimately related to the lack of order in the moral world of Greeks and Trojans; it has far greater realism than *Romeo and Juliet* but the traditional, if less realistic, values of the latter play make it more congenial to satisfying dramatic form. Nicholas Brooke,[10] far from seeing any incongruity between romance and naturalism in *All's Well That Ends Well*, argues that the unique achievement of the play is its 'consistently naturalistic presentation of traditional romance magic'. He makes his case largely through a fine analysis of the play's reticent, bare language, from which it derives its unity of tone and vision.

In a dense and multi-faceted discussion which is difficult to follow Alexander Welsh[11] considers questions of death, generation, and the problematic relations of biology and social order in *All's Well That Ends Well* and *Measure*

[1] 'Shakespeares *Kaufmann von Venedig* im Deutschen Nationaltheater Weimar', *ibid.*, pp. 56–63.

[2] '„Jew" und „usury" in der Shakespeare-Zeit und in *Der Kaufmann von Venedig*', *ibid.*, pp. 45–55.

[3] 'Die Figur des Shylock in heutiger Sicht', *ibid.*, pp. 64–71.

[4] 'The Lost Days in *A Midsummer-Night's Dream*', *Shakespeare Quarterly*, XXVIII (1977), 317–26.

[5] 'A Local Habitation and a Name (Bemerkungen zum Sommernachtstraum)', *Deutsche Shakespeare-Gesellschaft West Jahrbuch 1977*, pp. 51–69.

[6] 'The Figure of Rosalind in *As You Like It*', *Shakespeare Quarterly*, XXIX (1978), 44–51.

[7] 'Malvolio's Fall', *Shakespeare Quarterly*, XXIX (1978), 85–90.

[8] ' "A Received Belief": Imagination in *The Merry Wives of Windsor*', *Studies in Philology*, LXXIV (1977), 186–215.

[9] 'The Uniqueness of *Troilus and Cressida*', *Shakespeare Quarterly*, XXIX (1978), 20–7.

[10] '*All's Well that Ends Well*', *Shakespeare Survey 30* (Cambridge University Press, 1977), pp. 73–84.

[11] 'The Loss of Men and Getting of Children: *All's Well That Ends Well* and *Measure for Measure*', *Modern Language Review*, LXXIII (1978), 17–28.

for Measure. David K. Weisser[1] offers a good study of irony in *Measure for Measure*. Irony, seen in ascending levels of awareness and self-awareness, is exemplified in the main characters; however, although the play presents in the Duke a detached ironic view of the world, that view is not an answer to the world's evils but makes answers possible, and the play in the end returns from ironic complexity to moral simplicity. Somewhat at odds with this view Christopher Palmer[2] argues against a process of transformation for the main characters of *Measure for Measure* whereby they finally harmonise in a moral pattern, insisting that they retain to the end an assertion of self and self-interest. Two opposed views of *The Tempest* round off this section on the comedies. Contrasting Marlowe's Faustus with Prospero Georg Seehase[3] takes an optimistic view of the play, seeing Prospero as a forward looking figure, a scholar who has attained a high level of wisdom in his resolve to return to the human community. Clifford Siskin[4] locates the significant difference between *The Tempest* and the other romances in its centring not upon husband–wife or father–daughter reunions but upon the *loss* of a daughter through marriage; fresh significance is given to Prospero's 'father' relationship to Ariel and Caliban, and the impending loss is seen as underlying Prospero's flashes of harshness and his final world-weariness.

The first part of a two-part study by Paul Bacquet[5] of Shakespeare's English history plays has appeared. This first part deals with the first tetralogy and *King John*, and is in the nature of a conspectus but with special emphasis on Shakespeare's developing dramatic powers. *King John* is seen as transitional because its critical note, going beyond the purveyance in the first tetralogy of traditional ideology, prefigures the element of critical detachment found in the later histories. The early chapters deal with the character of the Elizabethan age in general, the emergence of the Tudor myth (in particular the 'mythological' portraiture of Richard III and Henry V), the history play before Shakespeare, Elizabethan politico-religious thought with its strong vein of xenophobia. The plays are then analysed with a frequent weighing of connections with religious drama, Kyd and Marlowe, and the pressure of Elizabethan political events. The most substantial and interesting chapter is that on *Richard III*. In short, the book provides a useful introduction to the history plays, compassing in little many topics relevant to their genesis and character.

Among the large batch of essays on the history plays there are some good things especially on the later histories. Larry S. Champion[6] shows how the dramatic techniques of *2 Henry VI* develop out of and refine upon those of *1 Henry VI*, especially in centring the multiple plot structure on two individuals, Gloucester and York; he is concerned generally with the ways in which Shakespeare searches to achieve a balance between broad historical perspective and interest in individual character. Bridget Gellert Lyons[7] demonstrates Richard III's skill during his rise to power in manipulating traditional emblems and visual images associated with kingship, and how they fail him once he has gained the throne. Through a

[1] 'The Ironic Hierarchy in *Measure for Measure*', *Texas Studies in Language and Literature*, XIX (1977), 323–47.

[2] 'Selfishness in *Measure for Measure*', *Essays in Criticism*, XXVIII (1978), 187–207.

[3] 'Prosperos Aufbruch ins Gemeinwesen – oder, wunderbare Abenteuer des gesunden Menschenverstandes', *Shakespeare Jahrbuch*, CXIV (1978), 30–8.

[4] 'Freedom and Loss in *The Tempest*', *Shakespeare Survey 30* (Cambridge University Press, 1977), pp. 147–55.

[5] *Les pièces historiques de Shakespeare* (Presses Universitaires de France, 1978).

[6] ' "Prologue to Their Play": Shakespeare's Structural Progress in *2 Henry VI*', *Texas Studies in Language and Literature*, XIX (1977), 294–312.

[7] ' "Kings Games": Stage Imagery and Political Symbolism in *Richard III*', *Criticism*, XX (1978), 17–30.

discussion of the monetary terms and business language used by Richard III Paul N. Siegel[1] attempts a re-slanting of his Machiavellianism, seeing him as incarnating 'the spirit of the bourgeoisie at the time of its menacing approach to power'. Donald R. Shupe[2] presents evidence from modern theory that Richard's successful wooing of Lady Anne is psychologically plausible. (One would have supposed that Shakespeare had presented it as implausible in reinforcement of the demonic dimension of Richard.) In a reading of *Richard II* Leonard Barkan[3] draws attention to what he describes as theatrical *cause* (as opposed to theatrical *effect*) although his demonstration is hard to distinguish from any close reading of the emotional life of the text. He finds suppressed passion in the early part of the play balanced in the second part by explosive, often half-comic, releases; one is asked to detect a comic element in the handing over of the crown and in the murder of Richard. Peter J. Gillett[4] analyses Vernon's speech at *1 Henry IV*, IV, i, 97–110, pointing out how differences of effect between the two halves of the speech contribute to the impression of Prince Hal emerging transformed from his tavern wildness. Norman Sanders[5] neatly demonstrates the technique of shifts and correspondence of identity by which Hal's dissociation from court and tavern worlds is defined, a dissociation which is his only means of establishing his right to the throne in himself rather than as son to a usurper. J. A. B. Somerset[6] argues that the morality affinities of *2 Henry IV* are not with the earlier *humanum genus* type of morality (as is the case with *1 Henry IV*) but with the later social, or estates, type of morality. The argument is valuable in bringing into focus structural differences between the two plays and their differing perspectives on Prince Hal. With some reference to Renaissance fears of the restricted or specialist perspective on life John P. Sisk[7] counters the view of Falstaff as expressive of an enlarged life; Falstaff is a specialist in appetite in contrast to Prince Hal's breadth of perspective and intellectual flexibility. William Babula[8] interprets *Henry V* as a study of the maturing of a young monarch from one resembling the rash, rhetorical Hotspur to one who is more moderate and honest; the argument depends heavily on supposed parodic parallels. Norman Rabkin[9] rehearses the evidence for the sharply opposed readings of *Henry V* – the king as ideal monarch or Machiavellian militarist – arguing that neither alone is acceptable any more than a reading which attempts a compromise between the two. The value of the play is said to reside in a radical ambiguity which, forcing us to entertain alternative points of view, expresses 'the simultaneity of our deepest hopes and fears about the world of political action'.

Two essays on *Henry IV* point us to the tragedies. G. R. Hibbard[10] defines *Henry IV* and *Hamlet* as 'growing points' in the development of Shakespeare's dramatic art, indicating connections between the plays (e.g. in terms of style Hamlet develops out of Hotspur and Falstaff) and between them and the preceding

[1] 'Richard III as Business Man', *Shakespeare Jahrbuch*, CXIV (1978), 101–6.

[2] 'The Wooing of Lady Anne: a Psychological Inquiry', *Shakespeare Quarterly*, XXIX (1978), 28–36.

[3] 'The Theatrical Consistency of *Richard II*', *Shakespeare Quarterly*, XXIX (1978), 5–19.

[4] 'Vernon and the Metamorphosis of Hal', *Shakespeare Quarterly*, XXVIII (1977), 351–3.

[5] 'The True Prince and the False Thief: Prince Hal and the Shift of Identity', *Shakespeare Survey 30* (Cambridge University Press, 1977), pp. 29–34.

[6] 'Falstaff, the Prince, and the Pattern of *2 Henry IV*', *Shakespeare Survey 30* (Cambridge University Press, 1977), pp. 35–45.

[7] 'Prince Hal and the Specialists', *Shakespeare Quarterly*, XXVIII (1977), 520–4.

[8] 'Whatever Happened to Prince Hal? An Essay on *Henry V*', *Shakespeare Survey 30* (Cambridge University Press, 1977), pp. 47–59.

[9] 'Rabbits, Ducks, and *Henry V*', *Shakespeare Quarterly*, XXVIII (1977), 279–96.

[10] '*Henry IV* and *Hamlet*', *Shakespeare Survey 30* (Cambridge University Press, 1977), pp. 1–12.

plays. Many suggestive points are made but the subject could do with more elbow room than an essay provides. An important essay by Daniel Seltzer[1] also sees *Henry IV* as a 'growing point'. Seltzer distinguishes between descriptive and internalised modes of writing, the latter being first fully realised in the characterisation of Prince Hal; the technique was a prerequisite for the creation of Shakespeare's major tragic heroes, making possible the ultimate moments of inner perception which define their tragic stature.

Gerhard W. Kaiser[2] makes his attempt to define the essence of Shakespearian tragedy believing that this can be best achieved by a prior examination of Greek tragedy. Over a third of his book is devoted to a discussion of Aeschylus, Sophocles, and Euripides followed by an analysis of *King Lear, Macbeth, Othello,* and *Romeo and Juliet.* The section on Greek tragedy does not, in fact, provide a very illuminating perspective for the Shakespeare plays although it does bring out differences between Greek and Shakespearian tragedy in the roles of fate and character in determining tragic destiny. The analysis of the Shakespeare plays (and why *Hamlet* and the Roman tragedies should have been omitted is not stated) is fairly routine, focusing on the 'fatal flaw', the achievement of knowledge through suffering, and an asserted reconciliation of some kind at the end of the tragedies. There is more variety of viewpoint than that bare statement indicates but even so the book offers little that is unfamiliar. Charles J. Sugnet[3] outlines what he sees as the characteristic pattern of Shakespearian tragedy, an important part of which is the hero's final assertion of self, creating himself 'in a free space beyond morality, social relations'. Ursula Püschel[4] writes on the varying relationships of love to the social order in *Romeo and Juliet, Troilus and Cressida,* and *Antony and Cleopatra.*

Two essays deserve pride of place among the contributions on *Hamlet.* The language of the play is the subject of an impressive essay by Inga-Stina Ewbank.[5] Although conceding that there is something incommunicable at the heart of the play she challenges some claims that Shakespeare shows himself disillusioned about the power of words to communicate. *Hamlet* reveals an intense awareness of the complexity of communication; how, for example, characters adapt speech to situation and interlocutor, and – a key idea of the essay – the function of language in *translating,* in the sense of both interpreting and changing meaning. J. Philip Brockbank[6] studies the line of continuity between *Hamlet* and ancient sacrificial ritual, the central concern of the play being communal guilt, not revenge. 'The tragic effects of both *Hamlet* and the *Oedipus Rex* may be set down, therefore, to a sacrificial law, working through "accidents" as well as through human choice and disposition, towards the discovery and purgation of guilt.' The thesis is not reductive and is explored with tact; it sets in fresh perspective several structural features and problems of the play, notably, as one might expect, the 'delay', and suggests a special dimension for the audience's tragic catharsis in the face of the 'sacrifices' of Hamlet and Claudius. Four other pieces on *Hamlet* were noted. A difficult essay by Barbara

[1] 'Prince Hal and the Tragic Style', *Shakespeare Survey 30* (Cambridge University Press, 1977), pp. 13–27.

[2] *The Substance of Greek and Shakespearean Tragedy,* Salzburg Studies in English Literature (Universität Salzburg, 1977).

[3] 'Exaltation at the Close: A Model for Shakespearean Tragedy', *Modern Language Quarterly,* XXXVIII (1977), 323–35.

[4] 'Lebensanspruch und Menschenwürde: Shakespeares Frauengestalten', *Shakespeare Jahrbuch,* CXIII (1977), 7–29.

[5] '*Hamlet* and the Power of Words', *Shakespeare Survey 30* (Cambridge University Press, 1977), pp. 85–102.

[6] 'Hamlet the Bonesetter', *Shakespeare Survey 30* (Cambridge University Press, 1977), pp. 103–15.

Everett[1] argues that *Hamlet* embodies a concept of time to which the notion of delay is inappropriate. Michael Sheldon[2] draws attention to the imagery of restraint in *Hamlet* as revealing 'how deep is the sense of human impotence in the play'. Georg Seehase[3] finds that Ophelia is destroyed by the tensions between love and social-ethical conventions; R. S. White[4] also discusses the elements intertwined in the tragic love story of Ophelia.

An absorbing study by John Reibetanz[5] argues that 'much of what sets *King Lear* apart from Shakespeare's other tragedies is what it shares with Jacobean drama, rather than with earlier Elizabethan drama'. The author's concern is not with sources or influences but with Shakespeare's response to a context of living, evolving traditions, more particularly in matters of form. Connections made with the practice of contemporary dramatists include narrative discontinuity, the self-contained play world, improbability, the strong scene, emblematic techniques, and stage-managed actions. There can be no doubt that the author has gone far in isolating those characteristics of the play which complement each other to produce a unique design affecting us in a way no other Shakespearian tragedy does; also that the insistent reference to contemporary dramatic practice has been a useful analytical tool, even if one sometimes wonders about the validity of some of the connections made. Such doubts arise partly because the author, in general, eschews reference to Shakespeare's earlier plays, in which we can observe most of the features listed above being employed in some degree or kind. The book also provokes one to reflect why *King Lear*, alone among the tragedies, should take so much of its character from its immediate dramatic context. Despite such reservations this is a substantial addition to *King Lear* criticism; one comes from it with an enriched understanding of how the play *works*, and specifically how it works on our feelings. Bradley looms large as an admired

though erring guide, whose affective response is superior to 'floating in clouds of abstract speculation that could have no possible bearing on an audience's reaction to the play'. There is an excellent section on the play's embodiment of the *moriae encomium* tradition, but Reibetanz's concern is with meanings rather than with a grand Meaning. However, in the end he makes his stand, anchoring the play in the Christ-like truth of Cordelia; he is with Bradley and the seventeenth century rather than with modern adherents to ambiguity.

A less sophisticated book by Urmilla Khanna[6] seems to be directed towards introducing *King Lear* to students judging by the initial basic chapters on sources and characters. The chapter 'Some Thematic and Verbal Patterns', although drawing heavily on the work of others, contains some details of interpretation to interest more advanced critics. It is a pleasantly written and intelligent introduction to the play which, while not claiming to offer a new reading, makes a sensibly reasoned case for the play's ultimate optimism. In the same camp is David Ormerod[7] who relates the tree under which Edgar tells his father to shelter to Christian typology, the tree being an image of Gloucester's sin, purgation, and redemption. Opposing the redemptivist view of *King Lear* Edward Pechter[8] concentrates on the power of

[1] '*Hamlet*: a Time to Die', *Shakespeare Survey 30* (Cambridge University Press, 1977), pp. 117–23.
[2] 'The Imagery of Constraint in *Hamlet*', *Shakespeare Quarterly*, XXVIII (1977), 355–8.
[3] 'Hamlet und Ophelia', *Shakespeare Jahrbuch*, CXIII (1977), 81–9.
[4] 'The Tragedy of Ophelia', *Ariel*, IX (1978), 41–53.
[5] *The 'Lear' World: a Study of 'King Lear' in its Dramatic Context* (Heinemann Educational Books Ltd., 1977).
[6] *King Lear. A Critical Introduction* (Doaba House, Delhi, 1978).
[7] ' "The shadow of this tree": Fall and Redemption in *King Lear*', *Deutsche Shakespeare-Gesellschaft West Jahrbuch 1977*, pp. 97–108.
[8] 'On the Blinding of Gloucester', *English Literary History*, XLV (1978), 181–200.

the play to make us suffer, specifically by involving us with characters and then punishing us for such involvement. Wolfgang Weiss[1] analyses Lear's speeches to show that Shakespeare used the prosodic instruments of his time to as good effect as Sidney or Donne. The remaining three essays on the play are more colourful. Assuming that Cordelia's behaviour in the first scene requires apologetics Duncan Fraser[2] makes a case for her based upon psycho-sociological analysis; his further assumption, that all other explanations of her conduct must suppose a change in her character between I, i and IV, iv, seems unwarranted. According to the psychological analysis of John J. McLaughlin[3] Cordelia refuses to enter into the love contest because she realises her own inability to win and cannot bear to be frustrated, while Lear's rage is touched off by her shattering of his sexual fiction of living with her as virtual husband and wife; the explanations of the behaviour of Goneril, Regan, and Edmund are less novel. For those who would enliven their studies of the play Hovhanness I. Pilikian[4] offers his conviction that the king is a fertility symbol whose rewards of love to his daughters are really fertility blessings, and that Cordelia's refusal to respect the ritual invites the evil of infertility. Lear's curse of infertility which we have mistakenly thought directed at Goneril is really directed at Cordelia; further, Lear's bouts of sexual nausea are occasioned by his queen's adultery and the bastardy of Cordelia.

Othello and *Macbeth* have one essay apiece. On the basis of some ingeniously linked evidence John A. Hodgson[5] argues that Desdemona's handkerchief is not a symbol of true love but an emblem of her reputation, 'and as such it closely parallels in its progress through the play the career of her good name'. Robert F. Willson Jr[6] examines the banquet scene in *Macbeth* as a play-within-play which fails because Macbeth has imperfectly conned his part; the scene focuses many of the

tragedy's thematic concerns but the more forcibly because of the compression and tension of the play-within-play structure. Finally there is a group of essays on two of the Roman tragedies. Richard L. Nochimson[7] advances the possibility that the many readers and spectators who would attest to the tragic effect of *Antony and Cleopatra* 'have been responding to the myth of Antony and Cleopatra rather than to Shakespeare's play', a view which would seem to founder on the fact that for most people the myth would not exist without Shakespeare's play. The essay interestingly aligns the play with *Troilus and Cressida* in respect of deflationary techniques, although the play finally eludes a primly moralistic reading. L. T. Fitz[8] offers a spirited defence of Cleopatra against the male chauvinism of many critics which is said to have biased estimations of her character and stature as tragic heroine; the essay redresses some imbalances but the point that Cleopatra is a complex rather than inscrutable being does not take into account the poetic effects.

---

[1] 'Redeform, Rhythmus und Charakter: Das Beispiel König Lears', *Deutsche Shakespeare-Gesellschaft West Jahrbuch 1977*, pp. 70–83.

[2] 'Much Virtue in "Nothing": Cordelia's Part in the First Scene of *King Lear*', *Cambridge Quarterly*, VIII (1978), 1–10.

[3] 'The Dynamics of Power in *King Lear*: An Adlerian Interpretation', *Shakespeare Quarterly*, XXIX (1978), 37–43.

[4] 'Ancient Echoes in *King Lear*', *Drama*, 127 (1978), 25–31.

[5] 'Desdemona's Handkerchief as an Emblem of Her Reputation', *Texas Studies in Language and Literature*, XIX (1977), 313–22.

[6] 'Macbeth the Player King: the Banquet Scene as Frustrated Play within the Play', *Shakespeare Jahrbuch*, CXIV (1978), 107–14.

[7] 'The End Crowns All: Shakespeare's Deflation of Tragic Possibility in *Antony and Cleopatra*', *English*, XXVI (1977), 99–132.

[8] 'Egyptian Queens and Male Reviewers: Sexist Attitudes in *Antony and Cleopatra* Criticism', *Shakespeare Quarterly*, XXVIII (1977), 297–316.

Gisèle Venet[1] analyses images of dissolution and fusion in *Antony and Cleopatra* relating them to theme and action; the imagery of fluidity is said to signal Shakespeare's break with sixteenth-century values and to assimilate the play to a 'baroque' existential vision. Where then do the epiphanies of the last plays fit in? Joyce Van Dyke[2] characterises the language of Coriolanus as tending to the condition of gesture, an act of pure self-expression which disables him as an actor, although in the end, tragically, he must learn to play a role, 'and the role he plays on re-entering Corioli is that of the man he once was'. Hermann Heuer[3] writes on three passages in *Coriolanus* which have been subjects of discussion in recent publications. Of the comparison made by Ladislaus Löb and Laurence Lerner[4] of *Coriolanus* and Brecht's *Coriolan* one can only concur that Brecht has 'turned the play from a traditional tragedy into a committed left-wing drama'.

Of writings on Shakespeare in the theatre today only a few things can be noted here. Bernard Beckerman[5] discusses what has elsewhere been called a 'stage-centred reading of Shakespeare', an approach that attempts a combination of Shakespeare in the study and in the theatre. He insists that not all theatrical readings are defensible: 'Without being able to set the exact limits of interpretation, we know that such limits exist.' Homer D. Swander[6] writes enthusiastically of the 1977–8 Royal Shakespeare Company's productions of the three parts of *Henry VI*, illustrating his account with excerpts from interviews with the director, Terry Hands, and some of the principal players. The real significance of these productions is their demonstration of the dramatic richness of the plays; they have been at last 'found', in the place that best proves them, the theatre, and we should in future cease to doubt their authenticity or apologise for their immaturity. An interesting account of an actor's approach to a Shakespearian role is recorded in Michael Mullin's[7] interview with Emrys James about the latter's playing of King Henry IV for the Royal Shakespeare Company. Roger Warren[8] reviews the 1976 season of plays at Stratford-upon-Avon by the Royal Shakespeare Company, and Samuel Schoenbaum[9] writes very appreciatively of the same company's 1977–8 season of plays at Stratford and London. In an account full of interesting detail Berners A. W. Jackson[10] chronicles the remarkable theatrical adventure story which began to unfold in 1953 at Stratford, Ontario. *Shakespeare Quarterly*, XXIX, (1978) includes an extensive section of reviews by various writers of Shakespearian productions, chiefly in 1977; one notes that although the United States has the lion's share of Shakespeare festivals, Shakespeare is also flourishing on the boards in places as far-flung as Tokyo and Tel Aviv.

There is little on translation this year. Martin Lehnert[11] calls for translations which do not simplify Shakespeare's meaning, that are scientifically based, poetical, and true to the

[1] 'Images et Structure dans *Antoine et Cléopâtre*', *Études Anglaises*, XXX (1977), 281–302.

[2] 'Language and Gesture in *Coriolanus*', *Shakespeare Survey 30* (Cambridge University Press, 1977), pp. 135–46.

[3] 'Rehabilitationen: Überflüssige Texte im Coriolan?', *Deutsche Shakespeare-Gesellschaft West Jahrbuch 1977*, pp. 43–50.

[4] 'Views of Roman History: *Coriolanus* and *Coriolan*', *Comparative Literature*, XXIX (1977), 35–53.

[5] 'Explorations in Shakespeare's Drama', *Shakespeare Quarterly*, XXIX (1978), 133–45.

[6] 'The Rediscovery of *Henry VI*', *Shakespeare Quarterly*, XXIX (1978), 146–63.

[7] 'On Playing Henry IV', *Theatre Quarterly*, VII (1977), 15–23.

[8] 'Theory and Practice; Stratford 1976', *Shakespeare Survey 30* (Cambridge University Press, 1977), pp. 169–79.

[9] 'Seeing Shakespeare Plain', *Times Literary Supplement* (6 January 1978), p. 10.

[10] 'The Shakespeare Festival: Stratford, Ontario, 1953–77', *Shakespeare Quarterly*, XXIX (1978), 164–91.

[11] 'Shakespeare in der Sprache unserer Zeit', *Shakespeare Jahrbuch*, CXIV (1978), 65–9.

spirit of the original. Philip Grundlehner[1] analyses the radically opposed methods of Stephan George and Karl Kraus in their translations of Shakespeare's Sonnets. An edition of *Measure for Measure* has been prepared by W. Naef and P. Halter[2] in the dual language series of Shakespeare's plays under the general editorship of W. Habicht, E. Leisi, and R. Stamm. The edition is based on *The Complete Pelican Shakespeare* and will be indispensable to the German student of Shakespeare. The translation, which renounces any claim to independent artistic merit, is careful and reliable, and together with the notes provides an excellent guide through the verbal and textual complexities of the play. The introduction and commentary are sensible and modest, and provide the student with useful hints for further reading.

We are left as usual with a lucky dip of contributions which resists logical sorting. Anselm Schlösser[3] looks at Shakespeare's plays from today's viewpoint on such matters as racial intolerance and colonialism, and Thomas Metscher[4] examines in them the operation of social, economic, and political processes. Armin-Gerd Kuckhoff[5] attributes much of the wickedness of 'wicked women' in Shakespeare's plays to frustrated self-expression for they can only fulfil themselves through men; Ljuben Groiss[6] distinguishes between Shakespeare's positive and negative women characters, those who do, and those who do not, experience moral growth. Ina Schabert[7] discusses the changes in Shakespeare's use of rhyme from the early to the later plays. Stephen C. Schultz[8] argues that William Poel's views on the speaking of Shakespearian verse have serious deficiencies, in particular that false ideas about metre 'led him to conclude that one must choose between chant and "lifelike" reading', thus implying a dilemma alien to the actual conditions of English metrics. Volker Schulz[9] uses the examples of structuralist analysis of *Othello* and Sonnet 129 to illustrate some of the limitations of the structuralist approach. Alvin Kernan[10] reminds us of the various uses to which Shakespeare put the two-place structure, noting the opposition of civic and 'natural' worlds and the cyclic pattern of departure and return.

Since its first publication in English in 1951 Wolfgang Clemen's study of Shakespeare's imagery has been many times reprinted, sufficient testimony to the value of a pioneering study and justification for the second edition that has now appeared.[11] Changes from the first edition are confined chiefly to the updating of the bibliography and the addition of a preface critically surveying subsequent work and directions in imagery study. Reading the book again one is struck by its balance, by the author's awareness of the complexity and pitfalls of his subject, and by the rightness of his early insistence that 'Every image, every metaphor gains full life and significance only from its context', and that imagery must be

[1] 'Kraus vs. George: Shakespeare's *Sonnets*', *Deutsche Shakespeare-Gesellschaft West Jahrbuch 1977*, pp. 109–28.

[2] *William Shakespeare, Measure for Measure* (Francke Verlag, Munich, 1977).

[3] 'Von Fremden, Eingeborenen und Barbaren bei Shakespeare', *Shakespeare Jahrbuch*, CXIV (1978), 7–21.

[4] 'Zum Wirklichkeitsbezug des Shakespeare-Dramas', *Shakespeare Jahrbuch*, CXIV (1978), 39–56.

[5] 'Versuch über die „bösen Weiber" bei Shakespeare', *Shakespeare Jahrbuch*, CXIII (1977), 72–80.

[6] 'Shakespeares Frauen unterwegs', *Shakespeare Jahrbuch*, CXIII (1977), 90–2.

[7] 'Zum Reimgebrauch in Shakespeares Dramen: Reimende Personen und reimender Autor', *Deutsche Shakespeare-Gesellschaft West Jahrbuch 1977*, pp. 84–96.

[8] 'William Poel on the Speaking of Shakespearean Verse: A Reevaluation', *Shakespeare Quarterly*, XXVIII (1977), 334–50.

[9] 'Conflicting Ideas of "Structure" in Literary Criticism: Reflections Based on Examples Taken from Shakespeare', *Études Anglaises*, XXX (1977), 273–80.

[10] 'Place and Plot in Shakespeare', *The Yale Review*, LXVII (1977), 48–56.

[11] *The Development of Shakespeare's Imagery*, 2nd edition (Methuen and Co. Ltd., 1977)

correlated with all other constituents of the drama. The original aim of the book to be inclusive in its approach is the source of its strengths and weaknesses but, as the author says, to attempt a massive re-writing from hindsight would produce a less original work.

The *Mississippi Folklore Register* has devoted a special issue to Shakespeare and folklore. Louis Marder's[1] account of Elizabethan folklore culture and of its presence in Shakespeare's plays allows folklore to include more areas of human experience and literary motif than the uninitiated might have supposed proper. However, his illustration of its significant functions in several plays establishes the claims of folklore on the critic's attention. The title of C. J. Gianakaris's[2] essay is rather misleading since it has little specific to say about folk ritual or *The Merry Wives of Windsor*; his primary concern is with the psychoanalytic dimension of comedy and its therapeutic functioning through comic catharsis. Whether or not David M. Bergeron's[3] discussion of Othello's phrase 'monumental alabaster' really comes under the heading of folklore he provides the phrase with an interesting social context concerning funerary monuments, finally relating it to the staging of Desdemona's bed; the tomb deaths of Romeo and Juliet are recalled, and the 'tragic loading' made to evoke the effigies of husband and wife on Elizabethan tombs. Linwood E. Orange[4] surveys the literal and figurative progeny of the folklore motif of extraordinary birth in Shakespeare's plays. Monstrous birth, according to Barry Gaines and Michael Lofaro,[5] is our most important clue as to the appearance of Caliban; the popular connection between devil-mating and deformed offspring is generally discussed, and specifically illustrated from a 1609 woodcut of a monstrous child which, it is suggested, may bring us close to contemporary expectations about the appearance of Caliban. In an essay which is conceptually and verbally high-flying Phyllis Gorfain[6] considers the prophetic utterances of

the Witches in *Macbeth* as formal riddles, and analyses their structural affinities with elements of paradox and disorder. Unlike the hero of romance Macbeth fails to solve the riddles posed by the agents of chaos and thus brings chaos upon self and kingdom; the riddles are answered in the action of the play 'which converts fatal contradictions and dangerous images into natural rythms'. Philip C. Kolin[7] provides a bibliography on Shakespeare and folklore.

S. C. Sen Gupta[8] has gathered into a book six of his essays, the first three of which have been published before. These three cover broad topics: 'Shakespeare Through the Ages' is a brisk historical survey of the major phases of Shakespearian criticism, concluding with the author's view of the special nature of Shakespeare's achievement and appeal; 'Shakespeare the Man' is conscious of the limitations of trying to derive his character from his works yet in the end attempts to do so; 'Shakespeare and his Sources' considers some general characteristics of his sources. More stimulating than any of these broad and relaxed pieces is a comparison of Barabas and Shylock seeking to point the difference between tragic and comic conceptions; his argument that it is Shylock's 'odd mixture of incompatible traits...in which no passion can assimilate others, that makes him a comic character' is persuasive; so is his reading of Portia's manipulation of Shylock in the trial scene. An essay on *As You Like It* shows

[1] 'Folklore Stress in Shakespeare', *Mississippi Folklore Register*, x (1976), 115–37.
[2] 'Folklore Ritual as Comic Catharsis and *The Merry Wives of Windsor*', ibid., 138–53.
[3] ' "Let's talk of graves"; *Othello*, v, ii, 5', ibid., 154–62.
[4] 'Despised in Nativity; Unnatural Birth in Shakespeare', ibid., 163–74.
[5] 'What Did Caliban Look Like?', ibid., 175–86.
[6] 'Riddles and Tragic Structure in *Macbeth*', ibid., 187–209.
[7] *Ibid.*, 210–33.
[8] *A Shakespeare Manual* (Oxford University Press, 1977).

how Shakespeare develops the pastoral romance of his source into the characteristic form of his romantic comedies, a juxtaposition of mutually qualifying ideas held in unity by a pervasive ambivalence. The last essay is startling; it proposes what the author with some understatement calls an unorthodox approach to textual problems – all emendation (including punctuation, lineation, prose and verse confusions) whether 'inspired' or deriving from bibliographical hypothesis, should be eschewed by modern editors since in the last analysis all are conjectural. Sen Gupta also includes a lecture, 'The Substance of Shakespearian Comedy', delivered by Sir Mark Hunter in India in 1912. It attempts to do for comedy something akin to what Bradley had done for tragedy in the first of his celebrated lectures. Asserting that the substance of Shakespearian comedy is romance it examines the characteristics that sustain the integrity of this mode of comedy. Whatever else may be said about this lecture its critical breadth and largeness of mind are refreshingly unfamiliar today.

If one needed any more evidence that the Shakespeare industry is highly productive there has been published a collection of fourteen essays edited by Walter Edens, Christopher Durer, Walter Eggers, Duncan Harris, and Keith Hull[1] which addresses itself to the question of teaching Shakespeare. Some of the essays are really critical studies with only a passing nod at the classroom. Among the few to engage closely with teaching problems is one by John W. Velz which discusses some of the play programmes, examinations and seminars that he has devised on the principle of guiding students to the point of discovery for themselves. Two other essays should be included here. Jay L. Halio takes a balanced look at the critical use of Shakespeare in performance, both as performed by students and viewed by them. Norman Rabkin considers the question of teaching Shakespeare to graduates whose

specialism lies elsewhere; from a lively account of his own teaching experiences emerges the suggestion that they would be most rewardingly taught through an undergraduate, 'unprofessional', type of course, and that graduate time might be devoted to other disciplines believing as he does that some of the best recent books on Shakespeare have resulted from illumination brought from other intellectual fields. The best essay in the collection, bubbling with witty metaphor, is by Robert B. Heilman which uncovers some manifestations of two kinds of pedagogic stance – 'Shakespeare as scientific object and Shakespeare as immediate experience'. Although opting for some kind of middle course he has scant respect for untutored gut reaction (also dubbed 'intestinal carillon'), nor for trendy programmes stemming from overanxiety to appease student demands. Shakespeare must not be adjusted to the taught; the taught must adjust to him. Albert Wertheim discusses *Macbeth* and Paul M. Cubeta *As You Like It* and *King Lear*, both writers being concerned in their different ways with the virtues of crossing the boundaries of genre. There is a skilful exposition by David M. Bergeron of questions raised by forms of play-within-play as a method of teaching the comedies. Brian Vickers advocates what he calls multifocal criticism, a weighing of the validity of several given (and interested) perspectives, exemplified here in the perspectives of patricians, plebs, and Volumnia on *Coriolanus*. There are also essays by Bernard Beckerman (on the distinctively dramaturgic features of the plays), by G. Wilson Knight (on the vocal realisation of Shakespeare's dramatic poetry), by Winfried Schleiner (on comparing versions of similar literary motifs), by A. C. Hamilton (on studying the individual play in the light of its place in the canon), by Ray L. Heffner Jr (on 'solving' *Much Ado*

[1] *Teaching Shakespeare* (Princeton University Press, 1977).

About Nothing in the manner of a detective story), and by D. Allen Carroll whose counselled approach, 'wherein extremities are tempered and the elements mixed', will doubtless soothe the conscience of many a teacher.

Richard Levin[1] offers the second part of a sustained refutation of the strategies and assumptions of the critics who refute Shakespeare's 'face value' meanings, those who find irony everywhere, and find Shakespeare's plays 'to mean something quite different from – often the opposite of – what they seem to mean, and what they have been taken to mean by virtually everyone up to the present'. This witty piece has perhaps some underground affinity with an inaugural lecture by J. M. Nosworthy[2] which reflects on Shakespeare's remembrance of things past, his variations on the themes of *ubi sunt* and the sad remembrance of happier times. The long lineage of these themes is sketched with an impressive literary range, and the dramatic capital Shakespeare made of them is illustrated, particularly in *Hamlet* and *Coriolanus*. The latter choice of play is unexpected, and Nosworthy's thoughts draw from this example of a hero of outstanding merits destroyed by a 'disaffected mediocrity' a kind of *ubi sunt* message for our own times.

[1] 'Refuting Shakespeare's Endings. Part II', *Modern Philology*, LXXV (1977), 132–58.
[2] *Shakespeare Puts the Clock Back* (University of Wales Press, 1978).

© R. F. HILL 1979

2. SHAKESPEARE'S LIFE, TIMES AND STAGE

reviewed by E. D. PENDRY

Leslie Hotson's latest book[1] is in its way biography. It is not based directly on some new discovery in the archives but upon an elaborate study of a portrait miniature, dated 1588, that has long been known to exist in two versions by Nicholas Hilliard. Hotson contends that the sitter (who was accepted before 1700 as the Earl of Essex) is in reality William Shakespeare. With the arcane knowledge and something of the ingenuity of a Sir Thomas Browne, Hotson amasses the evidence of iconography to sustain his argument that the mysterious linked hands in the portrait signify at once the sitter's association with Lord Strange's Men, who may conceivably have worn some such badge, and with some mortal friend to whom the sitter is as a Mercury to an Apollo. Building upon the foundations of his own *Mr. W. H.* and other books, Hotson identifies the Apollo-like friend as the Young Man amongst Roses (depicted in the miniature that is Hilliard's acknowledged masterpiece), as the Fair Friend of the Sonnets, as Mr W. H., and as William Hatcliffe, Prince of Purpoole in the Gray's Inn revels. There are links between Shakespeare and Mercury in the minds of contemporaries who admired him.

For criticism of Hotson's methods with miniatures, the non-specialist must turn with relief to art experts such as Roy Strong, who reviewed the book in *The Times*.[2] Strong is sufficiently unimpressed to propose a Rival Sitter in the person of Thomas Howard, 1st Earl of Suffolk. But even the non-specialist may have his doubts. He may wonder at the ease with which a miniature is treated as if the principles and conventions of this art-form were exactly those of an impresa. The precept laid down by Tasso and Contile that human

[1] *Shakespeare by Hilliard* (Chatto & Windus, 1977).
[2] 6 October 1977, p. 20.

figures should be excluded from the impresa unless they represent the classical gods (overtly, one would have added) thus prepares the ground for saying that the feather in a man's hat may help to thicken the proofs that do demonstrate thinly that the man is represented as Mercury.

Anyone who has undertaken research, however slight it may be on Hotson's scale, will know how coincidences and analogies of fact, idea, image and word eerily recur to remind him of what he has read: but these are will-o'-the-wisps. It is a haunted twilight, not the broad light of day, that Hotson eagerly extends over Shakespearian biography. For it is not only Hotson's main argument that fails to convince: it is almost every part of it.

Also in the land where learning and speculation meet, without shaking hands, A. L. Rowse elaborates his portrait of Emilia Bassano, whom he insists is the Dark Lady of the Sonnets.[1] In 1611 Emilia published a long-winded pious poem entitled *Salve Deus Rex Judaeorum*, which Rowse declares establishes her as one of the foremost poetesses of the age. His further claim that the poem 'is a unique feminist manifesto all the way through' is not borne out by the quotations he gives, which bemoan the seduction of beautiful women.

On terra firma, the close connection of the Sadler family of Stratford to Shakespeare has long been acknowledged. A relative of theirs and, by marriage, of the Quineys, was an Elizabeth (*b.* 1623) whose father (*b.* 1587) sought his fortune, and found it, in London, and who married a clergyman, Anthony Walker. After her death Walker wrote *The Holy Life of Mrs Elizabeth Walker* (1690) which embodied extracts from her own autobiography.[2]

Two articles set out to place Shakespeare in the cultural traditions of his time. With some warmth, Anca Vlasopolos[3] insists that the connection of *A Midsummer Night's Dream* with the rites of midsummer is specific and

essential, and that the play cannot be properly understood without a full sense that the lovers are brought into a harmony both pagan and Christian with one another and with the natural world. But she does not add much to our skimpy knowledge of the folk traditions involved.

Saad El-Gabalawy[4] traces an unorthodox strain of Christian Communism in works by More, Shakespeare and Milton. Like many others, the writer is inclined to confuse Communism and philanthropy.

Literary source-study has of late yielded a surprisingly rich harvest. Pride of place must go to Kenneth Muir's book, *The Sources of Shakespeare's Plays* (1977)[5] which, together with his earlier *Shakespeare's Sources 1* (1957), spans the period from 1957 to 1975 in which Geoffrey Bullough's eight authoritative volumes appeared. The 1977 *Sources* is at once a thoroughly revised edition of and the promised sequel to the 1957 book: Muir brings us up to date, drawing upon Bullough as well as upon new contributions to learning, including his own, and on private communications and unpublished dissertations. Where a choice has to be made between competing theories or a path found through conjectures, this is done with judicious good sense. No doubt this book will be used widely as a work of reference: but its lightness of touch and the telling examples make it readable seriatim as an ordinary book.

It is because the book hangs together so admirably that the reader finds himself looking about for a reassuring thesis, for a rationale of

---

[1] *The Times*, Saturday 22 April 1978, p. 14.
[2] Allan Pritchard, 'Elizabeth Walker and Shakespeare's Stratford', *Notes & Queries*, n.s. XXV (1978), 156–60.
[3] 'The Ritual of Midsummer: A Pattern for *A Midsummer Night's Dream*', *Renaissance Quarterly*, XXXI (1978), 21–9.
[4] 'Christian Communism in *Utopia*, *King Lear*, and *Comus*', *University of Toronto Quarterly*, XLVII (1978), 228–38.
[5] Methuen.

source-study (which does indeed stand in some need of one). Muir suggests that it teaches us something of Shakespeare's conscious and unconscious artistry. He sees Shakespeare much as John Livingstone Lowes saw Coleridge, as a writer gifted with an imagination capable of unifying the literary impressions he has received, some of them personal and some shared by contemporaries and in part now lost to us. True, such an artistic process may allow of quite strange and sophisticated associations of thought and image beneath the level of consciousness: thus the weaver Bottom is apparently named after a silkworm's cocoon; the devil Modu in Harsnett (Modo in *Lear*) may conjure up in Shakespeare's mind the Latin word *modo* and its context in Horace. But no theory of the esemplastic imagination will account finally for Shakespeare's genius; and, at its crudest, the picture of the learned Shakespeare carrying out some programme of research before writing each play looks suspiciously like the mirror-image of a scholar going about his work of source-study.

Muir concentrates, in the the traditional way, upon where the sources differ in detail from the plays. Chaucer is of course not overshadowed by Shakespeare, and consequently when Muir discusses the alleged dependence of *Troilus and Cressida* on Chaucer's poem, there is example enough of how a comparison between works will be of reciprocal critical interest. But elsewhere the implication is constantly of Shakespeare's crushing superiority, and the minor authors who provided the plots of, for instance, *As You Like It, Measure for Measure, Lear* and *The Winter's Tale* do not come in for serious attention on their own modest merits. This is a pity: it is to lose a valuable opportunity. If we understood more of Shakespeare as a literary critic, or at least as a critical reader (it was, after all, he who chose those sources), we might understand more of him as a playwright; but first we need to understand better the works as they were before he transformed them.

Ann Thompson has written a full-length study, the first of its kind, on the specific debt of Shakespeare to Chaucer.[1] It must be admitted that on the most generous estimate this debt does not extend much beyond *Troilus and Cressida* and *The Two Noble Kinsmen* as complete works, and *A Midsummer Night's Dream* and *Romeo and Juliet* in parts or aspects. Chaucer's *Troilus and Criseyde* and *The Knight's Tale* are said to lie behind these plays. Ann Thompson is thorough in gathering together the scattered facts and opinions of others, lucid and very properly tentative in expounding her own. Chaucer, she shows us, was accorded a considerable, almost legendary status in the sixteenth century as father of English literature. But, following her case as she makes it, both on points of detail and of general design, one must remain unconvinced that Chaucer was more than an uncertain and minor influence on Shakespeare, and something much less on other Elizabethan playwrights. There are at most six surviving plays outside Shakespeare which may owe something to Chaucer, and it is disconcerting that of these Chapman's *Sir Giles Goosecap* is said to show the keenest critical intelligence. Like Muir, Ann Thompson is not greatly interested in taking the work of Shakespeare's undistinguished contemporaries on its own terms, but only in so far as it reflects on the great.

Discussing the different approaches of Chaucer and Shakespeare to similar stories, Ann Thompson comes to the conclusion that, in both *Troilus and Criseyde* and *The Knight's Tale*, Shakespeare found a complexity or contrariness of tone and judgment that he cut down in the interest of a simple intensity, making cynicism the dominant characteristic of *Troilus and Cressida*, and romantic sentiment of *The Two Noble Kinsmen*, whereas Chaucer is at times idealistic in the first, and humorous in the second. There is the startling but stimu-

[1] *Shakespeare's Chaucer: A Study in Literary Origins* (Liverpool University Press, 1978).

lating suggestion that Pandarus in *Troilus and Cressida* may be a degraded, parodic version of the merry Chaucer-persona to be found in the poem. Fortunately, as in Muir's book, our appreciation of the critical comment does not depend on our accepting as proven the argument that Chaucer was indeed Shakespeare's immediate source.

Ann Thompson does not try to put her finger on those specifically dramatic qualities that might have caught Shakespeare's eye in Chaucer; and it would not be easy, though not impossible, to do so with the principal poems she discusses. In contrast, there is nothing novel or difficult in demonstrating that Shakespeare's art owes something to another medieval product, the morality play. Scholars have often – too often, indeed, and with too much wearisome particularity – traced its ramshackle progress all through the sixteenth century to Shakespeare's doorstep. For Edmund Creeth[1] such scholars, whom he dismisses as 'evolutionists', are wrong to limit the major influence on Shakespeare to the most recent Tudor hybrid moralities. Unless plays preserve the full structure of the morality play, with its phases of innocence, temptation and enlightenment, then they are not truly of the genre. On these terms few Elizabethan plays qualify. Thus the figures of Faustus and Falstaff are to be regarded as no more than superficial allusions to Everyman and the Vice. It is central to Creeth's thesis that only in *Macbeth*, *Othello* and *Lear* does an Elizabethan dramatist compose plays in the true spirit of the pristine morality play. So it is that he takes the unusual step of comparing *Macbeth* with *The Castle of Perseverance*, *Othello* with *Wisdom who is Christ*, and *Lear* with *The Pride of Life*. That three fifteenth-century plays have something in common with Shakespeare's, nobody would deny, since a common moral and religious tradition underlies them all. But the plays are really very different. Mankind in *The Castle of Perseverance* is corrupted by avarice, in *Wisdom*

who is Christ by revelry, and the king in *The Pride of Life* is brought to face the truth through death. To save appearances, Creeth is obliged to represent Cordelia and Desdemona as allegorical figures of Our Lady and Anima, and to make large claims for the initial innocence and ultimate wisdom of Macbeth, Othello and Lear. At worst, the Witches in *Macbeth* become the World, the Flesh and the Devil.

More conventionally, the classics may be explored for sources and analogies. J. J. M. Tobin[2] believes Shakespeare was influenced on more than one occasion by his reading of *The Golden Asse*. The arrest of Lucius by the nightwatch is reminiscent of the Dogberry episodes in *Much Ado*. Much less convincingly, Tobin argues for a debt to Apuleius in the deaths of Jack Cade in *2 Henry VI* (IV, x) and of the two Princes in *Richard III* (IV, iii, 1–22). According to John H. Betts,[3] *Henry V* bears the marks of Shakespeare's reading, and perhaps studying at school, Virgil's *Georgics*, with its images of the bees for social order and weeds for disorder. Anthony Brian Taylor[4] shows that *Titus Andronicus* (II, iii, 14–20), with its reference to 'the babbling echo', goes back to Golding's translation of Ovid, in which, at odds with his original, Golding represents Echo as a gossiping bawd. The same personal associations seem to be conjured up when Aaron calls the Nurse he has killed a 'long tongu'd babbling gossip' (IV, ii, 151). Moreover, as Taylor reveals in another article, Viola characterises Echo in a famous speech in *Twelfth Night*

[1] *Mankynde in Shakespeare* (Athens: The University of Georgia Press, 1976).

[2] 'On the Asininity of Dogberry', *English Studies*, LIX (1978), 199–201; 'Shakespeare and Apuleius', *Notes & Queries*, n.s. XXV (1978), 120–1.

[3] 'Shakespeare's "Henry V" and Virgil's "Georgics" ', *Notes & Queries*, n.s. XXV (1978), 134–6.

[4] 'Golding's "Metamorphoses" and "Titus Andronicus" ', *Notes & Queries*, n.s. XXV (1978), 117–20; 'Shakespeare and Golding: Viola's Interview With Olivia and Echo and Narcissus', *English Language Notes*, XV (1977), 103–6.

(I, v, 294) as 'the babbling gossip of the air', and she thereby relates her larger dilemma in the plot to Golding's rendering of the Narcissus story.

Other translated and foreign works come in for attention. In *All's Well* (I, ii, 31–48) the King has much to say to Bertram about the shortcomings of the modern courtier. Sentiments of a similar kind are to be found in 'Ermino Grimaldi', a tale in Painter's *Palace of Pleasure*, where Shakespeare could have found the tale on which *All's Well* as a whole is based. Whether such a general similarity amounts to a debt, as John Edmund Price[1] argues, is quite another matter. James Hoyle,[2] following up a suggestion by Roy Battenhouse, finds the best analogue to the main plot of *The Tempest* in the Genesis story of Joseph, who like Prospero is favoured by Providence and prefers virtue to vengeance on his enemies, in stark contrast to the merciless custom of the cannibals noted by Montaigne elsewhere in Shakespeare's reading. Katherine Duncan-Jones[3] suggests that in composing the Duke's speech against the fear of death in *Measure for Measure*, (III, i, 5–41), Shakespeare may have been partly recalling a treatise by the Huguenot theologian Philippe du Plessis-Morney. This was translated in 1590 by the Countess of Pembroke soon after the death of her brother, and published in 1592 as *A Discourse of Life and Death* along with her translation of Garnier's *Marc Antoine*, a minor source of *Antony and Cleopatra*. There are undoubted similarities between the treatise and the Duke's speech, although this is not wholly unexpected in reflections on a subject so rich in commonplace. However, it is fascinating to notice (what Katherine Duncan-Jones does not urge) that a thread may connect Claudio and his sister, with Sidney and his.

Then there is the influence of Shakespeare's own English contemporaries. Ann Pasternak Slater,[4] though uneasily aware of the pedantries of source-study, suggests that Shakespeare had

at least browsed through Nashe's *Terrors of the Night* (1594) and Lavater's *Of Ghostes and Spirits* (translated 1596). One can at least admit that the three writers treated the same subject in something of the same spirit. Shakespeare's Sonnet 21 has some likeness to those sonnets of Sidney's in which he mocks both himself and the conventions he is working in. Jacqueline E. M. Latham[5] suggests that the likeness is not fortuitous, but may come from Sidney's influence on Shakespeare. The popularity of the anonymous play *Mucedorus* has some bearing on Shakespeare's turning to romance in the last period of his writing career. Richard T. Thornberry[6] points out that the Epilogue of Q2 (1606) differs from Q1 (1598) in referring to King James instead of Queen Elizabeth. Since the 1606 title page speaks of sundry performances in the City of London, it might be supposed then that the play was revived between 1604 and 1606, thus well before the court performance recorded on the Q3 titlepage (1610), and in time to have influenced Shakespeare. Unfortunately, Thornberry does not seem to have noticed that the claim on the 1606 title page merely repeats that of 1598.

William Keach[7] gives a new and distinct identity to a group of long Elizabethan poems which include *Venus and Adonis*. What are they

---

[1] 'Painter's "Ermino Grimaldi" and Shakespeare's "All's Well That Ends Well" ', *Notes & Queries*, n.s. xxv, (1978), 141–3.

[2] '*The Tempest*, the Joseph Story, and the Cannibals', *Shakespeare Quarterly*, xxviii (1977), 358–62.

[3] 'Stoicism in *Measure for Measure*: a new Source', *Review of English Studies*, xxviii (1977), 441–6.

[4] 'Macbeth and the Terrors of the Night', *Essays in Criticism*, xxviii (1978), 112–28.

[5] 'Shakespeare's Sonnet 21', *Notes & Queries*, n.s. xxv (1978), 110–12.

[6] 'A Seventeenth-Century Revival of *Mucedorus* in London Before 1610', *Shakespeare Quarterly*, xxviii (1977), 362–4.

[7] *Elizabethan Erotic Narratives: Irony and Pathos in the Ovidian Poetry of Shakespeare, Marlowe and Their Contemporaries* (The Harvester Press, 1977).

to be called? Erotic narratives, Ovidian poems, *epyllia*? At all events, it is Keach's thesis that such problem poems as Lodge's *Glaucus and Scilla*, Marlowe's *Hero and Leander*, Marston's *Metamorphosis of Pigmalion's Image*, Weever's *Faunus and Melliflora* and Beaumont's *Salmacis and Hermaphroditus* belong together in taking their tune directly and freshly from the Ovid of *The Metamorphoses* rather than from the over-simplified moralisations of Ovid current in the sixteenth century. Reproductions of continental Renaissance pictures illustrate the tradition of mythology available. For the non-classicist Keach's chapter on the subtleties of Ovid's self-conscious art is especially revealing. Elizabethan poems on the Ovidian model deliberately yoke together the sensual, the airily witty, the decorative and the violent in their account of sexual love, and respond readily to the development of fin-de-siècle satire. The map of Elizabethan poetry is largely re-drawn by Keach's clear dissociation of the work of such poets, so keenly aware of their own place in fashion, from the Muses' garden of *The Faerie Queene*. Keach gives us a sensitive and observant reading of *Venus and Adonis*: this, and *Hero and Leander*, which he has already written so well about in *English Literary Renaissance*, are two undoubted swans amongst the geese. But his manner remains open, honest and tentative, and gives promise of further elucidations yet to come. One might look some day for some further definition of the irony and pathos that are claimed for the poems.

S. Clark Hulse[1] explains away what might seem to be the failure of *Venus and Adonis* to make a coherent statement about love by relating the poem to myth in art. Shakespeare does achieve a unity of opposites but it is not that of paradox in a verbal discourse so much as the aesthetic unity to be found in the structure of a picture. Mythical tradition, which is not logical or systematic, thus has the unifying function in the poem that visible stage action

may have in the plays. Donald G. Watson[2] declares that the world of Venus and Adonis is one of 'elemental strife and sexuality' in which the death of Adonis is arbitrary and senseless, and not to be seen as the direct outcome of passion: Venus embodies the *appetitus concupiscibilis*, but Adonis the *appetitus irascibilis*, in no clear relation to it.

Like Keach, Harriett Hawkins[3] also treats of Shakespeare in the company of other writers. The large terms of her title are not to be taken too earnestly: hers is (aptly enough) a free-ranging discussion that takes its force from an impatience with the self-important and small-minded modern criticism that tends to deaden the reverberations that great literature sets up in the mind. For her own part she enjoys her reading to the point of zealotry and truculence, and writes in a style that is at once throw-away and bellelettrist, handling quotations in the old-fashioned respectful way, for the sake of the golden reminiscence. She is interesting on *Hamlet*, showing how allusions to past times, persons and events, whether as trivial as Polonius's playing Julius Caesar, or as significant as a dead jest by a dead jester, lead to mysteries outside the action. At times, it must be admitted, it sounds as if Hawkins, in declaring for the freedom of the reader as well as for the writer, is advocating a criticism of paradox, irony and ambivalence, for which there is already coal enough in Newcastle; and her deprecating of 'moral convictions' antagonistic to, for instance, the creative liveliness and loveliness of a Volpone or a Cleopatra, is to substitute one narrowness for another. Moral values, far from being discountable in any work of literature, may and do shadow and colour the substance of the imagination,

[1] 'Shakespeare's Myth of Venus and Adonis', *PMLA*, XCIII (1978), 95–105.
[2] 'The Contrarieties of *Venus and Adonis*', *Studies in Philology*, LXXV (1978), 32–63.
[3] *Poetic Freedom and Poetic Truth: Chaucer, Shakespeare, Marlowe, Milton* (Clarendon Press, Oxford, 1976).

whether of fictional characters such as Tamburlaine, the Duchess of Malfi, Troilus or Macbeth, or of the author himself, and the writer is not set as free from the proprieties of his age, and the reader is not set as free from the proprieties of the author, as she would have them.

University Microfilms International have already begun to issue a series of twelve volumes for the American Theatre Association under the title *Shakespeare as Spoken: A Collation of 5000 Acting Editions and Promptbooks of Shakespeare*. These will be reviewed in a later number of *Shakespeare Survey*.

The usefulness of studies of theatre conditions during Shakespeare's own time is unquestionable. Neil Carson[1] argues that the complexities and obscurities of *Henslowe's Diary* may conceal, and may be made to reveal, a shifting but deliberate literary policy in the acquisition of plays and playwrights. Although Carson does not attempt (what may well be impossible) to define the taste and judgment shown in building up the repertoire, he throws doubt on the overriding influence of Henslowe himself in it, and points out that the sharers Robert Shaw, Thomas Downton and Samuel Rowley were most prominent in dealing with dramatists. They may well have seen things differently: the evidence, such as it is, suggests that Downton, for instance, was not so keen as the others on collaborative writing. With David George's[2] contributions, we now know of some thirty-five cast-lists of plays written before the closing of the theatres; most of these are in manuscript. Such lists increase our knowledge of, amongst others, actors known to have performed in Shakespeare's plays. Theatre studies drawn from a wider period than Carson's still have their relevance to Shakespeare's practice. In about 1628 Inigo Jones was commissioned to convert the Cockpit at Whitehall into a permanent court theatre. Scholars have understandably assumed that he would make provision for the use of more elaborate scenery there, and they have been inclined to regard certain scenic designs of his preserved at Chatsworth House as drawn up with the Cockpit stage in mind. Leonie Star[3] reviews the evidence and points out the difficulties of reconciling these designs with the layout of the playhouse, and comes to the conclusion that the arrangements at the Cockpit were actually very much like those at the traditional public theatre. James Shirley wrote almost exclusively for the Phoenix. David Stevens[4] illustrates James Shirley's sensitive use of the stage and the various auditory and visual effects available to him on it.

There is much still to be learned about theatrical costumes. Rhoda-Gale Pollack[5] provides information about the appearance of the Devil in mystery cycles that may make for a finer understanding of the supernatural in Shakespeare's imagination. An account book at St John's, Cambridge, contains inventories of players' garments in the college between 1546 and 1566 and perhaps earlier. The 'Lord In Christmas' each year was to be held responsible for handing them over to his successor. Sandra Billington[6] conjectures that a number of the costumes are for productions of Terence. Costumes for fools, the Devil ('a blak cote hose & cappe all of oñ for ye devel' and 'ij blak develles cootes wᵗʰ hornes') and

[1] 'Literary Management in the Lord Admiral's Company, 1596–1603', *Theatre Research International*, II (1977), 186–97.

[2] 'Pre-1642 Cast-Lists and a New One for *The Maid's Tragedy*', *Theatre Notebook*, no. 3, XXXI (1977), 22–7.

[3] 'Inigo Jones and the Use of Scenery at the Cockpit-In-Court', *Theatre Survey*, XIX (1978), 35–48.

[4] 'The Stagecraft of James Shirley,' *Educational Theatre Journal*, XXIX (1977), 493–516.

[5] 'Demonic Imagery in the English Mystery Cycles', *Theatre Notebook*, no. 2, XXXII (1978), 52–62.

[6] 'Sixteenth-Century Drama in St. John's College, Cambridge', *Review of English Studies*, XXIX (1978), 1–10.

for Death may also indicate the vernacular drama. T. J. King[1] takes a fresh look at the famous engraving from *The Wits* (1662) which is the earliest picture (after Peacham's sketch of *Titus Andronicus*) of Shakespearian actors on stage. The audience is dressed in a style popular in the middle of the century, while Falstaff's costume probably dates back to before the Civil War. The distinction seems a very fine one.

Shorter notes on the text may be conveniently listed in the common order of Shakespeare's works. G. Harold Metz[2] surveys the various and conflicting evidence for the date of *Titus Andronicus* and comes to the conclusion that, as the title page of Q1 suggests, it was performed before 1592 and, as echoes in other plays suggest, probably as early as 1590. Jane L. Donawerth[3] suggests that Nathaniel bases his praise of society in *Love's Labour's Lost* IV, ii, 161–2 on a passage in Ecclesiastes IV, 8–12. It is a well-known fact that in the first meeting of Romeo and Juliet the dialogue between them takes the form of a complete sonnet. Gideon Rappaport[4] points out that this is followed (I, v, 107–10) by the first quatrain of a second sonnet. The two sonnets reflect in little the course of the tragedy, and should be marked off from one another after line 106 by the stage-direction 'Kissing her', which Rowe arbitrarily placed a line later. The late J. C. Maxwell[5] contributes two notes on *Richard II*: the first tentatively tracing 'The frosty Caucasus' passage (I, iii, 267–72) to Cicero's *Tusculan Disputations*, was privately communicated to Kenneth Muir and is discussed in *The Sources of Shakespeare's Plays*; the second proposes a new reading for the crux at III, ii, 29–32 in Q1. Stuart Sillars[6] understands Bottom's 'Phibbus' car' (*A Midsummer Night's Dream* I, ii, 31) to be a garbled reference to Phoebe, the moon that is so significant an image in the play. In *The Merchant of Venice* III, ii, 43–7 Portia calls for music to accompany what may prove to be Bassanio's 'swanlike end'

should he choose the wrong casket. Anthony Lewis[7] makes the unconvincing suggestion that she has the death of Orpheus in mind. Norman Nathan[8] argues for a reading in *The Merchant of Venice* that was adopted by the New Arden Shakespeare twenty years ago; and apparently believes that Jessica eloped with Gratiano. G. West[9] tackles the difficulties of the principal crux in *1 Henry IV*, at IV, i, 99–100, and would have Hal and his fellows likened, not to ostriches, but to goshawks that 'withe', i.e. 'master', the wind and to eagles revived by bathing. The language used by Prince Hal to promise he will mend his ways (*1 Henry IV*, I, ii) is, Rosalie Osmond[10] claims, a parody of that used of Christ's redemption. Peter J. Gillett[11] shows convincingly, despite a tendency to over-read, that *1 Henry IV*, IV, i, 97–110 moves out of ambiguity in its description of Hal's preparing for battle into clear praise. From J. J. M. Tobin[12] comes remarkably far-fetched evidence for Shakespeare's dependence on Nashe and from Robert E. Jungman[13] and

[1] 'The First Known Picture of Falstaff (1662): A Suggested Date for His Costume', *Theatre Research International*, III (1977), 20–2.

[2] 'The Date of Composition of "Titus Andronicus"', *Notes & Queries*, n.s. XXV (1978), 112–7.

[3] 'Nathaniel's "Text" in "Love's Labour's Lost", IV, ii, 161–2', *ibid.*, 122–4.

[4] 'Another Sonnet in "Romeo and Juliet"', *ibid.*, 124.

[5] 'Two Notes on "Richard II"', *ibid.*, 124–5.

[6] 'Phoebe and Phoebus: Bottom's Verbal Slip', *ibid.*, 125–6.

[7] 'An Allusion to Orpheus in "The Merchant of Venice", III, ii, 43–7', *ibid.*, 126–7.

[8] '"A Iewes Eye" in "The Merchant of Venice"', *ibid.*, 127–8.

[9] 'Estridges that with the wind: A Note on *1 Henry IV*, IV, i, 97–100', *English Studies*, LVIII (1977), 20–2.

[10] 'Prince Hal's Parody of the Passion', *Notes & Queries*, n.s. XXV (1978), 132.

[11] 'Vernon and the Metamorphosis of Hal', *Shakespeare Quarterly*, XXVIII (1977), 351–3.

[12] 'Nashe and "1 Henry IV"', *Notes & Queries*, n.s. XXV (1978), 129–31.

[13] '"The Governance of England" and "The First Part of Henry the Fourth"', *ibid.*, 131.

Edward C. Jacobs evidence for his dependence on Sir John Fortescue. D. S. Bland,[1] stating that Inns of Court men at one time needed passwords to be let through the city gates after hours, hazards the rather desperate notion that Justice Shallow remembers one of them when he says 'Our watchword was, "Hem, boys!" ' (2 Henry IV, III, ii). The 'consideration' which has brought about a change of heart in Henry V (I, i, 28) is shown by Ruth M. Levitsky,[2] quoting an Elizabethan translation of Luis de Granada, to be a specific religious exercise (as some editors have long realised) and not merely meditation in general. Susan C. Shapiro[3] would have us believe, for no compelling reason, that Beatrice and Hero were modelled on Penelope, Lady Rich and Elizabeth, Countess of Southampton. David Blythe[4] informs us that 'marl' in Beatrice's characterisation of men in Much Ado, II, i, 63 should not be glossed 'clay' because clay clings and holds its form, while marl readily falls to pieces. Donald S. Lawless[5] wonders if Shakespeare had the circumstances of Marlowe's death in mind when, in As You Like It, he has Rosalind speak of a tapster as a confirmer of false reckonings. J. J. M. Tobin[6] finds, or thinks he finds, similarities of wording and theme in As You Like It, II, i, and six pages of Nashe's Pierce Penilesse. Martin Puhvel[7] finds in The Golden Bough examples of the practice in primitive societies of flinging stones at the spot where deeds of violence, including suicide, have taken place; the priest in Hamlet tells Laertes that Ophelia's grave has been spared such treatment. M. R. Woodhead[8] finds an explanation for Hamlet's false start in quoting Aeneas's speech about Pyrrhus (Hamlet, II, ii, 444): Pyrrhus is associated in his mind not with tigers but with dogs, loyal and revengeful, described by Montaigne. Frank McCombie[9] tries out the idea that Ophelia refers in her mad songs to a still-born child of hers, but even he has little confidence in it. In a none too cogent article Joseph J. Egan[10] accuses Shakespeare of

inaccuracy and anachronism in his use of 'gallowglass', who was properly a Hebridean footsoldier fighting as a mercenary in Ireland after the Anglo-Norman Invasion. M. E. Grenander[11] suggests the pricking of the thumbs felt by one of the Witches in Macbeth may have been a symptom of disease commonly attributed to witchcraft but actually brought on by eating mouldy rye. Joan Heiges Blythe[12] considers that in Lennox's 'Men must not walk too late' (Macbeth, III, vi, 7) the emphasis falls on walking as distinct from riding on horseback, rather than on lateness. Contemporary evidence adduced by E. B. Lyle[13] makes it likely enough that the regalia seen by Macbeth in the dumbshow of Kings stand, in the case of the twofold balls, for the united kingdom of Scotland and England (including Wales), and in the case of the treble sceptres for the kingdoms of Great Britain, France and Ireland. Jane Donawerth[14] links Lear's 'poor, bare, fork'd animal' to

[1] 'Justice Shallow's "Hem, Boys!" ', ibid., 132.
[2] ' "Consideration" as a Key to the Character of Henry V', ibid., 136–7.
[3] 'The Originals of Shakespeare's Beatrice and Hero', ibid., 132–4.
[4] 'Beatrice's "Clod of Wayward Marl" ', ibid., 134.
[5] 'Another Shakespearian Allusion to Marlowe?' ibid., 137.
[6] 'Nashe and "As You Like It" ', ibid., 138–9.
[7] 'The Background of "Shards, Flints, and Pebbles", Hamlet, v, i.', English Language Notes, xv (1978), 164–7.
[8] 'Hamlet's "Hyrcanian Beast" Reconsidered', Notes & Queries, xxv (1978), 139.
[9] ' "At His Heels a Stone" ', ibid., 139–41.
[10] ' "Of Kernes and Gallowglasses": An Error in Macbeth', English Language Notes, xv (1978), 167–71.
[11] 'Macbeth, IV, i, 44–5 and Convulsive Ergotism', ibid., xv (1977), 102–3.
[12] ' "Men Must Not Walk Too Late" ', Notes & Queries, n.s. xxv (1978), 153.
[13] 'The "Twofold Balls And Treble Sceptres" in Macbeth', Shakespeare Quarterly, xxviii (1977), 516–519.
[14] 'Diogenes the Cynic and Lear's Definition of Man, King Lear, III, iv, 101–9', English Language Notes, xv (1977), 14–18.

Plato's definition of man, which was so roundly refuted by Diogenes. Michael Cameron Andrews[1] argues, from evidence in other plays, that the Fool's 'I'll go to bed at noon' (*King Lear*, III, vi, 88) is a sexual innuendo, ironically expressing the unlikelihood of his spending the afternoon in loveplay. Reviewing the various attempts, some of them desperate, to explain what Lear means by 'This' a good block!' at IV, vi, 185, Winifred L. Frazer[2] desperately defines block as 'a nefarious scheme or bartering exchange of evil for evil'. Her case rests on Scottish usage. In the Folio *Lear*, V, ii, Edgar leaves Gloucester beneath a tree. The tree is significant, David Ormerod[3] suggests, because as an emblem it is traditionally associated with both the Fall of man and the Crucifixion: it therefore suits both the immediate context, with Gloucester's despair and consolation, and the entire play which, though full of conflicting forces, draws to a redemptive conclusion. Katherine Duncan-Jones[4] has noticed that the proper name Caius is used by Vincento Saviolo to illustrate the forms of entry into a duel. In *King Lear*, V, iii, 283 it therefore fits into the memory of swordplay which Lear calls up from the past and in which Kent may have had a place. A statistical analysis shows that *Timon* has more words in common with *King Lear* than with any other play in the canon. Eliot Slater[5] claims that this indicates closeness of date (rather than, say, similarity of theme). Three scholars have interested themselves in the naming of characters in *Othello*. Robert F. Fleissner[6] makes the point that the Roman Emperor Otho had marital difficulties and committed suicide. Samuel L. Macey,[7] noting that Iago is a Spanish name, looks for some of its connotations. Spain and the Spanish were diabolic in English eyes. And the patron saint of Spain, James (Jago) was famous as the Christian champion against the Moors, thereby earning the name Santiago Matamoros. William C. Woodson[8] thinks it more significant that one of

Lear's successors in Holinshed's history of ancient Britain was King Iago. When Othello says that Desdemona 'can turn, and turn, and yet go on/And turn again' (IV, i, 246–7), it could be, writes Allan Shickman,[9] that he is referring obliquely to the kind of Elizabethan trick picture which presents different aspects when viewed from different angles. Gordon N. Ross[10] has noticed, as Ann Thompson has, a resemblance between 'farewell our revel, all was ago' in *The Franklin's Tale* and Prospero's 'Our revels now are ended.' Shakespeare's Sonnet 21 has some likeness to those sonnets of Sidney's in which he mocks both himself and the conventions he is working in. Jaqueline E. M. Latham[11] suggests that the likeness is not fortuitous, but may come from Sidney's influence on Shakespeare. In Renaissance emblems, constancy in love might be represented by a magnetic compass and the polar star. The second quatrain of Shakespeare's Sonnet 116 similarly uses the star image. Peter M. Daly[12] accepts the view of John Doebler that there is a submerged image of a pair of

---

[1] ' "And I'll Go To Bed At Noon" ', *Notes & Queries*, n.s. XXV (1978), 149–51.

[2] 'King Lear's "Good Block" ', *Shakespeare Quarterly*, XXVIII (1977). 354–5.

[3] ' "The Shadow of this Tree": Fall and Redemption in *King Lear*', *Deutsche Shakespeare-Gesellschaft West Jahrbuch 1977*, pp. 97–108.

[4] 'Kent, Caius and Lear's Swordsmanship', *Notes & Queries*, n.s. XXV (1978), 151–3.

[5] 'Word Links Between "Timon of Athens" and "King Lear" ', *ibid.*, 147–9.

[6] 'The Moor's Nomenclature', *ibid.*, 143.

[7] 'The Naming of the Protagonists in Shakespeare's "Othello" ', *ibid.*, 143–5.

[8] 'Iago's Name in Holinshed and the Lost English Source of "Othello" ', *ibid.*, 146–7.

[9] 'A Turning Picture in Shakespeare's "Othello"?', *ibid.*, 145–6.

[10] ' "The Franklin's Tale" and "The Tempest" ', *ibid.*, 156.

[11] 'Shakespeare's Sonnet 21', *ibid.*, 110–12.

[12] 'A Note on Sonnet 116: A Case of Emblematic Association', *Shakespeare Quarterly*, XXVIII (1977), 515–16.

compasses in the first quatrain, and that there is indeed a submerged pun on 'compass' both there and in the third quatrain, with its 'bending sickles compasse'. Macd. P. Jackson's[1] study of the frequency of colloquial forms in the Shakespearian canon leads him to date Hand D in *Sir Thomas More* after 1600. He shows some limited awareness of the fact that

plays of different periods are on different subjects and in different styles, but none that a manuscript differs significantly from a printed book.

[1] 'Linguistic Evidence for the Date of Shakespeare's Addition to "Sir Thomas More"', *Notes & Queries*, n.s. XXV (1978), 155–6.

© E. D. PENDRY 1979

3. TEXTUAL STUDIES

reviewed by GEORGE WALTON WILLIAMS

The most significant contribution to the year's work has been the publication of the New Variorum *As You Like It* by the Modern Language Association of America. The New Variorum series, initiated by Horace Howard Furness in 1871, continued by his son, transferred to the Modern Language Association, has been near moribund since the publication in 1955 of *Richard II*, edited by the late Matthew Black. But hope has not died, and under the patient perseverance of James G. McManaway, now General Editor Emeritus, and the able direction of Robert K. Turner, Jr, General Editor, the giant has risen to new energies. Commenting on the vigor of this 'New New Variorum' Richard Knowles, the Associate Editor of the series, and the editor of the *As You Like It*, has announced in a paper delivered before the Variorum Committee that *Measure for Measure* was sent to the printer in December 1977, that seven editions are nearly complete, and that fourteen others are in active preparation. Some of these editions, like the present volume, are intended to supersede earlier volumes (the Furness edition of *As You Like It* appeared in 1890); others will present plays not previously included and thus complete the original design. As Knowles points out, the need for a Variorum has not decreased over the years, nor has its 'intellectual

voracity' been replaced by electronic devices; 'what is crucial [in a Variorum volume] is that a controlling intelligence [has been] able to see all aspects of the edition as interrelated parts of a whole'.

The volume runs to 765 pages, appreciably larger than the 461 of the 1890 version, but not remarkably more than the volumes of the 40s. The most striking and most welcome change is in the section of the page containing the textual notes. These are now confined to substantive emendations (or, as the volume describes them, 'significant'); accidentals in the tedious history of the transmission of the text are disregarded, and unused conjectures are consigned to an appendix. One result is that more space is left on the page for commentary, which is as thorough as possible, though 'early commentators are more fully represented' in the 1890 edition than in the present one (p. ix).

In light of the opinion of the Editorial Board that the editor of a play in the series should contribute to the on-going scholarship on the play and not merely collect or report, Knowles has provided a 48-page 'essay' on the text, which catalogues all the critical material on the composition and printing; describes the press variants noted by Hinman (Knowles has added to Hinman's work collations of another exemplar and of two facsimiles(!)); discusses at length the varying theories of the copy for the Folio; repudiates the theories on inconsistencies in the text and on early versions and late revisions; and analyzes the 'Staying Entry' for the play. The careful examination of the arguments on the nature of the copy for the Folio leads Knowles to question the prevailing view that the copy was the promptbook or a transcript of it, and to support the position advanced by Alice Walker and Fredson Bowers that the copy was a transcript from foul papers. Knowles has also observed in connection with the staying entry made on 4 August 1600 that Thomas Pavier visited Stationers' Hall on that day; and he shrewdly suggests that Pavier's 'expressed interest in acquiring rights to [*Henry V* and other plays] led the Clerk on Aug. 4 to list the...plays "to be staied" ' (p. 363), because he remembered the Lord Chamberlain's concern in the matter. The players, Knowles suggests, 'were interested not in stopping publication but simply in insuring that they made a rightful profit from it' (p. 362).

His most unexpected discovery dates the arrival of Robert Armin to succeed Kempe. Knowles (p. 375) has read literally Armin's comment in *Quips* (1600): 'I take my Jorney (to waite on..my Maister...) to Hackney'. As no reason has been advanced why the Lord Chamberlain should go to Hackney who lived in Blackfriars and was the next day in Richmond, the phrase could scarcely apply to him; seeking a master in Hackney, Knowles has found the Earl of Oxford who maintained his London residence there. He concludes that Armin was in the company of Oxford's Men or Derby's Men (Derby was Oxford's son-in-law), though he recognizes that there is no external evidence that either of these provincial companies was at the Curtain or in London at the time. If Knowles's thesis is correct, Armin could not have joined the Lord Chamberlain's Men before 1600.

Though earlier Variorum volumes have included the history of the staging of the play, Knowles's is the first to include a close analysis of 'The Text on the Stage'. This section of twenty pages records the differing forms and shapes that the text has taken in production: cutting, rearrangement of scenes, bowdlerization, transfer of speeches from one character to another, interpolations, 'improvements', and additions. It is to be hoped that this excellent section will be continued or expanded in future volumes. It is a valuable corrective to the necessary bookishness of the edition, and it could be of the greatest service to directors who, having the itch to better Shakespeare, may find where and to what advantage others have scratched.[1]

The Variorum Committee have also published supplementary bibliographies for *Richard II*, *Julius Caesar*, *1 Henry IV*, and *2 Henry IV*.

During the past year, three volumes have been added to the New Penguin Shakespeare: *The Two Noble Kinsmen*, *Antony and Cleopatra*, and *2 Henry IV*. Their simultaneous publication – bringing to thirty-one the number of plays already published in the series – is a fitting memorial to the late General Editor, T. J. B. Spencer, whose death all readers of these pages will lament. Since the texts of the first two plays both derive from a single substantive edition, it is not surprising that *2 Henry IV* (which derives from two) presents the greater textual puzzle. Rising to that challenge, P. H. Davison has provided the most interesting textual work of the trio.

N. W. Bawcutt's Introduction to *The Two Noble Kinsmen* handles well the awkward situations of that play. His conclusion, balanced and sane, is: 'if the play seems a rather isolated special case, it is partly because it has been so

---

[1] A similar study deserves mention here though its primary interest lies in stage history: P. J. Ventimiglia, 'Shakespeare's Comedies on the Nineteenth-Century New York Stage: A Prompt-book Analysis', *Papers of the Bibliographical Society of America* (*PBSA*), 71 (1977), 415–41.

often excluded from collected editions of Shakespeare' (p. 46). As it has now appeared recently in the Signet series (1966), in the Riverside (1974), and will appear in the Norton Edition, Bawcutt's wish that the play will soon enter 'the mainstream of modern thinking about Shakespeare' (p. 46) is more than a pious hope. Accepting the normal division of the play between the two authors, Bawcutt does not attempt to gloss over the fact that the joint labors are uneven; furthermore, he recognizes that 'the theme of the main plot ...is not one of the basic human situations with which an audience can readily identify itself' (p. 45).

Emrys Jones's *Antony and Cleopatra* gives us an Introduction which, among other virtues, is notable for its understanding of the intention behind the structure of the play. The constant changing necessitated by the many short scenes, so often thought a blemish, encourages 'an ironical comparative response' and lends a powerful 'illusion of life in free spontaneous motion'. The short scenes 'have no room for the grander movements of feeling' (p. 26), which appear only in the last and long scene of the play. Their 'perpetual mobility' has 'so conditioned us that it is inevitably with feelings of relief and pleasure that we...approach what we have all along been denied, a point of absolute rest' (p. 42) – the long last scene. This is structural analysis at its best and most productive. The Introduction concludes with comments on the style of the play – 'an economy and an exceptional elegance in the choice of words that give continuous pleasure ...incandescent' – in a word, 'Horatian'.

A few readings where Jones reinstates the Folio text deserve particular comment. At I, ii, 107 Jones keeps Folio 'winds' (editors read 'minds'); this reading is possible only if 'winds' is glossed 'furrows' (as in Riverside), but to claim enlivening breezes as *ours* is not tenable. At II, vii, 109 he keeps Folio 'beat' (instead of 'bear'); in spite of a splendid

Horatian analogy, the stamping of feet does not fit with the volleying of the sides in the next line. Two other decisions have more to recommend them. At V, ii, 87 Jones retains Folio '*Anthony*' in place of Theobald's 'autumn'. The delight in the emendation to 'autumn' has obscured the fact that a second emendation, 'it was' to "twas', is required to make it possible. The Folio line is an alexandrian. The change of the substantive is not a simple minim error (Wilson edn, p. 237); the compositor must have misread 'automne' as '*Anthony*' (Ridley edn, pp. 214–15), a misreading not very likely. Jones makes a good case for the Folio reading, first supported by Thistelton in 1899. At V, ii, 81 the restoration of Theobald's 'The little O o'th'earth' (Folio: 'the little o'th'earth') is, however, probably to be applauded. Jones considers it essential to keep 'o'th'earth' as a unit (it is certainly essential to keep 'th'earth' as a unit, though doing so without further emendation wrecks the line). The difficulty of 'O o'th'' is the awkward juncture between the two vowels.

In his 'Account of the Text' of *2 Henry IV*, P. H. Davison advances the hypothesis that the manuscript behind the Folio was a copy made up from actors' parts. He admits at once that this notion is unorthodox and improbable, but he counters with the idea that 'we have an improbable situation to deal with' (p. 293). Both of these statements are undeniably true. It would be comparatively easy to annotate a quarto by reference to actors' parts (and to supplement it as well), but to prepare a fresh script, annotating the parts, as it were, by reference to the quarto, seems needlessly unwieldy. Though Davison's theory does explain handily some of the curiosities of the Folio text, it leaves unanswered some of the others. It presents an additional difficulty in dealing with the common errors, the so-called bibliographical links between Q and F, by interposing another transcription in the process. Davison is refreshingly diffident about his hypothesis – he calls it a guess – and he is right in thinking that it deserves consideration.

Davison advances four new readings. One of these, a change of punctuation at I, i, 192, disregards the clear intention of the Folio at 'My Lord (your Sonne) had...'. Editors point with commas as an appositive, but Davison prefers to make the first two words direct address: 'My lord, your son had...'. Though this pointing continues the note of 'cautious deference', it denies an acceptable Folio reading. At II, iv, 47, Davison's 'Mary's joys', combining Q 'Yea joy' and F 'I marry', seems inventive and out of character with Doll and with the play itself. Shakespeare never uses the name of the Blessed Virgin in an asseveration. It is more likely that the Hostess's expression, 'O Jesu' in II, iv, 469 of Part 1 is echoed here (as Ridley suggested in 1934), thus contributing to the many parallels between Parts 1 and 2 in this scene. As his solution to the problem of speech prefixes at II, iv, 1–21, Davison brings Will on to speak the line 'Sirrah...' (l. 15) rather than the earlier 'Dispatch...' (l. 12) as most editors do. This trick avoids most of the problems that other schemes have, leaving only the problem of assigning 'Dispatch...' to the Second Drawer; though the tone of the speech coming from him seems a little odd (he is speaking to his superior), the oddity is not insuperable. This is a valuable emendation. The best of the emendations is that for the difficult crux at II, iv, 324; where Q reads 'divel blinds' and F reads 'Devill outbids', Davison reads 'devil binds'. Davison supports 'binds' with sound theological argument; his emendation is far superior to any that has yet been offered.

In some of the staging points of the play, Davison is less exact than one could wish. He adds between IV, iv and IV, v the direction 'They take up the king and lay him on a bed'; he would have been more helpful had he said that they bear the king across the stage in his chair and then lay him on his bed. Davison is clear, however, that the scene is continuous, and perhaps that is the most important point to make in this edition. Similarly he remarks the continuity of action at IV, i–ii though again he is insufficiently exact. Shakespeare has placed the stage directions in the dialogue; the editor should indicate them. The Archbishop's speech is divided, the first part to Mowbray (who then crosses the stage), the second part to Westmoreland (who then crosses the stage); Prince John, entering, also divides his speech, the first greeting to Mowbray (who reaches him first), the second to the Archbishop (who reaches him later). The speeches at the entry II, i, 1–7 are probably to be divided in like manner: Fang first addresses Snare, who is absent, then the Hostess (as Shaaber saw); the Hostess speaks to Fang in response and then calls for Snare. The sequential entries of the recruits at III, ii, 100–70 are properly placed by Davison. The massed entry of all the recruits at one time, as in F, requires that the five of them stand barefaced before the audience for some hundred lines and do nothing. That is not Shakespeare's way, nor the way of Betterton's acting version, *The Sequel* (1721?).

One matter in the extensive and useful Commentary requires notice. On Shallow's reassurance to Davy that William Visor of Woncot 'shall have no wrong' (v, i, 50–1), Davison remarks: 'Davy is concerned only to ensure that his friend has a fair hearing' (p. 269). Surely there is more to it than that. The episode is designed to show that so long as lawlessness obtains at the highest level of the state, the administration of justice will miscarry at the lowest. Davy expects that his place at Shallow's court entitles him at least once in a quarter to 'bear out a knave against an honest man'; in his small way, he expects that the laws of England shall be at his commandment.

In a supplementary article, Davison poses specific questions about the condition of the text in the Folio and answers them in a persuasive reconstruction of the history of its printing.[1] The problem of the unique eight-leaved gathering he explains as occasioned by the compositors who cast off the text on the basis of the Quarto without recognizing that it was some 125 lines shorter than the full text which they were then waiting to receive. Though Davison does not mention the possibility, if the compositors had before them a copy of Q (a), lacking III, i, another 108 lines, the casting-off would have been comfortably within the regular six leaves of the Folio pattern. Davison also speculates that the list of Actors' Names, intelligently analyzed into groups and handsomely displayed on the page, originated in the theater and served as the table of contents to the bundle of the actors' parts. Such an explanation for the list forms a part of Davison's thesis on the copy behind the Folio, but it seems to the present reviewer that the elegance and the literary quality of the list point away from the theater and that the list might more likely have accompanied the kind of fair copy of the manuscript that Alice Walker proposed as having been prepared in 1598.

In 'Greg's "Rationale of Copy-Text" Revisited', Fredson Bowers makes a major contribution to editorial theory, clarifying the application of Greg's rationale to post-Renaissance texts.[2] *En passant*, he is concerned to point out a lapse in Greg's use of the term 'substantive edition' for the texts of *Hamlet*, *Othello*, *Troilus and Cressida*, and *2 Henry IV*, plays which exist in two texts 'of comparable authority'. Greg's use of the term here is misleading, for these texts are of the type which he had earlier called 'mixed texts'. In fact, for none of these plays are the two versions of comparable authority, and therefore Greg's category has no examples; Bowers supplies examples from Beaumont and Fletcher and from George Herbert. Bowers returns to the definition of 'substantive' in an article in *The Library*;[3] here he proposes that the misused term be retained, now to signify that 'in some

manner there is a direct relation with the author of some feature of the text, in whole or in any part' (p. 106). Though this new definition clarifies some misconceptions, it may be too broad finally to be useful.

At the other end of the scale of editorial procedures Trevor H. Howard-Hill describes impressively the computer techniques now available to assist editors, though he warns that 'these machines can all too easily replace one kind of drudgery by another' (p. 220).[4] He records the success which an OCR (optical character recognition) method had in reading xerox copies of First Folio pages and finds that the 'outlook is encouraging' (p. 224). 'Although obviously many technical difficulties require to be overcome..., the means do exist to produce better editions more economically with computer assistance' (p. 232).

Editorial vicissitudes from earlier periods are described by John W. Velz, Frances N. Teague, William C. Woodson, and Yoshiko Kawachi. Velz and Teague make another foray into the correspondence of Joseph Crosby where they find background material on the 'abortive American Shakespeare edition begun by J. O. Halliwell in 1850 and the English piracy of it made by John Tallis' (pp. 280–1), and they confirm the disputed presence of R. G. White in finishing the American edition.[5] Crosby also speaks directly of White's plagiarism, and he gives information on the publishing of the first volumes of Furness's Variorum. Woodson reports on the printer's copy for the 1785 Variorum, now in the

[1] 'The Printing of the Folio Edition of *2 Henry IV*', *The Library*, XXXII (1977), 256–61.

[2] 'Greg's "Rationale of Copy-Text" Revisited', *Studies in Bibliography*, XXXI (1978), 90–161.

[3] 'McKerrow, Greg, and "Substantive Edition"', *The Library*, XXXIII (1978), 83–107.

[4] 'Computer and Mechanical Aids to Editing', *Proof 5* (1977), pp. 217–35.

[5] 'New Information about Some Nineteenth-century Shakespeare Editions from the Letters of Joseph Crosby', *PBSA*, 71 (1977), 279–94.

British Library in the form of a set of the 1778 Variorum, marginally annotated and with letters and comments contributed by critics of the time pasted to the pages of the volumes.[1] The textual value of this item lies in the control it offers to editors for identifying and correcting misprints in the 1785 volumes. Woodson sees it, however, primarily as a means of reassessing the quarrel between Steevens and Malone. Unfortunately, his brief note overlooks what may be the most significant evidence for that reassessment. In addition to the marginalia and the appended slips of manuscript, the volumes contain, similarly pasted in, passages clipped from unperfected sheets, inner and outer formes, of Malone's *Supplement* (1780) and his *Second Appendix* (1783), sheets which can have been secured only during the actual printing of the two publications. There is every indication that the cuttings of 1780 were added to the volumes at a date earlier than were those of 1783, that is, that the annotation was a continuing process; in at least one place (x, 507; *Oth.*, II, iii, 216), a cutting from 1780 has been pasted to the margin; a cutting from 1783 has been pasted to the first cutting; and a slip of paper containing a refinement in Steevens's hand has been pasted to the second cutting. (Wherever possible in any disagreement, Steevens saw to it that he had the last word. See also IV, 505; *Mac.*, II, ii, 60.) The presence of these datable slips strongly suggests that Steevens and Reed had begun the revisions for the 1785 edition soon after 1780, and were continuing their work on it throughout the first half of the decade. The friendship between Malone and Steevens that existed before their difference, Yoshiko Kawachi demonstrates in reprinting letters of the two men from the Folger and Huntington Libraries.[2] He also describes Malone's continuing efforts to produce an accurate dating of the plays: 'he opened a path for scientific and scrupulous research into the chronology' (p. 59).

Two texts have come to light in the past

year. Hans Walter Gabler announces that he has found in the Hochschulbibliothek in Darmstadt a copy of Q1 of the *Merchant of Venice*.[3] The nineteenth exemplar, it is uniform with Folger copy 1. John P. Cutts prints a new version of Sonnet 116, found in a manuscript at the Bodleian, and argues that it is a medial stage in the adaptation of Shakespeare's text between the printed version of 1609 and the version already recovered by W. M. Evans from a music manuscript of William Lawes in the New York Public Library.[4]

Three articles about Quartos – good and bad. It is generally accepted that the good Quarto of *Romeo and Juliet* (1599) derives in several places directly from the bad Quarto (1597). In their edition (1955), Wilson and Duthie proposed that IV, i, 83, was one such place; Sidney Thomas in support argues that the uniqueness of the Q2 spelling 'yealow' must derive from the Q1 'yeolow' and that in consequence the irregular Q2 form of the word following, 'chapels' (an error for 'chapless'), probably derives from the Q1 'chaples'.[5] Alice Walker's argument (also 1955) that the Q2 error must derive from a presumed holograph 'chaples' is thus considerably weakened. Karl P. Wentersdorf ingeniously argues for the inclusion of Q1 *Richard III* among the Pembroke bad Quartos by noticing in it the reporter's tags – 'Zounds' and 'I warrant thee'.[6]

[1] 'The Printer's Copy for the 1785 Variorum Shakespeare', *Studies in Bibliography*, XXXI (1978), 208–10.

[2] 'Edmund Malone and his Chronology of Shakespeare's Plays, *Shakespeare Studies* (Japan), XIII 1974–1975 (1977), 45–60.

[3] '"Merchant of Venice" Preserved', *Notes & Queries*, 25 (April, 1978), 128–9.

[4] 'Two Seventeenth-Century Versions of Shakespeare's Sonnet 116', *Shakespeare Studies*, X (1977), 9–15.

[5] 'Romeo and Juliet, IV,i, 83', *Shakespeare Quarterly* (*SQ*), 28 (1977), 524–5.

[6] 'Richard III (Q1) and the Pembroke "Bad" Quartos', *English Language Notes* (*ELN*), 14 (1977), 257–64.

He suggests that the memorial reconstruction of the play took place 'at the same time as the other Pembroke bad texts in 1592–94' (p. 262) and that Pembroke's Men toured the provinces with their memorially reconstructed texts from 1593 through 1596. When they returned to London in 1597 they sold their abridged text to the printer who passed it off to his public as the authorized version that the Lord Chamberlain's Men had been and were producing. Wentersdorf also questions the commonly held views (1) that it would be easier to make up a text in the provinces than to send a courier to London for the original, and (2) that a reduced cast automatically means a performance away from the metropolis. The printing of the bad Quarto of *Henry V* is discussed by the present reviewer in the Correspondence pages of *The Library*.[1]

Important and thoughtful reconsiderations address themselves to the major problems of text in *The Taming of the Shrew* and *Pericles*. Karl P. Wentersdorf returns to the problem of the Sly episodes in the *Shrew* and to the absence in the Folio of any closing scene for the 'frame'.[2] He suggests that the original form of Shakespeare's play included such a closing scene which was omitted in later productions to permit staging by small casts, and he supports this suggestion with an argument from the law of reentry. At the end of v, i, Katherina, Petruchio and Grumio leave the stage; they reenter immediately at the beginning of v, ii. This situation is so remarkable as to require a particular explanation. The explanation here advanced – it is almost unassailable – is that at this point in the original text a scene now lost intervened; the most logical assumption from that thesis must be that such a scene corresponded to the Sly scene preserved at this location in the bad quarto, *A Shrew*. If there was such a scene in the original text, then, it follows further, there must also have been a closing scene in which the drunken tinker was returned to reality. This is an excellent

contribution to the continuing discussion on the matter.

S. Musgrove counters the prevailing view that *Pericles* is a reported text with the hypothesis that the first part of the play (as far as E3) derives from foul papers, the latter section only being a report.[3] He supports the argument for foul papers (another author's) with examinations of variant spellings of proper names, of stage directions, and of dislocation of dialogue; he also supplies an ingenious analysis of the printing of sheet B. His conclusions on the first part of the play are that the Thaliard scenes and possibly the Simonides scenes give evidence of a report, but the rest of the section contains material of varying authority; 'sometimes Shakespeare himself seems to have intervened' (p. 399). In the latter part of the play, he suggests that the two speeches in which Marina denounces Boult's profession (IV, vi, 163–77) should probably be assigned to Lysimachus. The article is filled with perceptive and attractive suggestions and emendations; it deserves the closest attention from critics of *Pericles*.

Assuming the writer of Hand D in *Sir Thomas More* to be Shakespeare, MacD. P. Jackson demonstrates on the basis of the frequency of contractions and colloquial forms that the section must have been written after 1600.[4] This finding correlates with the statistics of D. J. Lake advanced in 1975. In another article Jackson analyzes the work of

[1] 'The Composition and Presswork of *Henry V*', Q1, *The Library*, XXXIII (1978), 170–1.

[2] 'The Original Ending of *The Taming of the Shrew*: A Reconsideration', *Studies in English Literature*, XVIII (1978), 201–15.

[3] 'The First Quarto of *Pericles* Reconsidered', *SQ*, 29 (1978), 389–406. James O. Wood in a less persuasive study, 'Shakespeare, Pericles, and the Genevan Bible', *Pacific Coast Philology*, 12 (1977), 82–9, assigns the whole play to Shakespeare, the first two acts deriving from his apprenticeship.

[4] 'Linguistic Evidence for the Date of Shakespeare's Addition to "Sir Thomas More"', *N & Q*, 25 (1978), 154–6.

Compositors B, C, and D in *Love's Labour's Lost* in the Folio, finding that the three men 'corrupted the text at roughly the same rate and in much the same manner' (p. 61).[1] His appendix categorizes the types of their errors.

Critics have been busy during the year interpreting or reinterpreting difficult words or passages and revising traditional glosses. Stuart Sillars proposes that the traditional 'Phibbus' car' of Bottom's rhetoric (*MND*, I, ii, 29) should be understood as Phoebe's car.[2] While the reference to the moon is apt in this play, the moon has no car, as Sillars admits; Shakespeare, however, regularly refers to Phoebus's car or his steeds. Furthermore, the phrase 'shine from far' does not strike the eye of this beholder as a phrase Shakespeare would use of the moon (at the only other reference to Phoebe in this play, the goddess is described as looking in a mirror – an image of reflection). Sillars would discount these technicalities as marks of Bottom's confusion; but if Shakespeare had intended to represent such confusion, the word would unambiguously have appeared in such a spelling that the audience would understand 'Phoebe's'. It does not seem that the spelling 'Phibbus' in the Quarto and the Folio does so. To the many interpretations of King Lear's 'good block' (IV, vi, 184) – headdress, mounting block, quintain, scaffold, stage, pulpit, blockhead, anvil, chopping-block – Winifred L. Frazer adds 'scheme, contrivance' (*OED*, IV, 17).[3] Though her argument draws on analogues and relates the interpretation to the play as a whole, this reviewer is not persuaded that the reference to a headdress is not the most significant that has yet been advanced. David Blythe objects to the common explanation of Beatrice's 'clod of wayward marl' (*Much Ado*, II, i, 52) as clay because clay is cohesive but marl readily falls to pieces, or is wayward.[4] As Shakespeare uses marl nowhere else, it is difficult to guess whether he had this idea in mind or not. But the *OED* defines marl as 'a kind of . . . clay' and

Shakespeare uses the word 'clod', as in *OED*, to suggest cohesiveness or coherence. It is not that the marl is to disintegrate, but that it is to go its own way, like other samples of earth. Benedick is one of Adam's sons. Explaining the rich 'emotional and thematic appropriateness' of Hamlet's 'let be' (V, ii, 217), Roger Lewis supports editors who follow Q2 in including these words though F1 omits them.[5] Klaus Bartenschlager suggests that the common gloss on the sycamore tree in *Romeo and Juliet* and *Othello* is incomplete.[6] The traditional attribute of the tree is its shadiness, as in Pliny and in *Love's Labour's Lost*. Shakespeare is responsible for the association of the tree with unhappy lovers, which he has based on the pun in the name of the tree. It is his own invention.

Mats Rydén suggests that in the song closing *Love's Labour's Lost* Shakespeare has coined the word 'cuckoo-bud' (V, ii, 883) to intimate the budding of horns on the head of the cuckold.[7] Though the *OED* lists 'horn' as one of the meanings of 'bud', Rydén does not show that Shakespeare uses the word in that sense; furthermore, as, new word or not, the cuckoo-buds are clearly flowers, growing in the delightful meadows beside the daisies pied, it is difficult to see how this gloss could be effective in this context. Another floral offering is more convincing: Karl P. Wentersdorf makes

[1] 'Compositors B, C, and D, and the First Folio Text of *Love's Labour's Lost*', *PBSA*, 72 (1978), 61–5.
[2] 'Phoebe and Phoebus: Bottom's Verbal Slip', *N & Q*, 25 (1978), 125–6.
[3] 'King Lear's "Good Block"', *SQ*, 28 (1977), 354–5. It might be noted that Collier had proposed that 'block' was a mishearing of 'plot' (see Variorum). See also the present reviewer's 'Second Thoughts on Lear's "Good Block"', *SQ*, 29 (1978), 421–2.
[4] 'Beatrice's "Clod of Wayward Marl"', *N & Q*, 25 (1978), 134.
[5] 'The Hortatory Hamlet', *PBSA*, 72 (1978), 59–60.
[6] 'The Love-sick Tree: A Note on *Romeo and Juliet*, I, i, 119, and *Othello*, IV, iii, 39', *English Studies* (Amsterdam), 59 (1978), 116–18.
[7] 'Shakespeare's Cuckoo-buds', *Studia Neophilologica*, XLIX (1977), 25–7.

a good case for replacing the common gloss for 'long purples. . . [or] dead men's fingers' (*Ham.*, IV, vii, 171–2), the early purple orchis (*Orchis mascula*), with the wild arum or cuckoo-pint (*arum maculatum*).[1] Pointing out that the older gloss is based on 'an improbable concatenation of guesses', he demonstrates how the characteristics, appearance, and lore of the arum make that flower more suitable than the orchid for Ophelia's coronet weeds.

The industrious Mr Wentersdorf supports the interpretation, first advanced by Tollet, that the shard-borne beetle in *Macbeth* (III, ii, 42) is the beetle born in dung, not borne on shards.[2] He attempts to argue away the connotations of wings, a common gloss, in this passage and in parallel passages (*Ant. & Cleo.*, III, ii, 20 and *Cym.*, III, iii, 20), but as Muir has pointed out in the Arden edition, (though he follows Tollet's gloss), it is while the beetle is in flight that it hums. In the same passage the bat flies (ll. 40–1) and the crow makes wing (l. 51). Perhaps Shakespeare was inexact in his use of this word. E. B. Lyle interprets the twofold balls and treble scepters that Banquo's descendants carry by reference to Sir George Buc's *Daphnis Polystephanos* and Matthew Gwinn's *Tres Sibyllae*.[3] The double orb intimates the union of Scotland and England (silently embracing Wales) and the treble sceptre intimates the king's rule over Britain, France, and Ireland. It is likely that Shakespeare was not imprecise in these numbers and that Lyle's interpretation, in that it flatters James, is the correct one. The customary glosses on a third passage in *Macbeth* are inexact, Joseph J. Egan suggests; Shakespeare follows Holinshed in ignorance as to the precise nature of the 'gallowglasses' (I, ii, 13).[4] The term, anachronistic in Duncan's Scotland, refers technically only to Scots foot soldiery when employed as foreign mercenaries in Ireland.

The year's work has produced several interesting discussions, confirmations, or rejections of emendations. Victor Skretkowicz renews the suggestion first made by Perring in 1886 and disregarded since, that the Folio 'At Grecian sword. *Contenning*, tell Valeria', (*Cor.*, I, iii, 43), which has been emended since Collier to 'at Grecian sword, contemning', might more economically be emended to read as if the troublesome word were the stage direction 'Continuing'.[5] This word constitutes a most unusual direction for dialogue, and its removal from the metrical system of the line destroys the pentameter. The late J. C. Maxwell suggests 'when' in place of Pope's 'if' to fill the supposed lacuna at *Richard II*, III, ii, 30.[6] This is a scene rich in temporal conjunctions, and 'when' 'could most easily have been lost by homoeteleuton before "heaven"'. T. H. Howard-Hill supports the suggestion of M. J. H. Gross that five sequential prefixes in *Richard III* (I, i, 134–44) have been misplaced, arguing that the scribe who prepared the manuscript from which the Quarto was printed 'wrote the speech prefixes in a column at the left of the leaf separately after the main text was written out' (p. 312).[7] This argument would be more convincing if there were some consistency in the degree of mislocation – if, for example, the prefixes were mislocated one or two lines uniformly above or below the 'correct' lines. The proposed arrangement maintains only a random relationship with the arrangement in the Quarto. The number of lines between successive prefixes in the Quarto (ll. 132–44) is 2–1–3–5–1; the number of lines between successive prefixes in the proposed correction is

[1] '*Hamlet*: Ophelia's Long Purples', *SQ*, 29 (1978), 413–7.

[2] 'Shakespearean Shards', *Studia Neophilologica*, XLIX (1977), 195–203.

[3] 'The "Twofold Balls and Treble Sceptres" in *Macbeth*', *SQ*, 28 (1977), 516–19.

[4] ' "Of Kernes and Gallowglasses": An Error in *Macbeth*', *ELN*, 15 (1978), 167–71.

[5] ' "Coriolanus" (I, iii, 15): An Alternative Emendation', *N & Q*, 25 (1978), 153–4.

[6] 'Two Notes on "Richard II" ', *ibid.*, 124–5.

[7] Correspondence, *PBSA*, 71 (1977), 311–2.

3–3–1–2–2. The proposed scheme places its first altered prefix one line after the first prefix in the Quarto and its last prefix one line before the last prefix in the quarto. The argument requires two assumptions: first that sequential mislocation occurred; second, that it was random. One would have more confidence in this hypothesis if it did not confess that the disposition of the later mislocations was not 'shrouded in obscurity', yet it cannot be denied that Howard-Hill has provided a bibliographical argument that could, under certain circumstances, account for such mislocation.

David Haley comes near to solving the problem of the 'sledded Polacks' that Old Hamlet smote on the ice (*Ham.*, I, i, 63).[1] He recalls the early tradition that Q1–2 'pollax' is not the Polacks but the poleaxe, and he cites in support Spenser's description of Grantorto's 'huge Polaxe' which was 'yron studded' (*Faerie Queene*, V, xii, 14). His emendation of Q1–2 'sleaded' to 'studded' is most attractive; as the good quarto may simply be copying the bad quarto in this passage, the emendation presents no insuperable difficulties. It solves the awkwardness also that the old King would have smitten any opponent while in a 'parle', no matter how angry.

Three critics argue for the restoration of original readings and the removal of eighteenth-century improvements. Barry B. Adams seeks to restablish the Folio punctuation at *Twelfth Night*, I, i, 9–13, in the passage:[2]

> O spirit of Love...,
> That notwithstanding thy capacity
> Receiveth as the Sea. Nought enters there...
> But falles into abatement.

The emendation, traditional since Rowe, avoids the apparent misagreement between the verb 'Receiveth' and a second-person subject:

> O Spirit of Love...,
> That, notwithstanding thy Capacity
> Receiveth as the Sea, Nought enters there...
> But falles into Abatement.

Demonstrating that this particular form of misagreement is common enough, Adams points out that the Folio version provides a clearer sentence structure and a sharper meaning than does Rowe's text. Most modern editors fail to comment on the structure or the meaning of the traditional text that they print, but Adams remarks on Orsino's 'fervid eulogy' and his 'revisionary afterthoughts' (p. 57) which the Folio pointing makes specific. In correcting an error that does not exist, Rowe and his successors have blurred the meaning of the passage and produced a 'pointless non-sequitur' (p. 56). Gary Taylor would restore the prefix '*Clo.*' for Pompey at *Measure for Measure*, IV, ii, 40, which has been since the time of Capell regarded as an interpolation in the Folio text.[3] He correctly points out the aptness of the speech in Pompey's mouth where it is both humorous and thematically apt. Norman Nathan joins the critics (see Arden Edition) who reject Pope's emendation of *Merchant of Venice*, II, v, 42, to 'Jewess' eye', *metris causa*, in favor of a return to the proverbial form in Q 'Iewes eye'.[4] Shakespeare refers to Jessica as a Jew and indeed never uses the word 'Jewess'. There is no reason why 'Jewes' should not be scanned as a disyllable. And in a remarkable bibliographical proof, Jeanne Addison Roberts has resolved the long debate between 'wife' and 'wife' at *The Tempest*, IV, i, 123.[5] Though all copies of the Folio that scholars have ever consulted for this crux read 'wife', two copies happily discovered at the Folger read 'wife', and between five and seventeen other copies there

[1] 'Gothic Armaments and King Hamlet's Poleaxe', *SQ*, 29 (1978), 407–13.

[2] 'Orsino and the Spirit of Love: Text, Syntax, and Sense In *Twelfth Night*, I, i, 1–15', *ibid.*, pp. 52–9.

[3] '*Measure for Measure*, IV, ii, 41–46', *ibid.*, pp. 419–421.

[4] ' "A Iewes eye" in "The Merchant of Venice" ', *N & Q*, 25 (1978), 127–8.

[5] ' "Wife" or "Wise" – The Tempest, l. 1786 [IV, i, 123]', *Studies in Bibliography*, XXXI (1978), 203–8.

show the right arm of the horizontal crossbar in various stages of breaking. As such progressive deterioration disallows the possibility of a press variant, there is no conclusion but that the original reading was 'wife'. Mrs Roberts's account provides textual critics with an object lesson in technique.[1]

During the year the University Presses of both Oxford and Cambridge have announced plans to issue new editions of Shakespeare's works. The Oxford series, under the direction of Stanley Wells and Samuel Schoenbaum, will appear in two formats, in separate volumes and collected in a single volume; the Cambridge edition, under the direction of Philip Brockbank, will appear in separate volumes, the more complicated plays being treated in more than one volume.

[1] The alternative – that the original letter 'ſ' became an 'f' by some mysterious typographical accretion – though it should be mentioned, is without question untenable; yet precisely that situation has occurred in this article: in some copies of *Studies* a dirty or broken sort of the letter 'ſ' has contrived to turn the word 'wiſe' at its first appearance into 'wife' (p. 203)! That impossible coincidence demonstrates that Mrs Roberts has provided an object lesson in humility as well.

CORRECTION TO SHAKESPEARE SURVEY 31

We regret that in *Shakespeare Survey 31* (1978), p. 185, we were incorrect in stating that H. J. Oliver assigned Marlowe's *Dido, Queen of Carthage* to the Admiral's Men at the Rose in his Revels edition of the play. He did in fact express his belief that the play was written for and acted by a children's company. We apologize for this error.

INDEX

Abington, Mrs, 28, 33
Adams, Barry B., 246
Aeschylus, 220
Agate, J. E., 27n
Akbar, Jalaluddin, 87
'Alasco' (Łaski, Olbracht), 198
Albee, Edward, 4
Aldington, Richard, 138n
Alexander, Nigel, 153
Alexander, Peter, 51n, 73n, 153, 154n, 158n
Alleman, Gellert S., 139n
Allen, Viola, 20, 22, 24
Alleyn, Edward, 194, 196, 197
Allon, Daphna, 115
Altick, Richard D., 16n
Ames, Winthrop, 19, 20, 21, 22, 23
Anderson, Mary, 24
Andrews, Michael Cameron, 236
Angel, Louisa, 33
Archer, William, 18
Armin, Robert, 6, 238
Armstrong, E. A., 155n
Asche, Oscar, 19, 20
Ashcroft, Dame Peggy, 29, 31
Atkins, Robert, 31, 35n
Auden, W. H., 51n
Ault, Norman, 42n
Avery, E. L., 37n

Babula, William, 219
Bache, William, 8
Bacon, Roger, 110
Bacquet, Paul, 218
Bailey, Derrick S., 132n, 135n
Baker, Herschel, 73n
Baker, Michael, 25
Baldwin, T. W., 78n, 171n, 175n
Baldwin, William, 163, 169n
Barber, Charles L., 3, 4, 7, 47n, 50n, 68n, 70
Barclay, Alexander, 165n, 169
Barentz, William, 86, 87
Barish, Jonas, 6
Barkan, Leonard, 219
Barne, George, 90n
Barnet, Sylvan, 9

Barry, Lodovic, 94
Bartenschlager, Klaus, 244
Barton (Righter, Roesen), Anne, 7, 9–10, 48, 109n, 177n, 207
Barton, John, 17, 201, 204–5, 208–9
Bassano, Emilia, 228
Bates, Paul A., 214
Batman, Stephan, 87n, 89, 90
Battenhouse, Roy, 231
Bawcutt, N. W., 238–9
Beaumont, Francis, 93n, 232, 241
Beckerman, Bernard, 223, 226
Beckman, Margaret Boerner, 217
Becks, George, 21n
Beecham, Sir Thomas, 84
Beerbohm, Max, 19n
Bennett, H. S., 137n
Bennewitz, Fritz, 217
Bentley, Thomas, 97
Bergeron, David M., 225, 226
Berry, Francis, 4, 9
Berry, Lloyd, 167n
Berry, Ralph, 1, 9, 64n, 212
Beste, George, 88n, 89n
Bethell, S. L., 153, 154n
Betterton, Thomas, 240
Betts, John H., 230
Bevington, David, 174n
Bèze, T. de, 174n
Billington, Sandra, 233
Binns, J. W., 69, 70n
Birje-Patil, J., 130n
Black, Matthew, 237
Bland, D. S., 235
Bland, Marjorie, 205
Blayney, G. H., 138n
Blistein, E. M., 5
Blundeville, Thomas, 165n
Blythe, David, 235, 244
Blythe, Joan Heiges, 235
Boccaccio, 137
Boethius, 166
Bogdanov, Michael, 201–2
Bolte, J., 192n, 193n, 194n, 196n, 197n
Booth, Barton, 42
Booth, Stephen, 214–15

Borinski, Ludwig, 6
Born, Lester K., 167n
Bowers, Fredson, 11, 93n, 174n, 238, 241
Bradbrook, Muriel, 6, 52n, 63n
Bradbury, Malcolm, 5, 7, 48n
Bradley, A. C., 60n, 221, 226
Brandenburg, Christian Wilhelm, Margrave, 195
Brayton, Lily, 20, 24
Brecht, Bertolt, 223
Bridges-Adams, W., 29, 31
Brimble, Nicholas, 85n
Brockbank, J. Philip, 220, 247
Brome, Richard, 93–4
Brook, Peter, 201
Brooke, Nicholas, 217
Brooke, Paul, 202, 204
Brown, Ivor, 29
Brown, John Russell, 1, 2, 3, 4, 5, 6, 7, 11, 139n
Browne, Robert, 194, 195, 196, 197
Browne, Sir Thomas, 227
Brownlow, F. W., 213
Bruce, Dr, 198n
Brunton, Miss, 21, 30, 35n
Bryan, George, 194
Buc, Sir George, 245
Buckton, Florence, 33
Bullen, A. H., 99n
Bullinger, Heinrich, 133–4
Bullough, Geoffrey, 2, 174n, 228
Burby, Cuthbert, 109
Burford, E. J., 103n
Burghley, Lord, 87, 91n

Calle, Richard, 137
Camden, Carroll, 11
Camden, W., 198
Campbell, Lily B., 146n, 147
Campbell, Thomas, 17
Campbell, W. E., 173n
Capell, Edward, 246
Carberry, John C., 132n
Carroll, D. Allen, 227
Carroll, William, 217
Carson, Neil, 233

Cartwright, Faith Wotton, 94n
Cavalchini, Mariella, 183n
Cavendish, Thomas, 91n
Chambers, E. K., 49n, 106, 108, 109, 195, 196n, 197n, 198
Champion, Larry S., 218
Chang, Y. Z., 85, 86, 89n, 93n
Chapman, George, 229
Charles, Archduke (of Poland), 196
Charles I, King, 198
Charleson, Ian, 203
Charlton, H. B., 49n
Charney, Maurice, 98n
Chatwin, Margaret, 30
Chaucer, Geoffrey, 133n, 166n, 229–30
Chettle, Henry, 197
Cibber, Colley, 42, 43, 44, 47
Cicero, 171n, 234
Clarke, Charles Cowden, 17n, 25
Clarke, Mary Cowden, 15–16
Clay, W. K., 164n
Cleaver, Robert, 134n
Clemen, Wolfgang, 224
Clericus, J., 163n
Coghill, Nevill, 6, 8
Cohn, A., 195, 196n, 197n
Coleridge, S. T., 50n, 51n, 179, 181, 229
Colie, Rosalie, A., 10
Collier, J. P., 245
Collinson, Richard, 88n
Colman, E. A. M., 100n, 103n
Condell, Henry, 108
Cook, Albert, 57n
Cookman, Anthony, 35
Cooper, Thomas, 89–90
Coverdale, Myles, 134n
Cox, J. F., 22n
Craig, Edward Gordon, 19, 35n
Craig, Hardin, 158
Craik, T. W., 50n, 64n, 74n
Crane, Ralph, 108
Creeth, Edmund, 230
Crick, John, 11, 50n, 53n, 60n
Crosby, Joseph, 241
Crosse, Gordon, 28, 32n
Cubeta, Paul M., 226
Cumberland, Richard, 23
Curicke, Reinhold, 190
Curle, Walter, 104n
Curtius, Ernst Robert, 99n
Cushman, Charlotte, 35n
Cutts, E. L., 109n

Cutts, John P., 242

Dale, James, 32
Daly, Augustin, 18–19, 21, 23n, 25n
Daly, Peter M., 236
Danson, Lawrence, 216
Danter, John, 106
Davenant, Sir William, 38, 93
Davenport, Fanny, 20, 21n
David, Richard, 105, 108
Davies, John, 86n
Davies, Norman, 137n
Davis, Walter R., 50n, 51n, 60n–1n
Davison, P. H., 238, 239–41
Dean, Leonard F., 68n
De Burgh, John, 135
Dee, John, 90n
De Escalante, Bernardino, 90n, 91, 92
De Granada, Luis, 235
Dekker, Thomas, 93, 95
Della Mirandola, Pico, 170n, 174
De Mendoza, Juan González, 90n, 91, 92
Denzinger, Henricus, 132n
De Plano Carpini, Johannes, 89n
Derby's Men, 195, 238
De Selincourt, E., 73n
De Veer, Gerrit, 87
De Witt, J., 189, 191
Dickmann, I., 190n
Dietrichstein, Cardinal, 196
Diogenes, 236
Dionisotti, Paola, 202
Dodds, M. H., 153n
Dodsley, Robert, 94n
Doebler, J., 9, 236
Donawerth, Jane L., 234, 235
Donne, John, 222
Doran, Madeleine, 10
Dowden, Edward, 16, 17, 155n
Downton, Thomas, 233
Draper, John W., 86n, 87n, 94n
Dryden, John, 38
Dudley, Ambrose (Earl of Warwick), 89
Duncan-Jones, Katherine, 231, 236
Du Plessis-Morney, Philippe, 231
Durer, Christopher, 226
Durfey, Thomas, 98n
Du Sautoy, Carmen, 209
Dusinberre, Juliet, 63n, 96n
Duthie, G., 9, 242
Dyer, Sir Edward, 90n

Ebreo, Leone, 213, 215
Edens, Walter, 226
Edwardes, Michael, 87n
Edwards, Philip, 4, 158n
Edwards, Richard, 168n
Egan, Joseph J., 235, 245
Eggers, Walter, 226
Eggers, Walter F., Jr., 216
El-Gabalawy, Saad, 228
Eliot, John, 103n
Eliott, Mrs M. L., 16n
Elizabeth I, Queen, 87, 88, 106, 131, 134, 198, 231
Elliott, J. H., 90n, 93n
Ellis, George, 21n, 34n
Ellis, Herbert A., 100n
Ellis, Thomas, 88n
Elyot, Sir Thomas, 167n
Emery, Winifred, 31, 35n
Emmison, F. C., 103n
Empson, William, 54
Erasmus, 136, 163, 166, 168n, 169
Esmein, Adhémar, 132n
Essex, Earl of, 87n, 227
Euripides, 220
Evans, Bertrand, 3, 7, 8, 59n
Evans, B. Ifor, 128n
Evans, G. Blakemore, 129, 142, 177n, 181n
Evans, Hugh C., 7
Evans, Lewis, 165n, 174n
Evans, W. M., 242
Everett, Barbara, 12, 53n, 55n, 58–9, 220–1
Ewbank, Inga-Stina, 220

Falk, Doris V., 164n
Farmer, John S., 95n, 97n, 98n, 103n, 104n, 138n
Farnham, Willard, 163n
Faucit, Helen, 16, 20, 26, 27, 28, 32, 33
Feil, Doris, 63n
Felheim, Marvin, 25n
Felver, Charles, 6
Fergusson, Francis, 6, 50n
Fielding, J., 190n
Finkelpearl, Philip J., 95n, 104n
Fitch, Ralph, 86, 87
Fitton, Mary, 96n
Fitz, L. T., 222
Fitzgerald, Sheridan, 203
Flanagan, Richard, 27
Flatter, Richard, 152, 156, 157

Fleissner, Robert F., 236
Fleming, Tom, 203
Fletcher, George, 17
Fletcher, John, 93, 241
Florio, John, 164, 186n
Foakes, R. A., 9
Foote, Maria, 34
Ford, John, 103n
Forman, Simon, 97
Fortescue, Sir John, 235
Foss, George, 29n
Fox, Richard, Bishop, 133
Foxon, David, 96n
Frampton, John, 90n
Fraser, Duncan, 222
Frazer, Winifred L., 236, 244
Frederick V, Palatine of Rhein, 194
Freeburg, V. O., 63n
Freud, Sigmund, 117, 118
Friedberg, Emil, 132n
Fripp, E. I., 135n
Frobisher, Sir Martin, 88, 89
Frye, Dean, 6
Frye, Northrop, 3, 4, 5, 12, 54n
Furness, H. H., 17, 49n, 85n, 86, 95, 237, 241
Furnivall, F. J., 137n

Gager, William, 69, 70
Gabler, Hans Walter, 242
Gaines, Barry, 225
Gardner, Helen, 2, 4, 8, 9, 46
Garnier, Robert, 231
Garrett, John, 6
Garrick, David, 27, 30, 33n, 38
Garter, Thomas, 128n
Genest, John, 37, 38n, 39n
Génestal, Robert, 132n
Genet, Jean, 4
Gentili, Alberico, 69
George, David, 233
George, Stephan, 224
Gerard, Thomas, 107
Gianakaris, C. J., 225
Gielgud, Sir John, 29, 31, 32, 35–6
Gilbert, Allan, 11
Gilbert, Sir Humphrey, 89n
Gillett, Peter J., 219, 234
Gilliatt, Penelope, 209
Godwin, E. W., 19
Golding, Arthur, 73, 74, 75, 145, 146, 147, 148, 150, 174, 230–1
Goldsmith, R. G., 6

Gonzaga, Maria Ludvica, Queen of Poland, 191
Gorfain, Phyllis, 225
Görne, Dieter, 217
Gosynhill, Edward, 97
Granville-Barker, H., 23, 155–6, 159n
Graves, Robert, 214
Gray, J. W., 137n
Gray, Simon, 82
Green, A. W., 103n
Green, John, 192n, 194, 195, 196–7
Greene, Robert, 103n
Greg, W. W., 107, 108, 109, 161, 194n, 196n, 197, 241
Grenender, M. E., 235
Griffiths, Richard, 203, 208
Groise, Ljuben, 224
Grose, Francis, 99n
Gross, G., 195n
Gross, M. J. H., 245
Gruenspan, Bertha, 127n
Grundlehner, Philip, 224
Grundy, Joan, 214
Guevara, A. de, 167n
Gwinn, Matthew, 245

Haaker, Ann, 94n
Habenicht, Rudolphe, 164n
Habicht, H., 224
Hagen, E. A., 195n, 196n
Hair, Paul, 137n
Hakluyt, Richard, 86n, 87, 89n
Hakluyt, Richard (the elder), 87n, 88, 104n
Hale, David George, 95n
Haley, David, 246
Halio, Jay L., 8–9, 226
Hall, Joseph, 101n
Hall, Peter, 79, 201
Halliwell, J. O., 241
Halliwell-Phillips, J. O., 151–2
Halter, P., 224
Hamblin, Eliza, 23n
Hamer, Douglas, 43n
Hamilton, A. C., 226
Hands, Terry, 223
Hanke, Lewis, 93n
Harding, Davies P., 129n
Hardouin, Jean, 132n, 134n
Hardy, Barbara, 2
Harrington, William, 133
Harris, B., 1
Harris, Duncan, 226

Harrison, G. B., 100n
Harsnett, Samuel, 229
Hartman, Herbert, 168n
Hasler, Jörg, 4, 7, 10, 12
Hatcliffe, William, 227
Haughton, William, 198
Havely, Cicely, 155
Hawkes, Terence, 179n
Hawkins, Harriett, 130, 131, 232
Hawkins, Sherman, 5
Haydn, 79
Hayman, Ronald, 35
Hayward, Sir Rowland, 90n
Hazlitt, William, 17–18, 21
Heffner, Ray L., Jr, 226
Heidemann, Conrad, 193
Heilbrun, Carolyn, 63n
Heilman, Robert B., 226
Heminge, John, 108
Henderson, Jeffrey, 99n
Henley, W. E., 97n
Henry VIII, King, 194
Henslowe, Philip, 103, 194, 197, 198, 233
Henze, Richard, 8, 100n
Herbert, George, 241
Herbert, Henry, Earl of Pembroke, 89
Herbert, Louisa, 35n
Herford, C. H., and E., 40n
Herrick, Robert, 99n
Herz, S., 194n, 195
Heuer, Hermann, 223
Heywood, Thomas, 69, 95, 102n, 166n
Hibbard, G. R., 219
Hill, Christopher, 55n
Hilliard, Nicholas, 227
Hinman, Charlton, 237
Hobson, Harold, 32, 35n
Hockey, Dorothy C., 12, 49n
Hodgson, John A., 222
Hogan, C. B., 37
Holden, William, 104n
Holinshed, R., 198, 236, 245
Holland, Norman N., 152, 155
Hollar, W., 189, 191
Hooper, John, Bishop, 133, 134n, 141
Hordern, Michael, 203
Hotson, Leslie, 96n, 110n, 137n, 152, 227–8
Howard, George E., 132
Howard, Thomas, 1st Earl of Suffolk, 227

Howard-Hill, Trevor H., 241, 245–6
Howarth, Herbert, 10
Howe, P. P., 17n
Howell, Wilbur S., 171n
Hoyle, James, 231
Hudson, H. N., 16
Hull, Keith, 226
Hulse, S. Clark, 213, 232
Hunt, Leigh, 22n
Hunter, G. K., 2, 7, 10, 12, 55, 83, 93n, 214
Hunter, Robert Grams, 4, 59n
Hunter, Sir Mark, 226
Hyland, Peter, 216
Hysel, F. E., 190n

Innocent III, Pope, 132n
Irving, Sir Henry, 18, 19, 21, 27n, 29, 30, 31, 32, 33n, 35

Jackson, Berners A. W., 63n, 223
Jackson, Macd. P., 237, 243–4
Jackson, R., 19n
Jacobs, Edward C., 235
Jaggard, William, 108
Jago, David M., 217
James, Emrys, 223
James I, King (James VI), 134, 198, 231, 245
James, Henry, 183
Jameson, Anna, 15, 16, 17
Jamieson, Michael, 2, 9
Jamieson, T. H., 165n
Janakiram, Alur, 213, 215
Jenkins, Harold, 8, 45n, 64n, 80, 82, 83–4
Johnson, Charles, 37–48
Johnson, Samuel, 71, 154n
Johnston, Mrs H., 33
Jones, Daniel, 194
Jones, Emrys, 239
Jones, Ernest, 100n
Jones, Gwilym P., 43n
Jones, Inigo, 233
Jones, Peter, 213
Jones, Richard, 194, 196, 197
Jonson, Ben, 10, 40n, 79
Jordan, Mrs, 33
Jorgensen, Paul, 11–12
Joseph, Bertram, 174n
Joyce, George H., 132n, 135n, 137n
Jungman, Robert E., 234

Kaiser, Gerhard W., 220

Kantak, V. Y., 10
Karasholi, Adel, 217
Kawachi, Yoshiko, 241, 242
Keach, William, 231–2
Kean, Charles, 29, 35n
Kean, Ellen, 29n, 32, 33, 35n
Kellner, Leon, 116n
Kelly, Thomas, 9
Kemble, Charles, 30, 32, 34, 38
Kemble, Fanny, 28, 30
Kemble, J. P., 34, 35
Kempe, William, 6, 87n, 163n, 194, 238
Kendal, Mrs, 23, 24, 26n
Kendals, the, 19
Kermode, Frank, 1, 179, 181n
Kernan, Alvin, 224
Khanna, Urmilla, 221
King, Thomas, 194
King, T. J., 234
King, Walter N., 11, 49n, 52n, 56n–7n, 60n
Kinnear, B. G., 149n
Kittredge, G. L., 175n
Knight, Charles, 17
Knight, G. Wilson, 56n, 59n, 156n, 214, 226
Knight, Joseph, 26
Knights, L. C., 139n, 213, 214
Knoop, Douglas, 43n
Knowles, Richard, 237–8
Kökeritz, Helge, 100n
Kolin, Philip C., 225
Koltai, Ralph, 202, 208
Könnecke, Gustav, 189n
Kostial, Hermann, 97n
Kraus, Karl, 224
Karuse, W., 195n, 198n
Król-Kaczorowska, B., 192n
Krutch, Joseph Wood, 44n
Kuckhoff, Armin-Gerd, 224
Kuhl, E. P., 98n
Kupper, Hans Jürg, 217
Kyd, Thomas, 145, 146, 156, 158, 218
Kyle, Barry, 201, 205–7
Kyndersley, Anne, 88, 89

Lacy, Walter, 30, 31n, 35
Lake, D. J., 243
Lamb, Charles, 20, 63
Lamb, Mary, 20
Lampe, J. F., 42
Landon, H. C. Robbins, 81

Langer, Suzanne, 8
Lapotaire, Jane, 209
Lascelles, Mary, 9, 10
Latham, Agnes, 2, 6, 9, 37, 64n
Latham, Jacqueline E. M., 101n, 231, 236
Lavater, L., 231
Lawes, William, 242
Lawless, Donald S., 235
Lawrence, W. W., 135n, 156
Lawry, Jon S., 87n, 100n
Leavis, F. R., 139
Ledbetter, Robert, 196, 197
Leech, Clifford, 7, 8, 53n
Leggatt, Alexander, 4, 5, 7, 12
Legman, Gershon, 99n
Lehmberg, S. E., 167n
Lehnert, Martin, 223
Leishman, James Blair, 101n, 103n
Leisi, E., 224
Le Laboureur, J., 191
Lents, Cheryl Blair, 101n
Leonardo, 203
Lerner, Laurence, 2, 223
Lever, J. W., 107
Levin, Richard, 6, 227
Levitsky, Ruth M., 235
Lewalski, B. K., 49n
Lewis, Anthony, 234
Lewis, Roger, 244
Lilly, Joseph, 98n
Lloyd Evans, Gareth, 2, 6
Löb, Ladislaus, 223
Lodge, Thomas, 232
Lofaro, Michael, 225
Loftis, John, 42n, 46n
Long, John H., 6
Lord Admiral's Men, 194, 196, 197, 198
Lord Chamberlain's Men, 6, 194, 243
Lothian, J. M., 64n, 74n
Lowes, John Livingstone, 229
Lyle, E. B., 235, 245
Lyly, John, 166
Lyons, Bridget Gellert, 218

McCollom, William G., 6, 56n
McCombie, Frank, 235
Macey, Samuel L., 236
Machin, Lewis, 192n
Machin, Richard, 195
MacIntosh, Angus, 6
Mahood, M. M., 214
Mack, Maynard, 174

INDEX

Mack, Maynard, Jr, 164n
Mackenzie, W. Roy, 101n
McKerrow, R. B., 149n
McLaughlin, John J., 222
McManaway, James G., 10, 237
MacPeek, A. S., 11
Macready, Charles, 21, 30n, 32, 34–5
Maitland, Frederic W., 132n., 134n
Malone, Edmond, 242
Mandeville, Sir John, 89n
Manningham, John, 102n, 104n
Mansi, J. D., 132n
Marder, Louis, 225
Mares, F. H., 63n
Maria Eleonora, Duchess of Königsberg, 195
Marlowe, Christopher, 112, 218, 232, 235
Marlowe, Julia, 22, 23, 24
Marshall, F. M., 23n
Marshall, Norman, 36n
Marston, John, 10, 93, 95, 104, 159n, 192n, 232
Massinger, Philip, 93
Maxwell, J. C., 130, 141n, 149n, 234, 245
Meader, William G., 139n
Mehl, D., 154n
Melanchton, 194n
Melzi, Robert C., 2
Meriam, M., 190n
Merrill, Robert, 214
Metscher, Thomas, 224
Metz, G. Harold, 234
Meyer, C. F., 197n
Middleton, Thomas, 99n
Miller, Frank Justus, 75n
Miller, Paul J. W., 170
Milton, John, 228
Mincoff, Marco, 10
Mitchell, Donald, 81n
Modjeska, Helena, 24
Molineux, Emeric, 86n
Montaigne, 186, 231, 235
Moore, A. P., 136n, 137n
More, Sir Thomas, 173, 228
Moriarty, Paul, 203
Morley, Christopher, 204, 206
Mozart, 79–84
Muir, Kenneth, 2, 80n, 228–9, 234, 245
Mulcaster, Richard, 169n
Mullin, Michael, 223
Mulryne, J. R., 2, 11

Mundy, Peter, 196n
Murray, Isobel, 26n
Murray, Paul, 6
Musgrove, S., 243

Naef, W., 224
Nagarajan, S., 130
Nares, Robert, 85
Nashe, Thomas, 231, 234, 235
Nathan, Norman, 234, 246
Neill, Kerby, 56n
Neilson, Adelaide, 23
Neilson, Julia, 30, 33
Nettles, John, 205, 206
Nevinson, Charles, 134n
Newborough, Mary, 96n
Ney, Marie, 32
Nicoll, Allardyce, 38, 43n, 44
Nisbett, Mrs, 30
Noble, Richmond, 59n
Nochimson, Richard L., 222
Norden, John, 190
North, Thomas, 167n
Norton, Thomas, 102n
Nosworthy, J. M., 152, 157, 158n, 159n, 227
Nottingham, Earl of (Lord Admiral), 198
Novy, Marianne L., 216
Nowottny, Winifred, 214
Nuttall, A. D., 9

Oakeshotte, Walter, 90n, 91n
Oberndorff, John, 94n
Odell, G. C. D., 37–8, 41–2
Orange, Linwood E., 225
Ormerod, David, 221, 236
Osmond, Rosalie, 234
O'Sullivan, James P., 63n
Otho, Emperor, 236
Ovid, 73, 74, 75, 145, 146, 147, 230, 232
Oxford, Earl of, 238
Oxford's Men, 238

Page, Nadine, 56n
Palmer, Christopher, 218
Palmer, David J., 5, 7, 9, 48n, 94n, 100n
Paolucci, Anne, 217
Parks, George Bruner, 86n, 87n, 88n
Partridge, Eric, 100n, 103n, 104n
Paston, Margery, 137

Paston, Sir John, 137
Paul III, Pope, 93n
Paulfreyman, Thomas, 163n
Pavier, Thomas, 238
Payne, Iden, 35n
Peacham, Henry, 234
Pearn, B. R., 154n
Pechter, Edward, 221
Pembroke, Countess of, 88, 89, 231
Pembroke, Earl of, 89
Pembroke's Men, 243
Pennington, Michael, 206, 207, 208
Percy, Robert, 194
Percy, William, 101
Perring, Philip, 245
Pettie, George, 168n–9n
Phialas, Peter J., 9
Philip Julius, Duke of Wolgast, 197
Pilikian, Hovhanness, 222
Plato, 169, 236
Pliny, 244
Poel, William, 35n, 224
Pollack, Rhoda-Gail, 233
Pollock, Frederick, 132n, 134n
Pollock, W. H., 35n
Polo, Marco, 89n
Pope, Alexander, 42
Pope, Elizabeth M., 129n
Pope, Thomas, 194
Porter, Andrew, 84
Powell, Chilton L., 132n
Price, Cecil, 42n
Price, John Edmund, 231
Pritchard, Allan, 228
Prosser, Eleanor, 174n
Proudfoot, Richard, 106
Pryce, Jonathan, 202, 206
Prynne, W., 69
Puhvel, Martin, 235
Püschell, Ursula, 220

Quiller-Couch, Sir Arthur, 1
Quilter, Harry, 23n
Quiney family, 228

Rabkin, Norman, 4, 219, 226
Radday, Yehuda T., 115
Raines, James, 137n
Rainolds, John, 69, 70, 71
Ralegh, Sir Walter, 90n, 91n
Ransom, John Crowe, 214
Rappaport, Gideon, 234
Reed, Isaac, 242
Rees, Joan, 211

Reeve, Ralph, 195
Rehan, Ada, 21, 23, 24
Reibetanz, John, 221
Reinolds, Robert, 196
Reynolds, Miss, 29n
Rich, Mr, 103n
Rich, Lady Penelope, 235
Riche, Barnabe, 74
Richmond, H. M., 5
Rick, L., 73n
Riding, Laura, 214
Righter (Barton, Roesen), Anne,
    177n, 178n, 179n, 184
Rilke, R. M., 105n
Roberts, Jean Addison, 246–7
Robinson, F. N., 133n, 166n
Robson, W. W., 157
Rose, Ellen, Cronan, 65n
Ross, Gordon N., 236
Rossiter, A. P., 1, 6–7, 11, 12, 50n,
    54, 55n, 58, 60n, 129n
Rouse, W. H. D., 73n, 145n
Rowe, Nicholas, 234, 246
Rowell, George, 19n
Rowley, Samuel, 233
Rowse, A. L., 88n, 97n, 214, 228
Rudyerd, Benjamin, 102n
Ruskin, John, 15
Russell, Edward R., 18
Russell, Sir Edward, 28
Russell, Thomas, 137, 142
Rydén, Mats, 244
Rynell, Alarik, 109n

St Jerome, 133n
St John, Christopher, 16n
Sackville, Thomas, 145, 146
Sadler family, 228
Saker, Edward, 27
Salgādo, Gāmini, 2, 22n, 37
Salingar, Leo G., 5, 100n
Samuel, Irene, 183n
Sanders, Norman, 219
Santlow, Hester, 42
Sarbiewski, Casimir, 192
Saunders, Florence, 32
Saviolo, Vincento, 236
Schabert, Ina, 224
Schäfer, Jürgen, 89n
Schanzer, Ernest, 129–30, 134n,
    142n, 143
Schleiner, Winifred, 226
Schlösser, Anselm, 216–17, 224
Schoenbaum, S., 103n, 223, 247

Schoff, Francis F., 12
Schönmetzer, Adolfus, 132n
Schopenhauer, Joanna, 198
Schrevelius, 136
Schultz, Stephen C., 224
Schulz, Volker, 224
Scott, Clement, 21, 33n
Scott, W. I. D., 8
Scott, William O., 215–16
Seehase, Georg, 218, 221
Seiden, M., 7
Seltzer, Daniel, 220
Sen Gupta, S. C., 225–6
Seneca, 146
Shaaber, M. A., 5
Shakespeare, William
  editions
    Alexander, Peter, 51, 73, 153n,
      154n, 158n
    Arden, 85n, 98n, 103n, 116n,
      118n, 124n, 128n, 245, 246
    Folios: *Hamlet*, 157n.; *Love's
      Labour's Lost*, 106; textual
      criticism of, 237–47 *passim*
    Folio Society, 79
    Halliwell, J. O., 241
    Harbage, Alfred, 163n
    New Arden, 1, 2, 37n, 38, 64n,
      74n, 75, 234
    New Cambridge, 85n, 145n,
      151n, 152n, 153n, 156n
    New Penguin, 79n, 85n, 86,
      178n, 238–9
    Norton, 239
    Pelican, 224
    Penguin, 1, 100n
    Quartos: *Hamlet*, 153, 154n,
      157n, 158n, 165n; *Love's
      Labour's Lost*, 105–6; *Mer-
      chant of Venice*, 118, 128n;
      Sonnets, 214, 215; textual
      criticism of, 237–47 *passim*
    Ridley, 239
    Riverside, 129, 142, 177n, 239
    Variorum, 7n, 50n, 57n, 241, 242
    Yale, 98n
  plays
    All's Well that Ends Well, 63n,
      211, 217, 230
    Antony and Cleopatra, 64n, 109,
      112, 201, 220, 222, 223, 230,
      238, 239, 245
    As You Like It, 1–10 *passim*,
      15–26 *passim*, 37–48, 49, 53,

    54, 56n, 63–8, 155, 159, 160,
    216, 217, 225–6, 229, 235, 237,
    Pls. Ib & c
    Comedy of Errors, The, 49, 50, 78
    Coriolanus, 112, 212, 223, 227
    Cymbeline, 63n, 64n, 72, 93n, 245
    Hamlet, 127n, 151–61, 163–76,
      212, 219–21, 227, 232, 235,
      241, 245, 246
    Henry IV, 219–20
    1 Henry IV, 93n, 165, 177, 219,
      234, 238
    2 Henry IV, 219, 235, 238, 239,
      241
    Henry V, 25, 212, 219, 230, 243
    Henry VI, 223
    1 Henry VI, 218
    2 Henry VI, 218, 230
    3 Henry VI, 93n, 164
    Henry VIII, 213
    Julius Caesar, 103n, 238
    King John, 165, 212, 213, 218
    King Lear, 57n, 112, 177n, 184n,
      213, 220, 221–2, 226, 229, 230,
      236
    Love's Labour's Lost, 39, 49, 53,
      54, 55n, 93n, 105–14, 184n,
      201, 208–9, 215, 234, 244, Pl.
      VIII
    Macbeth, 56n, 109, 112, 159,
      220, 222, 225, 226, 230, 235,
      242, 245
    Measure for Measure, 49, 53,
      93n, 108, 129–44, 201, 205–7,
      212, 217–18, 224, 229, 231,
      234, 237, 246, Pl. VII
    Merchant of Venice, The, 5, 63n,
      64n, 72n, 115–28, 201, 204–5,
      216, 217, 234, 242
    Merry Wives of Windsor, The,
      5, 64n, 85, 217, 225
    Midsummer Night's Dream, A,
      39, 42, 49, 53, 54, 112, 155,
      201, 217, 228, 229, 244
    Much Ado About Nothing, 1, 2,
      3, 4, 6, 7, 11–12, 15–26 *passim*,
      27–36, 38–9, 40, 49–61, 93n,
      215, 216, 226–7, 235, 244
    Othello, 53, 211, 220, 222, 224,
      230, 236, 241, 242, 244
    Pericles, 213, 243
    Richard II, 37, 39, 93n, 165,
      171n, 213, 219, 234, 237, 238,
      245

Richard III, 37, 145–50, 212, 218, 230, 242, 245

Romeo and Juliet, 184n, 212, 217, 220, 229, 242, 244

Taming of the Shrew, The, 38, 64n, 201–2, 243, Pl. III

Tempest, The, 49, 53, 177–87, 201, 202–4, 212, 213, 218, 246, Pls. IV & V

Timon of Athens, 213, 236

Titus Andronicus, 95, 230, 234

Troilus and Cressida, 184n, 212, 215, 217, 220, 222, 229–30, 241

Twelfth Night, 1–10 passim, 15–26 passim, 39, 41, 49, 50, 53, 68–72, 73–8, 79–84, 85–104, 152, 155n, 216, 217, 230–1, 246, Pl. Ia

Two Gentlemen of Verona, The, 63n, 64n

Two Noble Kinsmen, The, 213, 229, 238

Winter's Tale, The, 109, 113, 213, 229

poems

  Rape of Lucrece, The, 73

  Sonnets, 213–15, 224, 231, 236

  Venus and Adonis, 73, 93n, 213, 215, 231, 232

Shapiro, Susan C., 235

Sharpham, Edward, 95

Shattuck, Charles H., 15n, 19n, 20n, 21n, 22n, 23n, 24n

Shaw, George Bernard, 15, 18, 26

Shaw, John, 8

Shaw, Robert, 233

Sheldon, Michael, 221

Shepherd, Geoffrey, 166n

Shepherd, R. H., 95n

Shickman, Allan, 236

Shirley, James, 233

Shirley, Robert, 86, 87n

Shirley, Sir Anthony, 86, 87n

Shoham, Hanna, 127n

Shupe, Donald R., 219

Sidney, Lady Mary, 88

Sidney, Sir Philip, 89, 166n, 222, 231, 236

Siegel, Paul N., 219

Sigismund III, King of Poland, 196

Sillars, Stuart, 234, 244

Silvette, Herbert, 102n

Simpson, Percy, 40n

Simpson, R., 156n

Sisk, John P., 219

Siskin, Clifford, 218

Sisson, C. J., 152

Skretkowicz, Victor, 245

Slater, Ann Pasternak, 231

Slater, Eliot, 236

Smith, Charles G., 163n, 166n, 168, 169n

Smith, James, 50n, 51n, 55n, 56n

Smith, J. C., 73n

Somerset, J. A. B., 219

Sophocles, 220

Sorge, Thomas, 217

Sorlien, Robert Parker, 102n, 104n

Southampton, Countess of, 235

Southern, A. C., 103n

Spedding, J., 23

Spencer, Christopher, 38, 44

Spencer, John, 192n, 194, 197

Spencer, T. J. B., 238

Spenser, Edmund, 73, 74, 149, 150, 246

Sprague, A. C., 23n, 31, 32n, 33n

Sprague, Richard S., 163n

Stamm, R., 224

Star, Leonie, 233

Starnes, De Witt T., 168n

Steele, Richard, 44

Steevens, George, 85, 92–3, 96, 242

Stephens, Thomas, 194

Stevens, David, 233

Stewart, Patrick, 205

Stoker, Bram, 33

Stokes, John, 19n

Stookey, Lorena, 214

Storey, Graham, 12

Strachey, Lytton, 179n

Strakowski, Jerzy, 190

Strange's Men, 194, 227

Strong, Roy, 227

Styles, Philip, 95n

Suchet, David, 202, 203

Suffolk, 1st Earl of (Thomas Howard), 227

Sugden, Edward H., 93n, 103n

Sugnet, Charles J., 220

Summers, Joseph, 7, 68

Sussex, Countess of, 88, 89

Swander, Homer D., 223

Swinburne, A. C., 15

Swinburne, Henry, 136, 140n

Swinden, Patrick, 5, 7, 11

Talbot, Lady Anne, 88, 89

Talbot, T. H., 198n

Tallis, John, 241

Tasso, Torquato, 183n

Tate, Nahum, 38

Taverner, Richard, 168n, 174

Taylor, Anthony Brian, 230–1

Taylor, Gary, 246

Taylor, John, 103n

Taylor, Marion A., 86n

Teague, Frances N., 241

Terence, 233

Terry, Ellen, 16, 21, 22, 27, 29, 30, 32, 33, 35

Terry, Fred, 28

Terry, Kate, 33

Thamara, Francisco, 90–1

Thauer, Friedrich, 134n

Theobald, Lewis, 239

Thistelton, A. E., 239

Thomas, Sidney, 242

Thomspon, Ann, 229–30, 236

Thomson, Elbert Nevius Sebring, 70n

Thornberry, Richard T., 231

Thorndike, Sybil, 28, 32

Tilley, M. P., 163n, 164n, 166, 168n, 171n

Tillyard, E. M. W., 3

Tobin, J. J. M., 230, 234, 235

Tollet, 245

Traversi, Derek, 180n, 181n, 182

Tree, Sir Herbert Beerbohm, 25, 27, 28, 30, 35n

Tree, Marion, 22

Trewin, J. C., 31, 32–3

Tromley, F. B., 8

Turner, Frederick, 9

Turner, Robert K., 98n, 237

Tutin, Dorothy, 79

Underhill, Arthur, 129n

Ungerer, Friedrich, 91n

Vanbrugh, Violet, 28, 33

Van der Keere, Peter, 190n

Van Dyke, Joyce, 223

Van Laan, Thomas F., 212

Vele, Abraham, 97

Velz, John W., 226, 241

Venet, Gisèle, 223

Vernon, Elizabeth, 87n

Vickers, Brian, 5, 226

Victor, Benjamin, 42

Vining, Frederick, 29
Virgil, 230
Visscher, Claes Jansz, 190n
Vladislaus IV, King of Poland, 190
Vlasopolos, Anca, 228
Vorberg, Gaston, 100n
Vyvyan, John, 5

Wagner, Bernard M., 183n
Wain, John, 11
Walbrook, H. M., 22
Walker, Alice, 238, 241, 242
Walker, Anthony, 228
Walker, Elizabeth, 228
Wallace, Charles William, 128n
Waller, A. R., 93n
Wallis, Charles G., 170n
Walpole, Horace, 42
Walter, Wilfrid, 31
Warren, Roger, 223
Warren, William, 21n
Warwick, Countess of, 88, 89
Watson, Donald G., 213, 232
Watson, S. R., 152
Webster, George, 195
Webster, John, 138
Weever, John, 232
Weil, Herbert S., Jr, 4

Weiss, Wolfgang, 222
Weisser, David K., 218
Wells, Stanley, 2, 247
Welsh, Alexander, 217
Wentersdorf, Karl P., 242–3, 244–5
Wertheim, Albert, 226
West, G., 234
Westwell, Raymond, 207
Wharton, Edward, 103n
White, R. G., 21n, 24n, 49n, 241
White, R. S., 221
White, William, 106
Whitforde, Richard, 133
Whiting, B. J., 163n, 164n, 166, 168,
    169n, 171n
Whitney, Geffrey, 167n, 171n
Wilde, Oscar, 25, 26n
Wilkins, George, 138
Wilks, Robert, 42
Willbern, David, 217
Willeford, William, 6
Willer, Peter, 190, 195n, 199
Williams, Clifford, 201, 202–3
Williams, Porter, Jr, 8
Williamson, C. F., 214
Williamson, Marilyn L., 10
Willson, Robert F., Jr, 211, 222
Wilson, Edwin, 15n

Wilson, F. P., 2, 6, 7, 10
Wilson, John, 17n
Wilson, John Dover, 1, 7, 11, 50n,
    96n, 106–7, 108, 145n, 151,
    152, 153, 155n, 156, 158n, 239,
    242
Wilson, Robert, 106n, 109
Wilson, Thomas, 163n, 164n, 171n,
    174n
Wimsatt, James I., 168n
Wingfield, Lewis, 19
Winter, William, 19n, 24, 26, 37
Winters, Yvor, 214
Wood, H. Harvey, 104n
Wood, James O., 97, 98n, 243n
Woodhead, M. R., 235
Woodson, William C., 236, 241–2
Wolfe, John, 91n
Wright, Edward, 86
Wright, Louis B., 97n
Wright, W. A., 95n
Wynward, Diana, 29, 32

Young, David, 10

Zins, H., 198n
Zitner, Sheldon P., 177n